THE ESSENTIAL M1 GARAND

THE ESSENTIAL M1 GARAND

A Practical and Historical Guide for Shooters and Collectors

JIM THOMPSON

Skyhorse Publishing

Skyhorse Publishing books may be purchased in bulk at special discounts for sales promotion, corporate gifts, fund-raising, or educational purposes. Special editions can also be created to specifications. For details, contact the Special Sales Department, Skyhorse Publishing, 307 West 36th Street, 11th Floor, New York, NY 10018 or info@skyhorsepublishing.com.

Visit our website at www.skyhorsepublishing.com.

10 9 8 7 6 5

Library of Congress Cataloging-in-Publication Data is available on file.

Cover design by Tom Lau
Cover photo by the author

Print ISBN: 978-1-5107-4012-9
Ebook ISBN: 978-1-5107-4014-3

Printed in China

Inspirations and Dedications

If not for my daughter, Anna, it's unlikely my literary efforts would have undergone these restorative and resurrection efforts.

If not for my late brother-in-law, Lyman H. Pollock, my focus on the rifle he so smoothly operated and stashed during the war in his half-track would never have been so intense or long-lived.

If not for the smart, tough smiths and armorers encountered and worked with since the 1960s, all but one now deceased, loads of false rumors would've never been properly analyzed, and some events "unrecorded" at official and industrial levels might never have been passed on. Their insights proved much more meaningful and valid than crackpot "conventional wisdom" garnered from very narrow sources, and repeated as if passed down from mountains on stone tablets. A couple had serviced the M1 from the late 1930s, and were still prepping precision shooting Garands fifty or sixty years later. In my work, only those who gave permission to do so are quoted by name.

The collectors with whom I have consulted, too, have proven illuminating. Their privacy is likewise respected.

Lyman H. Pollock, Jr. 1925–2000.

Table of Contents

Warning viii
By Definition ix
Preface xiii

BOOK I: THE COMPLETE M1 GARAND

Chapter 1: The M1 Garand: An Overview and History **1**
- The Rifles by Manufacturer 3
- The Rifles by Stateside Source 6
- The Old Rifle Rejuvenated: The Safe, Accurate, Smart, Complete M1 10
- M1 Fodder and Feed: Ammo for the Warhorse 15
- Straight and True Downrange: M1 Garand and Accuracy 17

Chapter 2: The Practical M1 Garand **19**
- Quick Rules of Thumb (and Other Body Parts) in the Care and Maintenance of John Garand's Big, Heavy Rifle 19
- Troubleshooting and General Maintenance 22
- National Match, Accuracy Rifles 44

Chapter 3: The Garand, Illustrated and Explained **66**
- Early and World War II Garands 66
- World War II Serial Numbers, as Allocated 77
- The Postwar Garands 82
- Special-Purpose Rifles and Rarities 94
- Spin-Offs and Derivatives of the M1 Garand 99

Chapter 4: Your Garand and the Garand of Tomorrow **102**
- Parts Compendium–Special Notes to Collectors 102
- Front Sight Span Chart 106
- Loading for the Garand and Similar Semiautos 109

Bibliography 114

BOOK II: THE CLASSIC M1 GARAND

Preface 117

PART I: THE ONGOING HISTORY OF THE M1 GARAND 126

Chapter 1: The Tactical History of the M1 Garand: Some Thoughts, Recollections, and Analysis **128**
- Combat 131

Chapter 2: The Industrial and Developmental History of the M1 Garand 133

Chapter 3: New M1s for the 21st Century: The Danish Kits and Beyond **137**
- The Parts 137
- A Combination of New Merchandise and Old Artifacts for Shooting Pleasure 143

Chapter 4: M1 Garand's Multiple "Flaws": A Realistic View of Perceived Problems **152**
- Gas Trap Is a Powder Trap 152
- The M1 Is Too Heavy 154
- Magazine Capacity 155
- The Handguard System 155
- Ah, Sweet Mystery of Training 156

Chapter 5: The M1's Delivery Chronology: World War II and Postwar **157**
- Springfield 1937–1945 158
- Winchester 1940–Late 1945 160
- Post-World War II Date Information: Exceptions and Notes 163
- Interesting Subgroups 164

PART II: COLLECTING AND SHOOTING THE M1 GARAND IN THE NEW MILLENNIUM: MYSTERIES SOLVED, TROUBLE AVOIDED, TARGETS HIT 167
- M1 Garand Collector's Piece 167
- The Overall View 171

Chapter 6: Answers to M1 Puzzles Found in the Mail and Elsewhere **172**
John Garand 172
Bayonets and Blades 173
Gas Cylinders and Sights 180
Authenticity and Peripherals 181
Using and Smoothing the Civilian M1 182
Smooth, Reliable, Durable: The Brilliant M1 Firing Mechanism and How to Do a Trigger Job Where You Almost Can't Break Anything 186
Fun and Safety: Ammo and Avoidance of Danger 195

Appendix I: Sources: A Pooled Bibliography 198
Appendix II: The Marketplace 200
About the Author 203

Warning

By Definition

The author's 1943 M1, about 1986, by which time the barrel had been replaced, displayed and photographed here with vintage ammo and U.S.M.C. militaria, on a World War II vintage camouflaged shelter half. Much of what's here goes back to what amounts to a rummage sale of doo-dads from a closing Marine Reserve facility about 1960, so had real provenance.

This is *NOT* an industrial history. There are more than a half dozen of those on the market concerning the M1 Garand and its derivatives. My work is practical and functional, at once operational manual and historic delineation, but as to which parts were alleged correct for, say, May of 1943, that's peripheral to this project, and always was.

There are industrial history *aspects* and *comparisons*, tads of information here and there, but the droning chronologies are not the core of this project. Practical considerations are the guts of this beast, from economy to preservation and much, much more.

In the 1970s and '80s, I spoke to veteran, mostly retired factory workers who built M1s, long ago, in Springfield and New Haven, looking for details and insights, but the blueprints and machine tools and their operators aren't the primary places where the rifles made their actual mark in history.

That was done at firing lines, on battlefields, and even during training exercises.

By the time I began to publish magazine pieces on the M1, I'd already been studying the rifle functionally for over thirty years, shooting for two-thirds of that.

Manufacturing processes and so on are important, indeed, and so are part numbers, but they are not the primary thrust of this work.

The author test fires his grandson's rifle before delivery.

The author pops a few precision test rounds with a postwar .308 competition-level test rifle used for the very last of his eleven-year "Molycoat" bullet wear and accuracy tests. This rifle was being "fine fitted," but needed only a cosmetic touchup on the upper ("front") handguard. The molycoat work—fads fade rapidly, it seems!!—will never be published.

THE BEGINNING, THE MIDDLE

As sages remark about death and taxes, my long, fascinating, and very expensive involvement with Mister Garand's great rifle was inevitable.

As a kid, every adult male figure I knew had been somehow involved in World War II. Almost all were Army infantry or Marines, and those ground pounders had all trained with the M1 Garand.

Not long before Christmas of 1957, when a relative was working on a Holiday Christmas radio program, it became necessary to record some "snow sounds," the thud-thud-thud of the Browning Automatic Rifle, and of course the very distinct sound of the M1 firing rounds and ejecting its clip with the characteristic, crisp "ping." The weapons in the car were all legal, crammed in the trunk with at least two fairly huge reel-to-reel tape recorders.

The B.A.R. and M1 were in the custody of the local Marine Corps recruiter, and the "sound man" was a local disc jockey.

At the ripe, old age of eleven long years, I was there because the sound man needed an assistant to manipulate wires, to shovel snow, and of course, because I foolishly—as I have often done since!—was working for no remuneration.

Little did I know I'd be the one doing the firing, all at a partly shredded target some 200 yards downrange. All of 85 or 90 pounds, and having fired a single barrel shotgun and a .22 before, none of that was why I did the shooting. There wasn't much snow removal required, so, succinctly put, it was the available job. When the bullets ventilated, then severed the bottom of the remaining piece of target, I was hooked. It was downright fascinating.

It was also predictable. Sundays were spent at my sister and brother-in-law's place, frequently watching *You Are There* or *Twentieth Century,* regularly involving

It was amusing to read recently how rare and esoteric the M1 Garand was until the 1980s. This is manifestly untrue. The author owned several by 1965, and these 1963 American Rifleman ads from June of '63 are just three sources. Shows where there weren't fifty or a hundred available were rare. And NO, that figment of the imagination that any without stamped-in importer's data are "bring backs" is likewise a massive falsehood. However, the Garand WAS expensive, so the rifles didn't circulate as much as one might imagine.

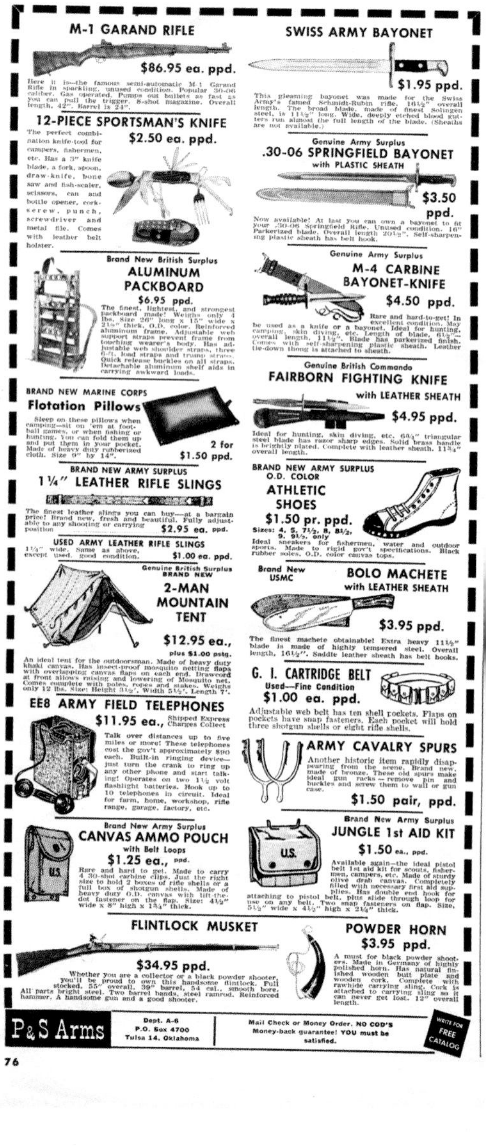

subject matter from the Second World War, and listening to Lyman Pollock tell us about Patton and Italy and Bastogne and the M1 rifle. Much of what he told us, we didn't immediately accept, but as time wore on, it all turned out to be correct.

Contrary to some recollections, many of which seem to be outright fantasies, M1s were not truly "rare" or even especially "uncommon" in civilian markets then. What *was* unusual was to see them change hands. The sporting goods stores seldom stocked them, but they were at all the gun shows, generally selling for around one hundred dollars. That was the price of three to five or more rather nice Enfields, Lee-Enfields, or Mausers, and near perfect specimens of the much-vaunted '03 and '03A3 bolt rifles were seldom over fifty dollars. M1911A1 and M1911 pistols rarely went over twenty-five dollars. A couple of local veterans who'd served very late in the war had purchased their M1s, paying around ninety-two dollars, direct from the government, somehow securing permission to have them forwarded home, and over time even showed me their paperwork, proudly.

By spring of 1963, via mail order, with all the permission necessary at the time, a "Remilitarized" (cut/rejoined with welding) rifle was purchased, and by summer of '64, work had commenced on upgrading an "original" (unwelded) rifle.

Half a century after that first "personal" M1, in 2013, for his fourteenth birthday, my grandson, Adam, was presented with the M1 Garand he had requested after test firing an elite selection of military arms, including a fully match-prepared Remington M1903. His father, of course, was the effective "owner" for the four-year interim.

It became a full circle of sorts.

The author presents his grandson Adam with his M1. That's my son-in-law, Dan, right, contemplating a handgun we had shot.

Adam practices shooting his M1 at fourteen years old.

The author tests a heavy bullet load on one of the M1's built to test new Lapua bullets. This rifle bears a heavy Citadel barrel in .308. Almost all of the sad Internet twaddle about heavy bullets in the M1 is nonsense, but it IS correct that at about 190 grains, careful thought about powder and pressures becomes more important.

A late 1954 Springfield M1 Garand rifle, .308 with "very heavy" custom commercial barrel, prepped and personalized with some aftermarket smith-supplied markings for the author's grandson's fourteenth birthday. This is what most of us call a rationalized rendition, generally intended to look "issue," but light years from being a fake. This upsets a lot of purist collectors, but the scholarship and intention is completely valid. This rifle was a true competition-worthy piece by about May of 2014, and will soon be hard bedded with reinforced fiber glass. The large CMP cartouche was deepened slightly as well. That's done with a very sharp knife. *Do not* do this on a G.I. cartouche.

Someone recently asked how many Garands I had owned. I can document several hundred on my FFL's over the decades, but I was most active with the rifles when I was an unlicensed hobbyist. A thousand or more is probable but not definitive.

Add the ones I've restored or helped friends refurbish or match condition and the figure is probably much higher than that.

Four ca. 2004 CMP "rack grade" rifles, cleaned up and minimally set up for shooting. These are all wartime, and the rightmost and second from the left have late-style locking bar sights. All but the rifle on the left have chamber flags in place. All of these had cracked GI walnut stocks when received. I actually PREFER that for shooting rifles, since the cracks can be prepared, the rifle(s) bedded or reinforced with epoxy, and no valuable wood goes on the firing line. In this time frame, most of the rifles came from US military facilities or were returns from Denmark, and the metal was at least decent. The barrels on all of these were tired to near useless when received, but I had a "stash" of commercial and unused G.I. surplus units, and most were .308s within six hours of receipt.

Old DCM rifles, many still in heavy grease, some purchased by N.R.A. officers and veterans as far back as the early 1950s, were purchased from former owners and their estates, to the tune of over one hundred specimens. Some had sat in closets, still in their ancient boxes, for decades when acquired.

One hundred fifty-six "Arlington Ordnance" post-1985 import-marked rifles were ordered in a single year, most refurbished, many rebarreled, all cleaned up and photographed. Before that enterprise shut its doors, I seem to have amassed over 300 of their rifles.

Short answer to the "how many" query: I don't know!

The entire M1 venture has primarily been a money *losing* enterprise. This is especially so when one values time which might have been spent in financially productive endeavors. Had I not done magazine firearms writing for a while and played wheeler-dealer over the years, the losses would be of even more monstrous proportions.

This tome is a sort of re-integration of the original concept; if you will, the merging of once-separated conjoined twins, available until 2017 as missives entitled *The Complete M1 Garand* (copyright 1998) and *The Classic M1 Garand* (copyright 2001). Those were my second and third books in international publication, originally composed as a single volume.

Now, the divided is again reunited, and some of the portions which fell through the cracks are folded back in. The previous versions were updated/upgraded and otherwise modified roughly twenty times during their long lives, before the original publisher folded tent in 2017. This is the next step, and it appears, the final one in which I shall be able to participate.

Some more detailed explanation is reintroduced, some small rivulets of information upgraded and clarified, and some of the images nominally enhanced or replaced.

Key motive for this work: *Creating and/or enhancing the life expectancy and enjoyment of the M1 Garand.*

If a single line can synopsize what characterizes this work, it's one I hear many times both from family members and veterans: "Shooting the M1 was actually *fun*."

Some days one can't do anything right, other days one cannot seem to do anything wrong. Here the author managed to take a "foot switch" shot (an electronic switch reposed under his right boot, tripping as he shot with his X-570 camera firing off 3.5 shots per second) of the M1 *en bloc* clip in the air, whilst still punching eight rounds of Federal Match in a 1-inch circle. And he'd never say that unless there were two witnesses, both still alive. That was about 1985. Can I do it now? Please . . . don't ask.

Preface

No American military firearm boasts the distinguished and victorious reputation the M1 Garand earned in nearly forty years of service. From the seriously flawed and controversial .276 prototypes, to the production "gas trap" rifles, all the way through the subsequent "gas port" guns, many times revised, the rifles were built in the United States until 1956–57, and in Italy much later. In a cast, non-specification form, Springfield Armory, Incorporated (*Nothing to Do With The Original Military Arsenal or Armory System*, by the way!), Century Arms, and others, presented to the public into the twenty-first century, the "last buttstroker" was known for its reliability and power. The service rifle outperformed match-prepped, venerable '03 and '03A3 Springfields as early as 1946, shooting scores with service ammo the ancient bolt gun never equaled in its finest form with match ammonium. *

A little uncommon and very pricey until fairly recently, they weren't commonly seen in civilian hands, at least not as frequently as the older bolt guns, which ceased to be "first line" issue in the 1930s. Galef in New York had sold off some imported specimens, mainly UK "lend/lease" specimens, as early as 1946, and so had Abel. Driblets were released from military inventory via the N.R.A.-affiliated Department of Civilian Marksmanship programs, most on a "once in a lifetime" basis. That organization and its name were "retired" ca. 1996, legal sources substantiate, Title XVI of the National Defense Authorization Act for Fiscal Year 1996 (Public Law 104–106, 10 February 1996) created the Corporation for the Promotion of Rifle Practice & Firearms Safety (CPRPFS) to take over administration and promotion of civilian shooting matters as the CMP. The CMP no longer features the tight relationship with the National Rifle Association for qualification, and also gone is the "one rifle per lifetime" limit, but pricing based on the World War II cost price of eighty-nine dollars to ninety-four dollars is also long gone. Just as with the old DCM, other firearms are often featured, and parts are available, but again, the cut-rate prices of the past are obsolete.

Authentic and "unfiddled with" rifles were rarely sold to troops "on the spot," although it has been my pleasure to view a few such rifles and their authorization paperwork. In the mid-'60s, some welded up, "remilitarized" rifles, made from the halves of sliced "demilitarized" M1 specimens condemned for reasons as varied as irreparable click detents on rear sights to simply being at the wrong installation when transportation became difficult, began to show up. The shipments of unmarked, early imports or "re-imports" (not an accurate term, but a common one, for foreign cash-purchased rifles whose re-entry to the US for private sale was authorized and executed), particularly in numbers from Europe, accelerated at about the same time. That last grouping included some of the very least likely to be extensively "mixmastered" and non-original Garands, since most had seen little or no use since 1945.

Since the changes to the gun control act of 1968 rendered by Congress in 1985, vast quantities of civilian-market Garand rifles have entered from Italy, Morocco, China, Korea, the Philippine Islands, and elsewhere. These, by regulation, must carry the name of the importer marketing, the caliber, and the nominal country of origin. Earlier private market imports did NOT require such emblazoning.

CMP has also imported rifles, which are *not* so marked, from Denmark, several Latin American countries, Greece, Turkey, the Philippines, and so on. While some wags refuse to use the term "imported," in the literal sense, it is correct. Anything which arrives in one country from another is an "import." The difference is solely that, being imported under quasi-governmental auspices, no special marking is required when done by the Army, when such arms are then provided to civilians. The gray area is simple; the legal distinction is not so easy. Since these are mainly returns of military aid program items, where there is no exchange of funds, one may technically claim such a transaction is not *in a fiscal, legalistic sense*, imported under duty or customs restrictions.

This tome deals mainly with the *practical* M1 rifle from

collecting, shooting, and loading points of view. If you own a Garand, something herein should help you, if only one of the troubleshooting or parts notations or compendiums. Collectors who do not shoot might find the categorizations by illustration in many of these portions handier than the rest of the text.

Few modern users have cleaned up M1s as they were shipped from the old DCM The military quit using COSMOLINE by the early 1970s for preservation, but it was packed much heavier on most of the civilian rifles shipped under that old, NRA-linked program than shown in these photos. In fact, many I bought from estates, unpacked, were identifiable as rifles only by general shape. Magazine wells were filled solid, and the older stuff was much more colorful (brownish) than depicted here. I still have nightmares about removing the stuff. COSMOLINE is basically petroleum jelly with additional heat buffering capability, mixed-in preservatives, and staining agents. Once, in Mesa, Arizona, I tried cleaning off about 20 such preserved rifles at a car wash, with the owner's full permission, and selected trucks blocking the view. There was nothing illegal about washing rifles in a car wash, but the act still attracted the unseemly and grossly inappropriate, hostile, erreoneous interventions of of the local police. It took about nine unpleasant hours to sort out the fools and send them on their way. This stuff is unpleasant, at best, and the CMP now degreases rifles sent to consumers under the new programs. This is one of those "good old days" things *no one* misses.

One issue covered inadequately in almost *all* firearms writing is overall preservation. A particularly excellent but under-analyzed piece on the uses of waxes, oils, and greases to preserve firearms was presented in *The Garand Collector's Association Journal* (Volume 20, issue 3—Summer, 2006), starting on page 19. Written and researched by none other than then-conservator at the Springfield Armory National Historical Site, it dealt with moisture and related damage to museum firearms and related specimens, in the wake of flooding. Dealing mainly with museum specimens never to be fired, the real KEY findings were that thin oils as preservatives are almost useless. Greases work much better, and *WAXES* are especially more viable than most firearms buffs ever imagine or discuss. Some look at the article and summarize, "Well, I shoot mine, and I carry them, so this is *useless." WRONG!*

A sharps carbine hung upon a friend's fireplace mantle many years ago by its owner and "oiled every few days" had rusted pretty much solid after a decade or so. It should've been treated with car wax or Johnson's paste wax. Oil migrates with gravity and also diffuses and disperses. Wax, rubbed and buffed a little, does not. An only slightly younger Winchester 1886 in worse cosmetic but better mechanical condition when emplaced on its mantle at about the same time, in the 1980s, waxed and wiped and buffed *but never once oiled,* remained in such fine condition when I returned to Wisconsin from Arizona in 2003, after digging some rather uncommon ammo out of the ether of the Internet, we were shooting it—and rather well, I might add!—for the first time in at least four decades.

Lesson: thin oils are not usable preservatives over the long run. Grease is, but it's very inconvenient. Waxes don't migrate after drying/buffing, and their patina directly resists better than watery liquids.

I have used gun oil on firearms as a light solvent, but not as a lubricant or preservative for over forty years. Guns don't deteriorate in my care since then.

The intention is to offer the practical information in a greatly condensed form, stripped of a lot of verbiage and obsolete misinformation and commercial disinformation, and especially in regard to the big, old wood and steel battle rifle for which I have so long and so much cared. A lot of it applies to other weapons, too, and even to other

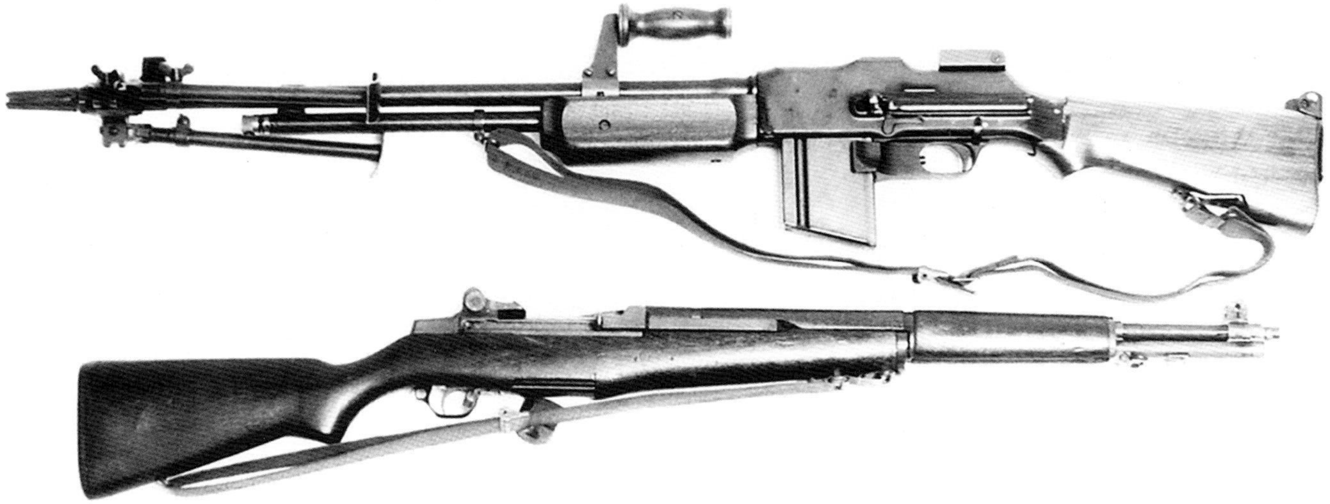

Launched by bloody lessons learned in "The War to End All Wars," massive efforts to increase the independence, versatility, and firepower of small American infantry units were championed by radicals in the Roosevelt administration. This meant vastly better communications; more mobility—some wheeled, some tracked; and a fast-firing rifle that was the core of the fire team and the squad, with all other small arms acting as support. The B.A.R. (a World War I veteran that saw some actual combat at the very end) and the M1 Garand proved to be the very guts of the weapons end of this approach, which was fought tooth and nail by traditionalists in the military and was the antithesis of the European approach. The B.A.R. on top is an old WWI veteran, upgraded to the M1918A2 form, apparently by Winchester, very late in World War II, and the M1 is a Winchester -2 receiver, one which apparently left New Haven at almost precisely the same time the old B.A.R. was refitted.

metal objects, but there is a litany of mythology and distortion unique to Mister Garand's rifle.

1. *SEVENTH ROUND STOPPAGE.* Not a myth, though it only ever truly applied to roughly the first 52,000 or so production rifles (basically all the unmodified "gas traps" and most of the first several thousand "gas port" rifles), the defect resulted from a potpourri of missed specifications and stresses involving the receiver's travel surfaces. But the hang-ups were quickly addressed and the underlying problems solved. Save for a very tiny quantity of rifles that somehow escaped the remedial welding and adjustment, no rifles evincing this defect exist today. Anyone who relays this tale either has a very rare rifle or a very vivid imagination. Most likely, it is another issue, "mis-nomenclatured."

2. The "*GOVERNMENT SUPPLIED RIFLE AS A PURELY VIRGINAL SPECIMEN*" myth. M1s were subjected to vast and irregular rebuilds and refinishes, and true parts interchange meant that swapping out whole assemblies even in the field was very easy. I have seen a very few DCM or CMP M1s that were truly "original" and undisturbed, and have only very rarely seen a Winchester so supplied that was close to original finish/markings. Often, the original markings are nearly gone. One I saw that belonged to a wonderful machinist who has since passed on had become a "Win ster," most of its logo material on the receiver heel having been excised with a belt sander. Someone had gouged out the serial number to make that clearer, but the maker's name wasn't so vital. There are surely exceptions, but the longer these rifles were in issue, the more likely they are/were to have been modified. Since coming home, I've seen rifles that left military ownership (stolen, later recovered) long before the end of World War II, untampered with since, and not one of them was "collector correct." Operating rods and trigger groups, in particular, tend to NOT conform to the hard copy literature.

3. The "*PARABLE OF THE MAGIC BRAND*" myth. This one is fascinating, if only because reality is almost a reverse image of "common knowledge," and no single myth about this rifle more clearly illustrates how twisted rumors, prejudices, lies, and disinformation gets injected into the arteries of what should be solid information. This and many other distractions have become far more common with the

growth of the Internet. There are differences in parts durability, mainly having to do with the older parts being less robust. And it is true that the later rifles tend to be more accurate and reliable, but these are matters of progress, not some voodoo of who made what. I have found late Beretta and Breda rifles to be especially excellent and uniform, but there's no magic involved, nor were they necessarily "better." They were made for foreign customers, sold to unbigoted customers, made much later, and the simple advances in machine tooling, measurement, and *lack of fatigue and combat* are the reasons they seem nominally more uniform and predictable.

4. The "ABSOLUTE RELIABILITY OF BORN ON DATES AND PARTS ARRAY/MATCH" I had seen a few before, and always presumed they were cases of battle damage. I am no longer so sure. The first "jump cut" rifle I saw was in California, about 1983, brought to my residence in Northridge, California, by a son who had inherited it from his father. It was a DCM piece from many years before, bearing a very early "gas port" serial number, just over 50,000, from late 1940 or so, but bearing every single part, including a cartouched, crisp butt stock, from well over a year later, probably some time early in 1942. Puzzled with what I found looking in Duff, Canfield, and/or whatever notes, literature, and scribbling on hand way back then, I paused for a moment and said it seemed to be a rifle "badly damaged in battle" which it seemed the armory or other related official facility had opted to repair with all new parts. I explained that was the best operative theory. Now I've seen a half dozen other so-called "jump cut" rifles, and I have another possible explanation/theory, buoyed up by one of my last conversations with an old armorer who trained during that period at the Massachusetts Armory. An approximate quotation amounts to: "If a rifle was somehow badly out of specification, it was torn down and the usable parts sent every which way. The pace was fast, *very, very* fast, and we got back to it when we got back to it, often quite a bit later." Some "jump cut" dates weren't far off; some were over a year. I briefly thought they were restorations by amateurs, gone wrong, but in 2012, a contact brought by an inherited late '43 dated rifle shipped from Rock Island, early '70s, still in grease, with paperwork, and it was a receiver *almost as old*, bearing black "soot" phosphate on the carbon steel parts, old panthermic paint in perfect condition on the gas cylinder, and a "GAW" cartouched stock, one of the best I've ever seen, and every other part appropriate until well into the 1944 production year. Obviously, the actual "born on" date of that piece was far more likely to be 1944, when it first saw the light of day, than its receiver "C.D.D." (Contract Delivery Date). This is where "correct" dating and parts and data array becomes "iffy." One clue: the paint finishes on the gas cylinders wore very quickly, and seem to have mostly disappeared by late '44. To find an unblemished one generally indicates a rifle or at least the cylinder had never been issued. Wooden stocks ding easily. The butt stock seemed too good, but wasn't. I originally thought this one was a very well-done fake. It wasn't. Or if there was something bogus, it can no more be proven than my somewhat educated hypothesis. No, not ironclad or bulletproof, just a slightly more rational explanation than the old one. . . .

Teaching rifle fitted with a re-stamped and clearly "unoriginal" butt stock, fitted with an NM 2 rear sight aperture for testing. The Boyd's logo in the barrel channel was left intact.

My intention is to provide photography that's closer, larger, and more detailed than commonly seen. Bear in mind, I owned most of the guns shown here. Many of them, if not most, are from groups purchased from now-defunct Arlington Ordnance. Others are specimens in whose restoration I participated, some kindly provided by collectors and dealers, notably the late Larry Kaufman, whose W.R.A. 100001 (the very first Winchester M1) and one of whose gas traps grace these pages. The others have chosen to remain anonymous, or at least haven't told me that I can use their names. I devoted a lot of work and money to finish identification, to be *certain* that oxide v. phosphate finishes were in detail chemically fingerprinted, to a certainty, and by multiple verified and corroborating sources, even though I knew there would still be arguments. One thing I notice is, when I present sources and name witnesses, none of those who spew challenges to the evidence has *ever* taken the time to contact the chemists, machinists, and engineers who drew the conclusions I duly reported to them.

A numbered gas cylinder on a W.R.A. 100001.

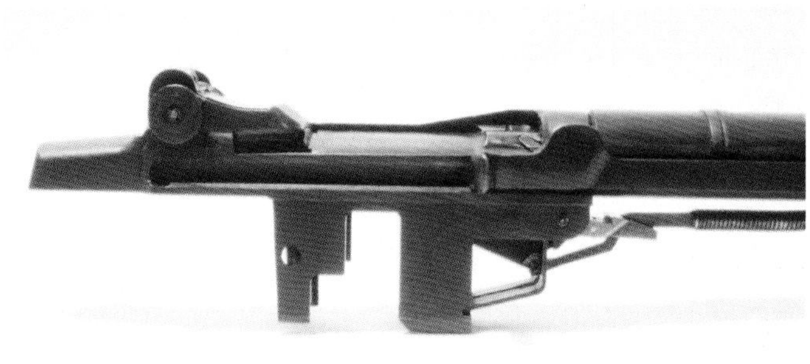

This is an intentionally overlit shot of Winchester M1 Garand rifle #100001, the very first "school" rifle they produced. It had to be lit with heavy handed studio lighting and aluminum burnished selectively because of the intense, satin black finish, which is quite common in early, and sometimes, later Winchester M1 Garands. This extremely valuable specimen wasn't chemically analyzed, but other low numbered rifles I actually owned myself were, and the universal result was, "This finish cannot possibly be phosphate, it is some kind of alkali-generated oxide." Old Winchester factory hands asked said some were actually finished by the Du-Lite firm.

Bottom view, showing operating rod catch, "square" op rod spring, and some other early aspects of the very FIRST Winchester M1 Garand, 100001. This general configuration of operating rod catch is typical of early versions of the rifle. The satin black finish of this specimen required heavy overlighting to show detail. The flattened out springs are extremely rare, and if a collector stumbles across one, it is probably imprudent to even keep it in the rifle, let alone shoot with it.

This is a "standard exposure" incident metered shot of Winchester rifle #100001, using the instrument literally. Notice: so dark, but with high sheen, and NO legible details. One wag advised me this was "highly polished Parkerizing." We tried that. Phosphate cannot reach this depth or sheen. The chemical analysis of the other like-finished rifles solved the mystery long before I saw this, roughly 1995.

Aluminum burnished rendition of the data panel on the "horseshoe" of Winchester M1 Garand 100001. This satin black finish was so dark and simultaneously shiny that polarized lights and camera (reflection control). And 2600 watt seconds of light would not render the information readable without gracing the surface lightly with aluminum foil. This, by the way, can be instantly removed with any industrial solvent, including Hoppe's or Outers. However, a word to the wise: Do NOT do this with a piece you're attempting to SELL if this is the image you send out. It will likely be presumed the piece is "gray" and "worn," which this rifle surely was not. Purpose of this exercise was to show the number, yes, but also to demonstrate the "puckers" from the lettering application, especially on the word "trademark," which we began using early on to try to figure out if these had been refinished. Obviously, this one hadn't. For the record for those photographers who used to do this kind of fine work, this was still "overexposed" by two stops from what my flash meters told me to use, or this might never have been legible. The alternative is to use multiple views with uncontrolled side lighting, and that gives way too many false impressions.

Burnished but NOT overlit shot of W.R.A. rifle #100001, showing minimal (almost no!) detail. The "first style" or "ungrooved" rear sight spring cover, however, is rather well depicted here. Oddly, those rear sight covers appear intermittently on what are supposedly "undisturbed" rifles, clear to the end of the war. It may, of course, be that those rifles are not as "undisturbed" as their owners think or claim.

The nature of the beast is such that by the time this missive sees ink or exposure on the web, my M1s may very well be all gone. Lesson: if someone imagines a living can be made researching firearms, well, it's not impossible, apparently. But it sure was for everyone I know who ever tried it. Most blew fortunes on "toys." I'm no different.

Least productive: "re-correcting" or "restoring" vintage rifles. And the older they are, the more this is so!

If portions of this seem radical, controversial, heretical, or blasphemous, I am pleased. I did my homework mostly with the hardware, albeit I did examine drawings and blueprints. My research was done with the rifles themselves, the documents the "greatest generation" allowed me to view, handle, report, and summarize, and many times, gems for photography or analysis showed up from unanticipated sources, including items that "cannot exist." Many are presented herein.

You'll notice when I have a hypothesis, no absolute statement is made.

One ought to recall: Military firearms collectors—and the more modern, the more this is true—are widely regarded as "riff-raff" by some other collectors and many laymen. The old operational lies are, "These are guns *only* for killing people!" and of course, "They're no good for hunting!" Shooters fall under the same dismissive blanket of quasi-condemnation. The M1 can still be an excellent high power competitor, albeit not without a lot of work, and one that I gave to a Marine returning from Iraq was used to kill the kid's first deer. But in some venues, truth and logic and perspective *don't matter at all.*

Please make no mistake. The M1 is a classic, in every way a fascinating instrument, but it will be and has been specifically attacked by both sides of the political spectrum, for reasons expedient at that moment, and sometimes even by name.

A hunting version of the semi-automatic German K43, top, compared to a laminated Breda M1 Garand stocked with contrasting laminated wood, below.

Technically succeeded by the M14, a great many National Guard and Army Reserve units, including my local ones, went right from this old rifle and the flimsy M1 Carbine to the M16, having only ever had quick briefings on the M14. Their M1s left inventory not in 1956 or even 1969, but well into the 1970s.

This handsome old beast survives because it looks good and because it's *FUN.* Oh, it really was in Manila and Bastogne and Cologne and Sicily and all those places, along the Chosin, and early in Vietnam. But its *LIFE* continues, part of tradition, part of our play, and every time I cram a clip into my Breda, in its laminated stock, with German Sauer bolt and South Korean gas cylinder, that whole legacy is in play.

ENJOY!

**[Note: The reference to "buttstroker" is not a veiled reference to anything but the M1 Garand's butt stock's ability to deliver a savage thrust strike to an opponent's chin or face, usually terminal to the recipient.]*

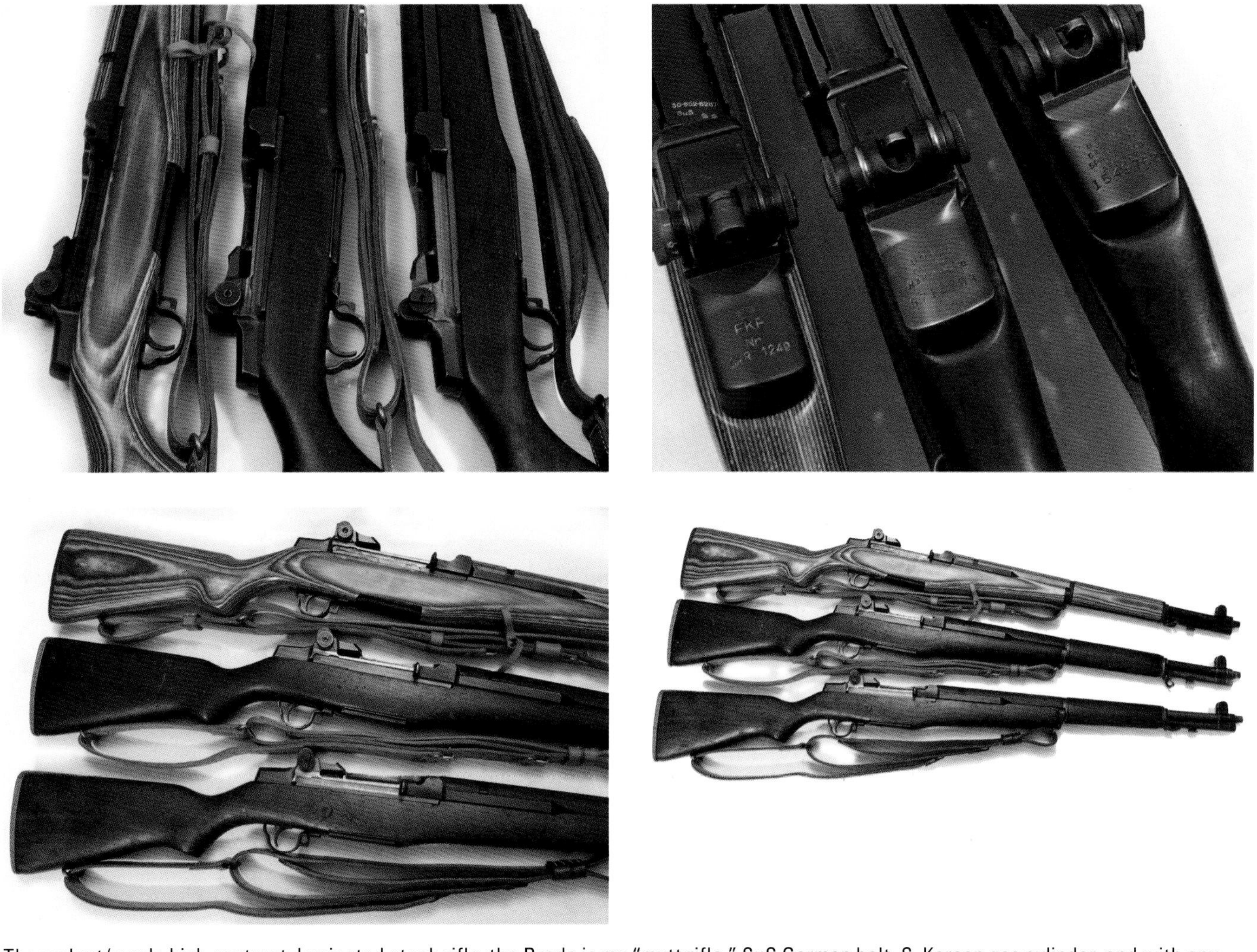

The walnut/maple high contrast, laminated stock rifle, the Breda is my "mutt rifle." SuS German bolt, S. Korean gas cylinder, and with any luck, one part from every major manufacturer involved in the Garand program, including Beretta, IHC, HRA, SA, and others I have forgotten along the way. It's a .308, of course. The 5.7 million range serial number HRA would've been a .308, too, but had a wonderful original barrel and almost all HRA parts, so I didn't convert the piece. It's in the middle, in the dark SA stock, not in a "collector correct" stock. The SA (1.5 million range) was also not a good candidate for conversion, bearing a rare original barrel and so on. I had an original midwar parts set around and some part real, part replica "locking bar" rear sights, so short term, I used it as an instructional/eductional piece. That one is in the reddish stock, and it bears the obvious dark rear receiver of one of the re-heat treated, "below about 2 million" annealed units, which has bled through what is probably an old refinish.

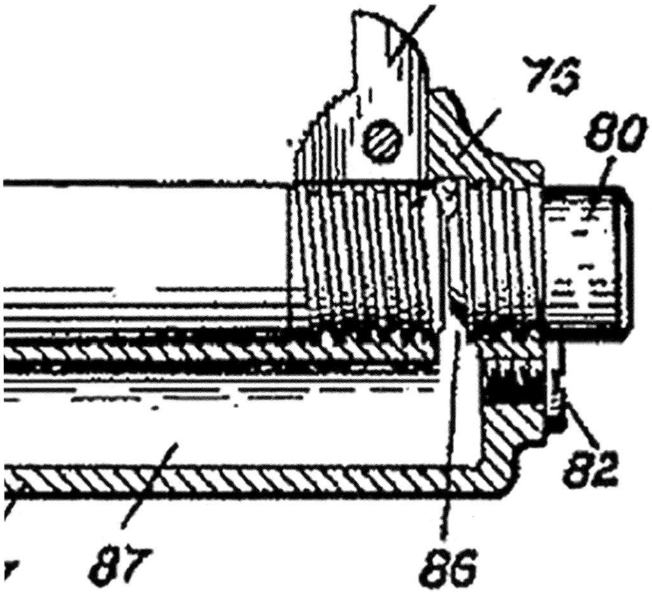

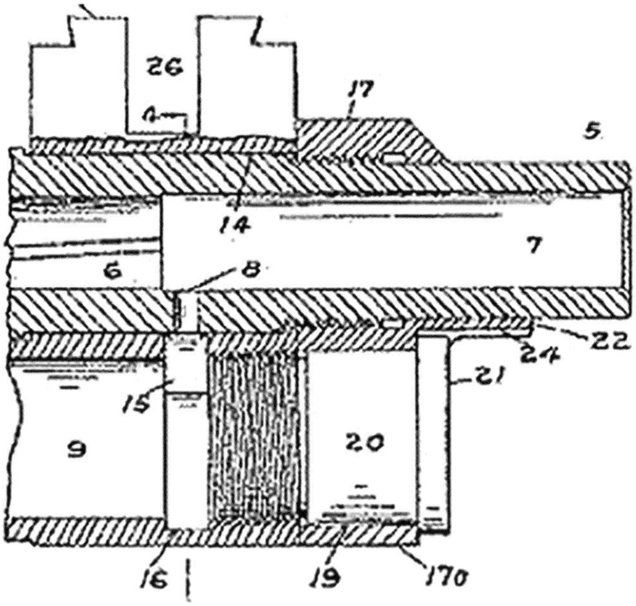

Dec. 27, 1932. J. C. GARAND
SEMIAUTOMATIC RIFLE
Filed April 21, 1930

June 23, 1942. J. C. GARAND
BARREL AND GAS CYLINDER ASSEMBLY FOR FIREARMS
Filed May 4, 1939

The gas trap had almost no service life and was never really practical in the "second choice" cartridge, the .30 06, and reversion to the ancient gas port system John Browning had used in his 1890s machine gun designs yielded a far more practical, reliable, and accurate firearm. It might have worked neatly in the .276 Pedersen centerfire, which was the truly original cartridge for which the M1 was prepared.

BOOK I

The Complete M1 Garand

CHAPTER 1

THE M1 GARAND: AN OVERVIEW AND HISTORY

Those who jot down the production life of John Garand's rifle as if it were a continuous span from 1936 to 1957 are not wrong but should add, at least parenthetically, that the original 1936 machine was basically a failed prototype. Most of the first batches of rifles, built exclusively at Springfield Armory, were welded up as/where required, reconfigured with new barrels and gas cylinders, and returned to service. Very few exist intact, though there is a surprising supply of early parts, many unused.

In the course of this book, the term "Model 1936" may turn up, but the term was never official. It refers to the first few thousand gas trap rifles and may refer to gas trap guns generically. To the military, they were all M1s, and subtypes exist only in relationship to specific parts.

The breakdown of manufacturers and rifles that follows is a primer for the rest of this book and its specialized parts and subsections.

To shooters, there is no magic to any particular manufacturer. Usually inaccuracy of the Garand involves something that is worn out, loose, or misinstalled—or, of course, a lousy shooter. Sloppy bedding, loose gas cylinders, tired barrels, lousy ammo are usually the causes. Only a very few parts are chronic problems, and this book will try to discern them all.

This book won't detail every marking on the Garand, though the photos should be helpful in gaining familiarity with the system. One should make some notations, however, to help determine the age of some parts and thus analyze a rifle's history. The maker's codes are very simply figured and are literal: "SA" = Springfield Armory, US (Springfield, MA); "WRA" = Winchester Repeating Arms; "SAI" or "SA" with ® to denote trademark = Springfield Armory, Incorporated (Springfield, IL, private firm); "IHC" = International Harvester; "HRA" = Harrington and Richardson; "PB" = Pietro Beretta; "BMB" = Breda (Beretta) Maschina Brescia, sometimes accompanied by subcodes to identify subfactories. While these are the major codes, ultimately hundreds of contractors produced parts and assemblies for the M1 program, and you'll find "RA" on operating rods, "SuS" (Sauer and Sohn) on some German-made replacement parts, and "LMR" on original International Harvester barrels. To the collector, some advice: on Springfield guns, almost everything comes from Springfield, but on all others, do not panic if a small letter or number code doesn't jive with the pattern of the rest of the rifle (see the photo sections for some details). There were hundreds of maker and material code markings such that "A" and "CM" appear on many wartime Winchester and even some Springfield guns, and collectors argue considerably over which tiny part is correct for a particular rifle.

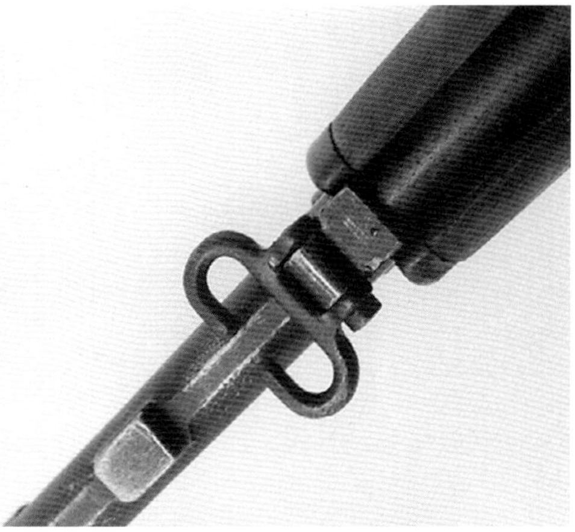

Virtually none of the mysterious letters on the gas cylinders of virtually all vintages of Garand from virtually all sources have been deciphered. Usually single letters, they were largely finish codes, used in a frantic effort to determine how best to make the stainless steel of the cylinder nonreflective. Acids, phosphates, plating techniques, and even paints were tried to increase permanence and darkness of the patina, and none seemed to work very well.

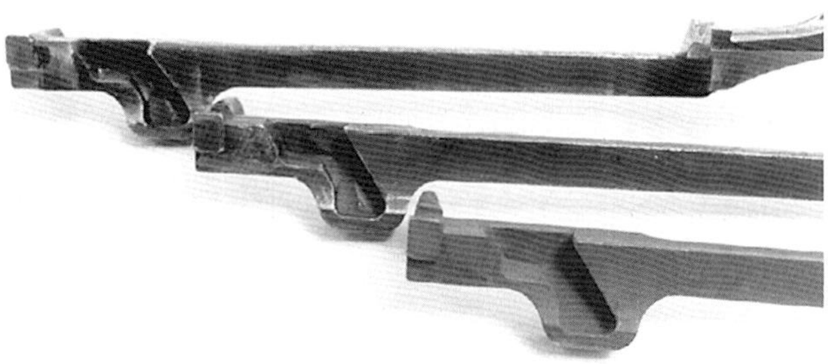

Three M1 operating rods: (top) -6 uncut, (middle) postwar replacement D 35382, and (bottom) "77" series National Match. Note stress crack and dislodged material at corner of bolt detent on the top unit, suggesting that this rod will soon fail and/or separate. The -6 rod does not belong on a rifle that is being fired.

The swept-back knuckle of this operating rod marks it as a very early style or a Winchester. This style was out of production at Springfield by mid-1940, but Winchester never adopted the changes to strengthen and modernize this part until after the the effective end of the war, roughly February of '45, with the WIN-13 series. This one carries the hemispherical relief cut added on rebuilds after the war.

Stainless steel pistons of typical M1 Garand operating rods. Note the thicker stock of the bottom unit, a "77" series. Note also pitting and erosion on the top unit, which has been repistoned, but which obviously saw extensive prior use with corrosive ammunition and was not properly cleaned. All three are usable.

Knowing the parts number code can save the unwary from a financial or medical disaster, such as paying a high price for a rewelded demilitarized receiver or, worse, suffering an injury as a result of a high-speed operating rod separation—chronic to the old, uncut World War II and earlier original rods but ordered off all rifles as early as 1946 (see the illustrations relating to operating rods). These rods can be worth two hundred dollars or much, much more to collectors, but shooters do not need or want them.

Somewhere in the parts number stamped on most major and some minor Garand parts is a five-digit core identification number. On the operating rod, for example, it's 35382, usually prefixed by a "D" for "drawing number," followed by suffixes to identify modifications. Don't memorize the system. The very first operating rods often bore no number at all. But the easiest identified "first model" is D 35382–0, sometimes overstamped and modified much later. Wartime

Three M1 Garand operating rods, a "6" variant wartime uncut from roughly 1942, original, a "D35382" postwar safety relieved replacement from roughly 1948, and from the 1960s, a "National Match" 7790722 - RA. The improved, cleaned up welds on the latest rod are obvious in the photo, and the parts are newer, too. Functionally, they are the same piece as the production 6535382 rods of a few years earlier. Many bearing the same part number were produced as replacements. The "SA" marked "77 series" are less common in both match and replacement versions.

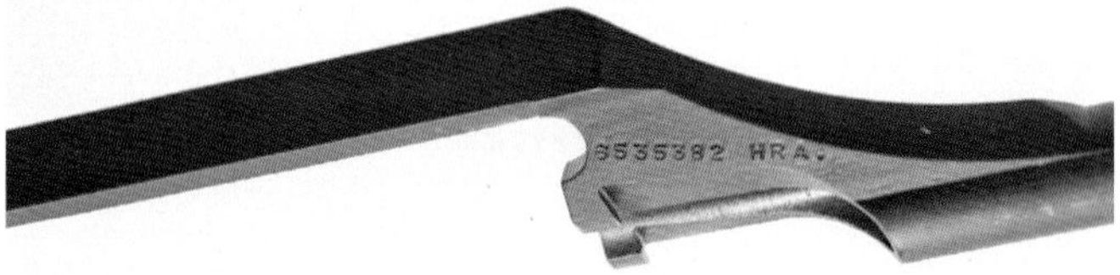

Typical 6535382 HRA Harrington and Richardson operating rod. These are all postwar and stress relieved.

rods ran to D 35382–9, with some small number of higher suffixed service and experiment specimens, common to 13, but once in a while, even higher suffixed. First-generation postwar production to accompany brand new rifles with cutout, were marked D 35382. First postwar production used a modified but still easily identifiable part number, prefixing the core number with "65" and using the maker's code as a suffix, such as in 6535382 SA.

The very latest (and, from the shooter's point of view, best and least likely to be worn out) parts were made after the rifle was out of production, often prefixed 77, as in the last Springfield operating rods. However, the rod was made sturdier and different welding techniques were used on these lots, so the final number became 77 90722. These were made well into the 1960s and perhaps into the 1970s. These distinctions are vital with some parts, such as when a Winchester receiver is encountered bearing the postwar receiver code up front right (e.g., 65 28291 3C SA, which tells one it's a postwar Springfield receiver up front, welded to a sought-after and fairly rare Winchester rear—or, in other words, a welded up demil/remil ca. 1960–64, and at the very bottom of the barrel in terms of dollar value). When the base part number changes, the part has been changed in a major way; prefix alterations (you'll see many specific applications in the photo and detail sections of this book) simply reflect later production indexed by a different drawing page number. However, as with a good reading of the rules before sitting down to play poker with strangers, forewarned is forearmed. The "D" letter for "drawing" was ultimately deleted on many parts. In fact, generally, as time wore on, fewer parts were numbered at all, and by the end of World War II, only more expensive parts bore numbers.

Easily identified Garand "business ends," obvious by the sight, gas cylinder lock, and gas cylinder lock plug configurations. From left: postwar (1955), late war (1944), and early World War II (1942). Details will be found in the following chapters and subchapters.

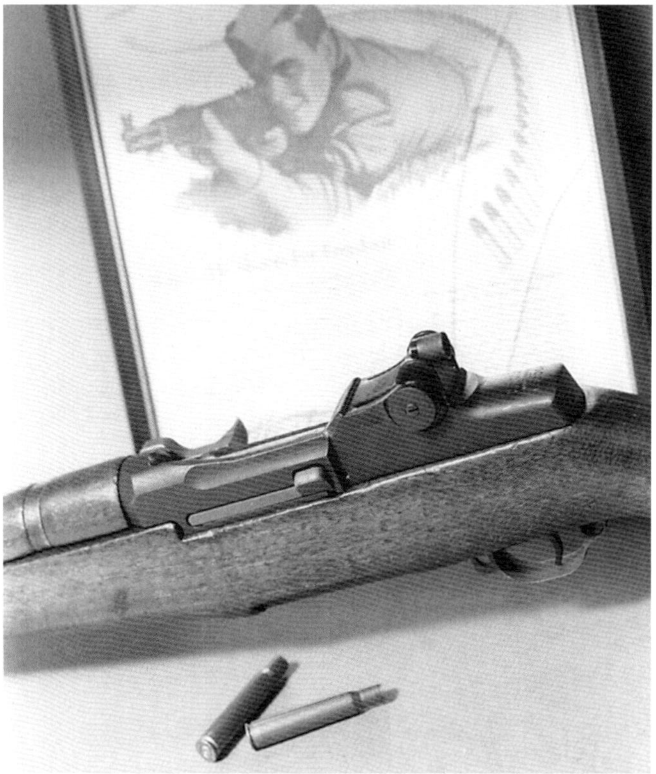

Early WRA M1 with Winchester-marked ammunition and World War II Winchester ad. Note that, for shooting convenience, this original Winchester rifle bears a late "National Match" rear sight aperture.

THE RIFLES BY MANUFACTURER

Springfield Armory ("SA" code). Manufactured from 1936–45 and 1952–56, with very few produced between late 1945 and early 1952. Some National Match rifles were delivered long after 1956. Springfield was the original M1 manufacturer; it built more than anyone, especially during World War II, and, depending on serial number ranges, generally evinced any and all changes first. World War II guns are most common, but there's absolutely nothing wrong with them unless some actual damage has occurred. Postwar Springfields of the last receiver variant are superb and those numbered over 6,000,000 quite rare.

All permutations of gray to greenish gray and black or charcoal will be found on Springfield guns, but most were very dark gray to black when first issued. The medium gray found on most extant guns is a fairly certain sign the gun has been refinished. Many different materials were used on the M1, and finish specifications were different for various parts. It is fairly accurate to say that a "virginal" Springfield M1 should not be absolutely uniform in finish color.

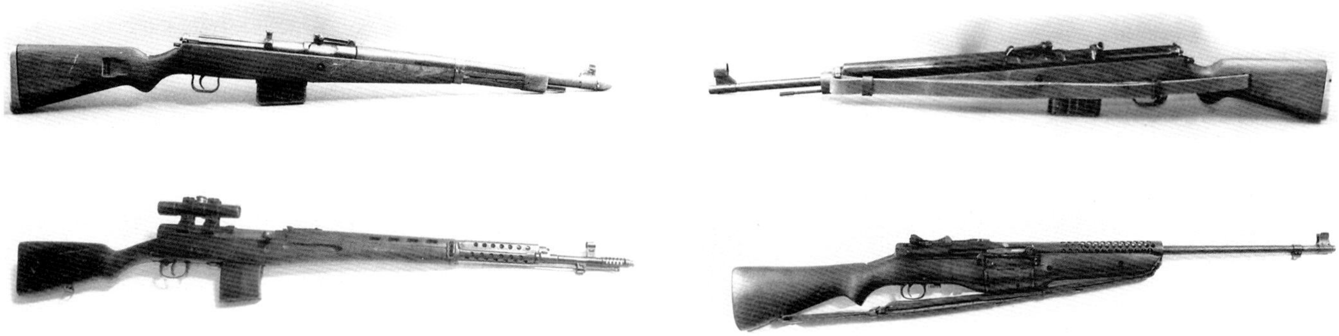

All the M1's contemporary competitors—full-power semiautos—evinced enough production or service glitches that they never saw extensive service in the field with ordinary infantry. They are, from top left to bottom right: [8] German G.41W, [9] German G.43/K.43, [10] Soviet Tokarev M40, and [11] US Johnson M.1941.

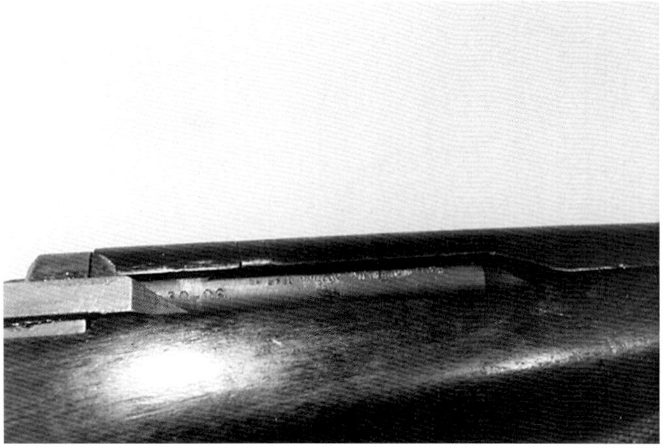

Postwar .30 06 Springfield Armory, Incorporated barrels were marked with caliber and "Geneseo, Illinois." This one has been marked by the installing smith with full data, similar to a military designation, including the date the tube was installed. These barrels were excellent shooters. This is the match version, installed on a ca. 1956 receiver.

A trio of early M1 Garand receivers, each of a different subvariation.

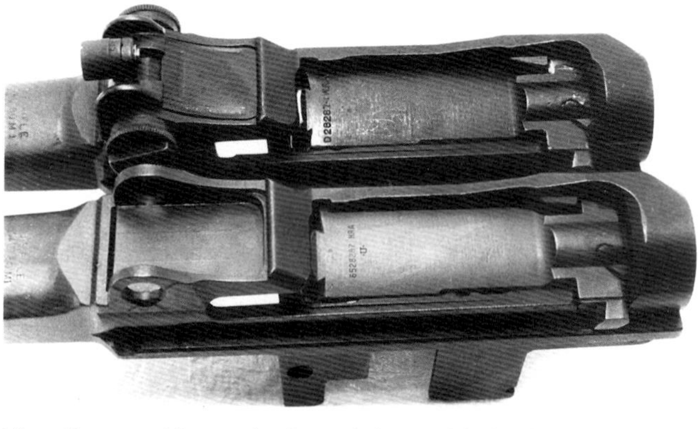

Virtually everything on the Garand changed during its long production life. The upper receiver in this photo is the crude, primitive Winchester -2 series; the lower a late H&R, numbered well over 5 million. The Winchester has been fitted with a National Match sight aperture in preparation for actual shooting, though the sight was not introduced until twenty years after this receiver was delivered (this is a convenience for shooters). Note the many detail and contour changes near the chamber area and the much heftier "horseshoe" area aft of the rear sight fitting on the postwar receiver. Most Winchester receivers and virtually all the bolts were out of true (basically out of specification). Not until the postwar WIN-13 series (ordered during the war apparently primarily delivered postwar, after contracts had expired), whose serial numbers overlap 1.6 million Springfields, did Winchester evince the willingness or capability to update its production by incorporating improvements. Later receivers are stronger and, obviously, tend to be less worn.

Springfield Armory experimented with many finishes late in the rifle's career, particularly on gas cylinders, and a few seemingly original rifles seem to have been oxided or black chrome plated at the armory.

Winchester Repeating Arms ("WRA" code). Manufactured in World War II only. Most Winchester Garand receivers are of the early 1940 -2 (dash two) configuration. Only the WIN-13 receivers, whose numbers overlap various Springfield contracts, showed any of the 32 major changes instituted at Springfield Armory during the war, as Winchester proved unwilling or unable to change its production line. Most early Winchester receivers were finished black/charcoal, though other parts may be various colors. Metal work on ancillary surfaces of Winchester M1s is quite rough, more so than on any other M1s, and many parts were

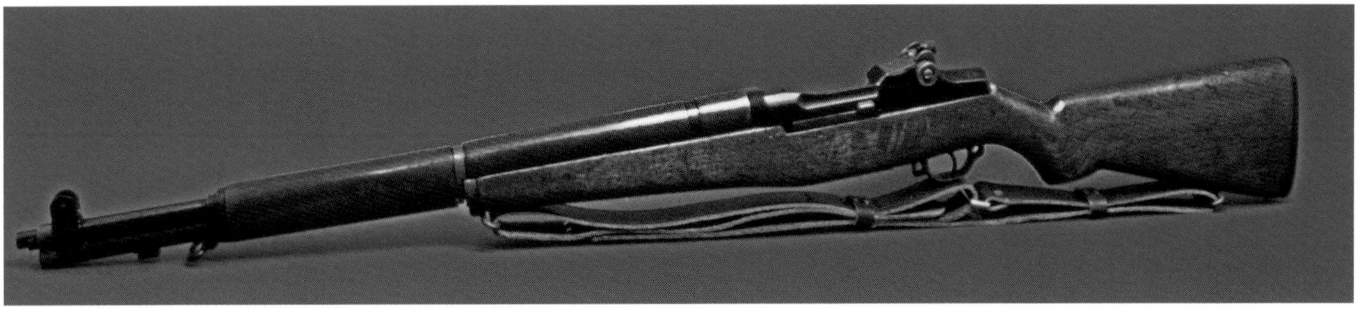

This old HRA Competition-style rifle was an oddity, and much of what it was and is remains speculation. It bore a black chrome finish (verified by chemical analysis) on most of its parts, and bore a heavy barrel of commercial origin when found. It seemed to have been at one time part of some sort of marksmanship demonstration and bore a thick yellow stripe around the butt stock, probably, one collector remarked, to "discourage theft by enlisted U.S.M.C. personnel." It was in no way collector original, bearing a post-1960 heavily bedded birch stock, milled trigger guard, and so on, but was a fascinating mystery.

marked in a nonregulation or very early manner. Wartime Winchester barrels were not customarily dated. Parts numbers are generally applied as on 1940 vintage specifications.

Springfield Armory Inc., Geneseo, IL ("SAI" code; note ® under logo). These are all postwar rifles, produced on investment cast receivers rather than specification forgings. As of this writing, new receivers are no longer being produced. Springfield began production in the 1970s, at first using GI parts almost exclusively. Later rifles use almost entirely new production parts. Their serial numbering began at seven million, and they are the *only* M1's bearing numbers that high.

International Harvester Corporation ("IHC" code). International Harvester had never built firearms before entering the program and did not deliver a rifle until late

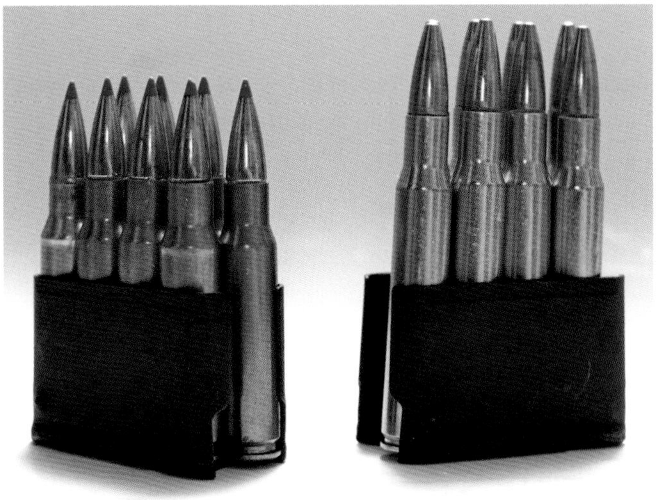

M1 Garand *en bloc* clips are usable with any Mauser based loading based upon the 1888 Mauser 8mm./7.92x57 cartridge, including .308/7.62x51 and .30 US Model of 1906.

1953, after much difficulty (including several bailouts by Springfield Armory, which actually produced many of the receivers). Because of marking and detail variations, the comparatively small quantities involved, and the history of the contract, the factory IHC is of little interest to shooters but fascinating to collectors (see the photo and detail sections). Serial numbers are all over 4,400,000. They are fairly common, but there are many variants/subvariants.

Pietro Beretta, Gardone val Trompia, Italy ("PB" code). At one time erroneously thought to have been produced on salvaged Winchester machinery (it was useless junk by 1950), the Berettas are among the very best fitted and finished Ml rifles ever made, not because of any magic from the manufacturer but merely because they were made under no combat pressure, largely to revitalize an ancient and respected firearms manufactory, and because many were made competitively to export orders. Almost every part of a Beretta rifle will carry the "PB" code and, since Beretta (and Fabrique Nationale ["FN"]) rebuilt M1s for the US military as early as 1947–48, it should shock no one that Beretta parts will sometimes be found on a US-issue DCM rifle. The Beretta M1s are quite rare in the United States. There are no parts interchange difficulties. As is true of the Winchesters, the Berettas command a considerable price premium, which is even more profound, since price pressure (a.k.a. demand) comes from both collectors and shooters. The Breda-built rifles are supposedly identical, made to the same tight specifications. Though I had never knowingly seen a Breda M1 Garand receiver before about 1999, I fully embraced the unusual nature of that brand name on my favorite rifle, and have since sopped up and used many.

Harrington & Richardson Arms Co. ("HRA" code).

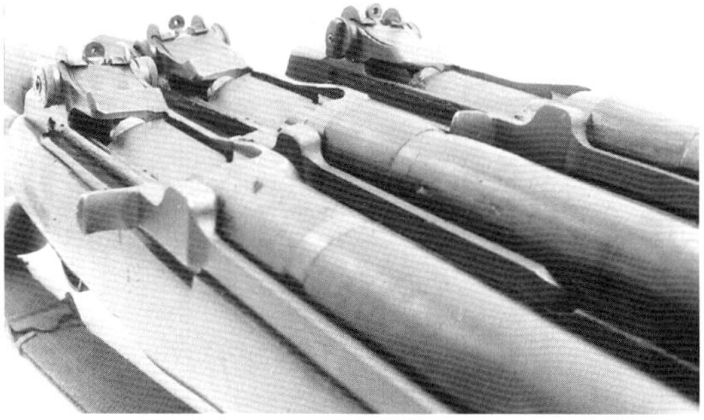

Various receiver vintages: from front, postwar, late war, and early war.

The "JLG" cartouche was the very last true cartouche marking on an M1 Garand stock. Technically ceasing to be standard in 1953, they show up sometimes on armory rifles a year or so later, seemingly original to the hardware. This likely reflects stocks being removed from rifles that required "further attention" and subsequently stripped of peripherals. But again: that's not proof; it's simply the most logical conclusion offered by most collectors and manufacturing consultants.

All H&R receivers were built and delivered from 1953 to 1957. One fairly often finds 7.62mm barrels bearing 1956–57 dates on very high-numbered HRAs. I am inclined to believe these were ordered and delivered as such, for by the 1950s H&R had gained a good reputation with the military for delivery on time and budget and seems to have been—along with the armories—the site of much M1/M14 development. All H&R receivers were to late specification and evince excellent craftsmanship throughout. They generally come closer to a true finish match than other M1s (excepting perhaps Beretta), and the serial numbers go much higher than the oft-quoted 5,700,000 seen in collector's books. H&Rs are fairly uncommon in truly superb cosmetic condition.

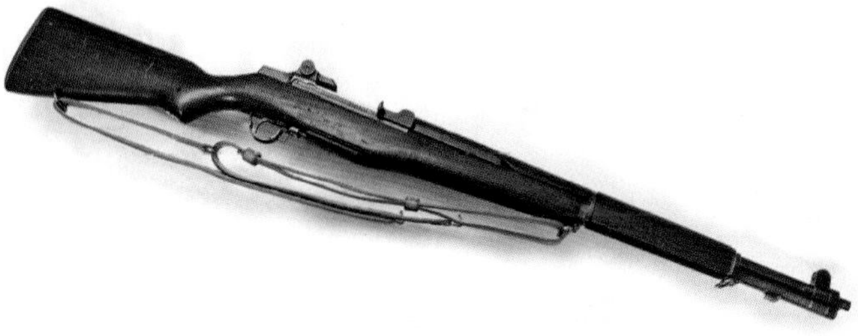

A great old H&R M1 in an SA stock of exactly the same vintage.

THE RIFLES BY STATESIDE SOURCE

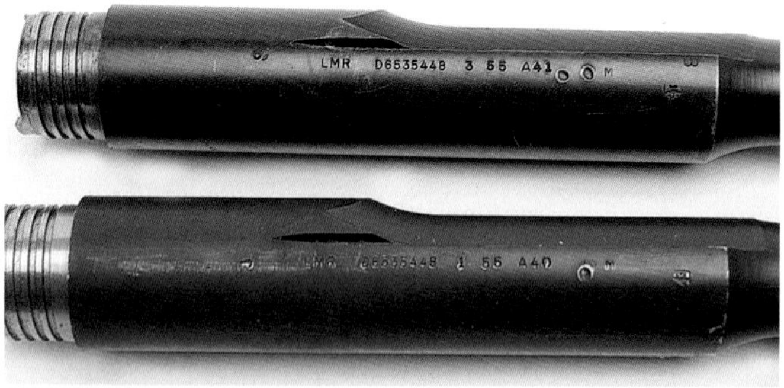

Two LMR M1 Garand barrels, these two both from 1955. The company was Line Materials, and the "R" was for "rifle." Had they produced marked pistol barrels, the sub-code would have been "LMP." These were used primarily with International Harvester rifles, from whence these two come, albeit there were also large orders for spares, and Harrington and Richardson also used some on some lots of their rifles. Supposedly, the punch marks adjacent to the lower handguard band identify IHC specimens, and also supposedly, unpunched specimens are spares or HRA's. A few of the detail markings used to be puzzling, but we've lately discerned, many of those were added by others, long after the barrels were made. My Air Force IHC competition "AFPG" rifle bore some very strange lettering that was apparently applied by its last military competitor, perhaps by an armorer who removed the barrel to check or measure something. One thing I've discovered: IHC CDD's (contract delivery dates) and barrel dates are often total nonsense, and both the highest and lowest numbered receivers I've logged bore barrels way outside their alleged born on dates. Yet, they were both DCM specimens, still wrapped and in cosmoline after being shipped from the Rock Island facility in the 1960s, undisturbed and surely untampered with by collectors. Ditto the specimens I've seen private purchased at facilities in the UK, also unfooled with.

Many snobbish types in the collecting community pooh-pooh the recent post-1985 reimport rifles as little more than junk, some of this stemming from the fact that all of them must be marked with importer's data, usually on the barrel, and the fact that, unlike DCM rifles and most pre-1968 imports, these barrels are often shot out. Like most overgeneralizations, though, this easy dismissal ignores some very important facts—primarily that the 1985–1990s imports represent a tremendous source of good receivers and parts. Plus, unlike with old DCM or current CMP rifles, one can choose a manufacturer or view the rifle before purchase. This section reviews rifles likely to be found by commercial or other source, and, while it is not complete (many thousands of M1s entered civilian hands by other means or importers), it'll provide the reader with some handy information.

As up-to-date as possible, this listing endeavors to cover all major stateside M1 importers/suppliers.

USA/DCM

The Office of the Director of Civilian Marksmanship provided M1 Garands to match shooters and N.R.A. members, duly qualified through authorized clubs. The last price under those old programs, ca. 1996, seems to have been $310. Under some conditions, the military released M1s to military personnel, particularly toward the end of World War II. Some were purchased far later, and many photographed for this book came off US bases abroad, with full paperwork. And it has to be acknowledged that some M1s left military ownership via extremely unauthorized means and can no longer be identified. Should anyone wonder, the stolen specimens were all "forgiven" ca. 1997.

While all these rifles, if not modified, are original issue, they have customarily seen some replacement of parts and/or updating/rebuilding, and may be in any parameter of condition. Significantly, they will not bear any physical identification as to source. In the last several months before first executing my 1998 M1 missive, I saw a smattering of DCM rifles shipped just before the name and function changes, including a collector-correct, totally unmodified lend-lease M1 ca. 1942 in mint condition with uncut operating rod; a Navy 7.62x51 Match rifle, pristine and properly bedded, with H&R receiver and birch stock; a grungy, disgusting Springfield with partially mashed gas cylinder, stock pounded badly, but no pitting and a virtually new ca. 1944 barrel (the barrel could be sold for more than the rifle's price to a collector who needed it, by the way); two very nice World War II vintage Springfield Armory M1s, one with all the Korean War vintage updates but, oddly, a WRA bolt, the other substantially unmodified; and a collector-correct IHC rifle, very nice, mint barrel, but totally incapable of holding 4 MOA on paper, even with match ammunition. The problem, as I worked with the owner, was straightforward: an incompetent had allowed a gas cylinder to become loose to the point of the absurd, and the receiver area of the butt stock was absurdly loose due to someone (this is a guess) wanting to make the rifle easy to strip. These ugly errors were corrected in a very straightforward manner. "Correct" has nothing to do with "undamaged."

Before a DCM rifle went out, it was certified in service condition. This certification was not the detailed check conducted by armorers when the gun was still in active service, but it at least certified, seemingly, the recipient that stocks will not be cracked in key areas, that parts work, and that the barrel is not excessively worn or eroded. This is now done almost infinitely better by the current CMP.

Pre-1968 Imports

M1s were sold or sent to many countries following World War II, partially due to Cold War pressures, but also because the Fascist forces stole all the local firearms and left their conquests unarmed. Since the Axis Powers' firearms—mostly left where they were dropped in defeat—were generic to parts and ammunition of out-of-business powers, the United States and England—and, in some of the world, the Soviet Union—rearmed the world. By the 1960s, M1 was viewed as too heavy, too powerful, and, since it was out of production in the US, a military lame duck. M1s began to arrive from Belgium, Germany, Italy, and elsewhere not long before the Gun Control Act of 1968 (GCA '68) cut off all surplus imports. As a group, these may be the best of all M1s, though they are also uncommon. Not marked as to origin, save where the recipient country attached some legend (usually in the buttstock), these rifles are very unlikely to have seen much use or heavy reconditioning/refinishing. Some rare rifles entered, too, including one IHC I have seen with British proofs. This was not a lend-lease rifle (IHC didn't produce any rifles until 1953) but was either used in British duty with some US-NATO attached unit or was in the UK on some nonmilitary function, for British proof laws require "resident" firearms be proofed and marked before even leaving customs. These guns carried very high prices for the time.

REMILs

In the 1950s, when M1 parts were cheap and plentiful, there were essentially no loose, independent receivers on the open market. Uncle Sam had determined that the best way to get rid of the leftovers from World War II and Korea was to torch them or saw them in half. However, some welders, machinists, weapons buffs, and dealers thought it might be a good idea to buy some of these pieces as scrap and see if the parts glut could be manipulated to produce some complete weapons. Back then this was all legal and more or less aboveboard. It began with machine guns, which even then had to be registered when completed. Fixture alignment was critical; sometimes little pieces had to fabricated, and about 50 percent of the assembled-reassembled receivers were junked (many of these were salvaged by less reputable dealers and resold). Naturally, the fronts and rears of the receivers didn't necessarily match by maker or style, so often late and early fronts and rears were butted together, even from different manufacturers. Much grinding and polishing was necessary to get these in a functionable condition, and a bump—either in the ridge line of the clip ejector recess area or the operating rod track on the receiver's right side—is the surest clue to a REMIL. Often, barrels were tack-welded in place because many of the receivers were already worn out. These are today the least valuable M1 receivers, though this does not mean they cannot shoot accurately and well. Some of the less reputable manufacturers even sleeved and arc welded two-groove Springfield barrels just ahead of the M1 barrel stub—another dead giveaway, for no production M1 barrel was made with two grooves. On the plus side, I've seen REMIL M1s with proper setup shoot excellent match scores. But these were extensively checked and modified guns. Any reweld is suspect, not because of class outfits like P&S, which checked all of its REMILs for straightness, hardness, and measurement specifications, but because of the bootleggers who pervaded the market with truly slipshod work.

Garands as received from the importer, all with "type 3" rear sights, representing (from left) mid-World War II, prewar ca. 1940, and late World War II receivers. Note the seam on the rightmost receiver, this line being apparently the effect of a worn mill blade stopping at the receiver's top ridge contour with each stroke, repeatedly. This line does not adversely impact the receiver's strength or value, and, in fact, the receivers like this that were examined were about .008 inch thicker in the rear horseshoe area than others. Note also the large, flat area of the postwar replacement stock, apparently designed to accept the revised selective fire, Remington-developed receiver, which never saw production. Note also small contour details among the various receivers.

Police Imports

Once GCA '68 was in effect, no military-owned firearm could be imported into the United States. However, there was an exemption for police officers and police-use items, and thus considerable numbers of H&R and IHC M1s (as well as the more common Springfields) got into the United States, primarily from Latin America, where they seem to have seen almost no use or modification. Some of these rifles carry the marks of the importers who brought them in; most do not. Most seem to have entered with new wood, primarily "SA" marked and cartouched. I have seen only a few, but all were essentially perfect mechanically and cosmetically, either rebuilt to new condition stateside or mint from shipment south to return north.

The Post–'85 Era

In 1985, significant modifications to the Gun Control Act of 1968 allowed reimportation/importation to the US market of all firearms then on the official Curios and Relics list, among which were M1s. Since the beginning of the Military Aid Program (MAP) in the late 1940s, however, shipment to the United States of any significant materials acquired from US military sources (substantially with taxpayer dollars) has been prohibited. After many customs, BATF, and other hassles and legal battles, however, this provision—intended to keep some of the more corrupt of our allies from enhancing their personal fortunes at the expense of the American taxpayer—was relaxed for what

Three just cleaned up M1 Garands from about 1985, imported from Morocco by Century Arms. On the left is a Springfield midwar piece, which I instantly fitted with an NM2A small aperture, a rather late Winchester, updated with postwar sights at some time during its long and storied life, and a rather early International Harvester. The IHC was almost 100 percent correct just as it was unpacked.

American shooters knew to be obsolescent military hardware, of use only to shooters and collectors.

This section is intended to be helpful in identifying Garands brought in since 1985. All such firearms are stamped with the importer's name or letter code, home city, and caliber. A summary follows, and, again, it is undoubtedly not complete, for many other small lots have entered.

Century Arms ("CAI" code). These rifles came from Italy, northern Africa, and China. Conditions run the gamut, but they were not freshly refinished just before or after entry, the lots were not very big, and most barrels are sound.

Blue Sky Productions ("Blue Sky" code). These rifles came from South Korea. Most barrels were not good; some even showed evidence of having been polished with high-speed rigs before refinish. Virtually all were refinished freshly before resale. Some markings are better than others. This lot includes many rare and /or unusual rifles, but most saw major rebuilds and so, for the collector, are mostly parts sources. To the shooter, however, these rebuilds are advantageous, for the later operating rods and other parts found on most of these rifles are superior performers and considerably less likely to be worn out. Many stocks are repaired with pins (a fix that was mechanically successful but cosmetically unappealing). Many are cracked and unrepaired. Many "NM" operating rods are seen on service rifles.

Federal Ordnance Incorporated ("Fed Ord" code). These rifles came from the Phillipines. Many were pitted in noncritical areas due to the humid climate, and virtually all were oxide-refinished before stateside resale. The importer applied markings on the front receiver strut rather than on the barrel. The wood was generally sanded heavily before resale, removing virtually all markings. Most barrels are better than those of Blue Sky rifles, and more than half I have seen were new or virtually new. These tend to be good shooters as is, but ugly.

Sherwood/Samco (several codes). These rifles were brought in from Israel by Sherwood and Samco virtually as soon as the law changed. Having spent parts of their careers in countries as diverse as West Germany and Yugoslavia (the Israelis apparently purchased some from the United States and some from Europe), these rifles have many odd parts but are of very high quality. Do not be surprised to find German, Yugoslav, or FN-Belgian barrels on these. There are many M1Ds, some M1Cs in this batch, most of them probably field-modified to that specification but technically correct. Some M1C variants with 1-inch rings (probably U.S.M.C. units by Griffin & Howe [G&H]) were in this lot, but without the glass. This lot was genuinely superb, and most of the rifles remain in splendid condition.

Arlington Ordnance ("Arl Ord" or similar code). Many

Garands and M1 Carbines bear this mark. Relatively late entries into the surplus market, the guns primarily come from Korea. These guns were not subjected to new refinishes before import unless it was really necessary, meaning there is a greater chance of finding an original finish rifle among these than among some others. More than one hundred fifty of these rifles were purchased in preparation for this book and examined in great detail. They were generally in better-than-average condition and import marked with some care and subtlety. Among them were several original, unmodified postwar rifles and a large number of almost original World War II rifles that were easily restored, including the Winchesters, H&Rs, and late Springfields heavily illustrated herein. Jack Williams, marketing director for Arlington Ordnance, advises me that it is Arlington's intention to quality control the rifles as far as fit and safety and not to interfere with old refinishes or original finish (whereas most of the Blue Sky guns were refinished pro forma). My favorite competition/accuracy rifle was an Arlington Ord M1 ca. 1954, fitted with appropriate high quality and ultra-precise parts. These are the best large lots of Garands available at the time of this writing.

Springfield Sporters ("SPR SP" code). Most of these rifles came from Colombia. They were received by the Colombians from the United States and Europe, and they include some Berettas. There are many "gray"—unmarked, probably US-MAP supplied—barrels on these rifles. All stateside-ordered rebuilds and specifications seem to have been adhered to, and there is no general pattern of receiver refinishing. These rifles all seem to have excellent barrels and are one of the best choices for the owner who wishes to shoot his rifle "as-is" and immediately. Should the shooter/collector wish to upgrade, restore, or match prepare a less-than-perfect M1 Garand, data provided in the last part of this text will give considerable information that will be of use. Suffice it to say, an M1 for four hundred dollars is almost always not a bargain, whereas one for a thousand or more dollars may actually be cheap. It depends on what the rifle actually is, and what the intended use happens to be. Almost no M1 from any of these subcategories is really a piece of junk, but it may very well have some pieces of junk hanging on it.

THE OLD RIFLE REJUVENATED: THE SAFE, ACCURATE, SMART, COMPLETE M1

While it's true that most any M1 receiver can be transformed into a reliable, straight-shooting rifle eventually, the process is not necessarily easy or cheap. Little known to collectors, who are sometimes even shooting rifles with original World War II bolts and unmodified operating rods, the process of shooting the M1 is also not necessarily safe. In fact, Technical Operational Orders issued to armorers from 1947 to 1949 ordered the replacement of all original operating rods and/or the addition of a hemispherical cutout at the first rearward 90-degree joint, since some deaths and injuries had been caused by the operating rods' breakage at that point. In the mid-1950s similar information demanding local inspection of IHC- and WRA-marked bolts for signs of bending, and of IHC operating rods for excessive hardness, was also dispensed. These are situations where the meaning behind specifications was locally misinterpreted or mishandled by the manufacturer. The IHC operating rods were not all defective, but the recent appearance on the civilian market of large numbers of new IHC rods causes one to wonder if these might be the ones in question. Most of the Winchester bolts I have seen and/or inspected showed the "too soft lug, too hard boltface" problem. Obviously, though the bending was already well along on the lugs, not all of these were destroyed or discarded as they were supposed to be. This is fortunate for collectors, unfortunate for shooters.

All the usual admonitions about headspace and ammunition applied to other arms, particularly semiautos, apply especially to the M1. But other specifications, such as gas cylinder integrity, size of gas vent (different in 7.62 and .30-06 rifles), lubrication (heavy grease, heavy grease only, and enough of it), condition of follower spring (most people call it the recoil spring, which is what it really is), and general cleanliness of the bore and gas system must also be checked and adhered to. Nowhere in any modern manual is oil mentioned as a lubricant, and that's 100 percent correct. Using oil on an M1 receiver is what truly bends operating rods and breaks parts. Use grease.

The most expensive parts on the M1 Garand are the operating rod, barrel, gas cylinder, and stock. The most likely to fail is the follower/operating rod spring (recoil spring). A troubleshooting chart analyzing M1 glitches is included in this book. It can be quickly summarized, though, by noting that an operating rod catch, bullet guide, follower/recoil spring, firing pin, and extractor are the most necessary spare parts. Clumsy folks who insist upon stripping the bolt in a hurry should order the ejector in multiples. Unrestrained, this heavily sprung part can be propelled with great velocity and—if not imbedded in the shooter's person—easily lost. For civilian shooters—and particularly for those who shoot the shorter, lighter 7.62x51 round—the ejector spring can be safely trimmed by two or even three coils. Stock Garands fling brass 20 or more feet, which was handy for the military but likely means nothing to you. Polishing the extractor surface means your brass is less likely to be damaged, and it will be located more uniformly as well. Where for parts? Check Part IV of this text. The remainder of this section breaks important parts down into information convenient for the shooter and likely useful for the collector as well.

Barrels

Garand barrels are expensive, and the wise shooter should appreciate that the cheapest of today's barrels will outperform even mint original GI issue from more than fifty or sixty plus years ago. The best of the civilian aftermarket heavy barrels can produce a whole new category of accuracy—and last longer to boot. Service bolt guns can't compete with the prepared Garand for accuracy, and, despite sniveling to the contrary, the Springfield '03 match rifles with match ammo couldn't equal the performance of selected but unaltered M1s with postwar service ammo. A new, high-quality custom barrel can put the semiautomatic Garand into a speed-with-accuracy combination not many other long guns can even approach. However, those who both collect and compete would be wise to pursue these activities with separate rifles. A Douglas or Krieger heavy profile match barrel on a properly prepared M1 may cost less than a ca. 1955 Springfield "NM" in pristine condition but will shoot far better and last longer to boot. That's why Marine Corps and Navy match teams began ordering special equipment outside ordinary mass procurement channels as early as 1951.

There is another important footnote about the Garand: provided you can afford the ammo, M1 tends to be shot more and in less time than most rifles. At 2,600+ feet per second (fps), copper fouling very quickly becomes a problem. I've bought shot-out M1s to which accuracy was restored instantly by careful treatment with copper solvents and/or Outers' reverse electroplate process. Williams sells a particularly handy copper solvent in a handy, unbreakable bottle that goes with me where my M1s go. I also use Kleenbore Copper Cutter and Hoppe's #9 in the Benchrest Copper Solvent version.

Now the barrels, by brand and category.

GI

Government issue and military aid program M1 barrels were produced by about everyone who could bore and contour the stock and cut the rifling. Winchester replacement barrels (mostly ca. 1953–64), use "electric writing" logo style and are sometimes mistaken for issue barrels. Winchester barrels sell for absurdly high prices. Only postwar replacement barrels originally carried manufacturing dates from the Winchester factory. One will find, as I did to my amazement, "dated" WW2 W.R.A.-marked barrels, but whose details were stamped in by US ordnance inspectors, primarily in Italy and Australia, and have *nothing to do* with the New Haven factory. They're not fake, either, and are a fascinating part of rifle's histories. They are *always* later, obviously, than the tube's manufacture date. Marlin, Savage, Remington (I've seen only two, and they seem to have been experimental) and many others produced replacement barrels, as did some other small contractors. Virtually all were four-groove, though I have seen five- and six-groove replacement units with military markings and one Marlin with many-groove button rifling. There were no two-groove M1 barrels, though some shady operators welded and recontoured combinations of shot-out M1 rifles and two-groove Springfield barrels and sold them as originals. Collectors will pay high prices for original barrels, but to the shooter they just aren't worth much. A Winchester barrel, original or replacement, which can cost over five hundred dollars, will not perform as well as the $120–$150 civilian barrel. GI match barrels are not much better than standard units unless they are of very late vintage.

Heavy Match

Unquestionably, the best barrel for the M1 is the Wisconsin-built Krieger. Douglas is a close second. The Krieger is very heavy, which demands reducing the rear handguard to a mere

In many ways, a rendition of rifle as art or idealized M1, visually and otherwise, this 5.4 million M1 Garand rifle was executed to full competition levels, again by Derrick Martin, on an import receiver acquired from Arlington Ordnance, with heavy barrel, grim tight bedding, all the relief and trigger job functions, and so on. But it's that flame-grained, military style walnut stock, a very rare late Fajen, which marks this extraordinarily accurate shooting machine as remarkable in every way. Note the extra-heavy third keeper hoop on the sling. In those days, I shot exclusively sling wrapped, and would slide that baby over any hooks that might tear me or my jacket. Also worth of note: the mismatched gas cylinder lock is very common, even on service rifles. Very few M1s ever finish matched, and on late rifles and match rifles, there were usually several completely different tones on metal parts. That reflects different steels and finish specification. Nothing in the specification discussed finish match, and indeed, sights were supposed to very, very dark, for reasons of obvious reflection control.

shell. The Douglas is only slightly smaller, and the handguard must be similarly sanded or routed. Both are available as stainless units, and both can be had in 7.62x51 (.308). Both should be ordered short chambered and then finish chambered to the shooter's bolt and receiver by a smith or armorer. Olympic/Safari Arms used to market a barrel similar to the Douglas, which I have not had an opportunity to test. Douglas offers six grooves as an option. Citadel offered a similar barrel in four or six grooves. These are the most durable and accurate M1 barrels, though also the hardest to fit and the most expensive.

Standard Configuration

Springfield Armory, Incorporated offers new barrels of six-groove pattern in both calibers to a slightly enhanced GI specification and also has a match specification version. The match units cost forty dollars more. Both were excellent. The option of four grooves is listed but apparently is not actually available. Citadel and others offered service and match barrels of standard configuration for very reasonable prices, but there are some borderline crooks out there selling rejects and remarked barrels at high prices.

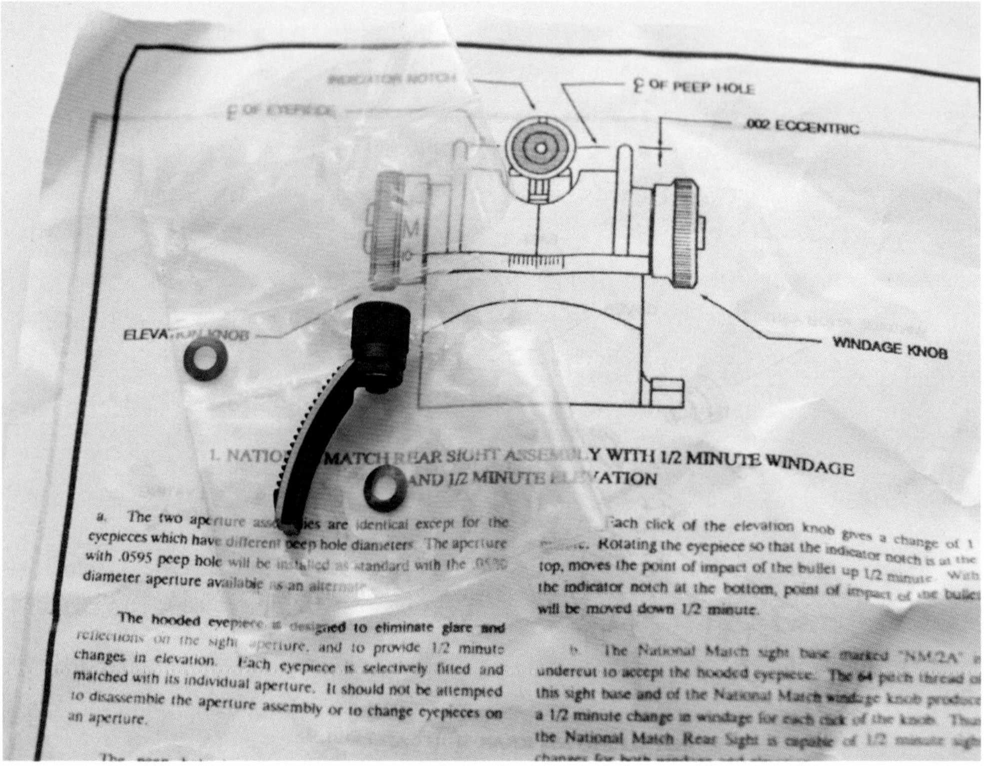

The NM2A hooded rear sight aperture was developed for the M1 and M14 ca. 1962 for National Match and service competition purposes. Generally available in .0520" and .0595" aperture diameters, these are still produced, and can be fitted by careful reduction of the outer slide panels to *any* rear sight base. Half minute-of-angle adjustments for elevation are done by rotation, using the notch to determine position. However, half MOA adjustments for windage require either reconfiguration of the standard base and threads, or an NM2A set. These are still produced, both by new manufacturers and by current and former military contractors.

.30 06 loads in clips and ready to shoot.

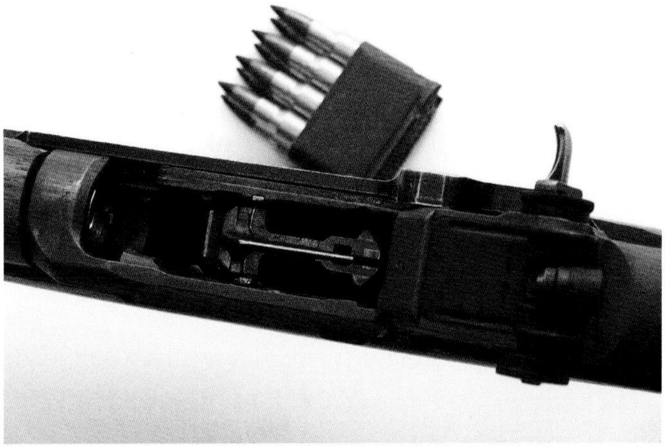

A presentation/recreational M1 in a functionable cross between World War II looks and match functionality is shown with black-tipped armor piercing ammo in commercial Winchester brass, .308 commercial, functionally identical to 7.62x51 NATO. The bullets are salvaged World War II AP, weighed and sorted to provide optimum accuracy. Note the small "NM" combined with reproduction locking bar rear sight apparatus.

Wood is an easily solved problem. I used, until the venerable firm folded, Fajen stocks on my fancy guns, and lately prices on stocks alone as well as on complete sets have been falling. At the time of this writing, there is a great deal of good, issue walnut on the market at very low prices. There are also plastic stocks available (see the data in the marketplace section of Part IV). It is wise to have spare handguards.

The late-issue match sight set used on the Garand was introduced in 1962. Many surplus dealers stock them. The hooded aperture can be used with the service base and knobs but will not give fine adjustments. (See the match section in Part II for details.)

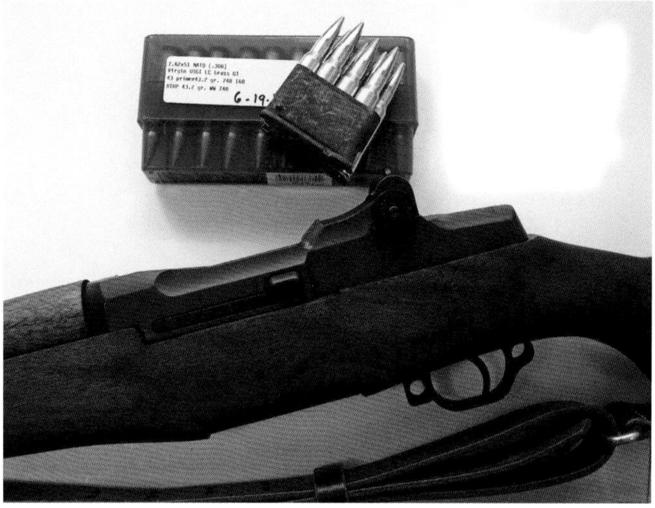

Precision loads on weighed, unfired, pull-down Lake City brass, utilizing WW 748 ball powder and detail measured bullets, plainly marked, dated, and displayed with a presentation rifle in the newer, shorter, more economical and more accurate loading. Note the use of the small aperture NM rear sight aperture on a reproduction locking bar sight setup. These may be Sierra, Hornady, or Lapua bullets, all three of which were used in various incarnations for accuracy testing by the author 2011–2017.

In a genuine G.I. clip, displayed here with a Citadel-brand, high-grade, heavy barrel (this firm was still in business effective 2019, but had ceased dealing with the public and with small orders), repose eight rounds which cannot be replicated by means other than handloading. They're US, never-been-fired, pulled down 7.62x51mm, brass hulls, the heavier military configuration, precision-measured and weighed and uniformed length, primer flash hole, and neck, and seated with Finnish Lapua 167-grain SCENAR boat-tail hollow pointed bullets. The powder loads were Varget, secured and measured to =/- one one-hundredth of a grain. This sort of precision, with a modern barrel and some rifle free-floating and decent trigger and similar prep, offers minute-of-angle and better accuracy out of Mister Garand's old rifle.

This is the muzzle end and gas cylinder area of an original "Type 2" National Match M1 Garand rifle, apparently originally departing the armory with the wartime low lock and poppet lock screw. Most of the actual competition rifles used the solid wartime lock screw, and no one knows why, but it seems a large minority of these, if not most, were shipped with the earlier lock. Note the scribed, not stamped, letters between the hoops of the gas cylinder. These were only cut in that way for a rather short period.

M1D barrels with blocks are now available new and used, and M1C drilling jigs are on the market. The wisest way to scope an M1 is probably with B-Square's unit, which doesn't require modifying the rifle.

BMF-Activator's Straight pull York Conversion kit changed the old semi auto into a straight pull bolt gun and saved several pounds of weight along the way. One advantage to the unit was that those parts that are hardest to clean are not on the rifle in its hunting, straight pull condition. BMF/York folded, apparently about 2001, but the principles illustrated when the old outfit was utilized helped explain the mechanism.

Smith/Western Ordnance in Tempe, Arizona, markets a compensator/muzzle brake for the Garand, furnished in Parkerized external finish, very convenient for extended practice fire, with no deleterious effect on accuracy. It seems to increase my shoulder endurance by about 10 percent to 20 percent. This unit replaces the gas cylinder lock and somewhat modernizes the old service rifle's appearance.

Smiths around the country market services to convert M1 into a sort of BM.59 clone, just as Beretta did many years or so ago. This is handy, but the twenty-round magazine capacity may cause users to run afoul of the gun confiscation lobby when it has its next couple of twitches.

.308/7.62 NATO conversions, however, are easy, handy, economical, and smart. Only a barrel change is required. The chamber bushings, sooner or later, will cause problems. The magazine spacers are not necessary, but if one operates rifles in both calibers, they will prevent the nightmare jams which occur when a .30-06 round meets a .308 chamber. The newer, shorter cartridge is more efficient, less powder-intensive, generates less gross heat, and, despite a higher chamber pressure, generates less down the spout—which is why about 1⁄64-inch enlargement of the gas port is required. Most important of all (as discussed elsewhere in this book), high-quality practice ammo is everywhere and cheap. The very nice HXP-marked Greek .30 Model of 1906 fodder will be almost entirely gone by the time this tome sees ink. Also amusing and factual: The truly original cartridge for the M1 Garand was the fascinating .276 Pedersen Center Fire, in its final incarnation, designed to use faster, more modern powders. The overall length of that cartridge is very close to that of the much more efficient and modern shorter loading.

Practical Parts for the Practical Man

The most common malfunction of the M1 Garand is the premature dumping of the clip, accompanied by one or more live cartridges. (See the troubleshooting guide and the photo on page 23.) Actually, the most common breakage is the snapping of the recoil spring, but, surprisingly, this often does not eventuate any malfunction at all. With the early ejection difficulty, the clip latch/clip ejector mechanism is rarely the problem. The correct fix prescribed in all manuals is the replacement of the bullet guide and the operating rod catch. Both should be replaced simultaneously. Of course, many overfinished and/or out-of-specification clips eventuate this issue, so it is wise to ONLY ever use actual G.I. clips, US or foreign. These are not expensive parts. Stamped bullet guides, which tend to work better, sell for as little as five dollars, and the operating rod catch is seldom more than ten dollars. Procedures for replacement are outlined in the manual included in this book. The time involved should be less than three minutes.

Contrary to conventional wisdom, match M1s are less fussy mechanically than even the robust Garand service rifle, if clean and properly lubricated with grease and otherwise correctly prepared. Keeping the stock tightly bedded can be a nuisance.

Special parts and preparations on National Match or "Civvy" accuracy rifles are generally as follows (as detailed in the National Match section of this book): 1) all wood relieved so as not to impinge directly on barrel, receiver, operating rod, or gas cylinder; 2) gas cylinder upper hoop bored out and shortened, so as not to contact handguard ferrule or barrel; 3) middle band and often handguard ferrule secured to front (upper) handguard, after boring or sanding out same to free float front of barrel; 4) trigger pull cleaned up, deburred, and if/when necessary, lightened to normal minimum of 4.5 pounds very clean pull; 5) tin operating rod guide/sleeve thrown away, though lately, I have seen some merely highly polished and drilled for heat relief on nicely working rifles; 6) stacking swivel's rear tab undercut, beveled, or otherwise reduced to eliminate any and all interference with the front handguard and/or handguard ferrule; 7) fitting of M1/M14 NM2A sight set, complete with knobs and bases, normally both front and rear; 8) often, exact and precise mating and lapping of bolt/barrel/chamber interface; 9) glass or epoxy bedding of the rifle's action and trigger group area, and, often, relief of the front well of the buttstock, or replacement of same with a polymer surface to minimize swelling and damage.

Certain other fits are often done to make M1 more reliable. Often, key moving parts are black-chromed or polymerized or hard- chromed—in particular the operating rod, bolt, and hammer. The military frequently marked bolts and trigger groups with the last three or four digits of the receiver serial number rather crudely with a scratch awl. Barrels were frequently, but not always, marked "NM," or sometimes "HG" (High Grade) on the left front, about 2 inches back from the front, upper "hoop" of the gas cylinder.

Most of these same detailed procedures were also followed with the later M14, many parts of which will interchange with the earlier rifle. The NM2A sights, in fact, were primarily intended for the M14.

Many of these operations can be done by anyone with minimal hand tool skills.

M1 FODDER AND FEED: AMMO FOR THE WARHORSE

The M1 Garand is a rifle with two personalities: the military rifle (rough 'n tumble, the collector's darling) and the shooting thoroughbred (still tough, but precise and accurate). It is therefore appropriate for the shooter who owns more than one gun or who enjoys both endeavors to—as I tried to do during my shooting/collecting career—clearly define two diets for his classic. There's plain old powder-burning, high-powered plinking, and then there's truly precise shooting.

For fairly casual shooting, there's no reason to be afraid of corrosive ammunition, provided one is willing to wash away the salts created by the primers. The proper and fast way is with a window-cleaner-like solution of detergent, water, ammonia, and alcohol followed by a normal cleaning with conventional solvents and brushes. The ammoniated solution is best applied while the bore is still hot to warm. Another vital step in prolonging barrel life and preserving accuracy is an aggressive attack on copper fouling. Specialized copper solvents and Outers' reverse electroplate kit are very helpful. A few folks with no chemical background inquire why the ammonia is used. It's simple. Ammonia is a fairly profound alkaline compound, and part of the process is neutralizing acid byproducts of primers. The stuff also loosens coupled copper molecules, which is why there's so much of it in the specialized solvents for removing that element from bores.

M1 runs dirty. Leaving it that way is never smart.

How you get it that way—having fun with the rifle—involves shooting what you aim at. Despite a great deal of Internet hooey to the contrary, the very best loads for the Garand are those calculated specifically for the rifle—and that means handloads, executed by a careful shooter who knows and follows the rules. But there are many alternatives. The first choice to make is, of course, which kind of cartridge to purchase or load.

There just isn't much low-cost, quality .30-06 on the market, and supplies must inherently decline as this now obsolete military loading dwindles on the surplus market. In recent years shooters have snapped up lots of Dominican ammo (actually, mostly made by Remington and almost entirely Boxer-primed), FN from Belgium, and ancient M1 and M2 ball and ca. 1942 armor piercing. French Gevelot is corrosive, and most of it is quite good, but like all French ammunition, powder stability can be a problem. Recent "remanufactured" military ball and armor piercing ammo from Gibbs/Navy Arms is fully reloadable and better than old M2 ball but will probably sell out soon. The Austrian ball ammunition on the market is fine but expensive. The Dutch ball was way too expensive and cost more than brand-new commercial ammo.

There is some very decent Ethiopian ammo reaching the market ca. 2019, but some of it has not had good storage, made obvious upon first sight. However, the best of it outperforms HXP for accuracy.

Very soon, the decent, Greek-produced "HXP" will disappear from the shooter's market. It was ball ammunition, to M2 specification, and accuracy was acceptable.

The non-G.I. Federal ammunition for the Garand uses an overall, generalized ball specification, but is quite soft, shooting considerably below hard specification G.I. ammo at all ranges. However, it functions an in-specification rifle nicely, reduces fatigue and recoil compared to military ball ammunition, and is *very* accurate compared to service fodder. Federal's motives for and execution of dedicated M1 Garand ammo bespeak solid reasoning, and shooters should use this fodder with confidence.

Among commercial items, the Prvi Partizan I acquire on the open market has performed well and is still quite reasonably priced. Federal's American Eagle is sensibly priced—cheaper than most surplus. Of course, Federal's Gold Match—retailing at well over a buck a shot!—is the standard by which all others are measured but is surely not plinking ammo for most of us. Occasionally some original GI .30-06 match becomes available, but it will not equal the Federal loading.

7.62x51 NATO (the slightly different commercial equivalent is .308 Winchester) ammunition poses far less mystery. Cheap, high-quality practice ammo is virtually ubiquitous, and virtually every maker in the world produces supplies of premium quality ammunition at competitive prices. The Argentine, Belgian, Israeli, Spanish, and Venezuelan surplus ammo from surplus suppliers is all suitable. The corrosive rounds from the Eastern Bloc are also fine but require the special cleaning procedures outlined earlier.

Federal's Gold Match is available in this loading, too. But Winchester and Remington also produce high-quality precision loads using 168-grain match bullets in the .308 caliber. All are superb.

When it's time for ultra-serious shooting, handloads are the prescription. Of late, my primary powders in both calibers are IMR 4064, Hodgdon's VARGET, Hodgdon BLC-(2), and Accurate Arms 2520. Generally, 168-grain to 190-grain match profile boattail hollow points are the bullets of choice, with IMI's bulk package 150-grain boattail hardnose providing an economical alternative. The best accuracy is always available with 165-grain and heavier projectiles.

I have lately standardized on Federal's Gold Match 210GM primer for ball powders and CCI's Benchrest Large Rifle for all other powders.

Semiautomatic rifles are somewhat more sensitive to pressure permutations than bolt actions: too little, and the gun will not run; too much and (if something doesn't get broken), at the very least, the brass may not land in the same county. Avoid 4350 and anything slower in full-power loads for the Garand, the M14, or any similar gas-operated rifles (though with reduced loads, at about a .30/30 power level, they work fine). This comes from a coincidence of their development of highest heat precisely where the gas ports live. Even Winchester/Olin 760 ball has been used in my testing through the M1, but loads were developed with great care, and for very specific purposes which day-to-day shooters will never encounter.

Sierra's manuals include accuracy data, though the loads chosen may not be appropriate for the Garand.

Much of the voodoo about M1 match loads consists of, if not bunk, then, at the very least, strange exaggerations. The GI match information suggests strongly that if 168–175 grain match bullets are held in the velocity range of 2,580–2,630 fps, accuracy will be close to optimal. That's more or less regardless of the powder or brass used, provided charges are precisely uniform and case volume and condition are carefully checked for consistency. Most any brass will suffice, but any and all controls to test for uniform weight and volume will pay off downrange.

Many combinations can work well, but the components must be as uniform as possible. "Batching" cases by weight and volume is important. Though it's true that I get fine results with setups claimed inappropriate for a caliber (especially in the Garand), my long-range findings are that consistency from one round to the next few means a great deal in overall results and, therefore, scores and group size.

One often-heard bit of poppycock—tested empirically and found to be false—concerns the use of match ammunition in service rifles. The slightly heavier bullets have no negative impact at all. Pressures are, if anything, a bit lower.

Lousy lubrication—that is, no lubrication, wrong lubricants, or insufficient lubrication—causes the bent operating rod syndrome sometimes associated with heavier bullets. It is, however, true that loading heavier bullets, even at comparatively low pressures and velocities, can beat up an M1—especially the operating rod. Surprisingly, this effect is often more profound with lower-pressure loads, and, again, the reason is simply understood through a little discussion of the physics involved. A bullet moving at, say, 1,200 fps (as a 230-grain slug might be in a Garand) exposes the entire gas system to pressure for more than twice as much time as a bullet at 2,600 fps+. There is, therefore, a tendency for the operating rod to be under rearward force long after it's fully back. Even this seems to be partially nullified by the use of heavy grease on the top rod rail of the receiver.

In 1986 I concocted an experiment to test the bendability of the M1 operating rod. From a retailer in Los Angeles, I acquired some 700 rounds of Browning 220-grain roundnose .30-06 loads. These I ran through an ancient, pitted M1 with a straight but pitted operating rod. After 691 rounds I had no bending, no malfunction, and no signs of serious peening. I was using an automotive MDS/graphite bearing grease rather heavily. Somewhat annoyed at being unable to induce a problem I had been told would become obvious in 20 rounds, I used turpentine to remove all the grease. Seven rounds later, the oiled rifle—remember, I told you about wrong lubricants—couldn't even be properly disassembled without heavy force, for the operating rod was on the brink of breakage, the spring had broken, and the right front bolt lug was heavily peened. Point proven, I gave the two remaining loaded rounds to a man firing a Remington 700 lightweight—he may still be angry with me—and satisfied myself that another little bit of scuttlebutt had been disproved.

A good M1 match barrel—and the military followed this pattern in M1 and M14 preparations—should get continuously more accurate for about 3,500 rounds. The tube should remain at a very high level for about 10,000 rounds. This can be extended greatly by careful cleaning and can be greatly compressed by failing to clean properly or by radical, repeated rapid firing. Without cleaning, a tight M1 match barrel will evince seriously compromised accuracy after only a few hundred rounds. Copper fouling impacts all high-velocity barrels and must be fought constantly. The higher the velocity, the more rapid the fire; the higher the heat, the worse the problem becomes.

With regular cleaning, gas ports do not corrode, though they tend to erode from heat about the time the barrel finally dies.

Slower-burning powders leave more residue in the gas system. Ball powders leave less residue than extruded powders of similar speed. Powder residue is *abrasive.* Abrasives abrade. That means, "remove material by friction." The rules of physics don't change because someone on the Internet so claims.

For handloaders who like to practice regularly, a good procedure is to work up a 150- or 168-grain load barely sufficient to operate the rifle. This will reduce fatigue on the shooter and rifle (the lower velocities contribute less copper fouling), and the good habits that come only from practice can thus be enjoyed more cheaply and with less work afterward. Each Garand will react differently, but with proper, heavy grease lubricants (never use oil, especially not on the receiver grooves and bolt corners) and a good polish on the upper surface of the operating rod, it is often amazing how little powder/pressure is required to operate this big, old, ugly rifle.

Even the old adage about heavy bullets tending to break or compromise the rifle is not necessarily correct if sensible caution is exercised. More details follow in subsequent sections of this book.

STRAIGHT AND TRUE DOWNRANGE: M1 GARAND AND ACCURACY

The military match manual for the specialized preparation of the M1 Garand is included later in this book, so it would be redundant to fully explore those processes here. Indeed, to diehard collectors, attempting such a recreation is blasphemous. A good, handy guide to quick accurizing of the Garand is included in the N.R.A.'s *The M1 Rifle.* However, even the "if it ain't issue, it ain't M1" hardnose should at least read the information in this section, for it explains some characteristics of the rifle that were once fairly mysterious and outlines the philosophy employed in setting up the accuracy rifle.

When the M1 first appeared in match competition in 1939 and 1940, any observer could quite reasonably and surely surmise that the M1's ninety-two-dollar (or more) procurement

The double cannelured bullet (right middle in this photo) shows up fairly frequently on G.I. ball. That's the odd striation set parallel to the cartridge's thrust line, intended mainly to provide grasp to the brass case. Non-cannelured bullets tend to be more accurate, as do uncrimped cartridge casings, especially in the M1 Garand. Another eccentricity of the Garand: It's most common one turn in ten inch barrels are a carryover from old, two-hundred-plus bulleted .30/40, and induces overspin on light bullets. This produces errant strikes, or "flyers." That's one reason the M1 *always* provides more uniform accuracy with bullets above 150 grains, proving most accurate with 175+ grain projectiles. One old machine gunner told me these double cannelures were used on machine gun ammo, belted, so that the assistant gunner (he said they were loaded about ten from the end of the belt) could see when a new belt might be required. Others have stated the oddity was just that: a miscellaneous fluke due to errant machines or machinists. Which is right? Your guess is welcome and probably as good as the author's.

price was plain, simple wasted money. The Roosevelt administration had persevered with the new spreading of firepower downward in the face of heavy opposition from inside the military, and the old "boondoggle" word was appearing again. A lot of tweaking was necessary to make the M1 into the rifle World War II vets remember so fondly. Later, more research would eliminate the strange and erratic patterns of inaccuracy some rifles evinced. The rhythmic stoppage problem was gone and understood by late 1940, and all specimens addressed by early 1941 or so. But often, rifles would evince strange flyers, putting typically one bullet in eight somewhere divorced from intended point of impact. The more loosely the front handguard wood was fitted, the less this seemed to happen. By the late 1950's it was discovered that oddments of stress and torque on barrel and receiver, especially when the rifle got hot, were responsible. Since, match-prepared rifles have used an extensive list of relief modifications to stand off wood and metal while bedding holds the receiver firm.

The first step in accuracy preparation has always been tightening up the bedding, which often involves fiberglass, epoxy, or even steel. There are other techniques, too. Derrick Martin, the now-retired founder of Accuracy Speaks in Mesa, Arizona a first-class riflesmith and Perry competitor, puts it simply: "A lot of simplistic, expensive fixes go on the wrong end of the rifle. A new barrel will almost always improve an M1, but glass bedding costs less and can often result in even more improvement."

Of course, also back there at the shooter's end of the rifle are the trigger, chamber/bolt and therefore headspace, and the operating rod rails, which can, if severely worn, mess up everything the rifle does, including shooting straight.

To me, a match-prepared M1 done by a first-class civilian smith is a relative bargain, and the logical place to begin the improvements is right there where you stick your face. I stress "civilian-prepared" because my experience with "authentic" M1 match rifles is that they belong with collectors. I've owned many, and most needed lots of fixing because they'd been improperly prepared or shot to death. Even a pristine ca. 1965 SA-updated gun wouldn't shoot close to any of my civilian prepared rifles until I set aside its issue National Match barrel and replaced it with a Douglas. Bear in mind that it met every shooting and mechanical specification and measurement, but while it was much more accurate than a run-of-the-mine M1, just replacing the barrel cut it from a "sometime" MOA shooter that could not hold a group when it got hot to a consistent sub-MOA gun that took 40 or more rounds to show any heat reaction at all. Had it been a 7.62, I might still own it. But it was .30-06, and it left my ownership with two barrels.

Therein lies a small lesson. An M1 can be both a war curio and a target gun, if one is wise enough to save the alternate parts. First quality Navy and Marine match rifles in 7.62 were bringing in as much as two thousand dollars in 2019, but most shooters want to test-fire such guns. Service guns in mint condition command often over $1000. Neither is common. The 2019 four-hundred-dollar wall hanger may properly belong permanently in a rack, but it can be often be made to look and shoot better than most civilians can even understand, and some of this is a small matter of elbow grease.

This most famous and successful of all US military rifles has much brilliant history behind it, but its best days may well prove to be in the twenty-first century.

CHAPTER 2

THE PRACTICAL M1 GARAND

After you unpack your M1, loading it up and shooting it are not your next steps. Learning how not to break it must be your next logical move.

That said, in the following sections you will find some rules of thumb, a heavily documented and researched military troubleshooting/analysis chart with notes (reprinted from an army manual), and the Beretta version of the military manual written late in the rifle's life that is the best "quickie" manual I've seen. Some small parts of it are a little dated, but it's presented here intact. The photos will help you deal with terminology and grasp the procedures involved in maintaining the rifle properly.

Remember: there would be far less appliances in the trash, fewer cars in the junkyard, and poorer mechanics and plumbers if consumers paid some attention to the instructions packed with almost everything they buy. The M1 is no more complex to maintain than any other firearm, but since it runs fast and strong, and since everything that can happen is well documented, the value of the rifle dictates preventive maintenance. Commercial semiautos are far more fragile, nowhere near as easily serviced, and not as much fun to shoot—nor do they feature as much history. Use the information. It will save you money and maybe even secure your health.

QUICK RULES OF THUMB (AND OTHER BODY PARTS) IN THE CARE AND MAINTENANCE OF JOHN GARAND'S BIG, HEAVY RIFLE

1. Never—under any circumstances—use oil to lubricate any major part of the M1 Garand. Use grease—heavy grease—in the four bolt points, op rod channel/receiver raceway, and op rod detent. I use a high-temperature, high-pressure wheel bearing grease, for which I pay $1.99 to $3.50 per tub at an auto parts store. You can buy the same thing in itty-bitty, teensy-weensy canisters labeled for firearms use at $3.50 per quarter-ounce, if you wish. Using no lubricants (or improper ones) will seriously attack your rifle's systems. Oil will slop onto the stock and you and just generally make a mess, without doing anything to help the rifle. Incorrect lubricants contribute to the premature death of operating rods, receivers, and, sometimes, shooters.

2. If one shoots corrosive ammo, bores must be swabbed or flushed immediately with water/detergent solutions, preferably with ammonia added, followed by a solvent cleaning shortly thereafter. As with any high velocity rifle whose owner wishes it to last any serious length of time, a copper fouling procedure must also follow extensive shooting *every single time the rifle is fired.* Although these techniques were controversial fifty years ago, benchrest shooters have demonstrated absolutely and empirically their value in prolonging barrel life and sustaining accuracy.

3. Never, under any circumstances, sand a military Garand stock that retains any original markings, and, most especially, use no abrasives in areas where the markings and stampings actually reside. This is a serious depreciation of the stock's value. Especially if one sands in the area where the receiver contacts wood, inaccuracy and cracking will become a problem, and very quickly.

4. There is seldom need to remove the gas cylinder, even for cleaning. However, if it is removed and reinstalled there is no need for it to contact the front handguard and/or ferrule, and, in fact, doing so can and will have a deleterious impact on accuracy. Minor peens on the channels that align and secure the cylinder can be used to resecure a loose gas cylinder, whose slop will definitely cause larger-than-necessary groups, since the front sight reposes up topside. Suggested standoff from handguard ferrule: .040 inch

5. Actually using unrelieved World War II operating rods is unwise, dangerous, and financially silly. They can work fine, up until the time they bend or break and something very unpleasant happens. Read some World War II unit histories and you'll find the information. Usually somewhat erroneously associated with high-pressure situations like grenade launching, separations were rare but did sometimes cause serious injuries and worse. Lefties suffer much more. And they are substantially more than relieved rods. Use the photos here to identify yours. Spares are not expensive.

Operating rod separations were never common, and in the literature and medical records found in 1964 at what was then Camp McCoy, all we stumbled into were related to pre-existing cracks and bores plugged with ice or frozen mud. Many—by no means all!—of the bits of evidence we found involved the 100th Infantry Regiment, and stuck in our minds because of the Japanese names. The orders and drawings and so on we found stressed how the pressure buildup in the gas system propelled the rod rearward at many times its customary speed, and if the barrel didn't burst first, and if there were pre-existing cracks, there were separations and, almost always, serious injuries. Importantly, the armorers and personnel were instructed to check for cracks, and muzzles checked before firing.

The armorers/smiths with whom we spoke while working on *The Valiant Americans* (an amateur film project) made clear this was the real impetus behind the very swift modification and relief of operating rods, and why all subsequent production included the hemispherical relief. This had to be verified and researched not because of any theoretical or collector's considerations, but because it was imperative that the staff of the project be physically safe.

By the way, the mundane cover story that the operating rod moves rearward at only about twenty m.p.h. is meaningless drivel when the gas pressure rises exponentially with a blocked muzzle.

One smith did notice that, if the ice plug went further behind the gas port, the result was generally a "banana split barrel," with no reaction from the operating rod at all.

6. The correct finish for the wood parts of the M1 Garand and most other military rifles is pure tung or linseed oil, sometimes mixed with glossy spar varnish. These are inherently shiny finishes that flatten down with age and exposure to heat and light. The matte finish many veterans remember or think they remember is nothing more than the ravages of time, ignorance, and neglect. Other finishes, such as lacquers, may be applied, but total lack of finish—which is what these old salts actually recall—is unwise, will cause accuracy and staining problems, and will ultimately cause the stock to crack.

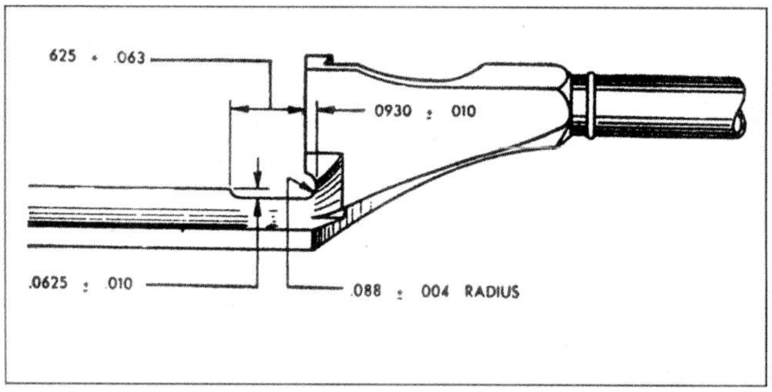

By the end of World War II, enough jammed-up rods and broken specimens made it pretty obvious the operating rods then extant would have to be modified, and indeed, some collectors and researchers suggest that "on the cusp" group of 3.8 million serial-numbered rifles with very late '45 and early '46 dated barrels left the armory with modified rods on their very first issue. No one *knows* that, but the initial date on this old drawing and dimension setup for modifying rods dates to about that time.

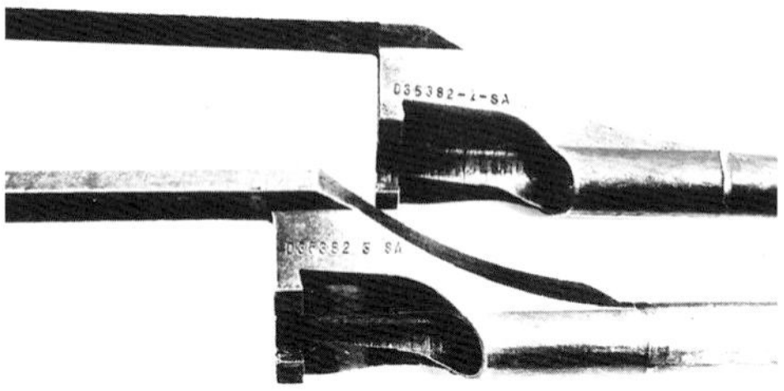

Use of uncut operating rods for the M1 Garand (these are two very early units) is dangerous and unnecessary. However, do not alter valuable originals. Simply purchase a relieved wartime specimen or a later postwar unit in nice condition. Note the uninterrupted square corner about ½ inch above the part number on these old units and the crude welding, especially on the-1 unit (top).

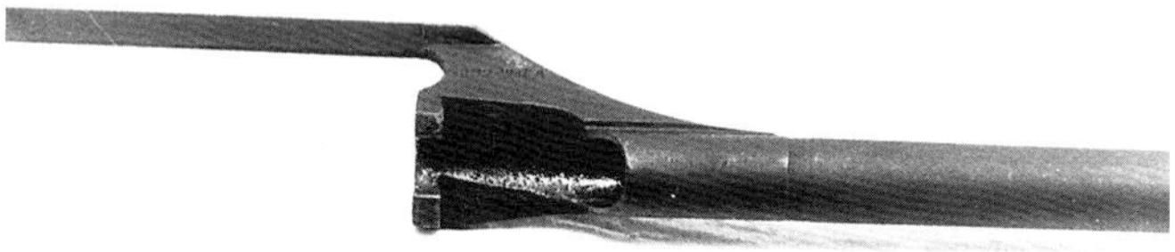

This cut (modified with hemispherical cut to relieve stress) Winchester wartime operating rod is far safer than unmodified originals, though of far less collector value.

7. With the correct gas system, .243, .308, .25-06, .270, and other caliber Garands can and do work absolutely

beautifully. However, properly mashed up and dinged by a well-meaning fool or one of the "I always wanted to fix a real rifle" crowd, even the .30-06 is iffy. M1 has suffered far more from derelict owners, clumsy smiths, and bad advice from various publishers who should know better than it ever has from any design deficiency or set of inherent glitches. The rifle is far sturdier than the M14 or any cast clone thereof, and it is surely the strongest semiautomatic high-powered rifle ever built. But some people can and do break anything, and they continually apply their ignorance, lack of skill, and bigger and better hammers to an ever more vast and continuing variety of inappropriate objects and devices. Idiots are what primarily and profoundly impact machinery, from your family car to your M1 Garand. If need be, pay them to stay the hell away from your rifle and everything else you own. You can, ultimately, destroy your property yourself . . . why pay a premium to someone else to do it for you?

8. Post World War II rifles (serial numbers about 4,200,000 and higher, or Italian Breda or Beretta) are considerably stronger than earlier guns; are far less likely to have been mashed up, dropped, or fired in anger than earlier guns; and have probably missed the clumsy attentions of at least one or two generations of that primary destroyer of military hardware, the clumsy recruit.

9. The original metal finish on almost everything M1 is some sort of phosphate. However, parkerizing—the GI name for the finish—took many forms and many different depths and colors according to the materials to which it was applied and the needs of the particular part. Even underlying polish level changed the color and reflectivity of the finish. The phosphate was post-application treated

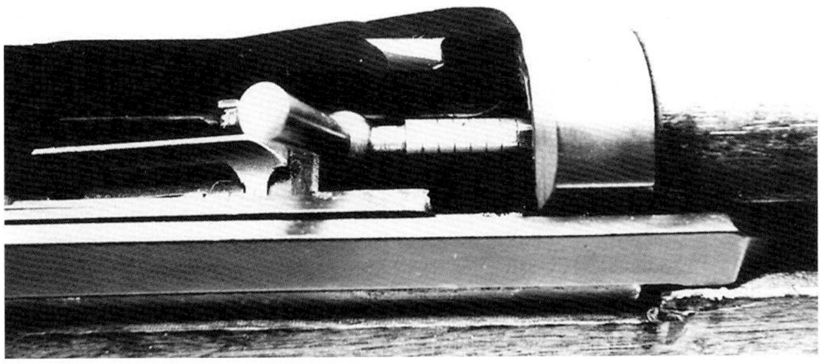

The military M1 TEG (throat erosion gauge) inserted in old ca. 1948 rebuild of any early World War II rifle, evincing an excellent 2.5 reading.

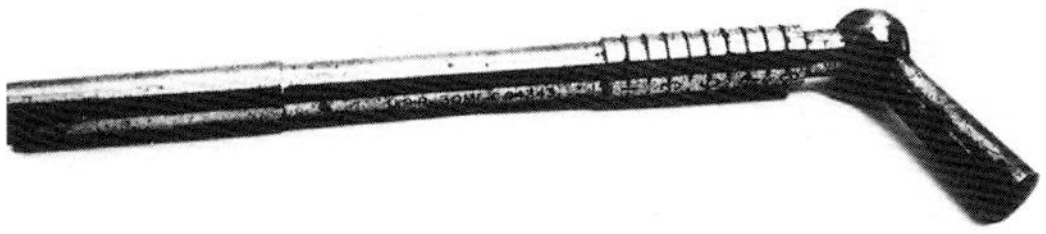

The M1 Garand TEG is the only reliable way to judge the condition of a military Garand barrel, and its information is far more vital than the degree of crud in the bore or the bore's polish condition. The numbers here index bore condition. Anything over five is heavily worn. However, because civilian barrels use gentler leades (one of several reasons they last so much longer and shoot better), even high-quality units may read 5 even when brand new.

in many different ways. Barrels, for example, were usually a different shade from receivers and sights. Most M1s left the factories far darker than the medium gray so common now. Most Garands were delivered with a rather dark base finish, somewhere between a very dark gray to charcoal and black. Winchester receivers and most other parts were black. Few rifles bore an absolutely uniform finish, and a uniform medium gray is a virtually certain sign that a rifle has been refinished—probably fairly recently.

10. Want to lose a thumb? The Garand can relieve you of an excess digit and inflict more pain in a heartbeat than you ever want to know about. Good pointers: a) your bolt is not fully back until it's fully back; b) pressure on the follower required to trip/release the bolt becomes less as the rifle wears, virtually always releasing when you least expect it; and c) there is no such thing as pulling the operating rod up, unless you actually wish to strip the rifle.

11. The proper instruments for checking a used or unknown Garand barrel are the throat and muzzle erosion gauges or porcine bullets for the muzzle, which can approximate the data to be gleaned there.

The eyeball, even assisted by optics, can only tell you if something has died there, and there are many charlatans (especially at gun shows) who specialize in polishing and dressing worn out barrels. Many good-looking bores on GI rifles I've checked out gauged 8 or more (virtually unusable) on the TEG. For .308/7.62 rifles, the M14 throat gauge is needed. Civilian barrels of modern design use gentler leades (one of the reasons they last longer) and may gauge 4 or 5 brand new, which is fine. However, what you need to know is this: an M1 bore that one has merely studied with the eye is an orifice about which nothing is known.

TROUBLESHOOTING AND GENERAL MAINTENANCE

NOTE: Experienced Garand shooters will note that freshly refinished rifles virtually never release the bolt the instant the clip is latched. For hundreds of rounds, a boosting pat to the operating rod is necessary to drive the first round into the chamber. Sometimes, they will not even eject the clip until worn in.

Many new California-produced clips are available, but their finish is too thick. They seldom function properly until used many times.

IMPORTANT: *Never pull up on the operating rod when opening the breech.* Pull the operating rod straight back, and straight back only! When you pull up you are asking the operating rod to slip out of the channel, and it will try to obey.

Though now quite old, the information in this synopsis from TM 9-1005-222-35 (US Army Ordnance) is still chapter and verse, despite Internet twaddle to the contrary.

That does *not* mean there are no new issues. Substandard, distorted, too heavily finished, and otherwise badly out of specification *en bloc* clips can cause misery such that it seems a splendid, virtually perfect M1 simply is non-functional.

Even worse, improperly cast and out-of-specification, civilian produced clip latches can cause premature ammo "dumping" much like that due to distortion of the bullet guide and/or operating rod catch, even exceeding the miseries promulgated by a badly distorting follower rod.

Variable gas cylinder lock screws and premium springs are another pair of solutions which, long term, have caused far more problems than they have ever solved.

Ditto there is too much worry about heavy bullets in the Garand and its M14 successor. Competition shooters have used heavy boat tail bullets in very powerful rounds for decades, and properly prepared rifles prosper under such loads. But the key term is "properly prepared." A rifle not greased or correctly checked before use *cannot* be properly prepared. The admonitions about avoiding commercial ammo are likewise mostly overdone.

Much of the "Garand specific" ammunition on the market is good for the rifle from the point of view of being quite gentle, and it's usually at the bottom of the power/velocity specification, but much of it shoots about two full inches below ball or match ammunition actually used by competitors. It's also not cheap!

I do hasten to add: the several samples I've had were *far* more accurate than G.I. ball. They were not as accurate as even relatively casual handloads, and the same is true of other standard quality factory ammo.

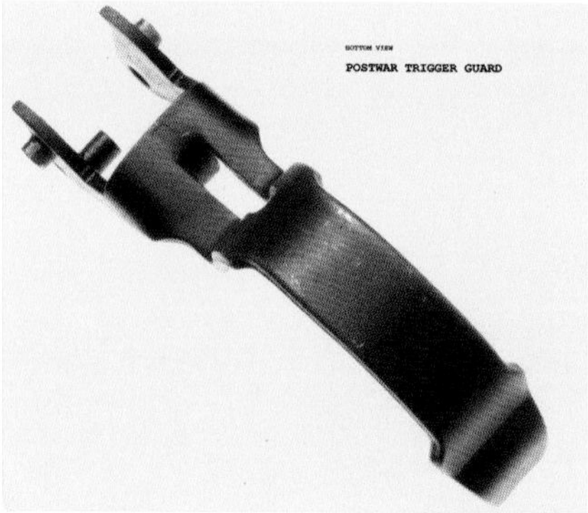

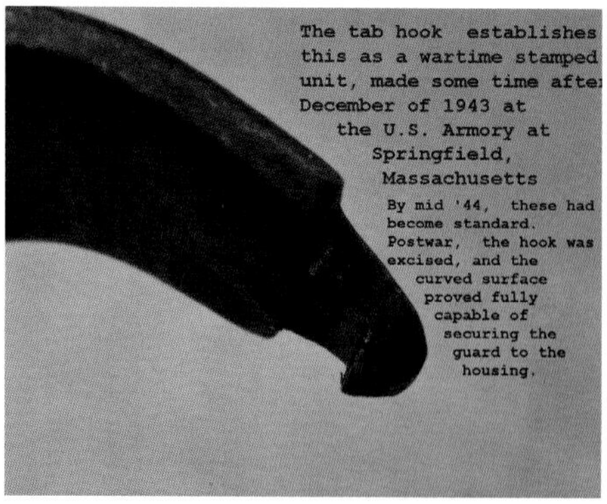

TROUBLESHOOTING AND GENERAL MAINTENANCE

Troubleshooting

Table 4-1. Troubleshooting

Malfunction	Probable cause	Corrective action
	RIFLE M1, M1C (Sniper's) AND M1D (Sniper's)	
Cartridge clip inserts with difficulty.	Deformed clip	Replace.
	Broken ejector	Replace.
	Interference between bullet guide and follower arm.	Replace bullet guide.
Short recoil	Undersized or out of round operating rod piston.	Replace operating rod assembly.
	Oversized gas cylinder	Replace.
	Undersized barrel at gas port	Turn-in weapon for replacement.
	Carbon in gas cylinder	Clean.
	Carbon or foreign matter in gas port of barrel.	Clean.
	Operating rod assembly binding	Replace operating rod assembly if damaged, or relieve wood from gun stock assembly, where operating rod binds on wood.
	Leak in gas cylinder lock screw with valve.	Replace gas cylinder lock screw with valve.
	Defective helical spring (operating rod)	Replace helical spring (operating rod).
	Bolt binding	Remove burs from bolt.
	Distorted or damaged receiver	Repair or turn in for replacement.
Bolt fails to close tightly	Extractor does not open enough to pass over rim of cartridge.	Clean bolt assembly.
	Operating rod assembly binding	Replace operating rod or relieve wood from stock assembly where operating rod binds on wood.
	Weak or broken helical spring (operating rod).	Replace helical spring (operating rod).
	Rust or dirt in chamber	Clean barrel chamber.
	Damaged cartridge, or frozen ejector	Repair or replace ejector.
	Damaged or deformed bolt and/or receiver.	Replace bolt or turn in weapon for replacement.
	Insufficient headspace	Replace bolt assembly by selective fit or turn in weapon for replacement.
Bolt does not release when clip is latched.	Insufficient radii on operating rod catch or operating rod hooks.	Repair or replace operating rod catch or operating rod assembly.
	Bullet guide low at accelerator bearing point.	Replace.
Bolt released before clip is latched.	Worn or broken clip latch	Replace.
	Worn or broken helical spring (latch)	Replace helical spring (latch).

Troubleshooting—Continued

Malfunction	Probable cause	Corrective action
	Excessive radii on operating rod catch or operating rod assembly.	Replace operating rod catch or operating rod assembly.
	Bullet guide high at accelerator bearing point.	Replace.
Bolt fails to be held rearward after firing last round of clip and clip held inside of rifle jammed by bolt.	Bolt does not move sufficiently rearward.	See short recoil.
	Binding latch ------------------	Replace latch.
	Arm or operating rod catch bent or deformed.	Replace operating rod assembly.
Failure to eject cartridge case ---	Low power, causing short recoil	Correct short recoil malfunctions.
	Weak, missing, or frozen helical spring (ejector).	Replace helical spring (ejector).
	Ejector binds------------------	Clean bolt ejector opening or remove burs from ejector.
	Short recoil ------------------	Clean gas port. Replace operating rod assembly or helical spring.
Failure to eject cartridge clip ---	Clip ejector worn, weak, or broken.	Replace.
	Operating rod catch deformed or broken.	Replace catch.
Failure of bolt to open after firing	Plugged gas port --------------	Clean.
	Loose gas cylinder-------------	Replace gas cylinder.
	Barrel undersize at gas port area	Turn in weapon for replacement.
	Gas cylinder lock screw with valve fails to close.	Replace.
Failure to fire-----------------	Light indent on primer ---------	Replace helical spring (hammer).
	Inadequate firing pin protrusion	Replace.
	Hammer spring housing damaged	Replace.
Pressure on trigger does not release hammer.	Deformed trigger, pin, or hammer.	Replace defective trigger, pin or hammer.
One or more live cartridges ejected with clip.	Operating rod assembly releases too soon when clip is inserted.	Replace operating rod catch and bullet guide.
Operating rod assembly disengages from bolt while firing.	Worn operating rod lug or kinked helical spring (operating rod assembly).	Replace operating rod assembly or helical spring.

"Failure of the bullet guide and/or operating rod catch can lead to the ejection of multiple live rounds, in addition to the spent case and cartridge clip," stated the author after having had just such an experience.

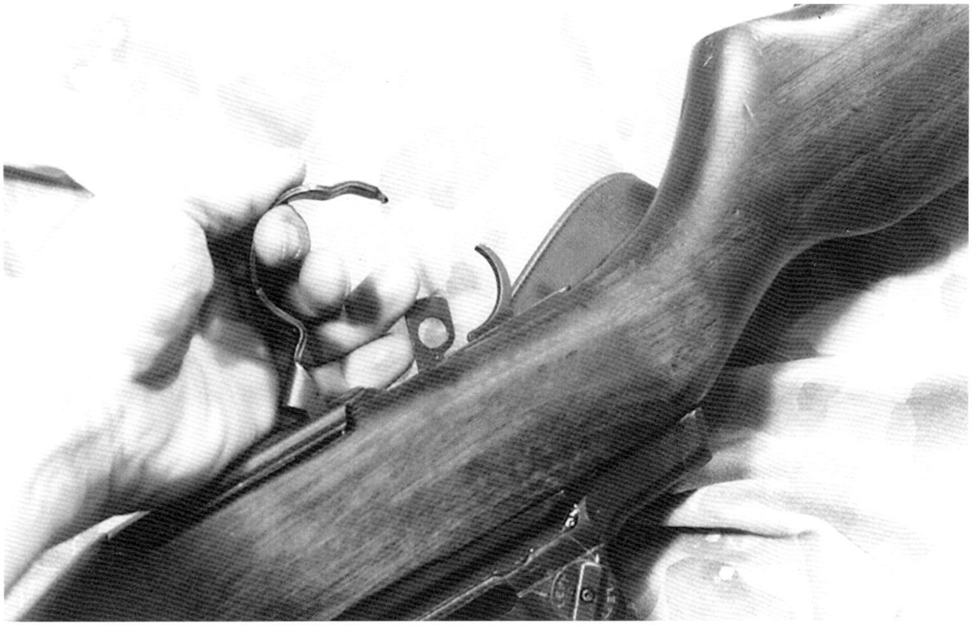

Stripping the M1 begins with opening the trigger guard to allow the trigger/hammer group to be removed from the stock and receiver assembly. The spring steel trigger guard, issue on all postwar rifles, is a much superior assembly to the older, heavier milled unit, which was easily distorted and allowed no easy readjustment.

TECHNICAL MANUAL

MAINTENANCE

U. S. RIFLE GARAND

Caliber .30 M1

BERETTA ARMS COMPANY - BRESCIA - ITALY

CONTENTS

		Page
Section I.	Introduction	1
Section II.	Measurements and Data	2
Section III.	Loading, Firing and Unloading	3
Section IV.	Field Stripping	5
Section V.	Assembling	12
Section VI.	Functioning	14
Section VII.	Care of the Rifle	16

SECTION I
INTRODUCTION

The U. S. Garand Rifle, caliber .30 M1, is a gas-operated, clip-loaded, air-cooled, semiautomatic shoulder weapon.

There are many features of the Garand M1 Rifle which make it one of the best among all the military semiautomatics. These include reliable functioning, ruggedness, protection of the shooter against gas leaks and blowbacks, excellent appearance, good balance, simplicity and relative fewness of parts, and a short receiver.

It is notable that the M1 rifle has only 82 components, including springs, screws and pins. It is also interesting to note that, in order to insure against premature discharge of the M1 Rifle, the hammer is so constructed that it cannot strike the firing pin before the bolt is rotated into a fully locked position. To provide an added safety measure, the firing pin is prevented from travelling forward until the same condition exists.

The Garand Rifle is probably the easiest to disassemble of any military semiautomatic ever developed. In an instant, it can be separated into three main groups consisting of the stock group, the barrel and receiver group, and the trigger housing group.

A feature of the Garand Rifle which is of interest to any target shooter is the type of the ignition blow applied by the firing pin to the primer.

In most weapons, the firing pin blow is either directly or indirectly caused by a compressed spring and the energy in the spring usually decreases as the firing pin moves forward. Thus, when the spring becomes fatigued, the impact on the primer is materially reduced and the result may be hangfires or misfires. In the Garand firing mechanism, the construction which controls the hammer is such that the leverage is increased as the hammer nears the point of impact, which tends to reduce the load on the sear, cause the trigger to pull easily, and increase the load on the firing pin at the time of firing, helping to prevent the extrusion of the primer into the firing pin hole.

Another point of interest is the lock time; that is, the time required from the moment the trigger is pulled until the moment the firing pin impinges on the primer. In the Garand Rifle, this has been designed to be just. 0057 second.

1

SECTION II

MEASUREMENTS AND DATA

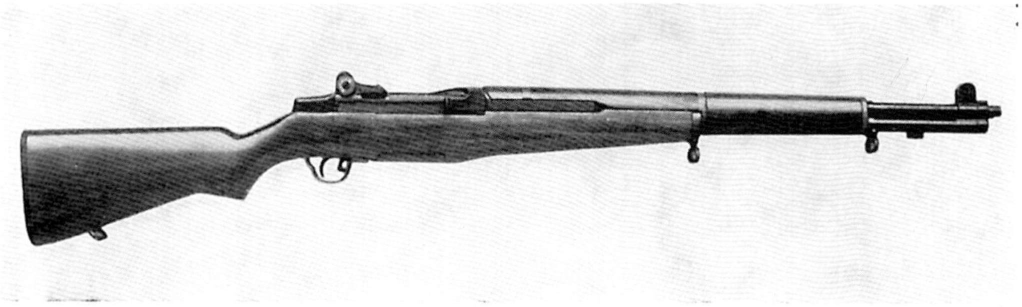

Caliber: .30 U. S.

Weight: 9.5 lbs. (The density of the wood in the stock varies from one gun to the next, changing the weight slightly).

Length (over-all) Rifle Only: 43.6 in.

Length (over-all) With Bayonet: 53.4 in.

Length of Barrel: 24 in.

Length of Rifling: 21.30 in.

Rifling:

Right-Hand Twist: 1 turn in 10 in.

Depth of Grooves: 0.0040 in.

Cross-Sectional Area of Bore: 0.0740 sq. in.

Type of Mechanism: Gas-Operated, Semiautomatic.

Magazine: Fixed box type in receiver loaded with clip.

Cartridge Clip: Capacity 8 rounds, clip is inserted in the Rifle with the cartridges.

Wen Last Shot Has Been Fired: Empty cartridge clip is expelled through top of the Rifle.

Rate of Fire: Semiautomatic.

Sights: Aperture, adjustable from 100 to 1200 yards.

Sight Radius: 27.9 in. at 100 yard range.

Trigger Pull: 7.5 lbs. max., 5.5 lbs. min.

Normal Pressure: 50,000 lbs. per sq. in.

Approximate Maximum Range: 3,450 yards.

Locking: By rotating bolt with two lugs which fit into recess in the receiver.

Ejection: Empty cartridge cases are ejected on the right, upwards and to the front. When rifle is empty, bolt will stay open. This serves notice that the weapon is empty and permits immediate insertion of a fully loaded clip, so that firing may be speedily resumed.

2

SECTION III

LOADING, FIRING AND UNLOADING

Loading and Firing

1. Grasping the rifle at the balance with the left hand; with the right forefinger, pull operating rod straight to the rear. It will be caught and held open by the operating rod catch.

2. Place the loaded clip on top of the magazine follower and, with right side of right hand against the operating rod handle, press down with right thumb on the clip, until it is caught in the receiver by the clip latch.

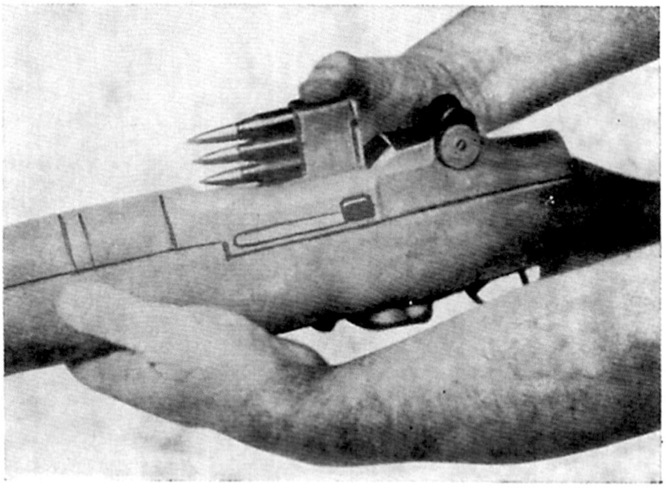

3. Remove the right thumb from the line of the bolt and let go on the operating rod handle, which will run forward under the pression of the spring. Push operating rod handle with heel of right hand to be sure that bolt is fully home and locked.

4. Pressing the trigger will now fire one cartridge. Weapon will be ready for the next pull of the trigger.

5. If weapon is not to be used at once, set the safety. The safety is in front of the trigger guard. Pulling it back towards the trigger sets it on safe, while pushing it forward is the fire position.
Note that the cartridge clip is reversible and may be fed into the rifle from either end.

3

Unloading the Garand Rifle

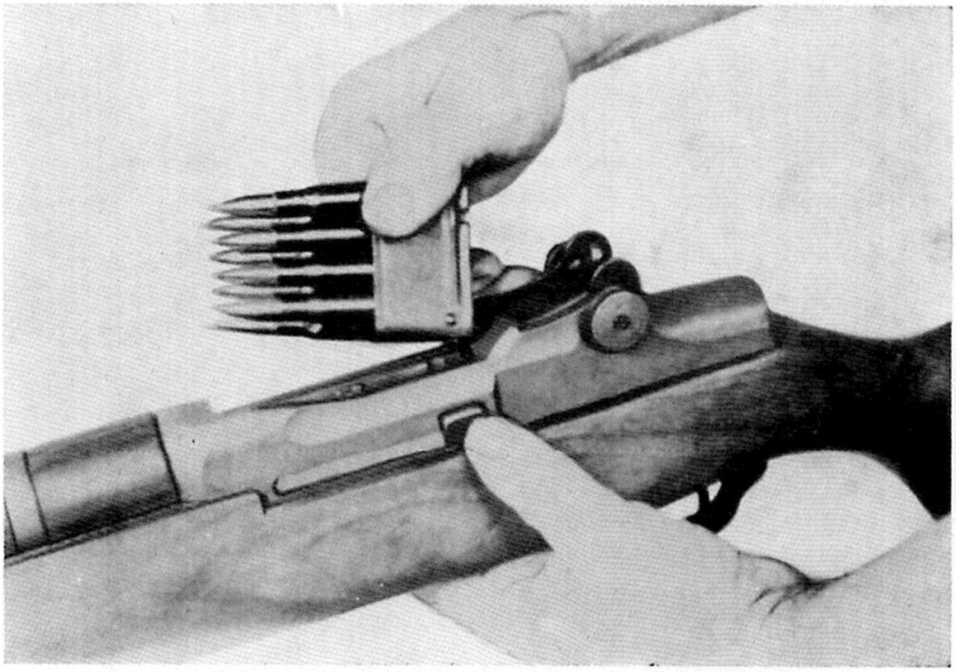

1. First check to be sure that the safety is set.

2. With the right forefinger, pull the operating rod back sharply and hold it in the rear position. This will eject the cartridge that was in the firing chamber. With the fingers of the hand grasp the trigger guard or the grip firmly. Hold the stock against the right hip to support it. Then place the left hand over the receiver and, with the left thumb, release the clip latch.

3. The clip and whatever cartridges remain in it will now pop up into the right hand and must be removed from the rifle.

4. With the right side of the right hand held against the operating rod handle, force the operating rod slightly to the rear. With the right thumb now push down the magazine follower and permit the bolt to move forward about an inch over the end of the follower.

5. Remove the thumb smartly from the follower and let go on the operating rod. The action will close under the tension of the spring. Now press the trigger.

4

SECTION IV
FIELD STRIPPING

To Dismount Stock Group

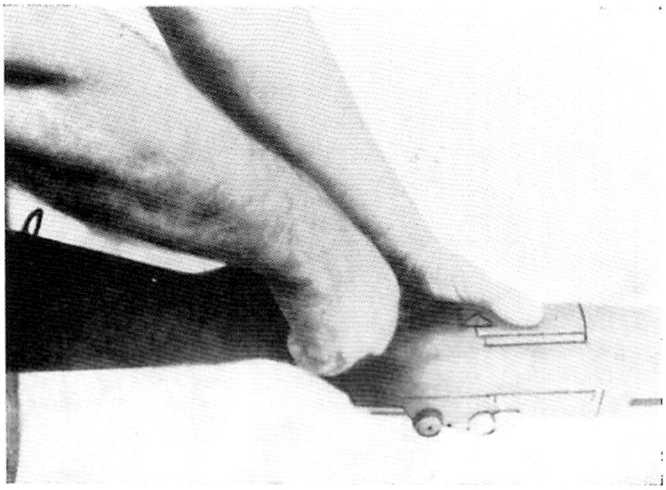

1. Start by placing the rifle upside down on a firm surface. Holding the rifle with left hand, finger firmly holding the base of the trigger housing, rest the butt against the left thigh.

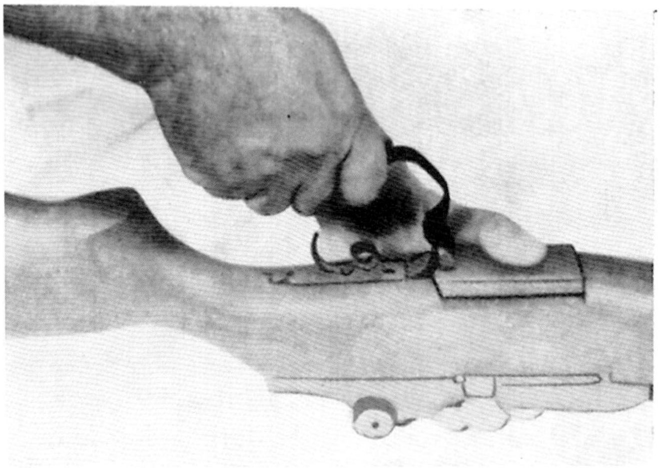

2. With thumb and forefinger unlatch the trigger guard by pulling back on it.

5

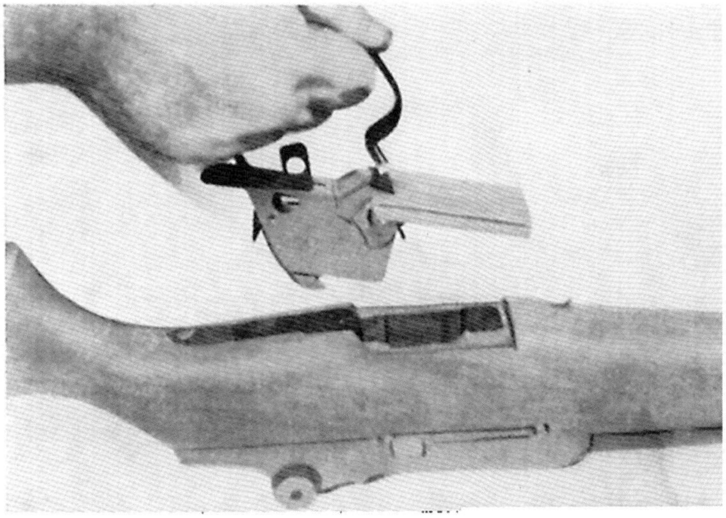

3. Continue the pressure and pull out the trigger housing group.

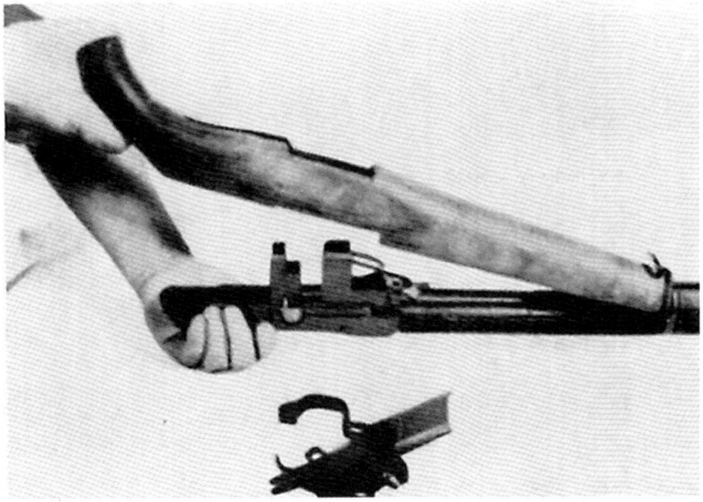

4. With left hand now grasp rifle over rear sight, holding the muzzle down and the barrel to your left.

With right hand strike down against the small of the stock, firmly grasping it at the same time.

This will separate the barrel and receiver group from the stock group.

6

To Dismount Barrel and Receiver Group

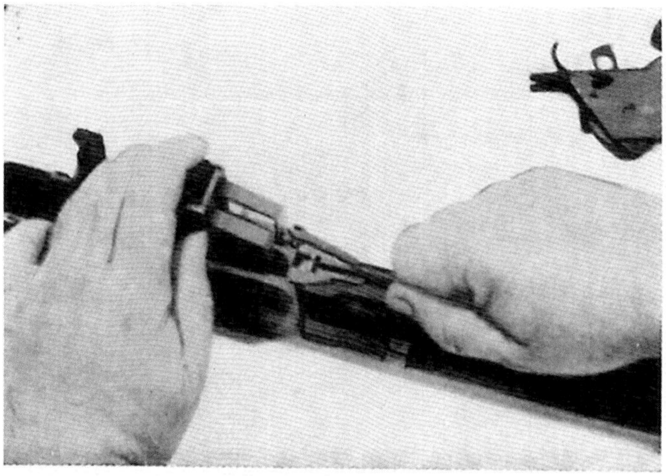

1. With the barrel down, grasp the follower rod with thumb and forefinger and press it toward the muzzle to free it from the follower arm.

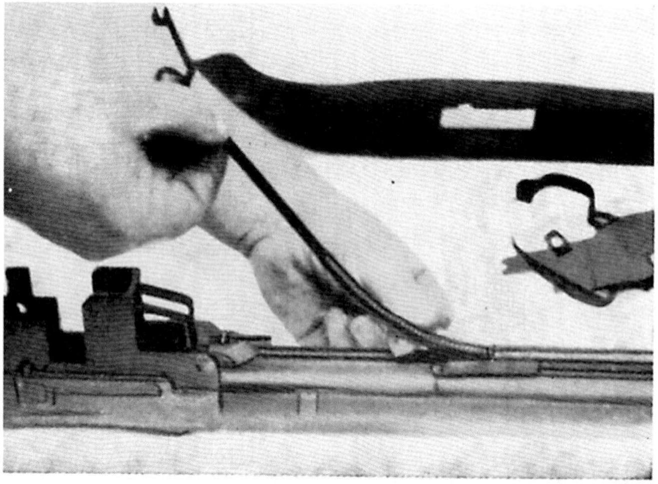

2. The follower rod and its compensating spring which is attached may now be withdrawn to the right. The compensating spring is removed from the follower rod by holding spring with left hand twisting rod toward the body with the right hand, meanwhile pulling slightly to the right.

7

3. With the point of a bullet, push the follower arm pin from its seat and pull it out with the left hand.

4. Seize the bullet guide, follower arm and operating rod catch assembly; pull these up until they disengage. The three separate parts may now be lifted out. Accelerator pin is riveted in its seat, so do not attempt to remove accelerator from operating catch assembly.

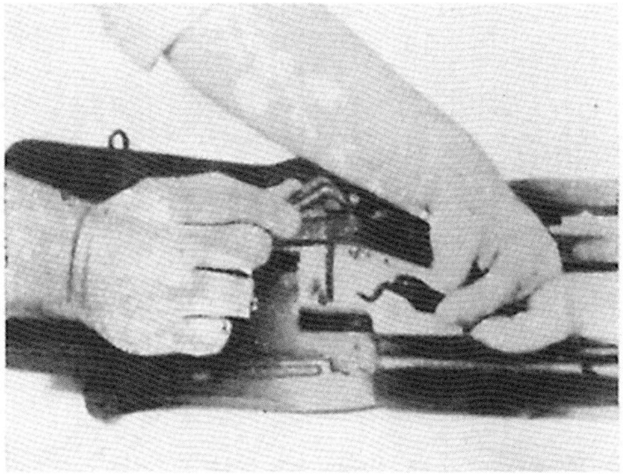

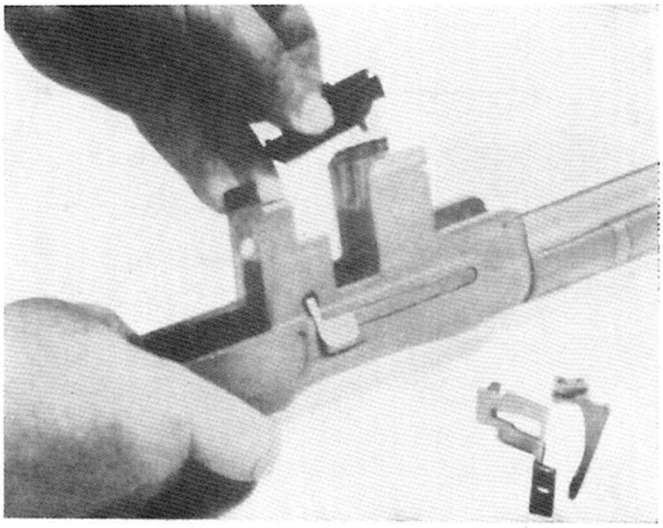

5. Lift out follower with its slide attached (do not separate follower from slide).

8

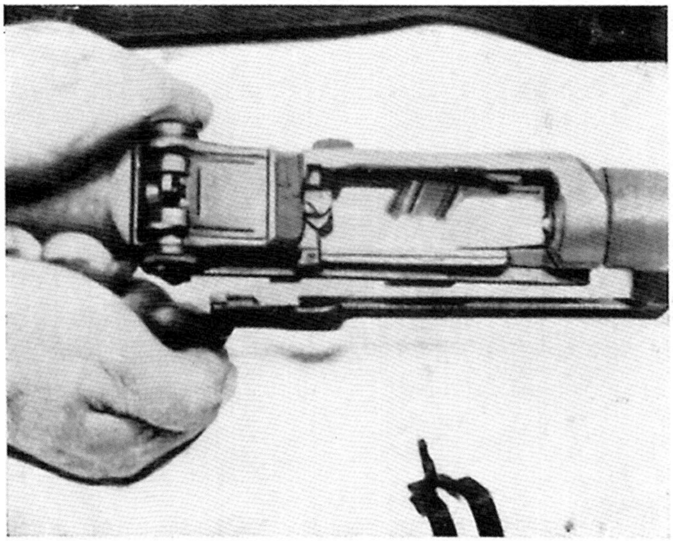

6. Holding barrel and receiver assembly with left hand, grasp the operating rod handle with rigth hand and move it slightly to the rear, meanwhile pulling the rod handle up and away from the receiver. (This disengages operating rod from bolt, when the lug on the operating rod slides into the dismount notch of the operating rod guide groove).

When operating rod is disengaged pull it down and back and withdraw it. (Note that the operating rod is bent. This is intentional. Do not attempt to straighten it).

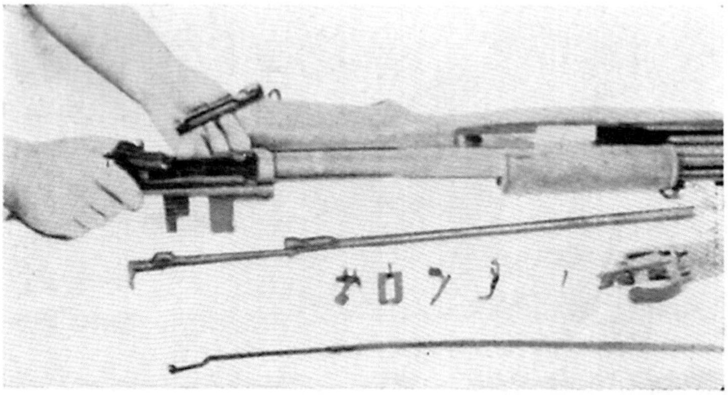

7. Slide the bolt from the rear to the front by pushing the operating lug on it and lift it out to the right front with a slight twisting motion.

9

To Dismount Gas Cylinder

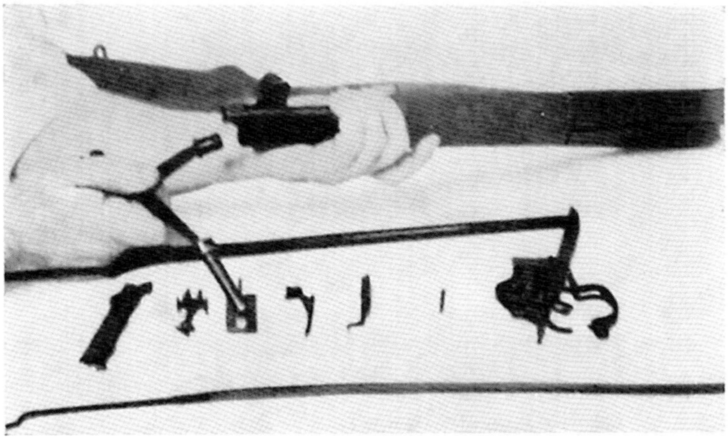

1. The combination tool is used to unscrew the gas cylinder lock screw.

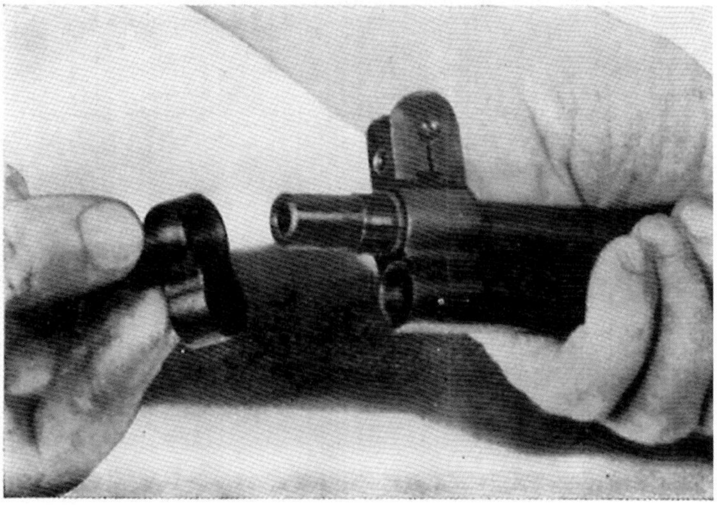

2. Next the gas cylinder lock is unscrewed.

10

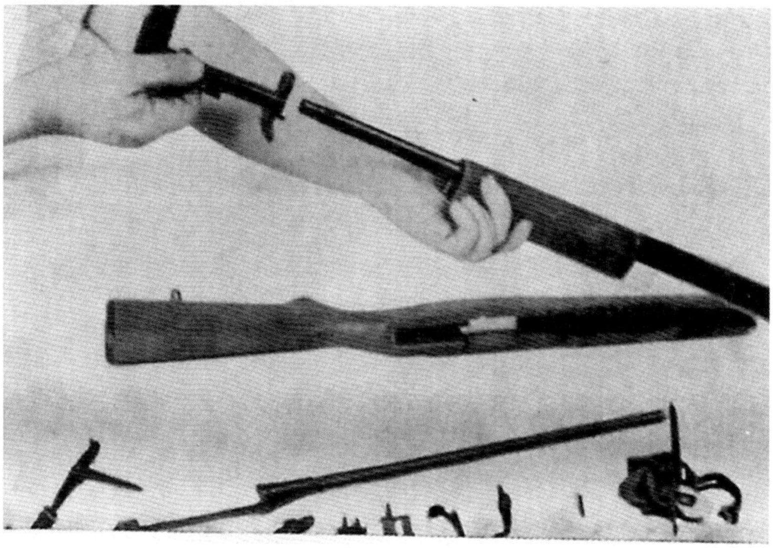

3. The gas cylinder is tapped toward the muzzle and removed from the barrel. The front sight is not to be dismounted from gas cylinder assembly.
4. Gas cylinder assembly should never be removed except when necessary to replace the front hand guard assembly.

11

SECTION V
ASSEMBLING

1. Replacing gas cylinder, if it has been dismounted, is done by merely reversing the dismounting procedure.

2. To assemble barrel and receiver group: tilt the barrel and receiver assembly, sight up and muzzle to the front to an angle of about 45°.

3. Holding the bolt by the right locking lug so the front end of the bolt is somewhat above and to the right of its extreme forward position in the receiver, insert the rear end in its bearing on the bridge of the receiver. Switch it from right to left far enough to let tang of the firing pin clear to the top of the bridge. Next, guide the left locking lug of the bolt into its groove just to the rear of the lug on the left side of the receiver and start right locking lug into its bearing in the receiver. Now slide bolt back to its extreme rear position.

4. Turn barrel and receiver assembly in the left hand until barrel is down.

5 Grasp operating rod at the handle holding it handle up, insert piston head into gas cylinder about 3/8". Be sure that operating rod handle is to the left of the receiver.

6. Hold barrel and receiver assembly in the left hand and twist to the right until barrel is uppermost.

7. Adjust operating rod with right hand so that camming recess on its rear end fits over operating lug on bolt. Now press operating rod forward and downward until bolt is seated in its forward position.

8. With barrel and receiver assembly held barrel down and muzzle to your left, replace the follower with its attached slide so that its guide ribs fit into their grooves in the receiver. The follower slide rests on the bottom surface of the bolt when the follower is in the correct position.

9. With left hand replace bullet guide fitting the shoulders of the guide into their slots in the receiver and the hole in the projecting lug is in line with the hole in the receiver.

10. With left hand, replace follower arm passing stud end through bullet guide slot and inserting stud in proper grooves in front end of follower.

11. Place the forked end of the follower arm in position across the projecting lug on the bullet guide, with pin holes properly alined.

12

12. Insert rear arm of operating rod catch into clearance cut in the bullet guide (be sure its rear end is below the forward stud of the clip latch which projects into the receiver mouth). Line up the holes in the operating rod catch, the follower arm and the bullet guide with those in the receiver and insert the follower arm pin in the side of the receiver towards your body, pressing the pin home.

13. Insert operating rod spring into operating rod and assemble follower rod by grasping the spring in the left hand and inserting follower rod with right hand, then twisting the two together until the spring is fully seated.

14. Seize the follower rod with thumb and forefinger of left hand with hump down and forked end to the right.

15. Place front end of follower rod into operating rod spring and push to the left, seating the forked end against the follower arm.

16. Insert U shaped flange of stock ferrule in its seat in the lower band.

17. Pivoting about this group, guide chamber and receiver group and press into position in the stock.

18. Replace trigger housing group with trigger guard in open position into the stock opening.

19. Press into position, close and latch trigger guard. This completes reassembling.

SECTION VI
FUNCTIONING

Starting with the rifle loaded and cocked, the action is as follows: The trigger being pressed, the hammer strikes the firing pin, exploding the cartridge in the chamber. As the bullet passes over the gas port drilled in the under side of the barrel, some of the gas escapes into the cylinder and blasts back against the piston and operating rod with strength enough to drive the rod to the rear and compress the return spring.

During the first 5/16" of the rearward travel, the operating lug slides in a straight section of the recess on the operating rod, after which the cam surface of this recess is brought in contact with the operating lug which it cams up, thereby rotating the bolt from right to left to unlock its two lugs from their recesses in the receiver.

During the moment of delayed action, the bullet leaves the barrel and the breech pressure drops to a safe point. The further rotation of the bolt then cams the hammer away from the firing pin and pulls the firing pin back from the bolt. The operating rod continues its backward movement carrying the bolt with it as the lug on the bolt has reached the end of its recess. During this rearward motion of the bolt, the empty case is withdrawn from the chamber by the extractor positioned in the bolt until it is clear of the breech; at which point the ejector, exerting a steady pressure on the base of the cartridge case, throws it to the right front by the action of its compressed spring.

The rear end of the bolt at this point forces the hammer back, rides over it and compresses the hammer spring; finally it stops in the rear end of the receiver.

As the bolt has now cleared the clip, the follower spring forces the cartridge up until the topmost one is in line with the bolt.

The operating rod spring comes into play at this point to pull the action forward.

Forward Movement of the Action: As the bolt moves forward, its lower front base strikes the base of the cartridge case and pushes it into the firing chamber. The hammer, pressed by its spring, rides on the bottom of the bolt. While it tends to rise, it is caught and held by the trigger lugs engaging the

14

hammer-hook, if trigger pressure has been released. Otherwise, the trigger engages the rear hammer hook until letting go the trigger disengages the sear from the hammer. The hammer then slides into engagement with the trigger lugs.

When the bolt nears its forward position, the extractor engages near the rim of the cartridge and the base of the cartridge forces the ejector into the bolt, compressing the ejector spring.

The rear surface of the cam recess in the operating rod now cams the operating lug down and thereby twists the bolt from left to right until the two lugs lock into their places in the receiver.

The operating rod drives ahead for another 5/16". The rear end of the straight section of the operating rod recess reaches the operating lug on the bolt, which completes the forward movement and leaves the rifle ready to fire when the trigger is pressed.

This cycle continues as long as there are any cartridges in the magazine and the trigger is squeezed.

SECTION VII
CARE OF THE RIFLE

The rifle must be kept clean and properly lubricated. Failure to do so may result in stoppages at a critical moment. The rifle is to be inspected periodically.

To Clean the Bore: A clean patch saturated with hot water and soap should be run through the bore a number of times. While the bore is still wet, a metal brush should be run through several times to loosen up any material which has not been dissolved by the water. Dry patches should then be pushed through the bore until thoroughly dry. The bore should then be coated with light issue of gun oil. Also use the chamber cleaning tool to give the chamber the same attention. Remember that powder fouling in the bore contains a salt which rusts the steel.

To Clean Gas Cylinder: The carbon must be scraped from the exposed surfaces, the front of the cylinder and the gas cylinder plug and piston head, after extensive fire. The mess kit knife or similar sharp bladed instruments should be used for this scraping process. Gas cylinder plugs and grooves in the gas cylinder should be cleaned so they will feed correctly in the plug.

Attention to other Parts of Rifle: Graphite cup grease is excellent for lubricating bolt lugs, bolt guides, bolt cocking cams, compensating spring, contact surfaces of barrel and operating rod, operating rod cams and springs, and operating rod groove in the receiver.

All other metal parts should be cleaned and covered with a uniform light coat of oil.

Rust should be removed from the metal parts with a piece of soft wood and oil, never with abrasive. Screw heads must be kept clean to prevent rusting.

Be careful not to use too much oil as any heavy coat will collect dirt and interfere with operations.

16

P I E T R O B E R E T T A S. p. A.

The Foremost Italian Manufacturer
of Shotguns, Pistols, Rifles
and Lightweight Weapons

Gardone V.T. - Brescia
Italy

A pair of M1 Garand rifles, the front one a prepped competition rifle based upon a "many times reborn" National Match rifle recently refurbished. Most old "NM" marked club and service match rifles are worn out from heavy use, and have had many parts replaced. They were never the equals of today's smith-prepped rifles in terms of accuracy, but many of us consider it distasteful to not make some effort to at least restore and record some of their status. There are ways to do this which do not upset collectors.

NATIONAL MATCH, ACCURACY RIFLES

The purpose of the National Match or competition Garand is to hit reliably at ranges that may reach as deep as 1,000 meters, and to do so in strings of fire involving a maximum of 20 rounds expended at a sitting.

This section contains data, photos, and illustrations relating to the M1 Garand's preparation as an accuracy rifle. The military text reproduced at the end of Part II is on the Rifle, National Match, M1 and was released by the US Army Material Command/Weapons Command at Camp Perry in 1963. It is obsolete, and no one today contemplating the best possible competition rifle seriously considers a military barrel. However, it does lay out excellent assembly and test procedures, and, though modern materials are much improved, every bit of practical information in the manual is useful.

Most civilian shooters will not bother with the marking procedures detailed in the text. Line and tension

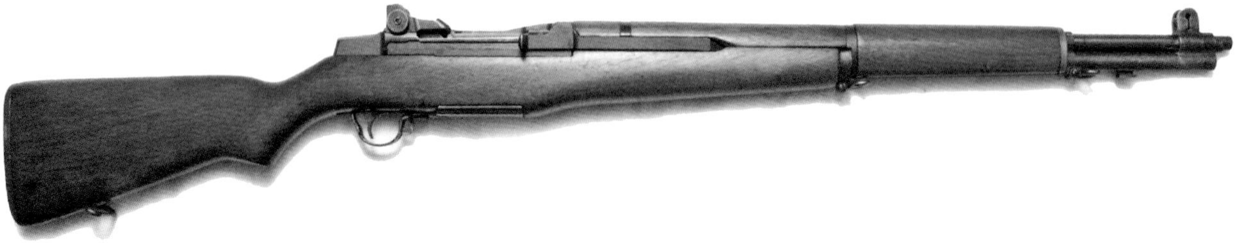

This tired, old "National Match" rifle is a relatively untampered-with ca. 1962–'63 Armory-produced competition rifle. Only the rear sight aperture has been changed out with the .0520 small, adjustable hooded version. The original aperture and the interim NM-marked aperture were in the butt well when sold.

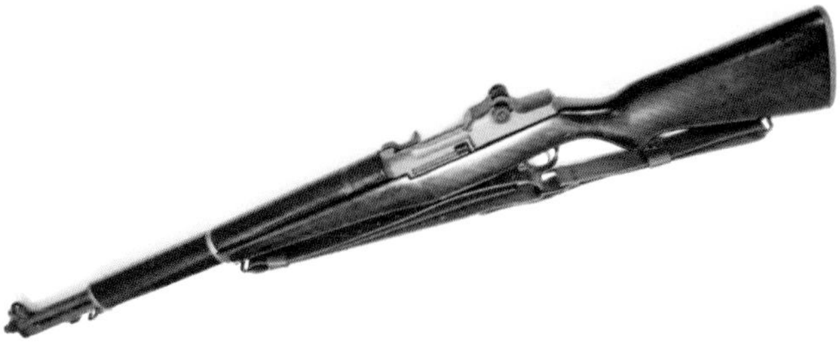

A very nice old "National Match" rifle purchased at Camp Perry in the late 1960s. It measured nicely, and like virtually all competition rifles actually used at the firiing line, bears a coat of very hard varnish, probably polyurethane, inside and out, done most likely by the first shooter to obviate moisture penetration and impact shifts and the necessity of re-bedding. This one bore a heavy barrel and was ready to go, but having been updated and upgraded, ironically, most likely at Parris Island, from a "Type 2" National Match, most collectors would not even be interested and would not even consider it "National Match" save in the status delivered direct from the armory. It was in the later, shorter 7.62x51 chambering, with barrel markings common to late Marine competition rifles from the late '60s to the mid-'70s, and was most likely one of those turned from commercial blanks. A magnificent rifle for a *shooter*, but one in which die-hard collectors would have little or no interest. Shortly after this shot was taken, the commercial lightweight M1907-style sling was replaced with a 60", 3-buckle/4 keeper match sling, civilian and custom made, and after duly greasing and adjusting a few things, it was firing most of a day at Rio Salado. Not as accurate as the specimens made for the author over the years at Accuracy Speaks, it was not far behind. The rifle was finished in a rather gray phosphate, probably when the heavy barrel was added.

straightening barrels should never be necessary any more. The procedure is sometimes done by manufacturers before delivery, but with today's broaching techniques and button rifling, the term itself has fallen into disuse and has become obsolete.

Likewise, the suggestion that cleaning the bore after firing is unnecessary has been known to be false since long before this literature was prepared. Removal of copper fouling in particular, especially after extensive shooting of a rapid-fire rifle with fast-moving bullets, has been proven many thousands—probably millions—of times, to be an absolute necessity for both barrel life and best shooting. One will still sometimes encounter some walking antique at a rifle range who suggests that cleaning a match rifle is somehow an error. This logic is as erroneous and tortured as the statement itself.

Just closed down as this book underwent its final edit was a project to develop yet more longevity for the paramount rifle of the 1940s. It was a two-part project to imbue the old musket with even greater durability. Examining inexpensive technology, it proved unpublishable and unproductive. But it remains amusing.

Cryo treatment involves immersing metal products subject to high stress into a tank of liquid nitrogen at temperatures fairly close to absolute zero, then precisely returning the assembly to normal temperature ranges. This is similar to heat treatment but has little or no impact on Rockwell hardness. It does, however, improve molecular cohesion at a near-atomic level, meaning metals so treated are far less subject to microfracture and fatigue.

Molycoating bullets involves using a complex polymer, coated with a high-temperature variant of Carnuba wax, in a special tumbler. Its primary effect is to minimize the shedding of copper, which tends to gall onto barrel steel. For now, this process is available and of use only to handloaders, though surely someone will find a way to market the processed bullets, loaded, to casual shooters of loaded ammo.

Between the two processes, it may now be possible to prolong the life of the Garand—especially its barrel, bolt, and operating rod—and to minimize the effects of heat and copper fouling on Garand barrels.

Unlike a lot of "panacea" mumbo-jumbo of the past, these two processes have real history and real impact. The question that may be explored is how much impact? Stay tuned . . .

However, the admonition that detailed disassembly of a tightly bedded rifle is both difficult and, in some ways, counterproductive is at least partially correct. Upon reassembly, such a rifle will require six to eight rounds to seat properly back into the bedding, and zero may shift slightly.

The variable gas cylinder lock screw is probably the most aggressively oversold accessory for the M1 ever devised. This one is from Accuracy Speaks. They should mainly be used for extremely powerful, long-range loads which might otherwise fatigue the operating rod.

So the procedure for cleaning the gas system without total disassembly becomes very important. Lubrication with more modern greases than were in military use in 1963 becomes much more important with match rifles because accessing the operating rod and spring is so awkward.

There were depot-prepared match Garands—and, likely, considerable activity at Springfield Armory as

Most depot-built and some arsenal competition rifles, when actually in service, acquired a lot of local markings and even painted bands, largely to discourage theft.

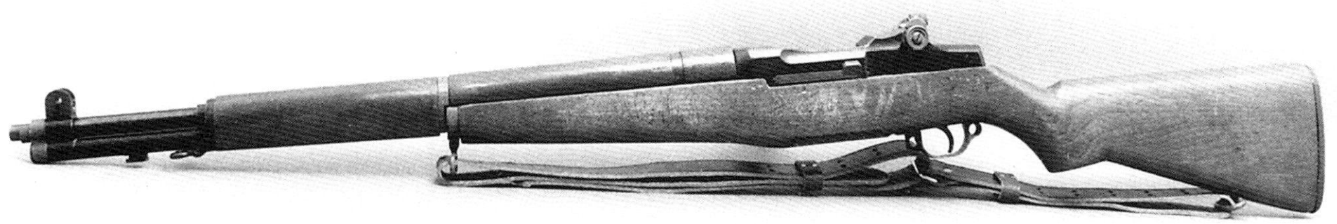

This 7.62mm U.S.M.C. Match gun was apparently prepared for demonstration use at Quantico and features a great many hard chrome and black chromed or oxided parts and a Douglas barrel with full local markings.

Properly set up, the ejector on the Garand will dump .308/7.62mm brass neatly and consistently where a shooter can find it quickly and efficiently. This H&R bears a custom barrel, and the bolt and ejector have received a great deal of detailed attention, which saves a great deal of time at the range and contributes to both accuracy and reliability. Rounds from this rifle land, reliably, about 3 feet in front of the rifle, perhaps a foot to the right.

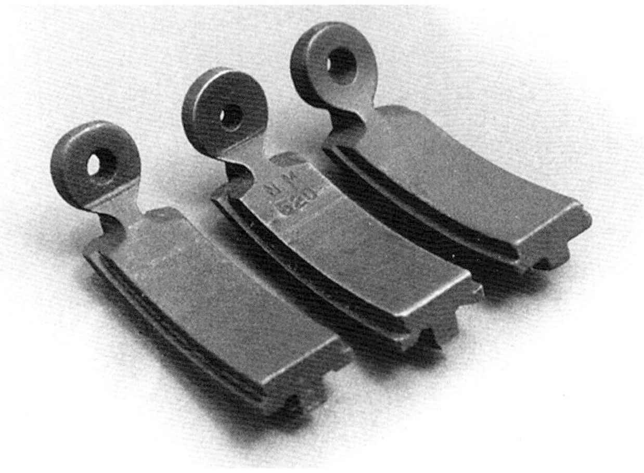

There were many stages in the evolution of the fine adjustment National Match sight, including the "small tin can" hooded version, shown elsewhere in this book, from the 1950s. Here are the standard H&R service sight, ca. 1 955; the rare first model small aperture National Match, ca. 1949; and a typical Winchester aperture from about 1 942, for comparison, from left to right.

well—long after 1963. Indeed, many of the navy's wonderful 7.62mm match rifles seem to have been rebuilt and reconfigured at H&R, apparently well into the 1970s.

One factor the military very thoroughly explored, which I regard as more or less gospel, is the curious inter-relationship between bullets and velocity for achieving maximum accuracy. Work done at Frankford Arsenal, Aberdeen, and Lake City led to conclusions that I tried for a long time to disprove and that I and every other serious researcher I know can only affirm: bullets of a given weight and design, virtually regardless of the type or brand of powder, will deliver best accuracy at a very specific velocity level. This is nothing new, but every handloader and many manufacturers keep trying to change this fundamental principle, with very limited success. This is not to say that your pet load is not at least partially dependent on the type and quantity of powder you use. What it does state, though, is that optimal performance appears at certain specific velocity "windows," even if different cartridges are used. In this case, of course, we're discussing 7.62mm (.308 diameter, or .30 caliber) virtually exclusively.

That said, I have noticed (and have spent ungodly amounts of powder working out this data) that there is far less difference in accuracy potential—given the use of any medium-slow rifle powder appropriate for this rifle and these cartridges—than some authorities would have you believe. I have gotten roughly equal results from carefully worked- up loads in .30-06 and .308 with Varget, IMR 4064, both versions of 4895, Winchester's 748 and 760 ball, and at least a dozen others, Slow powders like Win/Olin 760 must be approached carefully, and velocities will NEVER equal more appropriate propellants. However, decent accuracy is attained with careful work and research.

Several recent developments in products and processing bode well for the Garand shooter. While they'll surely be tried first to improve the durability and performance of match rifles of all sorts, there's absolutely no reason ***all*** can't be of benefit to the Garand collector and casual shooter.

First and simplest, Federal has re-entered the components market, and its excellent MUP match brass, including the nickeled fodder, is again available in both .30-06 and .308/7.62mm. To the precision shooter, this is particularly good news. No one seriously disputes that the very best shooting in the world is done by handloads, (especially on new, precise brass), although even reloads, carefully done, will generally outshoot all but a fraction of factory ammo. What MUP does is assure a consistent supply of the very best commercial brass, albeit at a premium price.

Second, polymer coating of bullets has become somewhat more economical for the reloader. This process involves tumbling bullets (essentially using a planar vibrator device, not a conventional tumbler/vibrator used for polishing brass) in combination with a molybdenum-based plastic medium. The plastic material thus deposited, generally with a coat of Carnuba wax, acts as a lubricant, which is intended to reduce heat buildup on the bullet itself and the barrel metal.

The claim is frequently made that the "moly" will increase accuracy and velocity. So far, I've been unable to see such a result. However, the friction reduction ***does*** reduce bore erosion and especially copper fouling, and therefore prolongs barrel life while reducing cleaning effort and time. Velocity increases per load are very minimal; I saw no accuracy increase whatever. But for the price per bullet, the increase in barrel life is very sensible. All testing was done with 175-grain Hornady boat-tail hollow point match bullets. The factories do not as yet apply this process to ***any*** of their ammunition. Some factory ammunition utilizes other polymer coatings. The "molycoating" may be applied to any caliber, and by the time you read this, ***all*** of my bullets will be so prepared.

The third development is also nothing really new but has been receiving a lot of attention lately; processes have improved, and prices for application are, correspondingly, decreasing. Cryogenic tempering subjects objects to temperatures below -300 degrees Fahrenheit for precisely controlled time intervals. Structure, stress, and crystalline arrangement are subtly modified, depending upon the material. The exposure to liquid nitrogen temperatures of this order sometimes eliminates specific accuracy problems related to tool stress and, with many materials, can greatly increase wear resistance. It has little to no effect upon the 8620 tool steel of the Garand's receiver but should significantly increase the life of most M1 barrels, particularly those which evince stress "bends" from machining processes. ***Guns and Ammo*** and ***American Rifleman***, among others, have run fairly detailed features on the processes and results.

Cryogenic processing seems to add considerable life to most barrel steels. It can increase accuracy, though usually with near-new barrels that have experienced machining stress (this sort of stress cannot usually be relieved with older techniques). The processes are not expensive, and my examination of M1 barrels thus prepared has so far indicated that the cryogenic treatment very slightly decreases cleaning time but considerably slows fatigue and throat burn.

All three can be good news to Garand shooters, and even to collectors.

The velocity peaks in the match barrels and high-quality GI barrels I've shot run about as follows:

BULLET AND TYPE	VELOCITY OPTIMUM "WINDOW" *
147–152 grain service-style ball USGI, PMC, Israeli, Winchester, commercial, flatbase or boat-tail—though flatbases actually have slightly less muzzle velocity latitude and are slightly more individual	**approx. 2,690–2,810 fps**
168–175 grain FMJ boat-tail match bullets, hollow points, and other	**approx. 2,590–2,660 fps**
180–190 grain boat-tail hollow point match	**approx. 2,400–2,540 fps**

Note: Some long-range shooters push much faster and make special gas system changes to shoot such rounds in the Garand. Do not do this in any standard rifle.

*These figures are all muzzle velocities.

For all the practical reasons noted elsewhere in this book, it is strongly suggested that today's match conversions of the Garand be executed in 7.62x5/.308.

Wise Garand shooters will polish the ejector and, especially, the knife edge of the extractor. Snipping a couple of coils off the ejector spring will keep one's spent brass closer to shooting position, and in better condition. These modifications will reduce ejector hickeys on caseheads. The Garand was designed so that casings landed far away from the rifle to minimize clutter in static combat positions. You're not likely to require that dispersion.

Presuming a receiver is not excessively worn, particularly in the operating rod raceway (and is hopefully a late World War II or postwar unit), there is no reason a properly prepared Garand with top-quality ammo cannot easily exceed minute-of-angle accuracy with regularity. Sometimes this can happen with far less than full match preparation. The barrel, of course, is critical to this formula. Whether a receiver has spent part of its life in a foreign country is irrelevant. (Regardless of who the last military owner was, virtually every M1 has seen service abroad, a very high percentage even of old DCM rifles having been foreign owned and/or operated at some time or other.) All of the very best shooting M1s I've fired were civilian workups on import receivers. In fact, entering competition with an arsenal "NM" rifle is a certain way to carefully avoid victory.

It is much better to begin anew and make use of some of the discoveries of the last thirty or so years.

Just as important to note is that an actual, certifiable GI SA NM rifle is an artifact. For half its value to a collector, a much better custom rifle can be concocted with brand new heavy Fajen stock and Douglas barrel.

The GI bedding specifications for the receiver are rather conservative. Most modern smiths put an "S" layer of hard bedding or even a steel "reclining L" piece at the receiver's foremost left corner wedge, ahead of the clip release, about 1 inch behind and below the receiver ring. Some also weld or bolt a heavy square wedge below the receiver "horseshoe" and inlet this into another bedded well in the buttstock. This increases bearing area and, in theory, stability—although with this robust receiver it may be unnecessary. Most smiths fiddle the stock ferrule around to provide a high level of upward spring tension to hold the barrel high. This is very helpful as the gun heats up. Springfield never did these procedures; nor was its bedding very secure.

Modern barrel crowns are less exaggerated and less fragile than thirty-odd years back. One of the best ideas I've seen was on a custom-turned barrel, some ⅛ inch of which was belled out and slightly countersunk. This shooter cleaned at the firing line with copper solvent—rapidly, at every opportunity—and was shooting scores way above his level of experience.

By the way, if you have some old USGI 173 grain M72 bullets, the original form of the manual makes very clear that their optimum specific velocity level (at the muzzle, of course) was 2,640 fps., which neatly fits my research parameters. Most any modern BTHP will, of course, outperform any of the old designs. That's why military personnel using .30/.308 machinery in accuracy applications now use high quality commercial match bullets.

There's a certain amount of pedantics, nostalgia, and romance associated with this old rifle, and I don't object to any of it. Indeed, I celebrate it. However, to me, the best way to celebrate this legend is to neatly plop bullets into paper, way downrange, one on top of the other. Good luck—and good shooting!

This manual dates from long before Kevlar-augmented epoxy bedding, laser-measured barrels, and some of the more radical techniques successfully used by America's best riflesmiths to build the best high- powered competition rifles in the country.

Despite the ravings of various hacks in the political realm, the M1 has never been popular with thugs, but its rapid-fire capability has made it one of the darlings of the competition firing line. Its offspring, the M14 and various cast copies, carry twenty-round magazines and have some advantage in the longer, timed strings, but are not as strong. Smith's semiautomatic M14, among others, is in the same accuracy class as the M1. The M14 was included in the original version of this manual but has been deleted in this excerpt.

The lubrication guide contained in the CMP's "Read This First" guide to the M1 Garand is adequate, but many shooters, mindful of the increased historic and monetary value of their rifles, go considerably beyond those fundamentals.

For example, the operating rod raceway on the receiver's right is usually lubed in the groove for its entire length with panthermic wheel bearing or other such greases. The detent in the operating rod behind the knuckle where the right-hand bolt lug engages is worthy of a substantial dollop of grease. The hammer spring plunger (the shaft inside the spring), its tube or barrel (inside, of course!), and the spring are generally also coated.

Many match shooters likewise apply grease to the frontmost five inches of the operating rod tube, as well as to the hook of the operating rod catch.

Where the follower (recoil) spring reposes inside the operating rod benefits from heavy grease, and since that area can also be a moisture trap, most shooters preclude the possibility of damage and lubricate there quite heavily.

Modern wheel bearing greases, machine assembly greases, and a variety of others can and will serve well.

And as a preservative, modern museum conservators and advanced shooters most often find waxes, which do not migrate with gravity, are vastly superior to oil in any and all preventative applications, including car waxes and products as fundamental as ordinary grocery store paste wax. I use Johnson's paste wax and whatever auto material first falls under the hand, and it has been decades since anything of mine acquired rust while I owned it. There are countless cases where oil was relied upon and repeatedly failed. The cause is, again, gravity, which means thin liquids move down and dry out.

There have been articles in the GCA Journal on this topic that put this even more in context and provide much more data than is appropriate in these volumes.

Austrian personnel with M1 Garand rifles, ca. 1957 or so (*"Ausbildung in der Gruppe"*) . . . The M1 did not service merely the US Army. Nor were they only US-produced. These are Austrian military personnel. Their rifles are American. In most European countries, the Garand was called the "G.50." Austrian Government photograph.

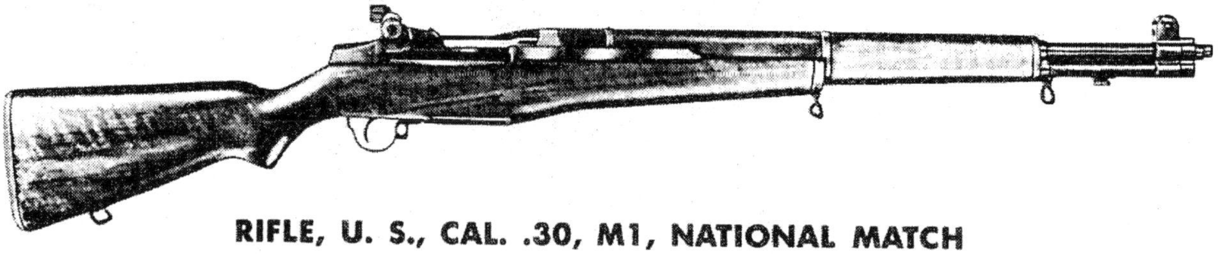

RIFLE, U. S., CAL. .30, M1, NATIONAL MATCH

PART I — HISTORY

1. In March, 1953, Springfield Armory was directed by Office, Chief of Ordnance to furnish 800 U. S. Cal. .30 M1, Rifles for use at the National Matches. These rifles were to be selected as being of excellent quality and workmanship and should possess accuracy (size of groups), and targeting (location of group), capabilities superior to the average service weapon. The Armory, at that time, was manufacturing new M1 rifles, a situation which naturally lessened the work required to produce the desired lot of match quality guns. Because of the high standards to which the service rifles were being produced it was necessary to apply only minor gunsmithing to any weapon to obtain National Match quality.

2. During the succeeding years from 1954 through 1963 the Armory produced National Match quality weapons by two methods, namely; (1) by applying minor gunsmithing operations to newly manufactured rifles as described in the preceding paragraph and (2) by rebuilding National Match weapons returned to the installation from various locations throughout the world. The latter procedure requires a considerable amount of inspection, refinishing, and rebuilding of weapon components. This work is necessary to eliminate parts which evidence excessive wear or which have been altered in the field for some particular reason. Each rebuilt National Match rifle is rebarrelled, restocked and glass bedded.

3. Inasmuch as production of new Cal. .30 M1 Rifles has been completely curtailed, M1, NM Rifles to be issued during the 1963 National Matches are rebuilt weapons. However, because of the critical acceptance standards applicable to National Match rifles, and because of the expert workmanship employed to meet these standards it is not likely the user will be able to distinguish between new and rebuilt weapons either in appearance or performance.

4. The following year by year breakdown indicates the quantity of National Match Cal. .30 M1 rifles produced by Springfield Armory:

Year	New	Rebuilt	Total
1953	800		800
1954	4184	499	4683
1955	3003	314	3317
1956	5050	550	5600
1957	4184	499	4683
1958	1295	731	2026
1959	2877	2652	5529
1960		8663	8663
1961		1410	1410
1962		4500	4500
1963		3639	3639

PART II — 1963 RIFLE

The 1963 model shown above represents the latest refinement of the M1 as a National Match rifle.

Over the years many modifications have been made to improve the accuracy and targeting capabilities of the M1. Those described on page 3 and illustrated on pages 4 and 5 have been found to produce the best results when judged by the performance average of large numbers of rifles.

This year's National Match M1 has a hooded eyepiece rear sight. This sight will make possible ½ minute changes in elevation, and will be available in two peep hole diameters. Scores will improve with the hooded eyepiece as the sight picture will be much more constant under changing light conditions.

In addition, new rear sight bases have been modified to considerably minimize movement between the aperture assembly and the mating surfaces in the base. The new rear sight base will be identified with the letters NM/2A.

The new hooded rear sight is shown on page 6. Operation of the sight, firing mechanism, and other points of interest are described on pages 7, 8 and 9.

Notes on inspection of barrels and of the completed rifle will be found in Part IV. Part V will provide useful information on rifle maintenance.

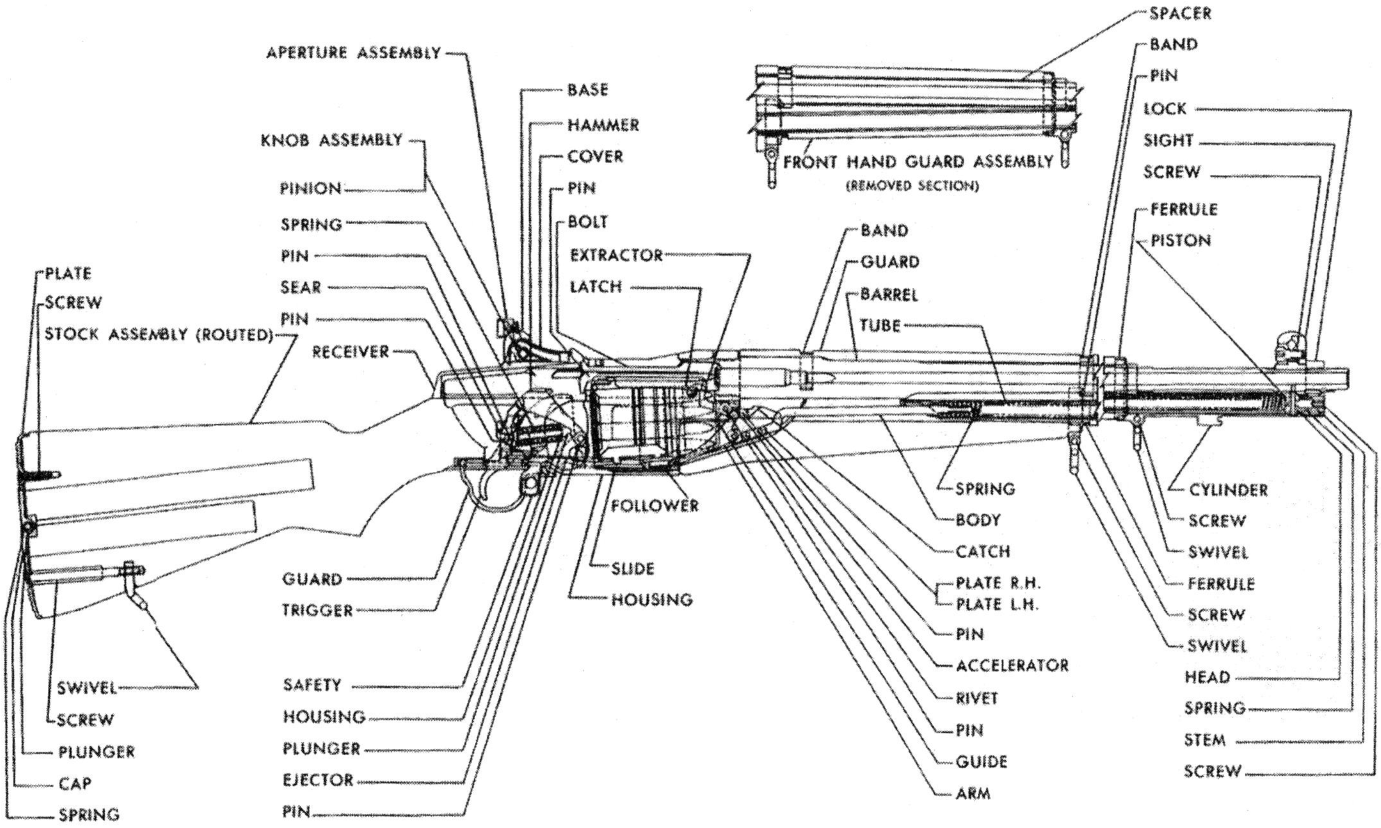

RIFLE, U. S. CAL. .30, M1, NATIONAL MATCH (SECTIONAL VIEW).

PART III — GENERAL REQUIREMENTS

1. All components shall be of latest design.

2. All wooden components shall be of solid heartwood with the direction of grain parallel to the longitudinal axis of stock.

3. All stocks shall be glass bedded and custom fitted to receiver and barrel assemblies and trigger housing assemblies. The stock assembly and the trigger housing assembly shall be identified with last four digits of the receiver serial number. These assemblies shall not be interchanged after glass bedding process has been completed.

4. The stock shall be free from contact with the barrel or handguard.

5. Stock ferrule shall not contact lower portion of lower band longitudinally; there shall be approximately 1/64 inch minimum clearance.

6. The stock shall have a clearance in the area between rear of receiver bedding surface and receiver rail bedding surfaces.

7. Clamping of the trigger guard shall have a definite resistance at a minimum distance of ⅜ inch from the full lock position.

8. Gas cylinder shall fit tightly on the barrel bearing diameter and the splines. There shall be no rotational movement.

9. Gas cylinder shall be brought forward against the lock before tightening the gas cylinder lock screw.

10. In assembly, the gas cylinder lock shall be hand tightened against shoulder on the barrel within a range of slightly beyond the 6 o'clock position but not in excess of 60° (8 o'clock) past the 6 o'clock position. The gas cylinder lock shall then be "backed off" the minimum distance necessary to align with the gas cylinder at the 6 o'clock position.

11. Gas cylinder splined hole and rear ring shall meet requirements of alignment gage.

12. The barrel muzzle shall be crowned – concentric with bore (60° included angle) to remove burrs.

13. The barrel shall be line straightened to meet the requirements of an optical straightness gage. Straightness of the barrel shall be such that the bore centerline established by a self-aligning expansion plug (2½ inches long with a pilot diameter of .2993 minus .0001) that fits and aligns itself in the bore at the muzzle end, the maximum allowable deviation from that centerline shall not exceed 0° 2' 23" throughout the length of the bore. Any resultant taper of the bore shall be within dimensional limits and be diminishing from breech to muzzle.

14. The operating rod assembly shall function freely without binding during a simulated firing cycle with the operating rod spring removed.

15. The trigger pull required to release the hammer shall be smooth, free from "creep," and within the limits of four and one-half to six pounds. Functional surfaces of the hooks of the hammer and trigger, and the related mating surfaces of the sear may have the phosphate coating removed by polishing to assure smooth trigger pull.

16. Aperture assemblies 7791133 and 7791282 produce ½ minute change of elevation by 180° rotation of the aperture. Aperture assembly 7791133 shall have an eyepiece with an .0595 peep hole. Aperture assembly 7791282 shall have an eyepiece with an .0520 peep hole.

17. Threads on windage knob shall measure 5/16-64 NS-3A. Threads on rear sight base shall measure 5/16-64 NS-3B.

18. Top of front sight blade shall be square with side and all edges and corners shall be sharp to .005 R. Max. Front sight shall be sharp and square and shall not overhang the sides of the gas cylinder.

19. Headspace shall be 1.940 to 1.943. Light finger pressure shall be used in checking headspace.

20. Identification mark shall consist of the letters "NM" approximately ⅛ inch high inscribed on the barrel approximately between the front hand guard and front sight.

1. ESSENTIAL POINTS AND AREAS

The essential points and areas established by these general requirements are illustrated on pages 4 and 5.

ALL WOODEN COMPONENTS SHALL BE SOLID HEARTWOOD WITH THE DIRECTION OF THE GRAIN PARALLEL TO THE LONGITUDINAL AXIS OF STOCK.

STOCK SHALL HAVE NO OPEN GRAIN WHICH MIGHT SWELL EXCESSIVELY IN HIGH HUMIDITY.

PROTECTIVE FINISH TUNG (CHINAWOOD) OIL.

REAR SIGHT MARKINGS MUST BE DISTINCT.

KNOBS MUST HAVE FREE MOVEMENT, INDEPENDENT OF EACH OTHER, DEFINITE CLICKING ACTION, AND POSITIVE RETENTION.

ELEVATING KNOB MUST BE ON 100 YD SETTING WHEN APERTURE IS ELEVATED 8 CLICKS FROM LOWEST POSITION.

SIGHT MUST BE FREE OF EXCESS OIL.

SCREW, REAR SIGHT SHALL BE TIGHTENED WITHIN 20 TO 25 INCH LBS.

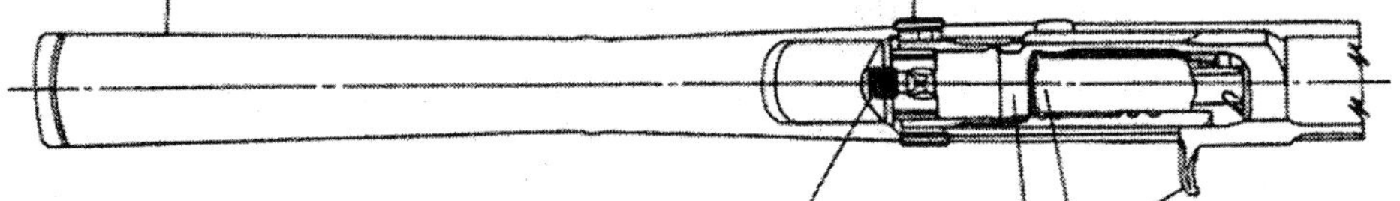

THE APERTURE ASSEMBLY PRODUCES 1/2 MINUTE CHANGE OF ELEVATION BY 180° ROTATION OF THE EYEPIECE. APERTURES WITH .0595 AND .0520 DIAMETER PEEP HOLES WILL BE ISSUED.

PRICK PUNCH RECEIVER AFTER PROOF FIRING.

PRICK PUNCH BOLT AFTER PROOF FIRING.

THE OPERATING ROD ASSEMBLY SHALL FUNCTION FREELY WITHOUT BINDING DURING A SIMULATED FIRING CYCLE WITH THE OPERATING ROD SPRING REMOVED.

HEADSPACE SHALL BE 1.940 TO 1.943. LIGHT FINGER PRESSURE SHALL BE USED IN CHECKING HEADSPACE.

AREA "A"
WITH THE OPERATING ROD SPRING AND ROD FOLLOWER DISASSEMBLED FROM THE RIFLE AND BY LIFTING THE ASSEMBLED RIFLE TO AN APPROXIMATE 60° ANGLE WITH THE MUZZLE UP, THE BOLT SHALL OPEN FULLY WITHOUT ANY MANUAL ASSISTANCE. NEXT, POINT THE MUZZLE DOWN ON AN ANGLE OF APPROXIMATELY 60°, THE BOLT SHALL CLOSE FULLY WITHOUT ANY MANUAL ASSISTANCE. WITH THE TRIGGER HOUSING AND STOCK DISASSEMBLED FROM THE RIFLE AND THE OPERATING ROD FULLY RETRACTED, APPLY A LIGHT PRESSURE TO THE HANDLE OF THE ROD INWARDS AT AREA "A." TENSION IN THE ROD MUST TEND TO RELOCATE THE ROD IN ITS ORIGINAL POSITION. THE VISIBLE OPENING BETWEEN THE RECEIVER AND THE HANDLE OF THE ROD IN THIS HORIZONTAL PLANE SHOULD NOT EXCEED .030 AND SHOULD GRADUALLY DECREASE BETWEEN THE POINT WHERE PRESSURE IS APPLIED AND THE ROD DISASSEMBLY SLOT ON THE RECEIVER. NEXT, APPLY PRESSURE DOWNWARDS ON THE ROD TOWARD THE RECEIVER RAIL IN THE SAME LOCATION AS ABOVE. THE TENSION IN THE ROD MUST RELOCATE THE ROD IN ITS ORIGINAL POSITION. THE VISIBLE OPENING BETWEEN THE ROD AND THE RAIL IN THIS VERTICAL PLANE SHALL NOT EXCEED .015 AND SHOULD GRADUALLY DECREASE BETWEEN THIS POINT WHERE PRESSURE IS APPLIED AND THE ROD DISASSEMBLY SLOT ON THE RECEIVER.

THREADS ON WINDAGE KNOB SHALL MEASURE 5/16-64NS-3A. THREADS ON BASE REAR SIGHT SHALL MEASURE 5/16-64NS-3B. IDENTIFICATION MARK SHALL CONSIST OF THE LETTERS "NM" 1/16 HIGH INSCRIBED ON THE RIGHT SIDE OF EACH PART.

AFTER PROOF FIRING, THE HEADSPACE WITH COMPONENT BOLT SHALL BE FROM 1.940 MIN. TO 1.943 MAX.

DEFENSE ACCEPTANCE STAMP (1/2 HIGH) (LEFT HAND SIDE)

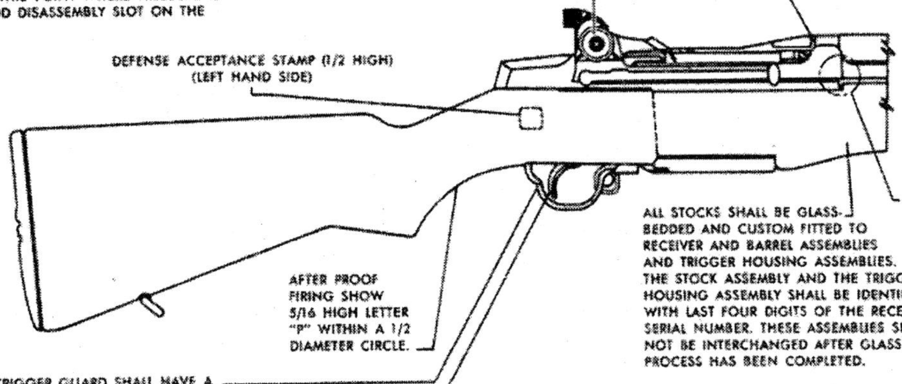

AREA "A"

AFTER PROOF FIRING SHOW 5/16 HIGH LETTER "P" WITHIN A 1/2 DIAMETER CIRCLE.

ALL STOCKS SHALL BE GLASS-BEDDED AND CUSTOM FITTED TO RECEIVER AND BARREL ASSEMBLIES AND TRIGGER HOUSING ASSEMBLIES. THE STOCK ASSEMBLY AND THE TRIGGER HOUSING ASSEMBLY SHALL BE IDENTIFIED WITH LAST FOUR DIGITS OF THE RECEIVER SERIAL NUMBER. THESE ASSEMBLIES SHALL NOT BE INTERCHANGED AFTER GLASS BEDDING PROCESS HAS BEEN COMPLETED.

THE STOCK SHALL BE FREE FROM CONTACT WITH THE BARREL.

THE STOCK SHALL HAVE A .005 MINIMUM CLEARANCE IN THE AREA BETWEEN REAR OF RECEIVER BEDDING SURFACE AND RECEIVER RAIL BEDDING SURFACES.

THE STOCK SHALL BE FREE OF ANY CONTACT WITH REAR HAND GUARD.

CLAMPING OF THE TRIGGER GUARD SHALL HAVE A DEFINITE RESISTANCE AT A MIN. DISTANCE OF 3/8 OF AN INCH FROM THE FULL LOCK POSITION.

THE TRIGGER PULL REQUIRED TO RELEASE THE HAMMER SHALL BE SMOOTH, FREE FROM "CREEP," AND WITHIN THE LIMITS OF FOUR AND ONE-HALF TO SIX LBS.

FUNCTIONAL SURFACES OF THE HOOKS OF THE HAMMER AND TRIGGER, AND THE RELATED MATING SURFACES OF THE SEAR MAY HAVE THE PHOSPHATE COATING REMOVED BY POLISHING TO ASSURE SMOOTH TRIGGER PULL.

ESSENTIAL POINTS AND AREAS

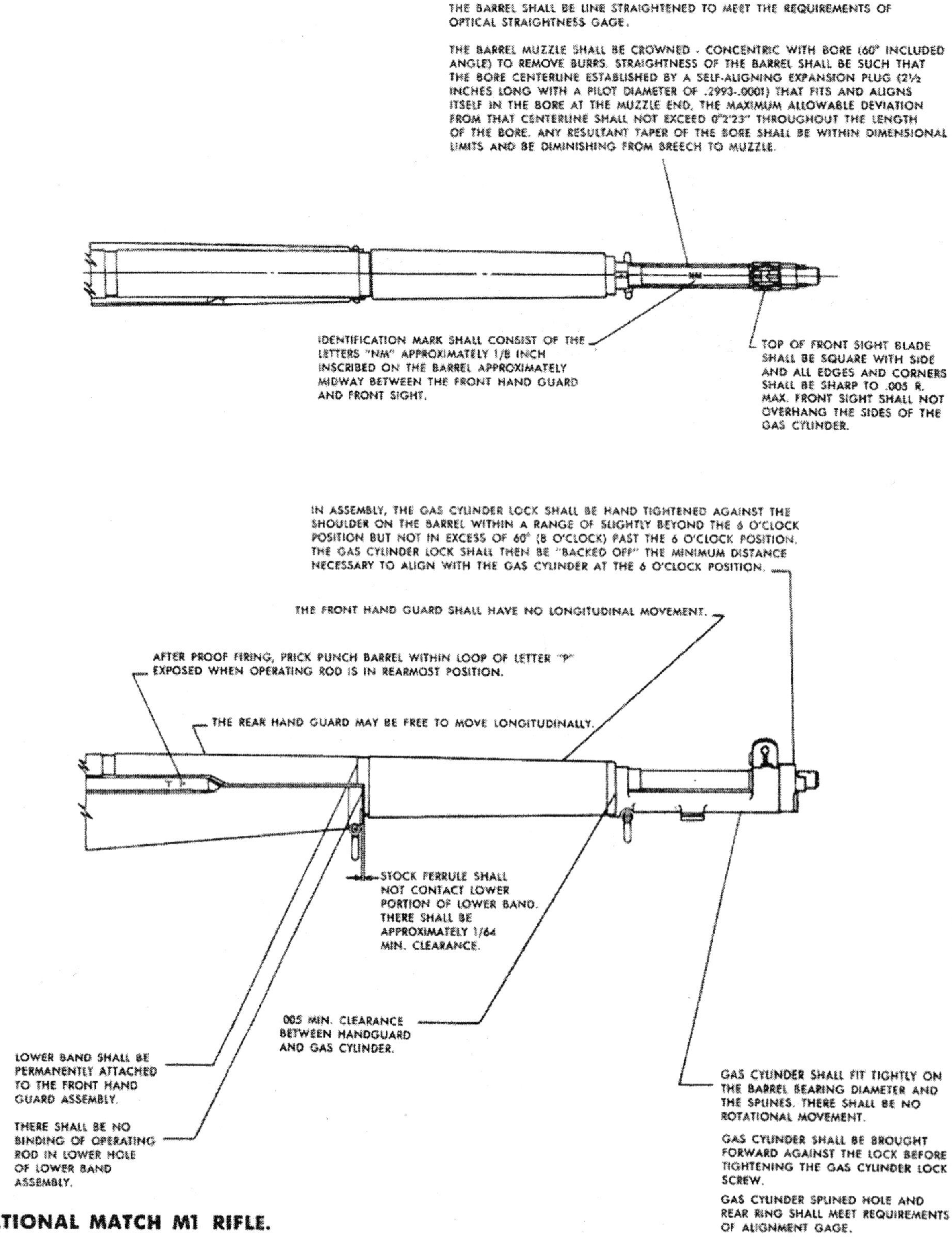

OF NATIONAL MATCH M1 RIFLE.

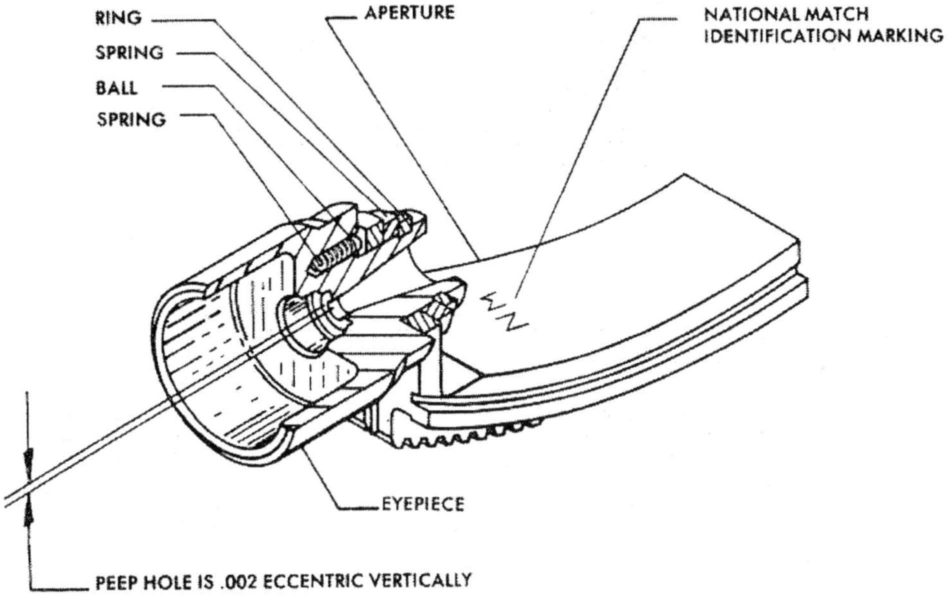

NOTCH INDICATES POSITION OF PEEP HOLE.
NOTCH AT TOP RAISES POINT OF IMPACT OF BULLET.
NOTCH AT BOTTOM LOWERS POINT OF IMPACT OF BULLET.

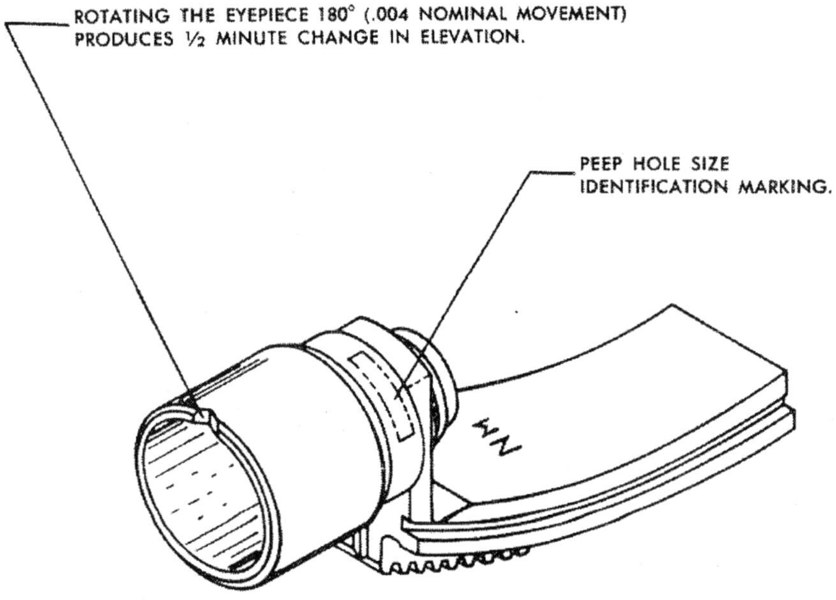

APERTURE ASSEMBLY STOCK NO. 1005-864-2926 (.0595 PEEP HOLE)
APERTURE ASSEMBLY STOCK NO. 1005-864-2928 (.0520 PEEP HOLE)

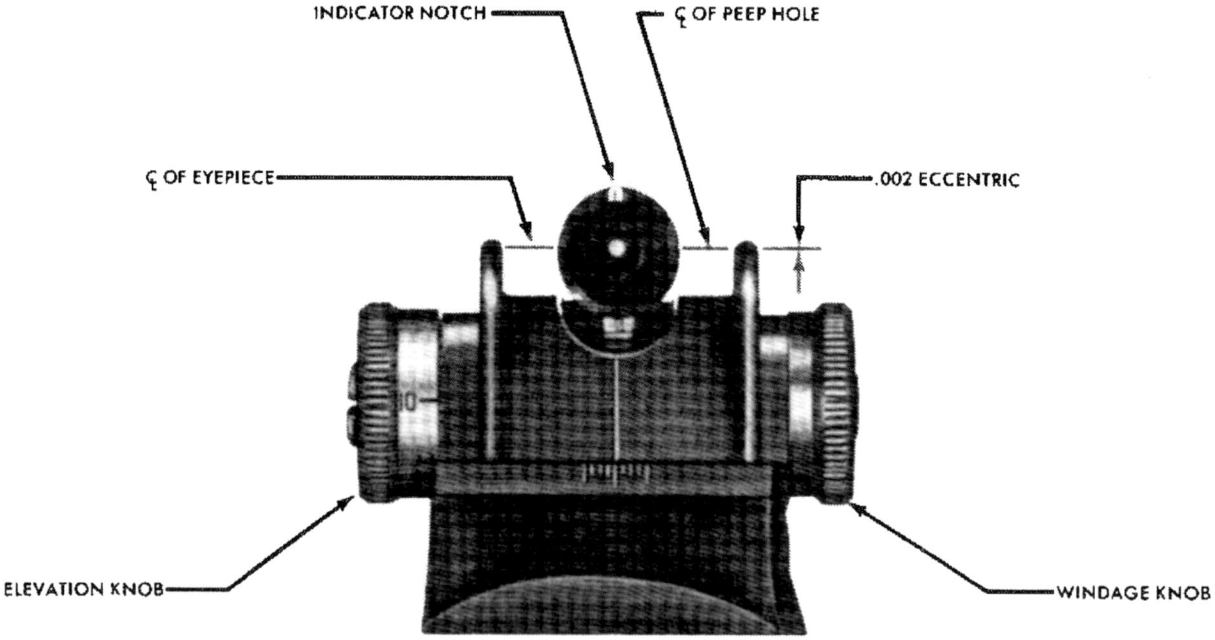

REAR SIGHT MECHANISM FOR ½ MINUTE WINDAGE AND ½ MINUTE ELEVATION

2. **SIGHTS**

a. The two aperture assemblies are identical except for the eyepieces which have different peep hole diameters. The aperture with .0595 peep hole will be installed as standard with the .0520 diameter aperture available as an alternate.

The hooded eyepiece is designed to eliminate glare and reflections on the sight aperture, and to provide ½ minute changes in elevation.

Each eyepiece is selectively fitted and matched with its individual aperture. It should not be attempted to disassemble the aperture assembly or to change eyepieces on an aperture.

The peep hole is .002 vertically eccentric with other diameters of the eyepiece. Rotating the eyepiece 180° clockwise or counter-clockwise raises and lowers the line of sight. Two spring loaded balls in the eyepiece engage a vertical "v" notch in the face of the aperture to retain the eyepiece in each position. The position of the eyepiece is indicated by a notch at the rear face of the eyepiece.

Each click of the elevation knob gives a change of 1 minute. Rotating the eyepiece so that the indicator notch is at the top, moves the point of impact of the bullet up ½ minute. With the indicator notch at the bottom, point of impact of the bullet will be moved down ½ minute.

b. The National Match sight base marked NM/2A is undercut to accept the hooded eyepiece. The change from 32 to 64 threads per inch of this sight base and of the windage knob produce a ½ minute change in windage for each click of the knob. Thus the 1963 National Match rifle is capable of ½ minute sight changes for both windage and elevation.

c. The National Match front sight has a blade width of .065 minus .005, and is identified by the letters "NM" and the numbers "062" on its right side. The width of the sight blade of the standard M1 rifle is .084 minus .010.

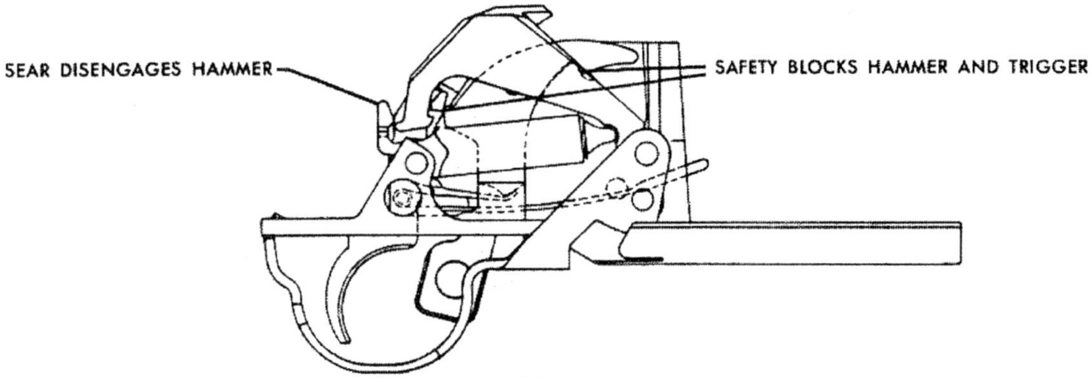

SAFE

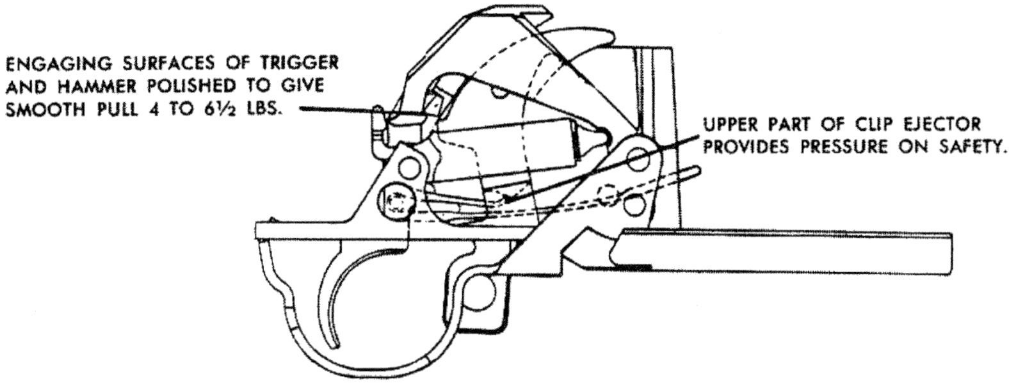

READY

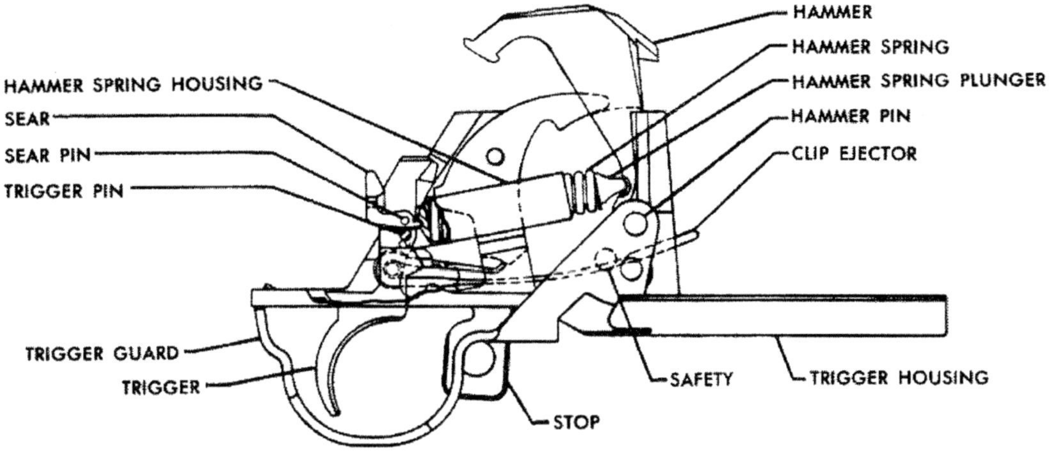

FIRED

FIRING MECHANISM

3. **FIRING MECHANISM**

The firing mechanism of the National Match M1 rifle is composed of standard parts specially fitted to meet National Match requirements.

The major components of this group are the trigger housing, trigger guard, trigger assembly, safety, hammer, and hammer spring. This group effectively controls the firing of the rifle. To prevent accidental firing, the hammer can be locked in cocked position by the safety. In the event of a misfire, the trigger guard may be used to cock the mechanism.

The rearward movement of the operating rod causes the bolt to move to the rear. The bolt cams the hammer down and rearward and compresses the hammer spring. If at this time the trigger has not been released, the sear engages the rear hammer hooks. Subsequent release of the trigger disengages the sear and allows the hammer to slide into engagement with the trigger lugs. Because of this, a separate squeeze on the trigger is necessary to fire each round.

When the safety is in the rearward (SAFE) position it blocks both the hammer and the trigger.

When the safety is in the forward (READY) position the hammer pivots forward to be engaged, at its front hooks, by the trigger. The hammer and trigger are free to move. Squeezing the trigger disengages the front hooks, and the hammer is driven forward under spring pressure to strike the firing pin and discharge the rifle.

The forward clamping shelf of the trigger housing covers the bottom of the receiver and prevents foreign matter from entering the weapon. The center upright section provides the hole for the hammer pin which serves as a pivot for the hammer and trigger guard. This section also serves as a vertical stop surface for the base of the cartridge clip. The clip ejector positioned at the lower left side of the housing extends through the upright section and exerts continual upward pressure on the clip. Another function of the clip ejector is to spring-load the safety in the selected position. A hole through the upper left side of the housing accommodates the boss of the safety. The trigger pin which passes through the rear section serves as a pivot for the trigger assembly and holds the rear end of the hammer spring housing. The trigger guard is locked in the closed position at the lower rear edge of the housing.

4. **GAS CYLINDER**

The gas cylinder is a special part and is identified by the letters "NM" on the flat at the rear of the stacking swivel. This gas cylinder is inspected to assure that it fits tightly at the barrel bearing diameter, and that there is no rotational movement of the gas cylinder on the barrel.

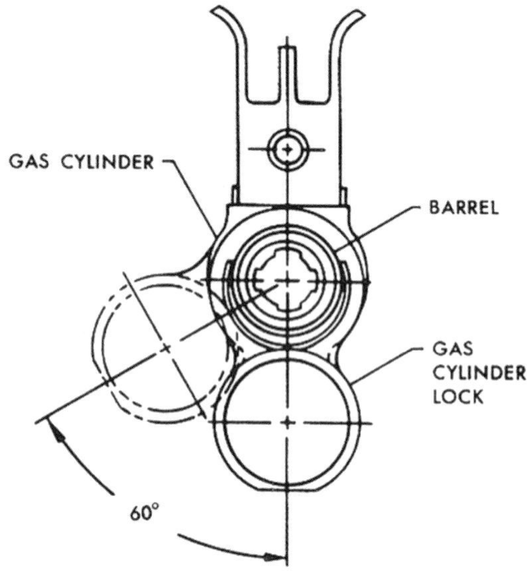

FIT OF GAS CYLINDER AND LOCK

The gas cylinder lock should tighten against the shoulder on the barrel within a range of slightly beyond the 6 o'clock position but not in excess of 60° (8 o'clock) beyond the 6 o'clock position. The gas cylinder lock is then "backed off" the minimum distance necessary to align the gas cylinder at the 6 o'clock position.

It is imperative that the gas cylinder lock screw be kept properly tightened.

5. **HAND GUARDS**

The front hand guard is permanently attached to the lower band. The lower band is pinned to the barrel which eliminates movement of the front hand guard assembly. The stock ferrule at the forward end of the front hand guard must not touch the rear of the gas cylinder.

The rear hand guard may be free to move longitudinally.

PART V — MAINTENANCE

1. CLEANING

When non-corrosive ammunition is used it is not imperative that the bore be cleaned after each day's shooting. If fouling accumulates it may be removed with bore cleaner or solvent. In damp weather a light coat of preservative oil should be left in the bore. Before firing the following day the oil should be removed with dry patches or solvent, and the bore checked for the presence of foreign matter or obstructions. The chamber should be kept clean by using a patch wet with solvent or cleaner on the brush of the chamber cleaning tool. Exterior metal surfaces should be kept clean, and protected with a light coat of preservative oil.

Limited cleaning to prevent fouling build-up in the gas port hole and on the head of the piston may be accomplished without disassembling the rifle. By holding the muzzle down and retracting the operating rod, a small amount of bore cleaner may be poured down the cylindrical portion of the rod and be worked into the gas cylinder. Cleaning without disassembling the rifle aids in maintaining its zero.

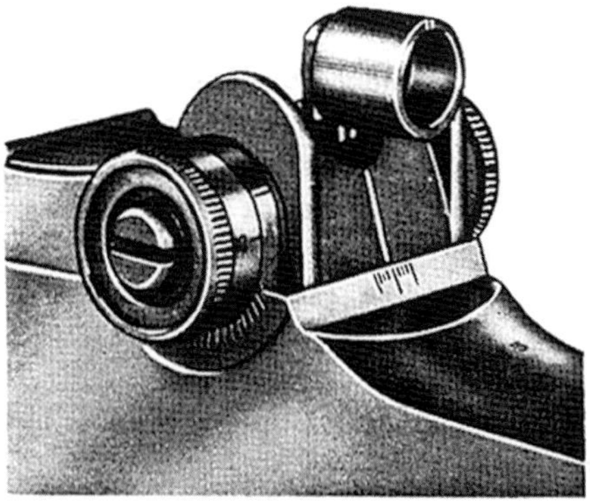

APERTURE REAR SIGHT MECHANISM FOR ½ MINUTE WINDAGE AND ELEVATION

2. REAR SIGHT

Sight bases marked NM/2A will accept hooded apertures with .0520 or .0595 peep holes, and also standard (unhooded) apertures. A plastic cap will be provided to protect the aperture assembly.

Changing apertures requires disassembling the rear sight mechanism. Extreme care should be used in handling the parts. Both the windage knob and rear sight base have a fine pitch thread. Because of the precision made threads, particular attention should be given the following, prior to, and during assembly:

a. Insert rear sight base through the opening of the cover.

b. Place the front lip of cover into the recess at the forward portion of rear sight receiver well. Raise the base slightly, exposing the rear portion of the cover. With a screwdriver, apply pressure to rear of cover in a horizontal direction until the cover snaps into place and is firmly retained by the receiver.

c. Insert the aperture, or aperture assembly, into the aperture groove in the base and lower until it bottoms against the receiver.

d. Caution should be exercised in starting windage knob threads into rear sight base to preclude danger of cross threading. Mating threads must be free of excess oil and all foreign matter.

With the left hand, apply pressure to the base forward and to the right of the receiver. Insert and turn windage knob carefully to engage the mating threads. Continue to turn windage knob until the base is tightly seated against the right receiver ear.

e. Insert pinion of elevating knob assembly through the hole on left side of receiver ear, meshing the pinion teeth with mating teeth of the aperture. Simultaneously align by feel, the flat at the end of pinion shaft with mating contour of the lock, housed in the windage knob. Thread the rear sight nut (in the windage knob) onto the pinion shaft. (Some manipulation of parts may be necessary to permit assembly). Tighten rear sight nut until both elevating and windage knobs become inoperative. By backing off the rear sight nut one or more clicks (one-half turn per click) both knobs will then be operative. The graduation mark on rear sight base can be aligned with graduation mark on the receiver.

f. Tighten the rear sight screw securely. Settings of various ranges are attained in terms of the number of clicks from the lowest position of the aperture once the sight has been "zeroed" in at the respective ranges. Once sight settings have been established, the rear sight mechanism should be left intact to preserve sight zero.

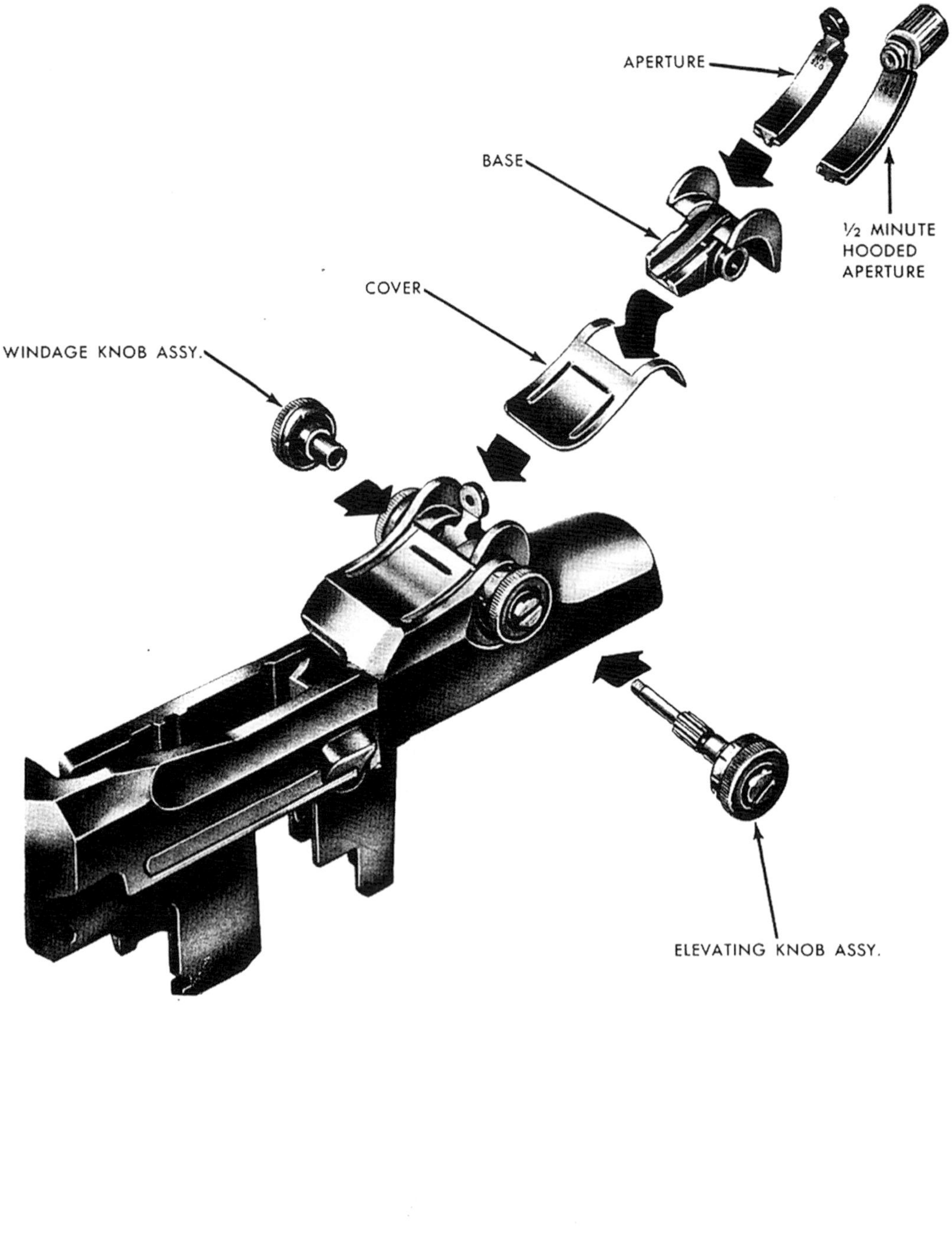

REAR SIGHT ASSEMBLY

3. **GLASS BEDDING**

It has been established that glass bedding improves both accuracy and maintaining of rifle zero.

Pages 17 thru 20 illustrate the method used for glass bedding M1 National Match rifles at Springfield Armory. Preparatory routing of the stock is illustrated below. Standard stocks may be glass bedded if similarly routed.

Materials required for glass bedding are commercially available employing an epoxy resin, milled fiberglass, polyamide resin and catalysts. Prior to using the above materials, it is imperative that a suitable release compound be applied to completely coat those parts of the metal components which will be in contact with the glass bedding. The mold release compound facilitates the breaking away of metal parts, thus leaving an exact molded impression of the metal components. In addition, a suitable solvent should be used for cleaning excess flash in the soft state prior to hardening and for sundry cleaning of equipment. It has been found that the most suitable method for applying glass compound is by the use of a syringe type polyethelene applicator having an orifice of approximately 7/64 or 1/8 inch diameter, effecting a smooth constant extrusion of material into the routed stock channels.

Whenever commercial products are used it is recommended that suppliers' instructions be followed.

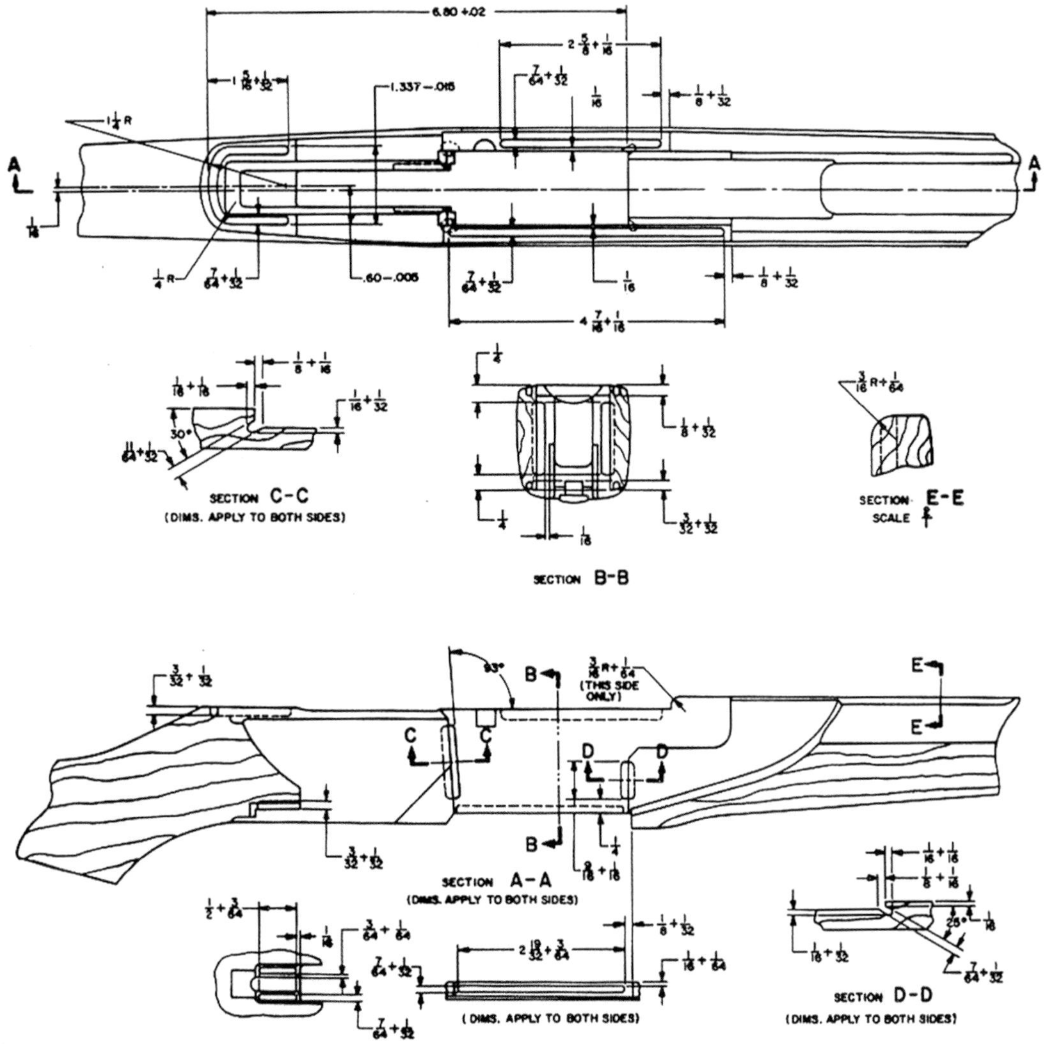

ROUTED STOCK

INSTRUCTIONS FOR GLASS BEDDING
RIFLE, U.S., CAL..30, M1 — NATIONAL MATCH

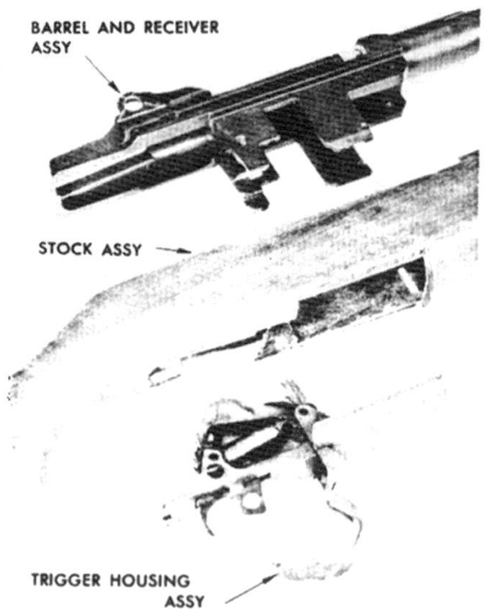

FIGURE 1

THREE MAJOR ASSEMBLIES USED IN THE GLASS BEDDING PROCESS.

IMPORTANT: THE STOCK ASSEMBLY AND TRIGGER HOUSING ASSEMBLY SHALL BE IDENTIFIED WITH THE LAST FOUR DIGETS OF THE RECEIVER SERIAL NUMBER. NOTE: IT IS IMPORTANT THAT THESE COMPONENTS BE KEPT TOGETHER THROUGHOUT THE GLASS BEDDING PROCESS.

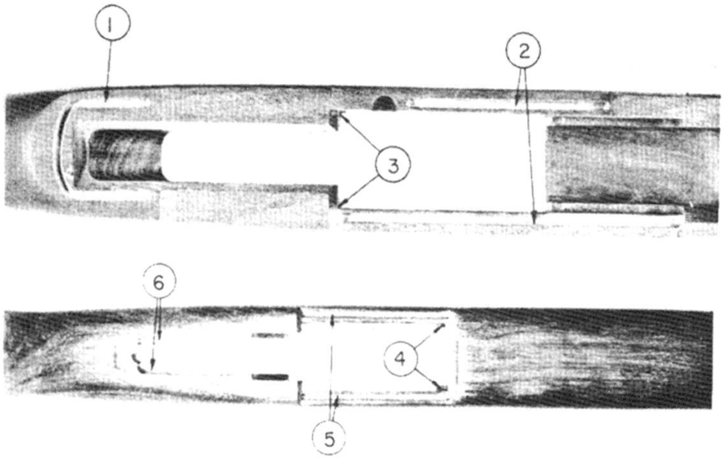

FIGURE 2

TOP AND BOTTOM VIEWS OF STOCK SHOWING ROUTED AREAS (1 THROUGH 6) OF BEDDING SURFACES OF RECEIVER AND TRIGGER HOUSING ASSEMBLY.

FIGURE 3

DIP AND COMPLETELY SUBMERGE BOTH THE RECEIVER AND TRIGGER HOUSING ASSEMBLY INTO THE RELEASE COMPOUND AND ALLOW TO AIR DRY.

IMPORTANT: DIP COATING INTO THE RELEASE COMPOUND IS NECESSITATED BECAUSE OF THE OUTSTANDING ADHESIVE PROPERTIES OF THE EPOXY GLASS FORMULATION.

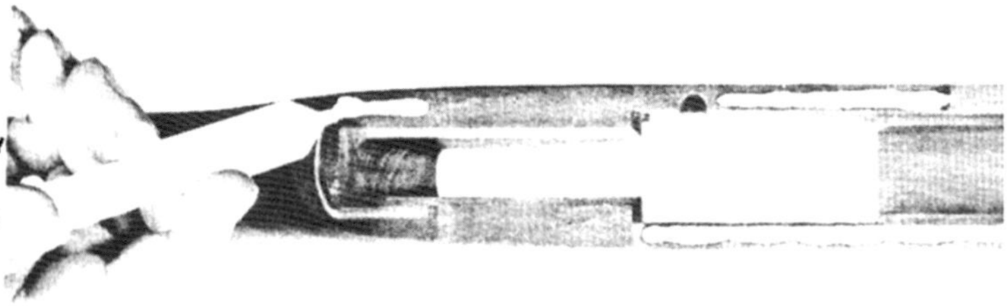

FIGURE 4

FILL ROUTED AREAS 1, 2 AND 3 WITH GLASS BEDDING COMPOUND. AN EXCESS QUANTITY OF GLASS COMPOUND IS REQUIRED IN FILLING THE ROUTED CHANNELS TO INSURE THAT THE INLETTED BEDDING SURFACES ARE COMPLETELY COVERED.

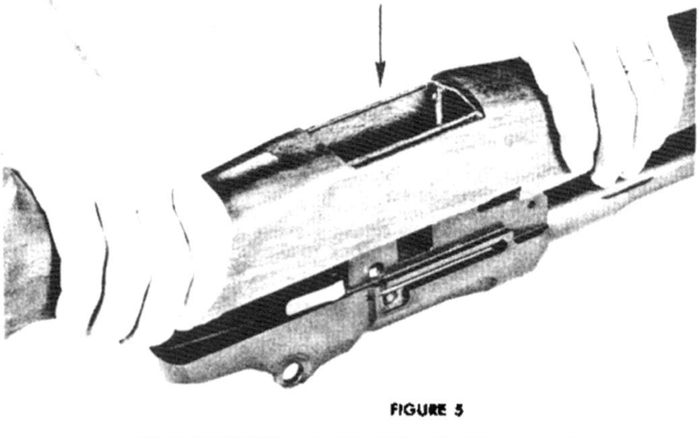

FIGURE 5

PLACE THE BARREL AND RECEIVER ASSEMBLY (RECOIL LEGS UP) AS SHOWN. ASSEMBLE THE GLASS FILLED STOCK ON TO THE RECEIVER IN THE DIRECTION INDICATED.

NOTE: WHEN THE STOCK IS FULLY SEATED ONTO THE RECEIVER, TAP THE BUTT END OF THE STOCK TO INSURE SEATING OF RECOIL SHOULDERS.

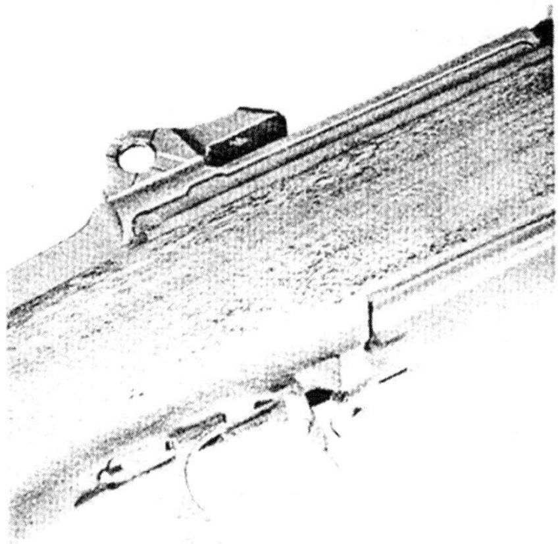

FIGURE 6

1. CLAMP THE TRIGGER GUARD TO WITHIN 1/4 INCH OF THE FULL LOCK POSITION. THE TRIGGER GUARD CAN BE HELD IN THIS POSITION WITH THE USE OF A U-SHAPED RETAINER AND/OR PIN.

NOTE: CAUTION SHALL BE EXERCISED TO INSURE THAT TRIGGER GUARD DOES NOT EXCEED ITS 1/4 INCH OPENING.
SAFETY SHOULD BE IN "SAFE" POSITION.

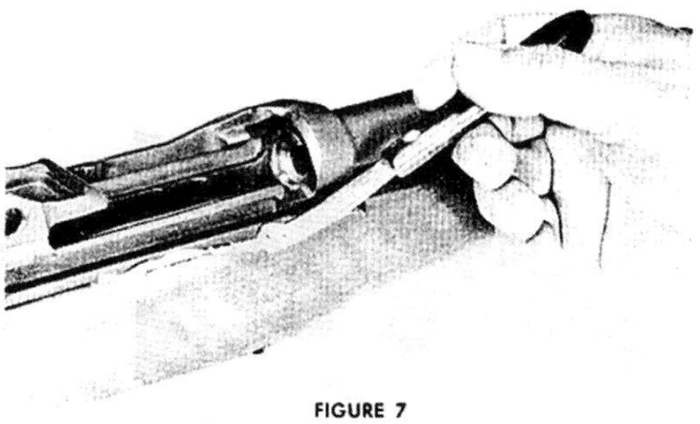

FIGURE 7

REMOVE EXCESS GLASS COMPOUND DISPLACED AFTER ACTION IS CLAMPED. FINAL TRACES OF GLASS COMPOUND SHOULD BE WIPED CLEAN.

THE COMPLETE ACTION SHALL BE ALLOWED TO DRY A MINIMUM OF 8 HOURS.

FIGURE 8

DISASSEMBLE THE BARREL AND RECEIVER ASSEMBLY FROM THE STOCK ASSEMBLY AS FOLLOWS:

1. REMOVE THE TRIGGER HOUSING ASSEMBLY.

2. HOLDING THE ASSEMBLY AS SHOWN IN FIGURE 8, STRIKE A SOLID SURFACE WITH THE BUTT END OF THE STOCK TO DISLODGE THE RECEIVER IN THE DIRECTION SHOWN.

3. EXAMINE STOCK TO INSURE THAT A DEFINITE IMPRESSION OF THE RECEIVER BEARING SURFACES HAS BEEN MADE OF THE GLASS BEDDED AREAS OF THE STOCK.

4. CLEAN ALL EXCESSES OF GLASS COMPOUND FROM METAL (RECEIVER & TRIGGER HOUSING ASSY) AND FROM ADJACENT AREAS OF BEDDED SURFACES OF STOCK.

5. IMPORTANT: MAKE SURE THAT THE MOLDED IMPRESSION OF THE RECEIVER BEARING SURFACES ARE NOT DISTURBED WHEN THE SOLIDIFIED EXCESSES OF GLASS COMPOUND ARE REMOVED.

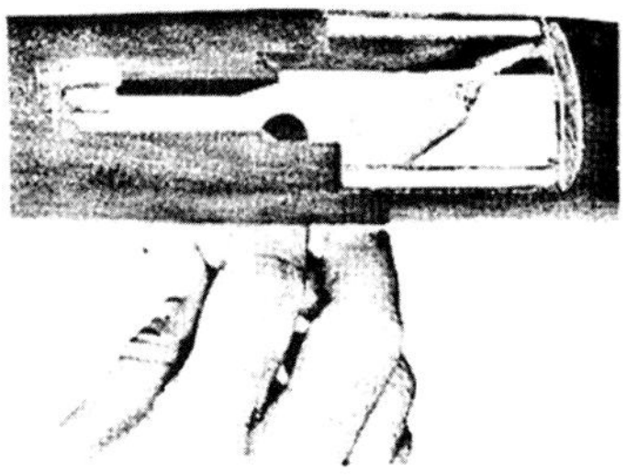

FIGURE 9

1. REDIP AND COMPLETELY SUBMERGE BOTH THE BARREL AND RECEIVER ASSY AND TRIGGER HOUSING ASSY.

2. FILL ROUTED AREAS 4, 5 AND 6 WITH AN EXCESS OF GLASS BEDDING COMPOUND.

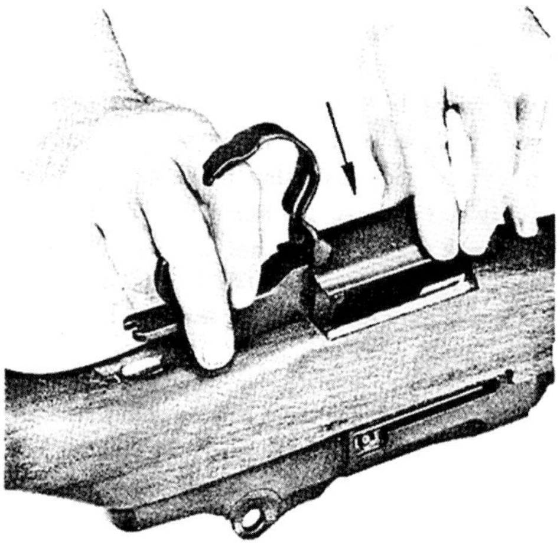

FIGURE 10

1. PLACE THE BARREL AND RECEIVER ASSEMBLY (RECOIL LEGS UP) AS SHOWN. ASSEMBLE THE GLASS FILLED STOCK (AREAS 4, 5 & 6) ON TO THE RECEIVER IN DIRECTION INDICATED.

2. CLAMP THE TRIGGER HOUSING ASSEMBLY AND POSITION THE TRIGGER GUARD WITH THE "U" SHAPED LOCK AS SHOWN IN FIGURE 11.

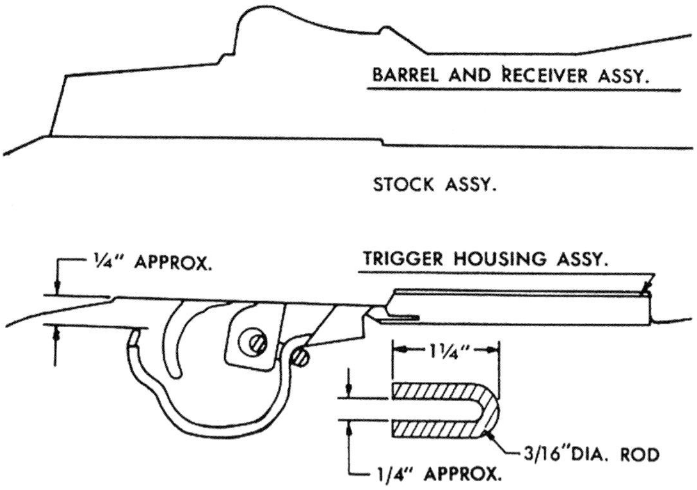

FIGURE 11

CONFIGURATION AND USE OF U LOCK.

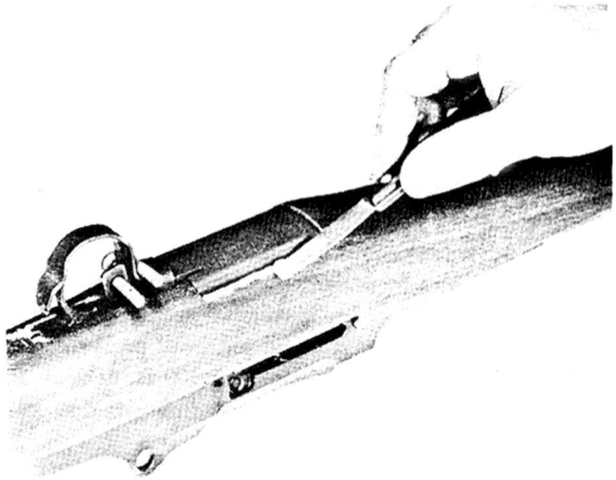

FIGURE 12

1. REMOVE EXCESS GLASS COMPOUND FROM ACTION AS DESCRIBED IN FIGURE 7.

2. ALLOW THE ACTION TO DRY A MINIMUM PERIOD OF 8 HOURS.

3. DISASSEMBLE THE BARREL AND RECEIVER ASSEMBLY FROM THE STOCK ASSEMBLY AS DESCRIBED UNDER FIGURE 8.

4. EXAMINE STOCK TO INSURE THAT A DEFINITE IMPRESSION OF RECEIVER AND TRIGGER HOUSING BEARING SURFACES HAS BEEN MADE ON GLASS BEDDED AREAS OF THE STOCK.

5. IMPORTANT: INSURE THAT THE MOLDED IMPRESSION OF THE RECEIVER AND TRIGGER HOUSING SURFACES ARE NOT DISTURBED WHEN THE SOLIDIFIED EXCESSES OF GLASS COMPOUND ARE REMOVED.

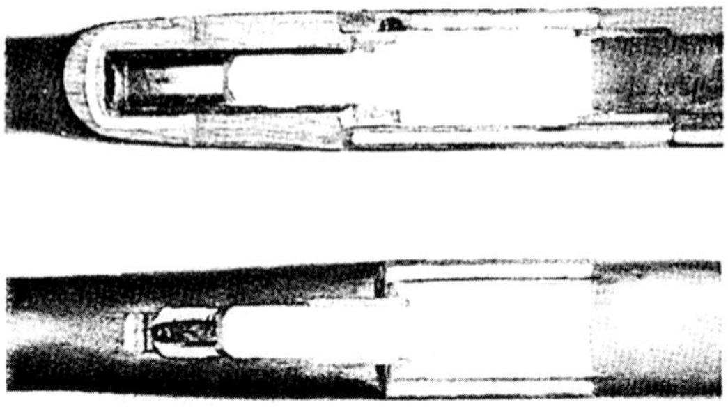

FIGURE 13
TOP AND BOTTOM VIEWS OF COMPLETED GLASS BEDDED STOCK.

In its long and illustrious life, the M1 Garand saw all sorts of uses, for at least four decades. Here, in this difficult-to-restore old image, from August 12, 1953, New Orleans, Louisiana reservists review some specialized weapons applications, including an M1D being shown by the instructor, with a grenade-launching rig on the table. That's a B.A.R. in the background. In Marine Corps units, many sniper/sharpshooter rifles incorporated the modifications/adjustments of the best competition rifles, and featured much superior, vastly more modern optics, along with smoothed, lightened trigger pulls. (Phone Credit: US Army)

CHAPTER 3

THE GARAND, ILLUSTRATED AND EXPLAINED

The M1 was produced more or less continuously, with a short breathing spell from about 1946 to 1952, in the United States for twenty years and in Italy for almost thirty continuous years. That's a gross military production life of about thirty-two years. Add on another twenty years of civilian production.

The photos and subsections in Part III describe the rifles and are intended to help the collector or shooter identify and categorize his rifle and its parts.

Later in this book are some further details in a special "parts" area, which will demonstrate how every single part of the Garand—even though most will interchange from the very first to the very last rifle—became a whole different item.

The background presented in the preceding history of the rifle should help put these photos in context easily.

EARLY AND WORLD WAR II GARANDS

Prewar and World War II Garands are the most active areas for collectors, the least active for shooters.

The gas trap gun with its 22-inch barrel and internal blast cone configuration, was a loser from the first day, just as similar designs failed in Germany, England, Belgium, and Russia. Nobody ever got the elegant theory to work properly in the field, mainly because of the tremendous mass of hot gas that had to be moved around. By serial #55,844, the gas trap rifle was pretty much a dead horse, though a few higher-numbered specimens have supposedly been identified. The experimental gas port rifle (a 24-inch-barreled gun with an approximately 5/64-inch gas hole exiting into a much smaller chamber in a new gas cylinder) comprised a considerable number of guns numbered below 50,000, of which numbers 43938 and 44602 are two confirmed specimens. Rifle #44702 may be another early gas port experimental, though it is impossible to prove. Most likely it was built as a gas trap gun but did not stay that way for very long. What you need to know is that you will never find a gas trap rifle that is both intact and cheap. And restoring one of the low numbered guns is a process that is brutally expensive, close to impossible, and ultimately amounts to taking a gun that probably works rather well and making it into a version of same whose function is, at best, questionable. Right now, the approximate dollar figure required to revert a low-numbered gun using mostly custom-made reproduction parts is a minimum of roughly two thousand dollars. With authentic parts? Forget it.

An import-marked M1, serial #44702, originally a gas trap rifle, was found among a shipment of rifles from Arlington Ordnance, and was ultimately restored, complete with short pinion/flush nut sights. Shown here with midwar-style locking bar sights, before restoration, the July of 1940 rifle had seemingly been reconfigured as a gas port before the end of that year. It was a decent shooter, once cleaned up, but the original barrel was kept with the rifle when sold, replaced for convenience purposes with a commercial unit. The earlier receivers are somewhat weaker, more valuable, and difficult and expensive to restore. At 2019 prices, the old-style flush nut rear sights, authentic and in nice condition, can top eight hundred dollars.

There are a *lot* of factors going into what is a collector's piece and that which is not. If one means to do both with the same piece, it's prudent to shoot a rare rifle with some parts—especially operating rods and barrels!—which can be more readily and cheaply replaced.

There are some other asides that intrigue some collectors, at least one of which is almost impossible to illustrate in normal photo reproduction. Suppose you find a Garand with a horrendous looking scorch mark, blackish at the rear, fading to dark grays and even browns at the front. A much-feared "REMIL"? A gun that's been in a fire? Sort of the latter. Firing and use of accessories about 1943 tended to crack some of the harder (as in more brittle) receivers, and so a new heat-treat configuration was applied to some existing receivers and a few that had not yet left the factory. This process is the source of the "two-tones." If the scorch mark is especially profound, the gun still bears its original finish and is therefore worth a little bit extra because of its unique and obvious background. Suppose you notice a hot spot of weld about ¾ inch back on the op rod channel (groove) front border on the raceway flat on the receiver's right. Is this a reweld? Sort of. If the serial number is below 80,000 or so, the hot spot marks some of the work required to prevent the much-vaunted seventh round stoppage. (Some rifles up to 96,000 were so treated; virtually all below 80,000 were.)

The single-slot gas cylinder lock screw and "no hump" gas cylinder lock were standard World War II parts. The one shown here is shown with a gas cylinder lock wrench in the tighten/loosen position, in this case BEFORE the lock is removed, for illustrative purposes. Aluminum wrenches are less likely to tear up old finish. This single slot solid gas cylinder lock screw is a very high quality repro. They and the postwar BM.59 metric Allen wrench versions, also one-piece machined, are considered far more consistent for competition rifles, and frequently show up on late competition rifles, even some G.I. "National Match" specimens.

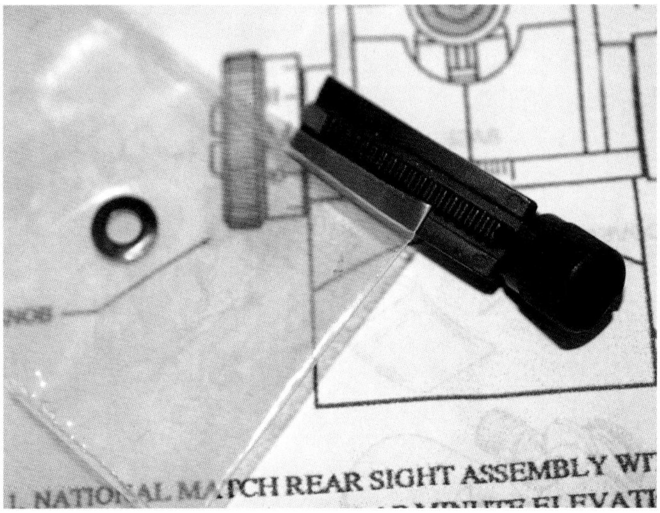

After the peculiar "flush nut" rear sights, their special tool, and the impractical setup, was abandoned, the earliest parts were applied to "short pinion, locking bar" sights, the rarest of all standard rear sight assemblies. There were two major styles of "locking bar" long pinion sights made, of which the more rounded is usually called the early style, and these—the later, more squared thumb locking bar—were the very last. The T105 sight was vastly superior, and did not "shoot loose." Most soldiers and armorers center punched the pinion, to preclude the securing bar departing the sight entirely. These were from the nineties, awaiting rifle cleanup and restoration. Note that sight parts were supposed to be as close to black as possible (it's in the specification) and thus, the rifles were not supposed to "color and shade" match, or if they did, it was merely an accident. This is commercial NM2A small sight aperture.

Some other notes: Virtually all Winchester receivers, up until the WIN-13 series, were of the very early -2 version, which had square cutout rear of bolt travel on the receiver—a feature that was gone from Springfield production by 1941. Winchesters are rough receivers, and many of their trigger parts are even rougher. While they are a poor choice for shooters because of the weaker earlier receiver design and the usual out-of-specification condition of many—if not most—of the parts, they can shoot fairly well with excellent barrels. These Winchesters are worth entirely too much money to devote much more to converting a receiver to anything like match configuration.

By 1945 the Armory was well into -35 receivers, which were much stronger than the units of 1941. The most common receiver variants are shown here along with some rare specimens, such as the very first Winchester rifle produced. Winchester never built a gas trap rifle.

The observer will note that many of my rifles of World War II vintage in these pages bear the much later National Match rear sight aperture. This takes a few seconds to install and is a much better sight than the military version;

I use it on any M1 I shoot. I generally change out only sights and operating rods when I shoot vintage Garands.

Certain standard equipment had to be replaced at war's end with almost indecent haste. Replacing or modifying uncut operating rods was a safety priority, but it is amazing how many show up on MAP returnees and even DCM guns. Both early sight styles were basically failures, and the third type was added to virtually all World War II guns during rebuilds. The many notations on rebuilds, match configurations, and various other photos in this book document these alterations.

Just as parts and receivers changed, so did markings. Early barrels did not carry dates. Standard Winchester barrels never carried dates, though I have seen what may be replacements or fakes that did. Ironically, these were cases where the low prices suggested to me that the barrels might have been authentic, though I very much doubt they were issue barrels of any sort. I suspect they were part of some kind of subcontracting deal that either fell through or comprised a very small lot of replacement units or experimentals.

Even into the postwar era, replacement barrels as late as 1951 used the World War II marking pattern, with the maker information atop the barrel. By 1953 (earlier at Springfield Armory) subcontractors placed maker and date information neatly in the operating rod cutout, between the buttstock and the rear handguard.

Everything on the Garand got continuously better as production wore on. By 1943 the early, intricate milled trigger guard was replaced with a spring steel stamping, which proved easier to adjust and more durable. By mid-1942 the gas cylinder's bulk and strength were increased. The "X-form" gas cylinder lock screw allowed the use of a new grenade launcher and introduced an additional safety factor.

Checking the parts details section later in this book will give the reader some idea as to how various complex parts were replaced with stronger, simpler items as time wore on. This may be the central lesson of the Garand's evolution: Simpler is better.

Wartime M1 Garand gas cylinder lock screws, real and functional reproductions: The ones on the left are authentic, original, and unused. The two on the right are the replicas, much higher than usual quality. For accuracy rifles, I prefer the replicas, which are less valuable and more robust. The center hole is not drilled as deep on the "repops." The originals are most often a sort of semi-gloss/satin BLACK finish, almost like a paint in appearance, whereas the repros are most commonly dark gray. However, this varied, and some are a flat soot/black. Winchesters are slightly differently contoured. These are Armory specimens. Either provides a more stable blast area than the poppet type, and unless you're using a grenade launcher, accuracy shooters usually prefer them.

Springfield

Gas trap rifles: Virtually all M1 Garands numbered below 50,000 were originally gas trap rifles, as were a few experimentals above that figure. However, virtually all have been reconfigured during their long lives to the ubiquitous gas port configuration. The rare rifle shown in the detail photos here is serial #26171 and remains in its original ca. 1939 configuration. Comparison of this rifle with other gas traps reflects the tremendous amount of fine-tuning done virtually continuously (though somewhat erratically) on all the early Garands.

The gas trap gas cylinder was much more massive and entirely different from all others. The barrel ended less than halfway down the upper "tube," and the gas cylinder was screwed on. This was secured by two screws. The muzzle was a false muzzle, in fact part of the gas cylinder. The sight and its attachment are entirely different from the gas port style. There were several other subtypes of this gas cylinder, all shaped more or less the same, but with tool grip flutes added to some.

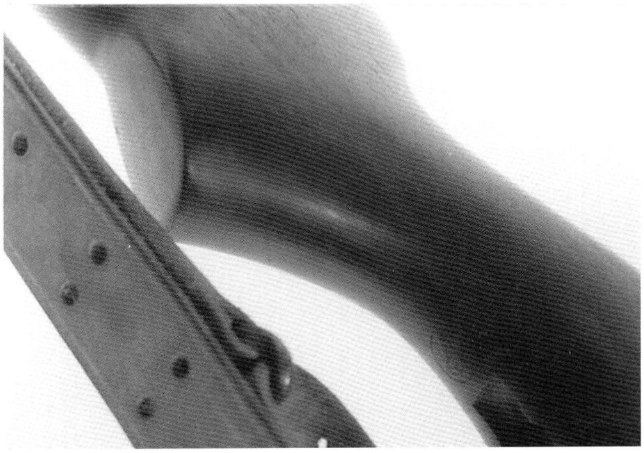

It seems that many early stocks did not receive cartouches at all. This one is Winchester #100001, which was retained by civilian management in New Haven, and thus never got any military acceptance cartouche marking.

Virtually every part of the gas trap rifle was different from the typical gas port rifle—even the square (flattened) configuration of the recoil spring. The entire operating mechanism—operating rod catch, follower rod and arm, bulletguide—is shaped very differently from later guns. Note also the creased surface of the handguard clip.

The original buttplate contained no accessory or oiler door at all.

The heavy creased and scalloped bands of the gas trap guns were carried over to early gas port rifles.

The early "First Model" sight and cover and early receiver configuration of rifle #261 71.

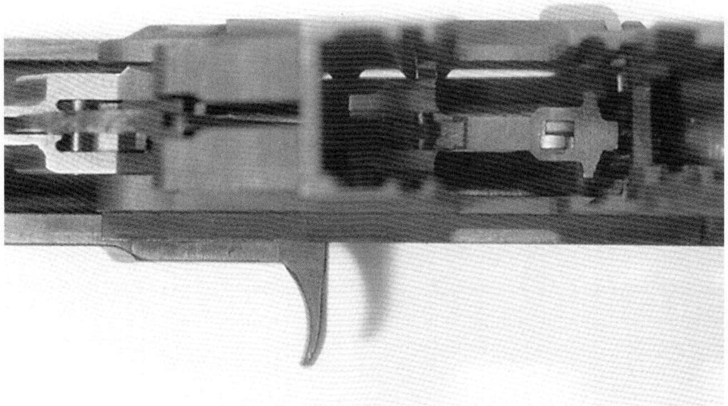

Many early rifles had their operating rod catches "in the white." This is rifle #26171.

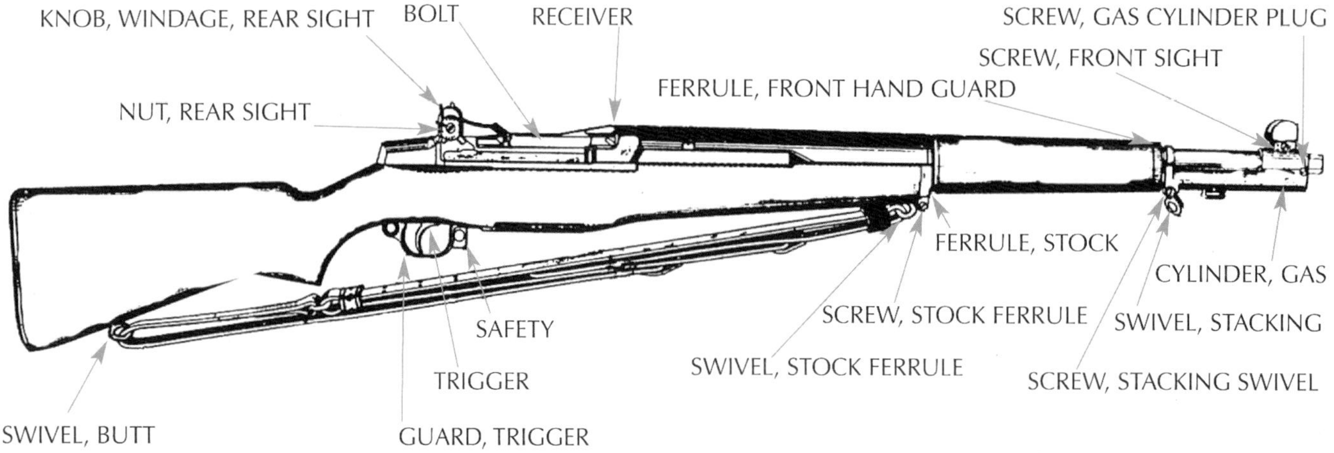

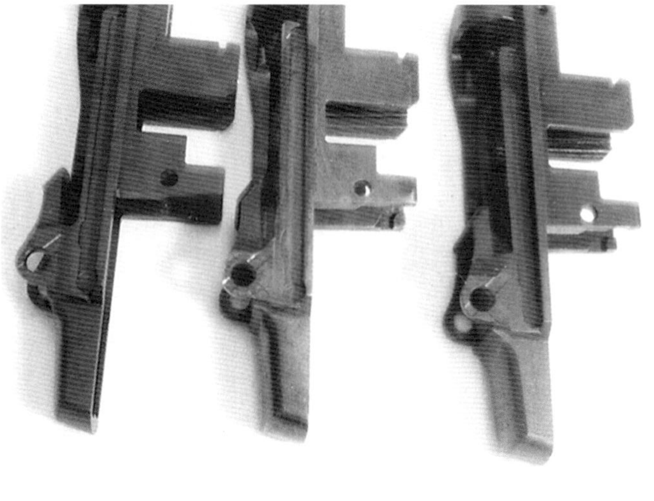

Garand receivers from the rifle's early production, from top, 97308, 7146, and 44555. Note squared-off rear receiver legs on all. Note also the traces of welding on 7146 and 44555, done during their changeover from gas trap configuration to obviate the "seventh-round stoppage."

Note that both receivers, at this stage, retained the square bolt cutout and that the leading edges of the rear stock engagement lug (strut) still had not received the softened edges standardized by 1942.

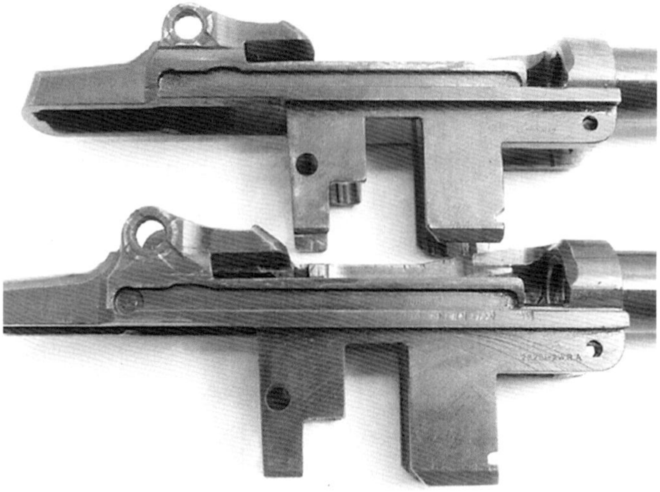

A direct comparison of -2 receivers from Springfield Armory and Winchester (the Springfield D2821-2 on the top and the Winchester on the bottom), both delivered by late 1941. Winchester's overall quality and conformance to specifications, even simple dimensional specifications, was very questionable, which can be proven very quickly with a micrometer. The poor machining on the Winchester is quite visible on the strut/lug area adjacent to the part numbers. Winchester continued to produce this comparatively primitive receiver type right up until the WIN-13 series, by which time the armory had produced at least 35 major improvements.

Rifle serial #44702 may have been an experimental gas port rifle (verifiably, #44602 was such an experiment), but it is more likely the gun was simply reconfigured to the later model very early in its service life. Note that, rebuilt or not, the rifle retained a lot of early parts, even the flush nut sights. However, in testing, I used T105 types.

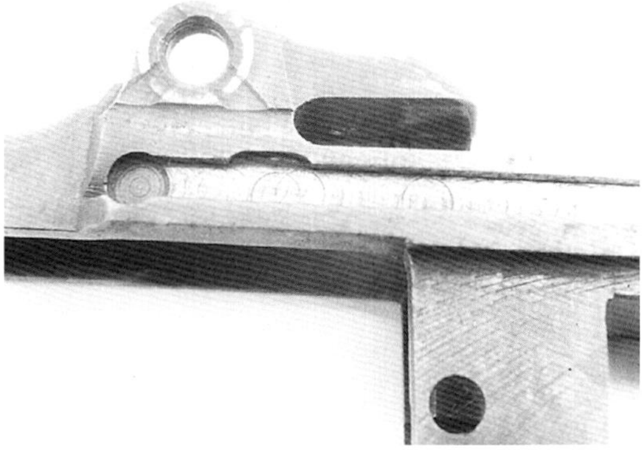

By the -3 revision, the Garand receiver was already becoming more streamlined and sturdy. This modification, with the rounded bolt cutout, seems to have been produced for a time alongside the earlier -2 type.

This nice old rifle was shown to me by its owner with both of its stocks, one (the one shown here) a quite nice subcontractor specimen, re-stamped with replica cartouches and "circle P" markings, as well as an "RS" (means "re-struck"), in which he fired the great old thing. The original wasn't as nice, but bore the same markings. Nearly unfired when he got it, it was most likely an import via Galef, Abel, or Interarms, bore British proof marks, and could've been a cash and carry rifle or lend/lease from very early WW2.

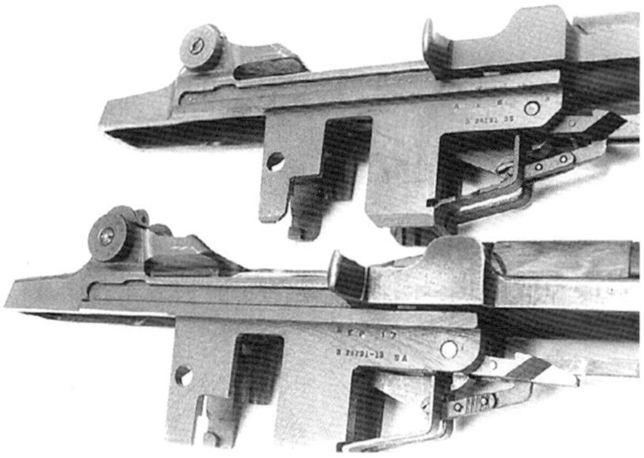

A comparison between a ca. 1941 receiver (-13, bottom) and a rebuilt ca. 1945 receiver (-35, top) reveals that machine tool quality and precision improved even as Garand production pace increased. Note the virtual absence of tool marks on the later specimen, as opposed to the severe drag marks on the earlier rifle. The later receiver is also considerably stronger in key areas.

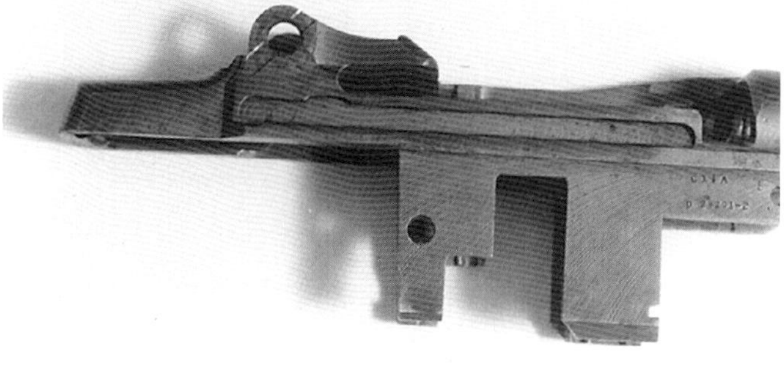

The rounded bolt cutout generic to the -3 receivers and some other improvements were incorporated earlier than sometimes believed, or perhaps unfinished -2 units were simply completed with the -3 improvements. This one is marked D 28291-2 but bears all the -3 modifications.

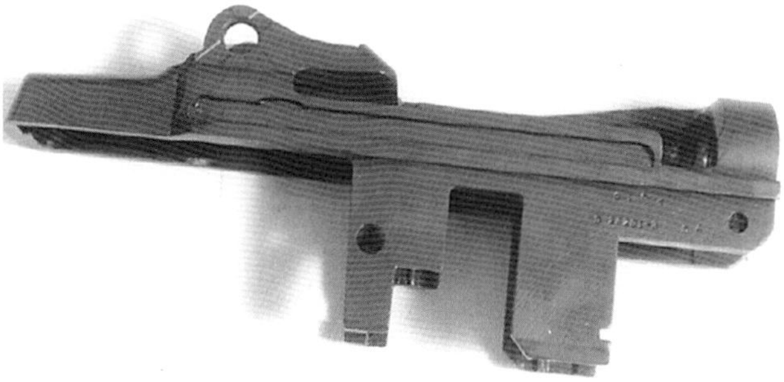

This -3 receiver overlaps the period of time within which only -2s were supposedly leaving the armory. But its other parts (cartouche, etc.) suggest an actual delivery date just when the receiver configuration would suggest.

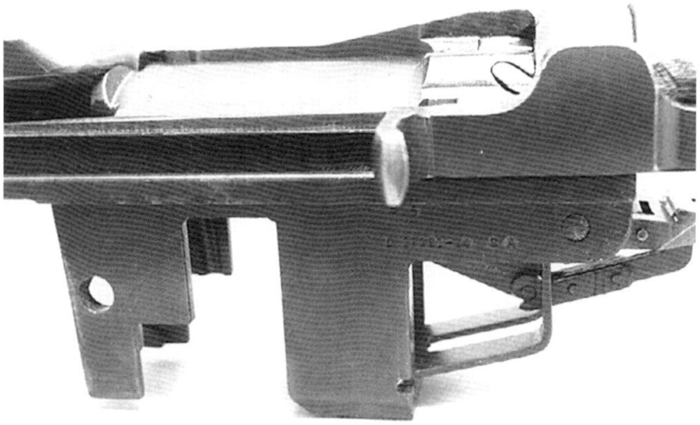

This -14 receiver shows fairly typical early midwar characteristics. Note the rounded receiver struts.

By the -17 revision, ca. 1942, the Garand hadreached its definitive World War II receiver configuration. The striations on this one are very rare by this vintage and are probably caused by a nearly worn-out tool. Note the various witness marks and codes above the part number.

Comparison photo of three M1 Garands: (top) 1940—note especially the "first model" flush nut rear sight; (middle) 1941; (bottom) mid-1942.

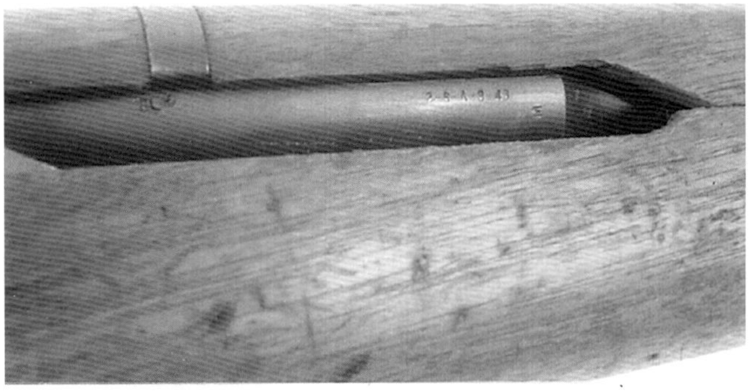

Typical Springfield barrel markings, these from August 1943.

Typical stock cartouches on as-issued rifles received from Arlington Ordnance. Both have been rebuilt once, and the top rifle has had its stamped trigger guard replaced with an older milled unit during the process. Both rifles date from 1945, though the lower rifle may not have been actually completed until after the war, and its 2-46 dated barrel may, therefore, be its original. The top cartouche is SA/NFR (Norman F. Ramsey), the lower, the rare SHM (Steven H. MacGregor), ca. 1946.

When World War II Garands had been sighted and test-fired and were ready to leave the armory, a seal was driven into the Allen screw at the rear of each rifle's front sight. Very few rifles retain these seals.

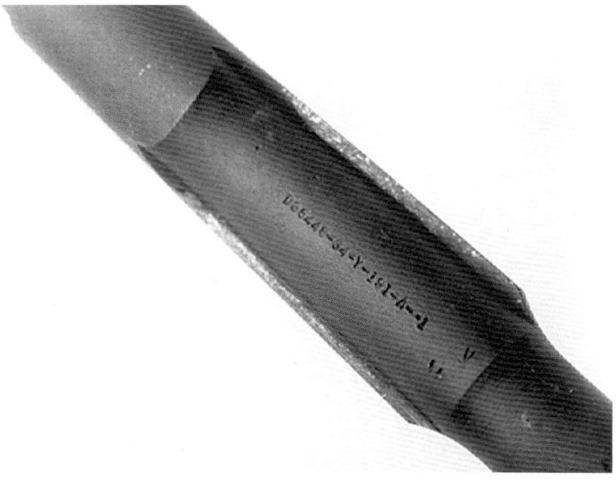

Late World War II Springfield barrels carried their part number and detailed information—lot and heat treat numbers—atop the chamber area, under the wood. Early war rifles, of course, carried all the data here, as Winchesters always did.

Winchester

Laying hands on Winchester's very first M1 Garand was an exciting experience, and studying the rifle was an education—just as this rifle itself was an educational tool for workers at Winchester. This first batch of rifles essentially consisted of handmade early gas port rifles of the -2 version then being made at Springfield. The gun seems to be satin blued, then hydroxide dipped to produce a semigloss black finish that resembles a nicely applied coat of black trim paint.

In order to photograph Larry Kaufman's rare rifle and get some contrast on the markings where necessary, I used a technique others might find convenient: a quick, temporary surface burnish applied simply by rubbing the area with aluminum foil. This allows the original stampings to show well without having to apply anything permanent and without impossible lighting problems that make the surface look artificial. This burnish may then be wiped off with thin oil, rifle bore cleaner, or any convenient petroleum-based solvent. Note the typical "electric writing" of the Winchester logo.

One of the very last Winchester M1 rifles bearing the dark Du-Lite finish.

The very first Winchester-produced M1 Garand, S #100001, was finished in a satin black oxide, and in order to see the markings in close-ups, it required a light and very tender burnishing. This was immediately removed with bore cleaner.

Winchester M1 Garand rifle, serial # 1300081, fitted with an NM2A rear sight aperture for shooting purposes. Almost all W.R.A. specimens until the last few months were very dark, and the very earliest bore what seems to be a hot salt oxide blue, similar or identical to "Du-Lite." The chemistry of that has been verified. This rifle was set up and "rationalized" (that's what amounts to a visual restoration) to test a very weirdly marked (I think custom made!) barrel acquired from a friend. The sights are the correct midwar vintage Winchester locking bars, so of course, the sight's windage adjustments were minute-of-angle, not the NM2A half MOA. This kind of shooting expedient may be rapidly reversed for a wall hanger or to please a collector.

The trigger group of the late Larry Kaufman's gas trap rifle. A very early Winchester would be almost identical, except that the hammer spring housing barrel would certainly be finished in the deep black the New Haven firm employed at that time.

The early, narrow-profile gas cylinder of 100001 carries its part number on the rear, upper hoop.

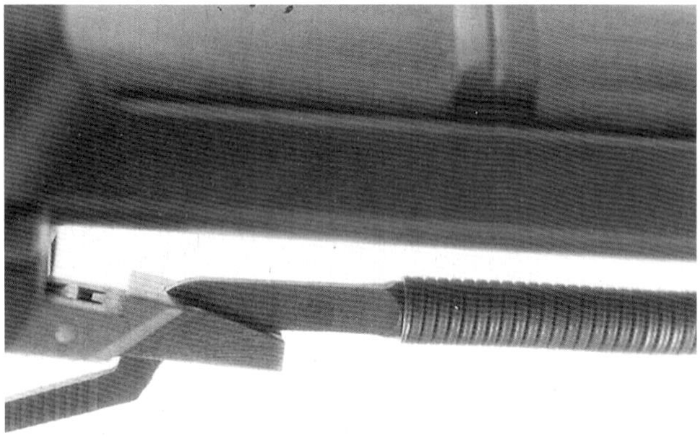

All of the first Winchester's operating rod assembly parts are typical, heavily marked, milled series similar to early Springfield parts.

Early and midwar Winchester M1 Garands: The Winchester Garand did not change much after the very first rifle. Virtually all parts remained the same or very similar, though some subcontractor parts (marked "A" or "CM") were used as the pace of production sped up.

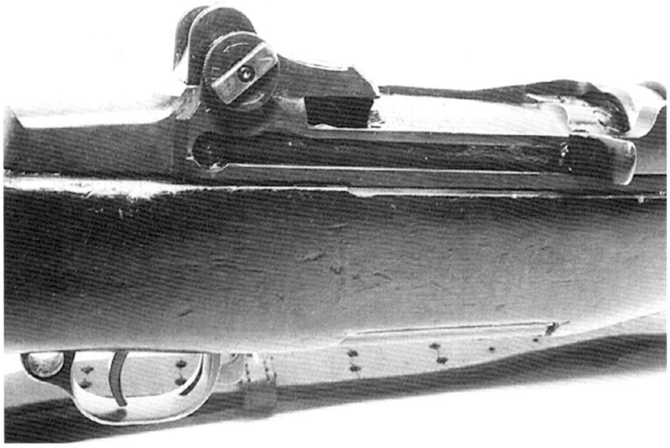

Midwar Winchester as rebuilt around 1947.

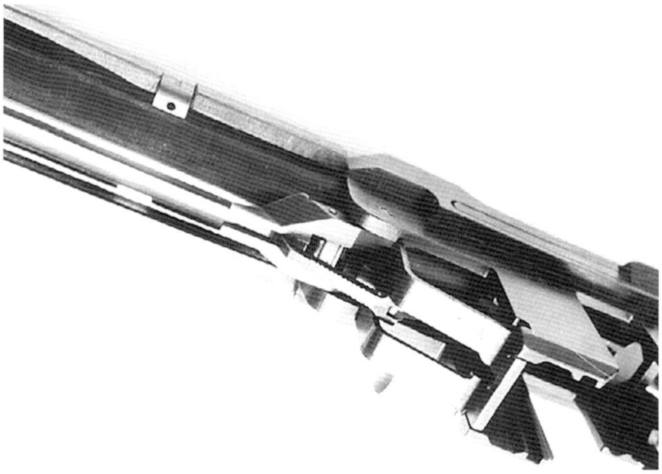

Bottom details, bottom receiver/bbl. view of a mid-war Winchester. Note short fork follower rod, milled with serrated finger grooves, crisply stamped "A" on bullet guide.

Midwar Winchester follower arm.

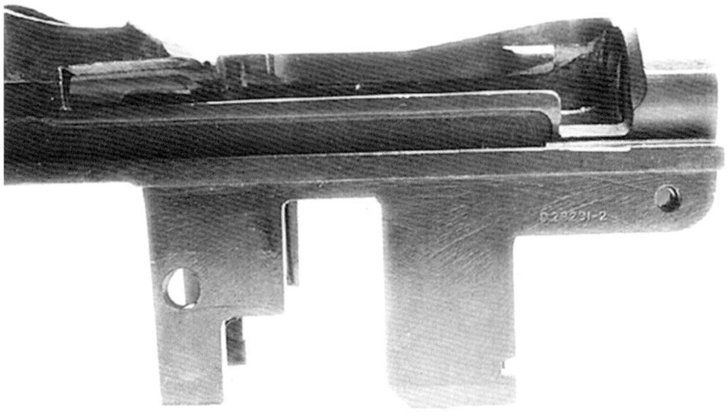

Side view, midwar Winchester receiver.

Trigger guard part number data stamping on mid-war Winchester M1.

Closeup of witness marks below front right bolt lug detent on receiver of a midwar Winchester M1.

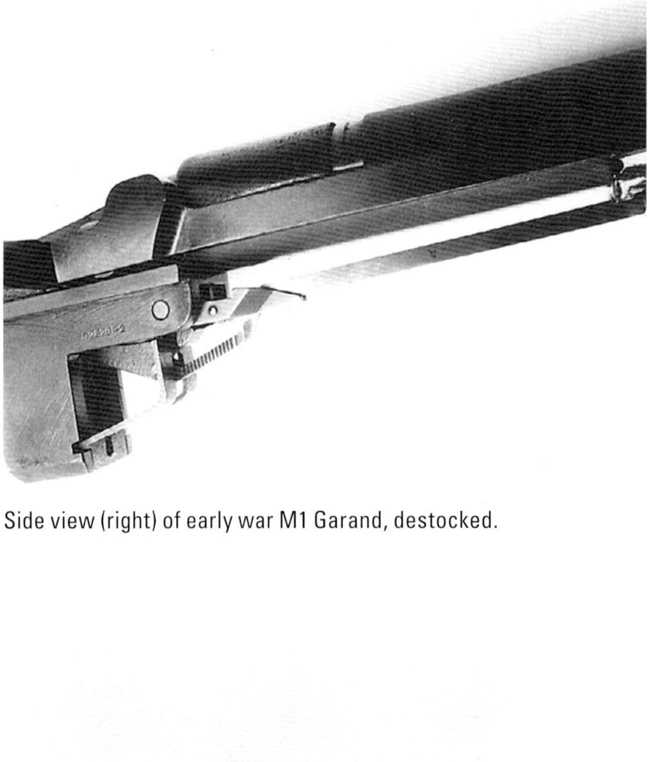

Side view (right) of early war M1 Garand, destocked.

Winchester receiver #130081.

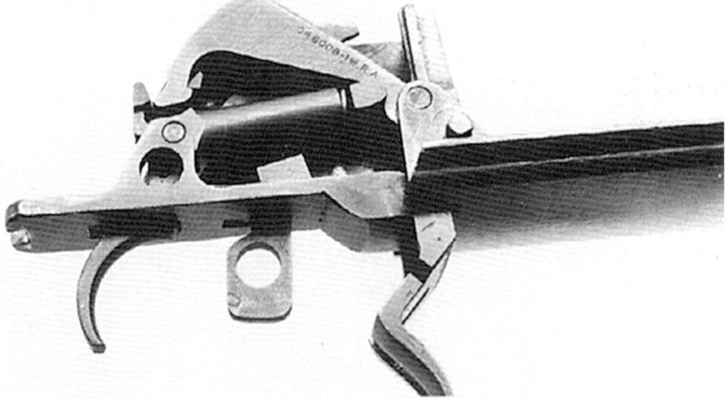

Midwar Winchester M1 Garand trigger housing.

Winchester receiver #1332557.

Winchester receiver #2310946. As with most of the Winchester receivers in these photos, this is an Arlington Ordnance "reimport" that has never been refinished.

The WIN-13 Series: The WIN-13 series constitutes the very last Winchester M1 Garands, in which some of the early parts array and configuration were discarded. These rifles are, at least in theory, the only American-made Garands whose serial numbers are directly duplicated. The close-ups here are of receiver #1617139, which (alone among the Winchesters pictured here) bears a fairly typical charcoal phosphate finish.

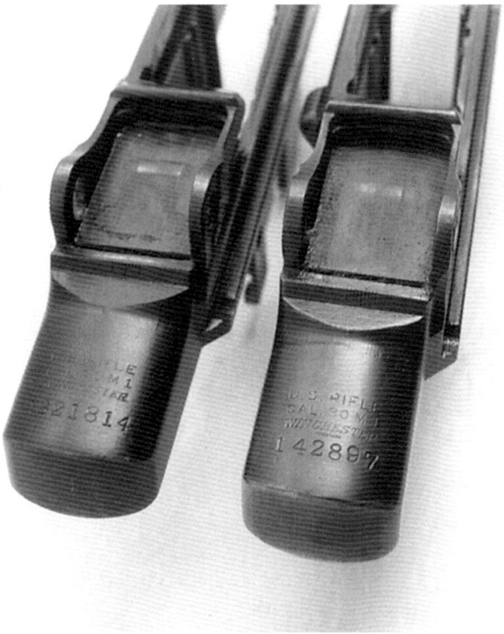

Comparison shot of late Winchester M1 receivers #2321814 (ca. 1945) and #142897 (ca. 1941) demonstrates how little these changed in the time frame in which the armory had instituted 35 major changes.

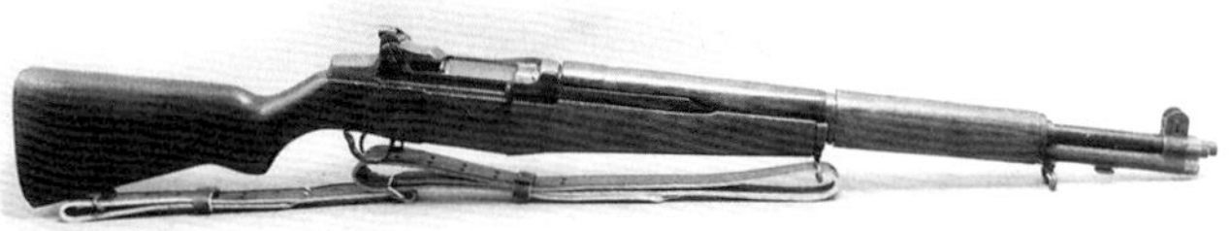

WIN-13 rifle with very late finish and -9 configuration operation rod. NOTE: National Match sight aperture was added by the author for firing convenience and is not authentic or original. Stamped trigger guard was on rifle when received and is not original, though finish does match receiver's charcoal exactly.

Close-up of WIN-13 receiver serial #1617139. This receiver carries a dark gray-green phosphate finish, probably original to this 1945 receiver. Almost all early Winchester Garands carried a virtually black "Du-Lite" finish, which involved iron-plating parts and then placing a deep satin blue-black finish on all parts, including the stainless steel gas cylinder. The subcontractor for this process is still in business. Winchester quickly discovered that phosphate finishes could be done in numbers for slightly less—sometimes in house, sometimes by vendors—and as a result, late Winchester rifles are most commonly seen with virtually random mixtures of "Du-Lite", satin black, and various gray and gray-green phosphate finishes, until this run at the very end, where the main parts were in a slightly more neutral finish, albeit by no means uniform. Winchester tended always to do that which was cheapest and fastest for it.

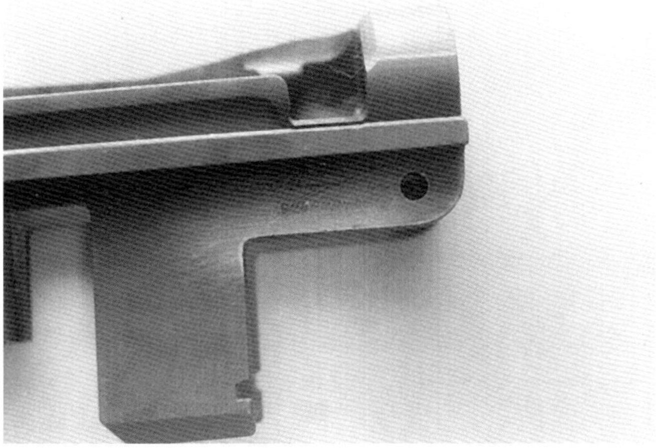

Burnished for visibility, this marking panel on #1 61 7139's receiver reads "D28291WIN-13."

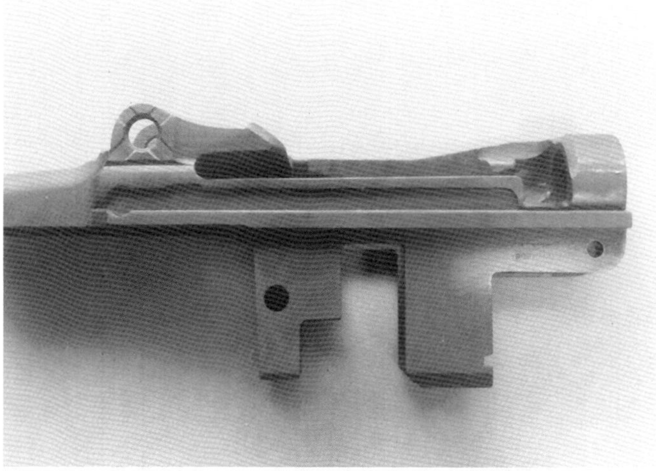

The WIN-13 receivers finally adopted the rounded bolt detent and later sight "click" cuts. Note the part number and updated overall contours.

WORLD WAR II SERIAL NUMBERS, AS ALLOCATED

Manufacturer	Blocks, as Assigned
SA	1–100,000
WRA	100,000–165,000
SA	165,001–1,200,000
WRA	1,200,001–1,357,473
SA	1,357,474–2,305,849
WRA	2,305,850–2,655,982
SA	2,655,983–4,100,000

Many of the very last M1 Garands produced off World War II contracts were not finished until well into 1946, nor were they delivered in absolute serial number order. 3.8 million + would've been the last Armory delivery while the war was still on, perhaps not quite that high. The Winchester Win-13 series was their attempt to recover funds and resources from the project, and were delivered after the contracts folded, at the very end and apparently after the end of the war. Serial numbers seem to have entirely replicated earlier SA contracts, approximating primarily 1,600,000 to 1,640,000, such that there *are* many duplicate M1 Garand serial numbers. Parenthetically, there are even *more* replica serial numbers, somewhere, among Italian M1s, as all save the Indonesian Italian M1 contracts began at "one." And there were at least 14 contracts!

The world abounds with date charts for M1 Garands, and they're generally close. However, the dates are always derived from contract information, and thus the actual delivery or barrel date of a Garand will frequently be later than the "book" date. Wartime and postwar cartouches, likewise, do not necessarily have much do with actual delivery dates. I've handled a WIN-13 Winchester, for example (none of which were delivered until after the war) that bore a WRA/WB stock, and, based on the circumstances of the rifle's acquisition, it almost had to be the "issue" stock for the rifle. Such anomalies are less common on Springfield guns but do exist, since factories tended not to throw away usable material of any kind, and perhaps their last concern during World War II was what some collector would think more than six decades down the line.

These letter combinations (as the illustrations make clear) appear right where your cheek goes in the firing position—stock's left side, just below the "heel" of the receiver and slightly to the front.

One of the earliest postwar M1 Garand rifle receivers, a Springfield (US) 4.21 million, fully to the postwar specification. Sometimes, in undisturbed, original condition, these will contain small parts from wartime "spares" production, and only the earliest bore lettered cartouches on their stocks. This one bore faint traces of a lettered cartouche box, but a "DAS" eagle somewhat lower and much deeper, possibly a postwar replacement stock from the late '40s drawn as new old stock and fitted to the rifle, or perhaps just a depot supplied, much later substitute that happened to be that way. After sixty years, there are precious few solid answers. M1s were assembled until early '46, supposedly, then went out of production until 1952. It is unlikely any of the Korean War era M1s ever got to Korea before the end of hostilities.

Cartouche	I.D. & service period	Appx. serial # range	Notes
SA/SPG	Samuel P. Green	1–80,000	all gas trap and early gas port rifles
SA/GHS	Col. Gilbert H. Stewart Mid 1940-June 1942	80,000–700,000	early WWII
SA/EMcF	Col. Earl McFarland June 1942-July 1943	700,000–1,800,000	midwar
SA/GAW	Col. George A. Woody July 1943-October 1944	1,800,000–3,260,000	late war
SA/NFR	Gen. Norman F. Ramsey Oct. 1944-Nov. 1945 rifles	3,260,000–3,900,000+	last wartime
SA/SHM	Col. Steven H. MacGregor Nov. 1945-Aug. 1947	—	small production, experimentals, much rebuild activity
SA/JLG	Col. James L. Guion	4,200,000–4,300,000	a very few "Korean War" rifles, by comparison, got letter cartouches before the defense acceptance stamp was standardized
WRA/WB	Col. Waldemar Broberg 1940–1941	100,001-appx. 1,220,000	
WRA/RS	Col. Robert Sears 1941–1942	1,220,000-appx. 1,357,473	
WRA/GHD	Col. Guy H. Drewry*	at least 1,357,473–2,655,982 and WIN-13 series	

*All Winchester cartouche data is to be taken with a grain of salt, as are many so-called rules of parts marking. Collectors have seen, owned, and handled enough rifles to know that so-called early wood was leaving the factory right up until the very end. Serial #100,001 (pictured in this book) has a certifiably original stock and never had a cartouche.

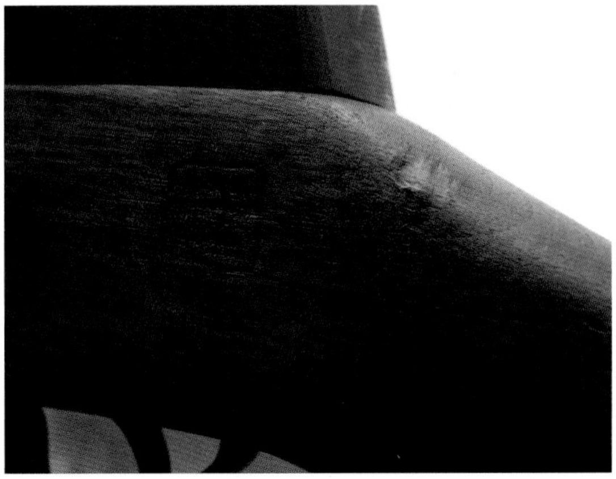

An absolutely authentic, quadruple verified Defense Acceptance stamp on a ca. 1955 Springfield Armory M1 Garand. This one probably hadn't been seriously sanded, but was never squarely applied. I had some doubts due to eyesight issues and having been burned earlier, but this came from the CMP, anyway. I still showed this photo and/or the stock itself to the most sophisticated, young (good eyesight!) collectors with whom I am acquainted, and compared it to the literature and a known fake I then retained for just that purpose, and this came up 100 percent. Still, I got attack e-mail from a so-called expert who said it was an obvious fake. It currently resides with one of the nation's most advanced collectors, and he pronounced it authentic. That sort of bickering often dominates discussions on collector's forums, and my inclination is to simply avoid the entire snake pit of that sort of conversation.

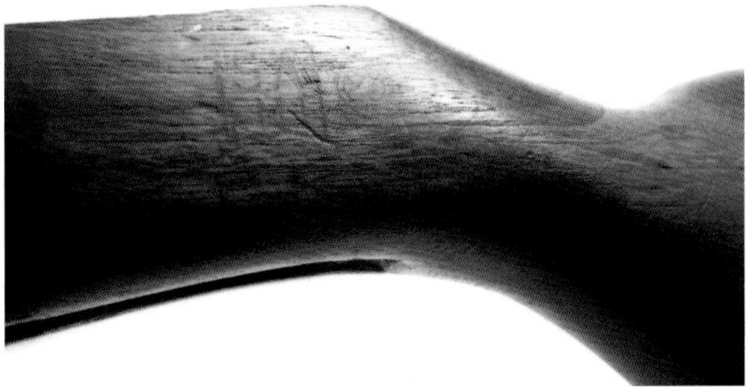

A faint but absolutely proven "EMcF" cartouche on a battered M1 Garand butt stock. Colonel Earl C. McFarland was inspector at the armory from June, 1942, to July of 1943, and this cartouche appeared on rifles from about 700,000 to roughly 1,800,000. A really crisp, verified original with a much deeper stamp impression, uncracked and not heavily sanded, would bring a market price in the right place approximating what one would pay for a complete service grade M1 Garand from the CMP. That price stuff is why people fake these things, and why, lately, I do all I can to avoid vintage wood, period. I don't even want to have those conversations. Wound up with some bogus wood myself purchased from a smith as takeoffs, and the startling thing I found out was, apparently people have been faking this stuff far longer than I realized. Main annoyance was, I had to degrease and sometimes remove *many* layers of paint to find that out, and I had to rely on others (an eyesight issue and a certain amount of apathy!) to find out what was real and what wasn't.

This is a verified original "SHM" cartouche, original on practically no M1s, but used on rebuilds and what few rifles were finished from wartime leftovers during the tenure of Col. Steven H. MacGregor, November, 1945, to August of 1947. The rifle it contains is a 1942 receiver, upgraded with T105E1 rear sight, a new barrel, a safety relieved postwar operating rod, and the "soot" dark phosphate refinish. The 1946 barrel date is probably quite close to the actual rebuild date. *many* so-called rebuilds amounted to nothing more than an inspection, testfire, and return to service. Others replaced almost everything. It always depended upon the condition of the rifle and safety factors.

A rather common and prosaic 1.7 million serial number M1 Garand rifle, rebuilt either during the war or shortly after, perhaps both, and nicely refinished, probably at the armory. Interestingly, the cartouche looked suspicious, so ultra-closeup photos were taken, an old fashioned onion skin "rubbing" taken, and in the presence of two sophisticated collectors, like old seers or soothsayers reading entrails, looked it over and pondered and considered. Conclusion: It's two cartouches, an old GAW and another one mostly obscured, plus something else stamped, probably Korean, carved in over that. The stock was probably worthless, dollar wise, but still fascinating

The actual, authentic, and quadruple-verified by the most knowledgeable collectors the author could locate, this is the genuine "GHS" cartouche from the same rifle shown on page 55. Its owner never shot the rifle in this wood, and had the replica/restrike hard bedded for recreational accuracy. This isn't a small thing. A cartouched stock is valuable, and a dent hither and thither greatly impacts value.

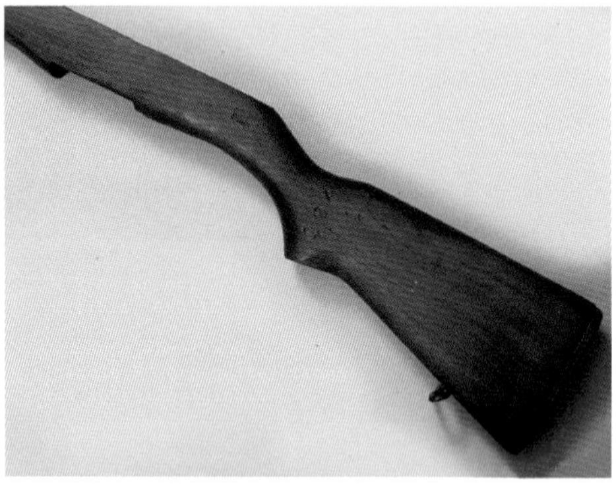

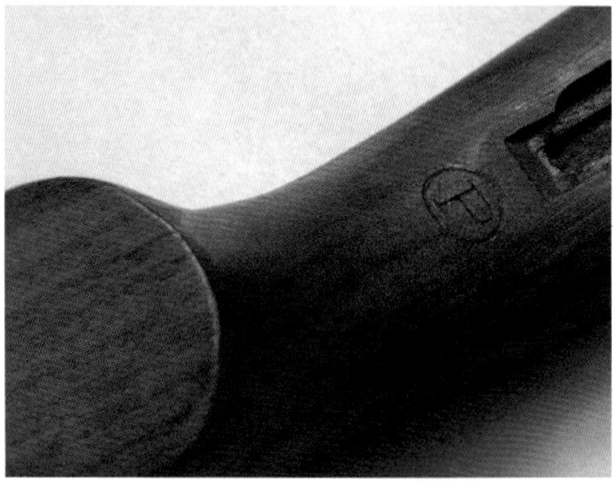

This rare WRA/GHD butt stock had been rather severely sanded, and the "WRA" portion disappeared. It bore authentic, original "WIN-13" buttplate, swivel, screws, and ferrule, but also had a very hefty rack/locator number heavily stamped. It was useless to me. I sold it for the price of about half a dozen brand new stocks and furniture. These are brutally difficult to find.

The last of the lettered cartouches, this SA/JLG marking was used until roughly September of 1953 on outgoing rifles at the armory. This came off an early postwar Springfield Armory rifle, just a tad short of 4.3 million, and had at some point in its life seen small repairs with ceramic bedding replacing compressed and chipped wood. These are quite rare, and there is some controversy about how late they might've seen use.

Rebuilds

Throughout their production career and long after (well into the 1970s) M1 Garands were rebuilt in a bewildering variety of facilities all over the world. A major book could easily be written dealing merely with the types, patterns, and remarkings of various Garand rebuilds. A great deal of the research would have to be based on speculation, though, for the records of bases all over the world would prove virtually impossible to reconstruct.

This small subsection on rebuilds is included separately to give the reader a flavor for what rebuild markings look like.

Certain details of early rebuilds—which began, incidentally, as early as 1940—were urgent. The conversion from gas trap to gas port operating system was a matter of great priority. Later, so were the removal of both the flush nut and locking bar sights. Most critical was the replacement or modification of uncut, square-cornered operating rods, which was a matter of safety.

Considering the clarity of the orders of the time, it is amazing that many of the old operating rods survived. In fact, many postwar rifles were rebuilt using World War II

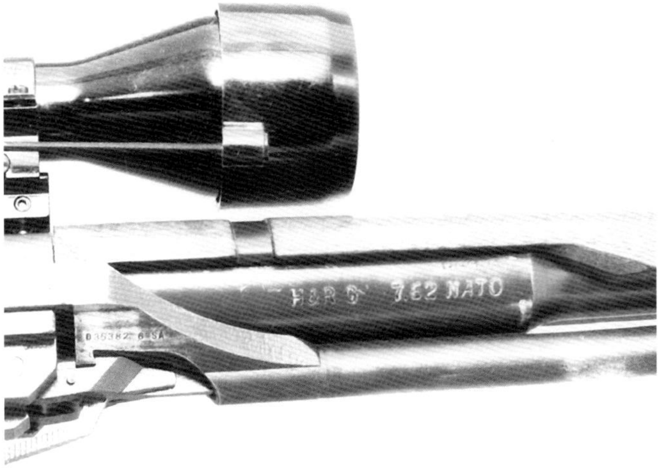

Rebuilding World War II rifles sometimes led to some strange anomalies. This 2,900,000 range rifle, shipped by the DCM and shown here wearing a B-Square scope mount and 3–9x glass, was received with a -6 uncut operating rod and this very unusual barrel (of Springfield manufacture, bearing an original 1 948 date) but in 7.62 NATO and not bearing a chamber bushing or sleeve of any kind, indicating that at least some of the armory's production must have been set aside with no chamber reamed at all. The rebuild seems to have been done at H&R sometime in the 1960s.

A Springfield Armory replacement barrel, produced in May 1951. The postwar part number is D 6535448, located on the barrel's upper surface.

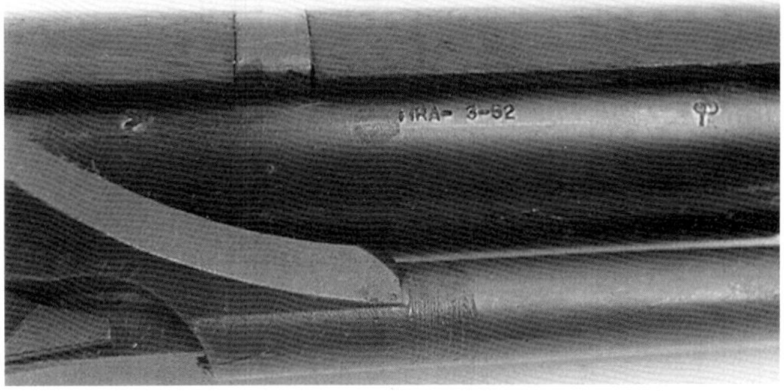

Marking on a 3-52 dated H&R replacement barrel. Though barrels marked in this manner are often found on rifles of approximately the same vintage, it is virtually certain that these are, in fact, replacement units from separate contracts, since issue barrels contained the full data panel on the rightside, and the original barrels at H&R did not enter production until a few months later.

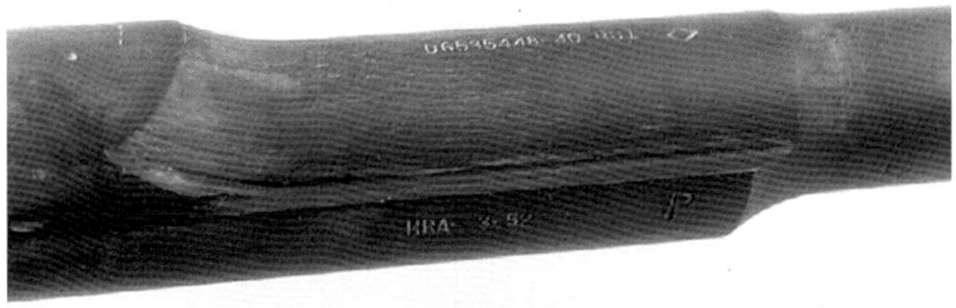

View of 3-52 H&R replacement barrel, showing both information panels.

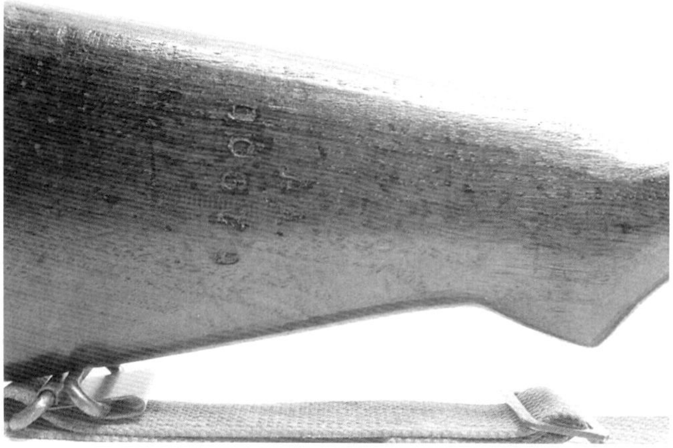

Aniston Arsenal often applied lot and order numbers to stock wood on rebuilds. This one is from the early 1950s.

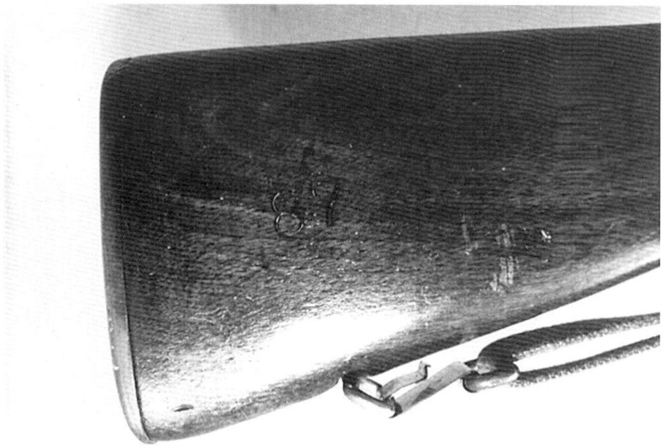

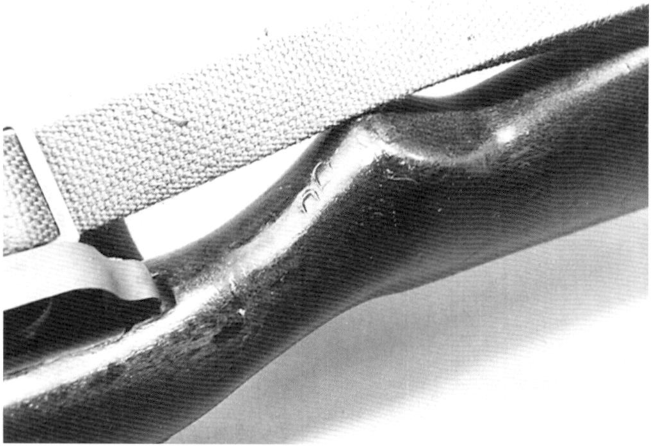

Commonly, postwar rebuilds replicate the "P" firing proof on the stock—usually without the serifs and quite large and deep with no circle around the letter—and often they replicate the last two or three digits of the rifle's serial number on the stock (if the stock required repair).

and even prewar parts as time wore on. That is the source of the mixed-up parts brand and vintages on so very many rifles. There is one fairly reliable rule of thumb, though: one can be reasonably certain that a wartime part on a postwar rifle did not go through Springfield Armory's rebuild programs, whereas a newer part on an older rifle—especially if the pattern is consistent—strongly indicates that the rebuild was executed either by the armory or by someone who read the Technical Operations Orders governing such refurbishments.

The following serial number information pertains to wartime lots allocated, which (as the reader will note from the data) does not necessarily indicate that a rifle was built, or built as allocated. For example, most of Winchester's WIN-13 series were numbered, almost spitefully, to overlap Springfield Armory's 1.6 million block.

About 220,000 of Springfield's last wartime serial number block were not manufactured, a great many of them having apparently been assigned to Remington in pursuit of the slightly longer upper-receivered selective-fire T22. Indeed, much later, H&R built a very few 7.62x51mm rifles in Springfield's very last (over 6 million) lot, apparently to serve as ammunition workup guns for the M14, which was about to enter production.

THE POSTWAR GARANDS

Common to all "as manufactured" postwar M1 Garands is the so-called "high hump" gas cylinder lock screw, designed for a new grenade launcher, but long term, found to be far stronger than older units. These appear frequently on rebuilds, albeit oddly, for replacement purposes, special runs of hardened "low" versions were also produced. Interestingly, some of the old style are found marked "PB" and "BMB," but they're American-made, re-marked by the Italian firms in the fifties, after inspection and finishing. They were furnished about 1949–51.

The wartime M1 Garand may be the typical, definitive, and most common M1 Garand, but the postwar rifles are unquestionably the best, and for very simple reasons: they're newer and have therefore been knocked around less; they were made without the pressure of an ongoing "hot" war; and they reflect all the technological and safety improvements of sixteen years' research, experience, and progress. The special purpose guns wound up seeing much of their use postwar as well, though many were based upon wartime receivers.

In 2001, looking over my paperwork, I realized the ancient DCM paperwork was addressed to a man whose initials were J. L. G. He'd had his M1 marked, or did it himself. The deceased owner had also had his social security number emblazoned upon the right rear butt stock. This is a replacement stock, but those "markings" don't fake anything. They're part of the rifle's history.

In addition to parts sections scattered throughout this book, this short preface to the postwar manufacturers (Springfield Armory [US], H&R, International Harvester, Beretta, and Springfield Armory, Incorporated [private firm]) includes some photos to give the reader some idea of the new assemblies incorporated into the 1952 and later guns.

Almost all postwar parts were improved and renumbered, prefixed "55," "65," and, in the case of the operating rod, "77" on the very last batches.

There were other manufacturers who produced non-specification cast receivers. The Breda organization produced many early Beretta receivers, albeit Beretta eventually was the *only* producer, delivering receivers two decades and more after US production concluded. I purchased the first Breda receiver I saw, and since then, have specialized in building them into accuracy rifles.

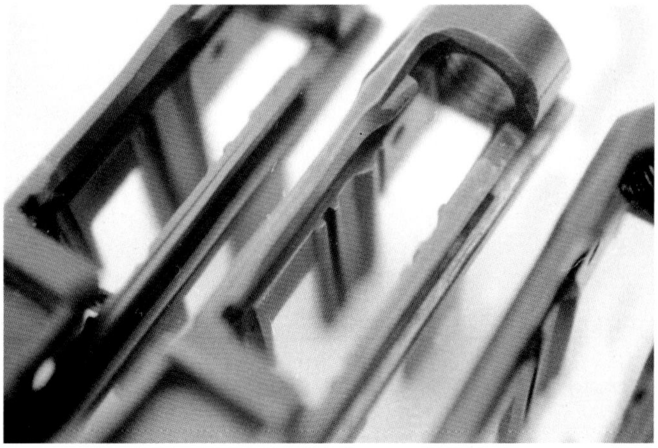

Generally, early receivers are slightly weaker, but also far more varied and interesting. These three are all 1941 or before, and the one in the middle carries the extra slot, or "mystery rail" for a tool which apparently was canceled shortly thereafter. Some other experts think the follower was going to be changed, and it never happened. Who knows? Both or neither could be correct.

Remington seems to have produced a considerable quantity of experimental T22 selective-fire receivers, which were longer and employed a trigger-based selector setup.

International Harvester rifles are a fascinating corporate and hardware study. Historians continually puzzle over why IHC was ever brought into any firearms procurement program, especially when there were competent, well-established precision firearms firms in the United States who could have used the work. The tractor and truck producer had no firearms background and had constant quality and delivery difficulties; one researcher estimates that roughly 15 percent to 20 percent of its production actually occurred at Springfield Armory and at least another 10 percent to 15 percent was finished or detail-inspected by Springfield staff. Two indicators of IHC's difficulties come from even a quick inspection of its receivers, which show odd contour permutations at random and large variations in finish color (often running to strange dark green), which most experts feel indicates poor chemical control or contamination of the phosphate chemicals.

All postwar Garands were issued with the stamped trigger guard, though in the rebuilding process many milled guards got stuck on postwar rifles. Most shooters prefer the stamped unit, made out of spring steel, which is more readily adjusted if it gets out of whack and evinces greater tensile strength.

Unique among Garands, most Beretta rifles carried their serial number and identifier data on the left rearmost receiver flat, just behind and below the elevation knob, on the left. Some very late rifles are marked on the horseshoe, just like their American counterparts. Beretta's production is covered in far greater detail than here in Vol. 7, No. 2 of the *Garand Collector's Association Newsletter*, in an article by Corso P. Boccia.

A closeup look at an H&R elevation knob.

Covered later on in this book are the spin-offs of the Garand, including the BM.59s, most of which actually began life as M1s and were modified to the later format.

That Beretta, F.N., and Sauer parts are found on M1s—even DCM guns, which saw NATO service—should amaze no one. Rifles were being rebuilt in Europe just as they were in the United States.

The M1 is the "daddy" of the M14, but the adoption of the 7.62mm.x51 cartridge in Europe prompted some changes in the M1 that, until recently, went largely unrecorded in the formal literature on the rifle. H&R unquestionably built some NATO-caliber rifles in 1955 and 1956. AMF, among others, produced replacement barrels. Beretta rebuilt M1s into .308/7.62 caliber (both remodeling original .30 tubes and producing new ones) and also delivered major quantities built for the shorter cartridge from the very beginning. There are Beretta M1 Garands that bear the BM.59 receiver legend, which indicates that Garands were being ordered and delivered after the Italian NATO rifle had become the Italian standard.

A closeup of an H&R barrel marking ca. 1955.

The following is a list of US contract figures and numbers of postwar rifles. Beretta is not included, since, like many European firms, it numbered and coded rifles to order—meaning that even if the information were available, which it is not (at least not to me), it would not be particularly meaningful, since there would be many duplicate numbers.

Many of the rifles on later contracts were not produced, or were delivered as match rifles years after the receivers were completed. As a result, the contract figures will have less correlation with the date lists toward their very ends. Also, several collectors have verified that H&R built some small lots of rifles bearing numbers well into Springfield Armory's last batches.

Closeup of the part number panel on an IHC M1 Garand operating rod. The rods are quite uncommon. Notice the hemispherical safety relief cutout immediately to the left of the part number. That's found on all postwar operating rods.

The postwar "type 3" rear sight assembly required no tools for adjustment and was locked without need for thumb pressure. These windage knobs are marked with their manufacturer's codes ("SA-WH" for Springfield Armory and "IHC-DRC" for International Harvester), indicating the subcontractor as well.

Postwar stocks usually carried the "stars 'n' eagle" Defense acceptance stamp, with the exception of some late replacements and the earliest lots from Springfield. H&Rs like this one were smaller than Springfield or IHC markings.

The "type 3" sight assembly gave birth to the fine adjustment 1962–63 National Match rear sight, with its half-minute adjustments, shown here with base and knobs, with standard IHC and SA windage knobs for comparison.

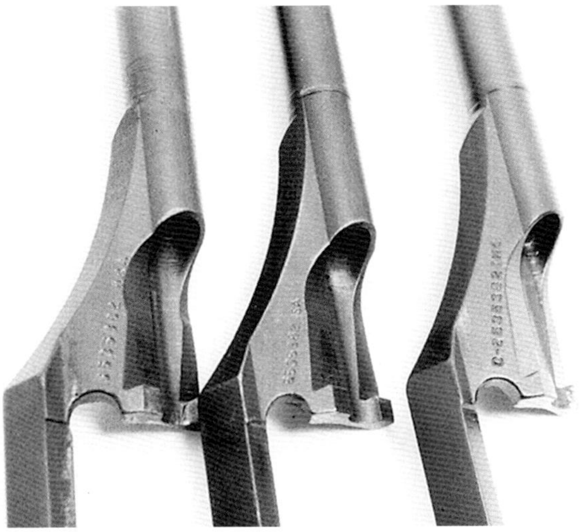

Postwar operating rods were not always uniformly marked. Top is an H&R marked "6535382 HRA"; in the middle, one marked "6535382 SA"; and on the bottom, one marked "D-6535382IHC." However, the suffixes used on wartime rods are gone.

Postwar bolts were numbered "D 6528287," and there were no longer any subtype suffixes. The other numbers are heat-treat lots and/or order numbers. The refined design was less subject to peening and was stronger.

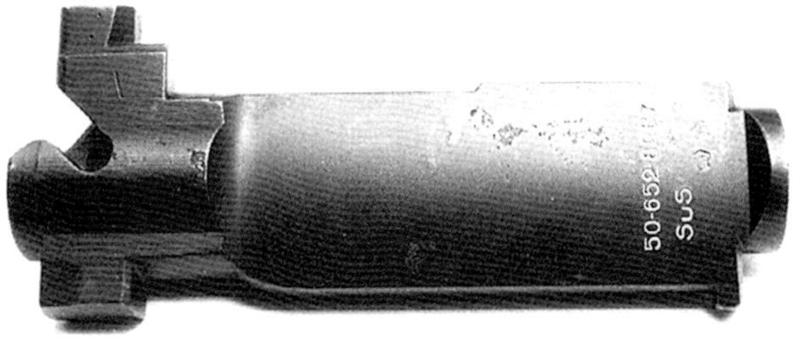

This Sauer and Sohn bolt was located originally on a Beretta-rebuilt, Springfield M1 Garand rifle, probably imported here from Germany ca,1967, in 7.62x51. The markings contain the NATO version of the M1's nomenclature. Yes, this is the same firm which today produces the largely Swiss-designed Sig-Sauer handguns, and who produced firearms long before most American manufacturers even existed. They produced barrels, too, and some say, operating rods. However, no one among my fairly wide circle of collector and shooter friends has seen such a rod.

German-made Breda M1 with an "SuS" (Sauer und Sohn) bolt from the postwar period. Note the unusual arrangement of the parts number code "50652-8287" and the fact that the type reads from the opposite end of American-made bolts. In all other respects, these parts meet every specification. The "50" code may refer to an adoption date or to a German code for the Garand. Note also the two proof/inspector's marks at the bolt's rear.

POSTWAR US GARAND PRODUCTION BLOCKS

Though almost none of these rifles saw service in the Korean conflict, some writers refer to these guns as the "Korean War Period" rifles. Save for the first group of rifles from Springfield (noted in the wartime section), none of these guns bore letter-cartouched stocks.

MANUFACTURER	International Harvester
Springfield Armory	Harrington and Richardson
Springfield Armory	4,400,000–4,660,000
International Harvester	4,660,001–4,800,000
Springfield Armory	5,000,001–5,000,500
Harrington and Richardson	5,000,501–5,278,245
Springfield Armory	5,278,246–5,488,246
Springfield Armory	5,488,247–5,793,847
SERIAL NUMBER BLOCK RANGE	5,793,848–6,034,228
4,200,001–4,399,999	6,034,229–6,099,905

NOTE: A very few experimental guns were manufactured in the 4,800,001–5,000,000 range, by various manufacturers. (Also note that in the serial number block ranges given, some numbers were allocated but never actually used.)

The Springfields

A shooter bench sights a postwar Springfield M1, the near-black finish of which is evident in this photo.

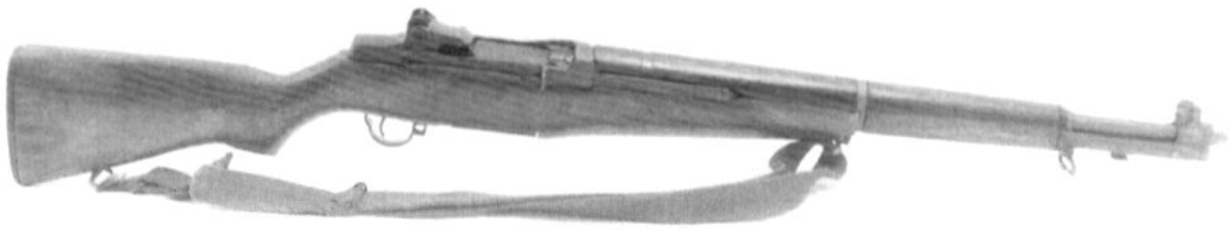

A very high-numbered (6,000,000+) postwar Springfield M1 in mint condition.

Close-up of postwar Springfield Garand issue barrel, this one dated September 1954 and bearing typical markings, including the postwar part number 65 35448 and several "P" proofs, at least one of which is usually upside down.

Close-up of postwar 5,000,000+ rifle with SA-WH marked sights. Note dark finish on metal.

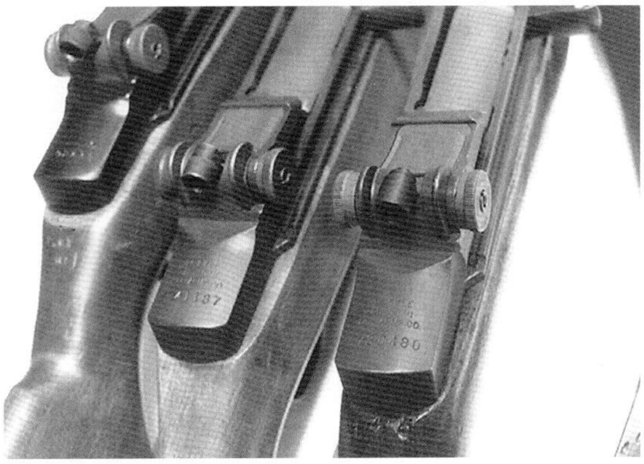

Three match-prepared M1 Garands on H&R receivers. From left: ca. 1964–65 U.S.M.C. on 5.7 miMion+ receiver, black-chrome plated; USN "Special Match" from about 1970 and apparently assembled by H&R, with new barrel, serial number range 5.7 million+; and a third, bearing a very early version of the "tin tea cup" nonrotating, hooded National Match sight ca. 1957–58. The rifle on the left was rebuilt at some time and tightly bedded on a World War II cherry (fruit wood) replacement stock. All but the center rifle are post-1985 marked imports. A little careful thought about the semantics: it really is slightly more correct to call the American rifles brought back "reimports," as they had already been imported once or more, and were then, after 1986, imported again, this time back to the US. Even Berettas here are linguistically and technically "reimports," as they went from Italy to another nation—usually Denmark, as that is the only large infusion of Beretta military rifles to the US—and then got imported from there back to the US, or more often, to Canada, and then illegally imported to the US. None of this matters much, but then again, neither do most of the other artificial distinctions and categorizations advanced and artificially and often erroneous titled outside the producing arsenals and organizations.

The postwar Springfield trigger housing, part-numbered 6528290-SA. There were virtually no changes from the late war units.

The H&Rs

Smith Derrick Martin test fires a re-barreled H&R Garand, left-handed.

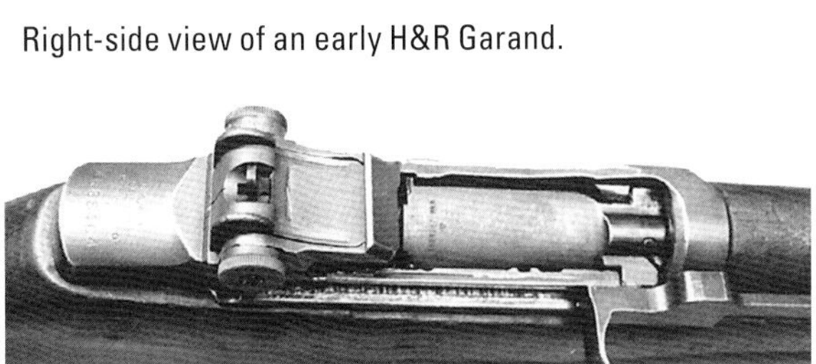

Right-side view of an early H&R Garand.

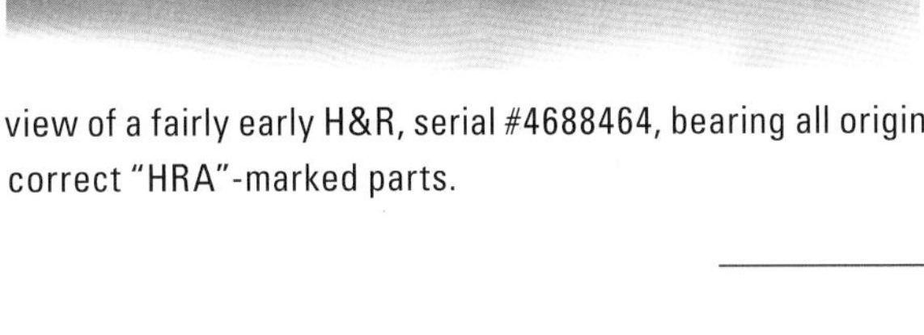

Top view of a fairly early H&R, serial #4688464, bearing all original and correct "HRA"-marked parts.

The International Harvesters

1954 "G" series International Harvester, serial #5170972.

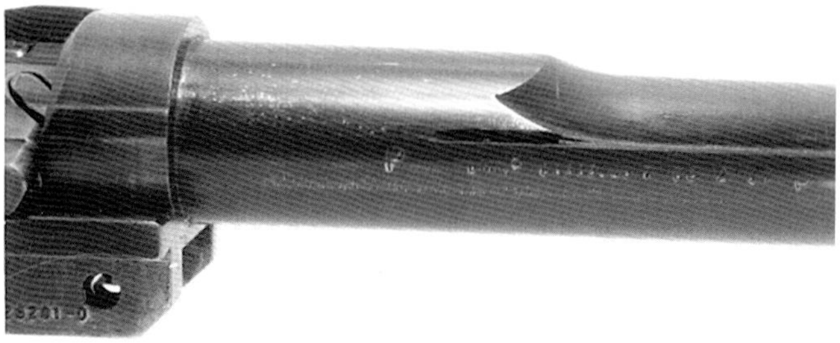

Typical "LMR" International Harvester barrel markings, this one dated 7-53. These barrels were also ordered as replacements, and some will carry "HG" or "AFHG" and even "NM" notations. "HG" is for "high grade," "AF" for "air force" (for their competition guns), and of course, "NM" denotes "National Match."

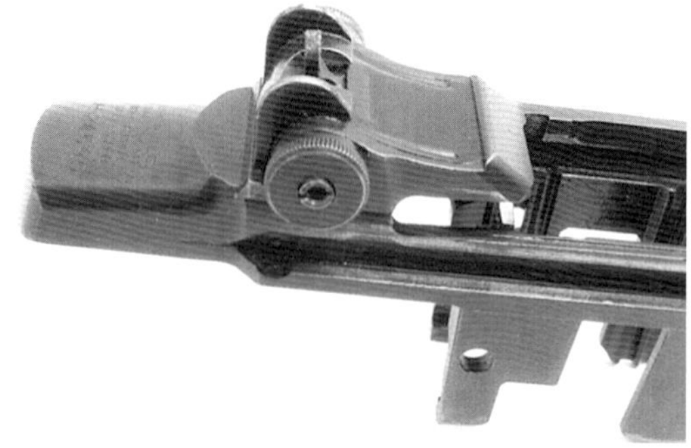

Early International Harvester receiver serial #4524595.

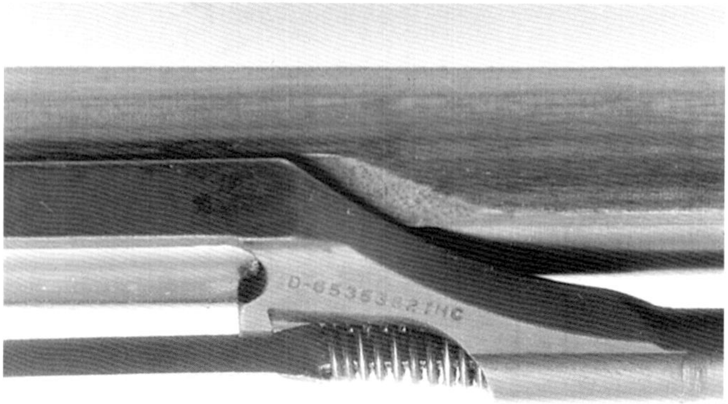

International Harvester operating rod data stamping. This rod is fairly early but was located on a very high-numbered rifle on which it was probably original equipment. Most IHC stocks were subcontracted to Overton Mills and will be marked "O" somewhere in the barrel channel.

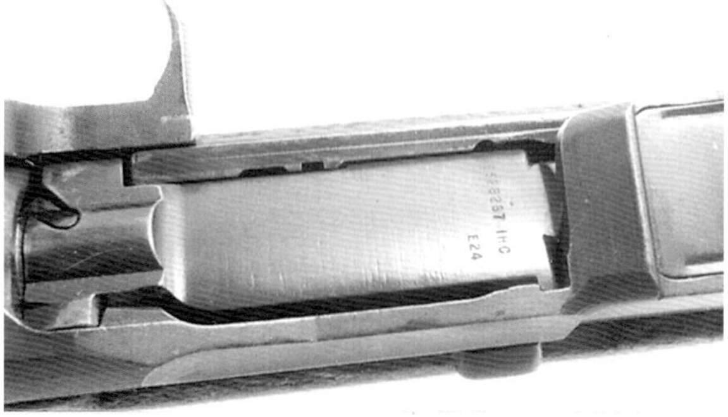

Bolt and receiver of a typical IHC rifle.

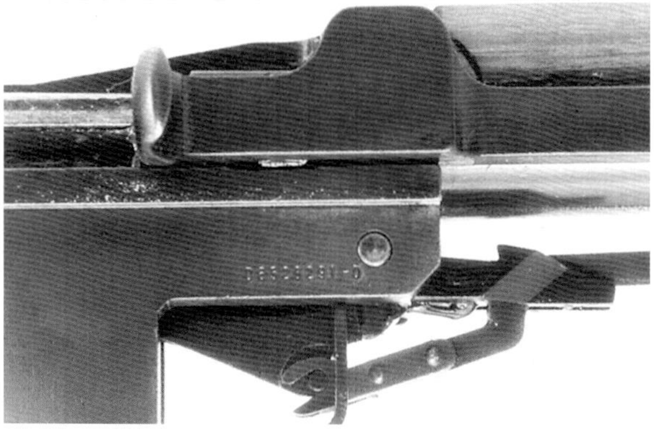

Marking detail of a "D" series International Harvester receiver, showing part number D6528291-D.

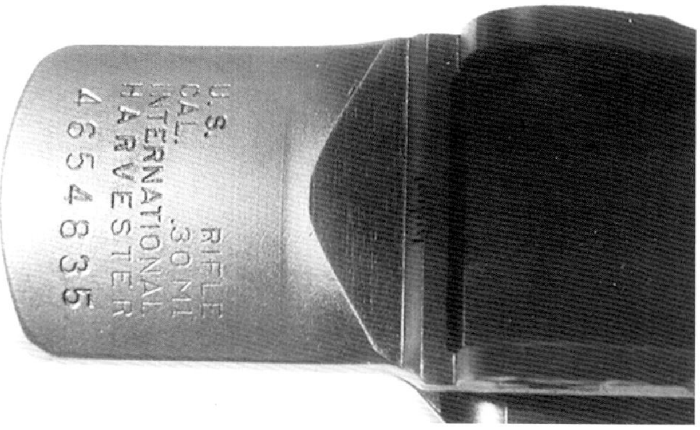

The rare International Harvester "gap letter" serial #4654835 illustrates the unusual letter justification with a large space in the middle, typical of the IHC receivers actually manufactured and completed at Springfield Armory. Note also the heftier contours of these postwar receivers, compared to those in the early wartime section of this book. The thickness of the flat aft of the sight is particularly important.

Part number of a "gap letter" International Harvester rifle, noted with heat treat number typical of other Springfield-built rifles, in this case: A 51 D I H C F 6528291. That Springfield actually built these constituted a bailout that should've been a scandal.

The Berettas

The Berettas: Beretta was the last producer of actual military M1 Garands. Delivered over two decades after US production ceased, the Beretta Garands—including many in 7.62x51 NATO—were true, forged M1s from the original postwar configuration.

An extremely rare Yemeni Beretta M1 Garand. At least one correspondent and advanced collector tells me this rifle is off the Ethiopian contract. I am inclined to doubt that. But crests other than Danish on Italian-produced M1 Garands are *all* extremely rare.

Side view of Beretta M1 Garand, serial #E 1139.

Left-side view of an Italian-issue M1 Garand. Note data legend, rear receiver.

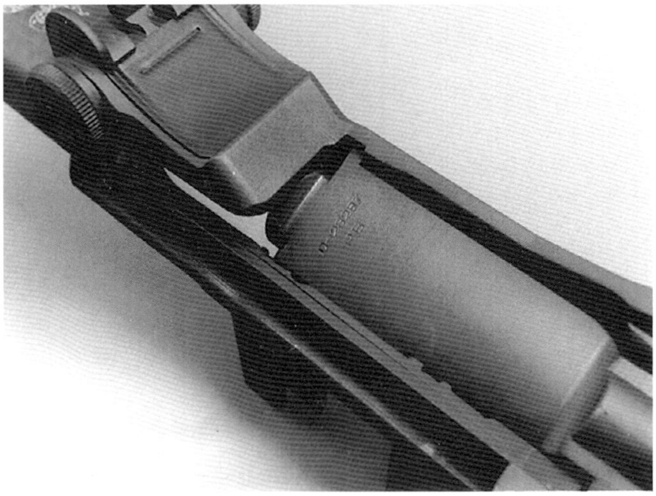

Top view of Beretta M1 Garand.

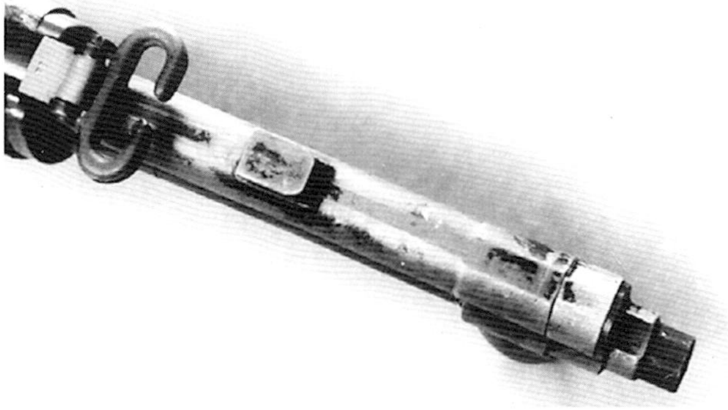

Along with the production tooling specimens, Beretta received many US parts, including trigger guards, front sights, and gas cylinders. This Winchester configuration "no toe" gas cylinder is not Italian made but bears a crisp "PB" marking aft of the stacking swivel, on the rear spacer lug.

Rare Allen wrench gas cylinder lock screw by Beretta, ca. 1 960 or later.

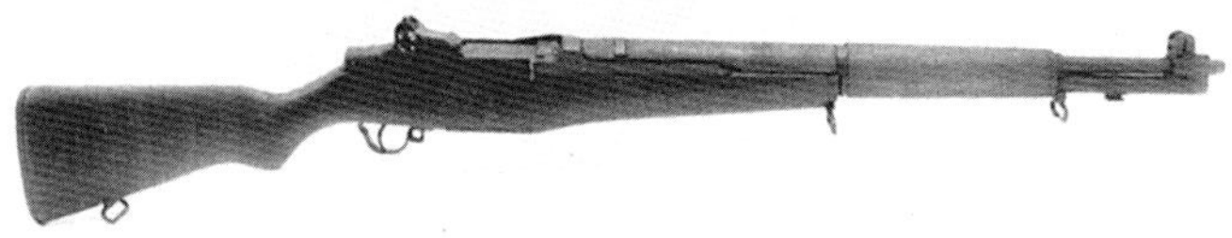

7.62mm NATO Beretta M1, as imported by Springfield, Incorporated sometime after the 1970s. Note the simplified, US-style markings. These were the last true military-specification M1 Garands completed and sold.

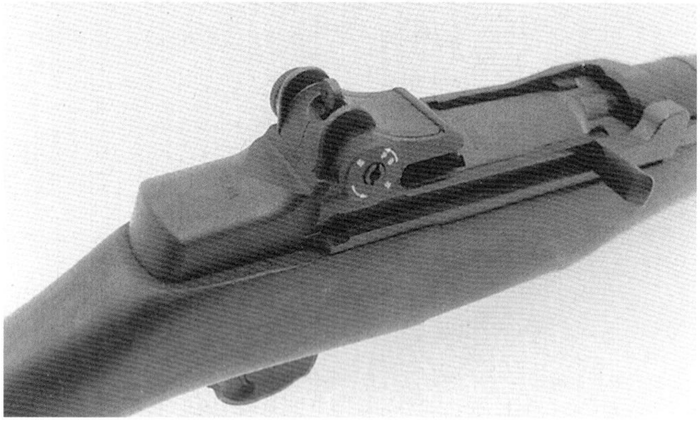

Right view, late Beretta M1 as imported to the United States from Beretta stocks by Springfield Armory, Incorporated (Illinois—not the armory), for the civilian market. This rifle seemed to be unfired and was chambered and marked for 7.62x51 mm NATO.

Very late Beretta M1 Garand receiver, serial #1 80, apparently off the very last contract. Beretta serial numbers were "to order," and if a country wished to begin its contract numbers at "1," regardless of previous orders, the contract numbers would begin at "1."

Italian M1 Garands generally carry their maker's name on the left side flat, bearing letter codes on the legs. A Beretta is on top, the Breda below. Both of these were readied as .308 rifles, albeit .30 06 barrels were retained. Many late Beretta full-length rifles were delivered in 7.62x51mm., especially on the last contracts. How many no one seems to know. There are pre-GCA 68 M1 Garands whose receivers are denoted "BM.59," and yet they were never fitted with the charger bridge or selector. Nor were they ever adapted to the twenty-round Italian magazine.

THE ITALIAN JOB

When *THE COMPLETE M1 GARAND* was first committed to ink in 1998, many say I was the first to say much of anything in print, in English, about the Italian M1 Garands. My information then came from collectors in the US, some old contacts in Italian ordnance, a few European collectors, and from vendors way back in the 1960s who had shown me Italian-made Garands when I initially found it hard to believe such things even existed.

I'd had fleeting "official" contacts with the manufacturers, too, but could never find an interpreter who spoke the kind of technical jargon in both languages that was necessary to assure what was intended by some passages.

So some of the information didn't go in that missive.

Indeed, it was only shortly *after* that volume came to life that I saw, handled, and photographed what was probably the very first Breda M1 to actually be placed in my hands. At one time I'd mused they "might be a rumor."

Two decades later, after correspondence much earlier with other sources, Jarno Antonelli, Beretta's official historian, was able to affirm much of what I had previously considered mere educated guesses.

For example, my circle of associates seemed to have evidence that the Italian M1 Garand production amounted to somewhere around 250,000 units of that rifle in their original form. That was apparently entirely too high. Antonelli specifies that, on all contracts, Beretta *alone* delivered from 60,000 to 80,000 rifles. Others suggest that Breda production was about half that. So perhaps 90,000 total Italian-produced M1s seem to have existed. That's the best estimate. Some think the 90,000 figure way too low.

The suggestion was made by a friend that perhaps someone had added known M1 supplies to the Danish contract, somehow. Perhaps it is from that source that the seeming error originates.

I'd seen Nigerian- and Colombian-crested M1s, and most of the colloquy of "experts" were sure those specimens were intermingled with the later BM.59 orders. No Italian source denied or refuted that. Of course, that doesn't guarantee it's absolute truth, but there literally seems to be no alternative explanation. The rifles existed.

Operating rod markings and leg codes on an Italianate Tipo 2 M1 Garand, based upon a late World War II USGI receiver.

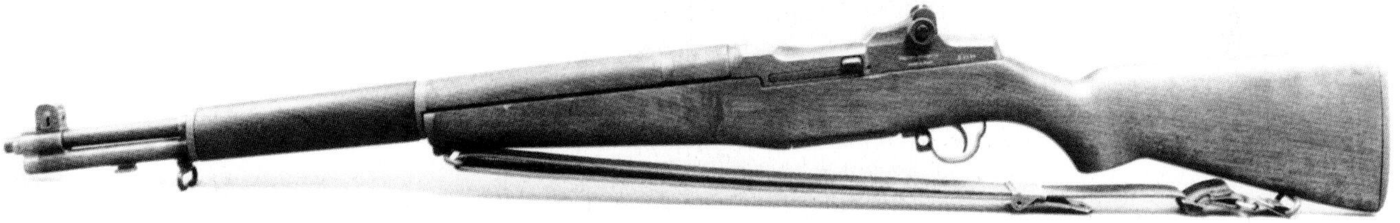

Full-length, left-side view of Italian-built Yemeni M1 Garand by Beretta.

The Tipo 1 and Tipo 2 and 2A rifles were, as we all surmised, all rebuilds (none ever left the factory in the ¼" shorter configuration), and almost all receivers were re-marked US M.A.P. This was figured out early on based upon a six-digit numbered, reconfigured and re-identified specimen which carried the square operating rod cutout of a standard Winchester M1 of the "dash two" type. Serial number was that of an early Winchester receiver, and the numeral face was unmodified, as was the number itself. The caliber was marked thereon (NATO 7.62), as were "type 2" designators, and we checked carefully. Microwelding had allowed the re-marking with caliber and the Beretta information. Another we examined not only had a serial number *entirely too high* for any Italian rifle, but carried the "US rifle" designator line. That was a much later receiver, originally from the armory, again, with the old markings microwelded and new information applied. This rifle was made by the American firm but marked as if made in Italy.

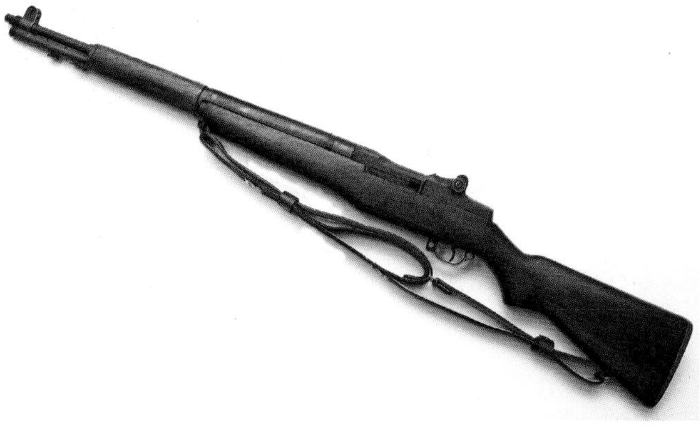

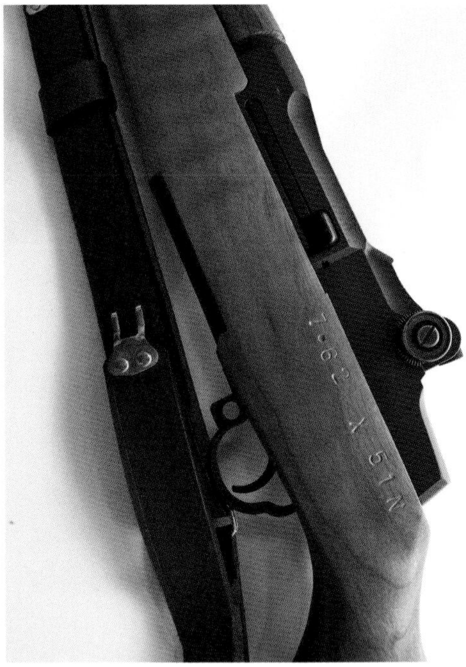

The Italian format "Type 2" ("Tipo 2") was a straightforward modification of the M1 Garand to the 7.62x51 NATO format cartridge, using shortened operating rod, lower handguard, butt stock, and barrel. NONE were ever built in this format, and US receivers, most often microwelded to obscure their origins but bearing their original serial numbers, were gernerated exclusively from M.A.P. and other US-supplied stores. The shortening of the barrel, from the rear, was a masterful and well thought-out process. These were introduced *after* the BM.59, as a cost reduction measure, along with new stocks produced at Terni and cut down from older units at various depots as well. They still served somewhat with non-infantry reserve units well into the twenty-first century. The rifles are about 12mm. shorter than standard Garands, as opposed to the "Tipo 1" conversions and new rifles, which were all full length. The modified operating rods with the visible knuckle "notch" and caliber markings and other notations were intended to provide guidance in determining caliber. When the author uses these, he often equips them with lighter, commercial-style M1907-style slings, but put together with rivets rather than regulation stitching. It helps keep track of which rifle is which.

We had long since discovered that both Italian and US barrels in the 23.75" (appx.) length had been reconfigured. Some barrels, but not many, were supposedly produced brand new in the reduced length.

7.62x51 rifles in standard length were delivered on many of the later contracts, new built, as we had all speculated was the case. Startlingly, the BM62—which was *never* a military designation or duty firearm—was indeed produced, in a lot of 1000, by the mother firm at Gardone Val Trompia, specifically for civilian export. Antonelli verified that in detail.

There is no definitive, published Beretta book or history to illustrate this particular sort of information.

Beretta-produced receivers were not common in Italian service, since the US had supplied the Italian services with 230,000 specimens off the Military Aid Program. The domestic production wasn't much needed.

For a long time, many collectors and military historians had thought that the Italian military used *not a single* domestic produced Garand in its original form. That turns out to have been somewhat incorrect.

Antonelli also surprised everyone by noting the M1 was being produced and delivered far longer than anyone else realized: from as early as 1952 to 1974 and even after. They, therefore, were in the "M1 business" longer than anyone else. Deliveries went past '74, and the Reese family acquired the remainder some two decades later, rifles and parts which had *never* been military pieces for anyone.

The conclusion by many researchers suggests that almost no single M1 Garand contract at Beretta carried a larger than low five-digit number. This appeared also largely correct with the Breda-produced specimens. Most were well below those numbers. The high-numbered units showing Tipo 2 designations carry US serial numbers, and seem to be microwelded (modified marking information) rifles with new "manufacture" data and a revised caliber notation. Indonesian numbers ran far higher than any other contract, at the request of the receiving government.

This was also done with BM.59s.

Surprisingly, there is no single comprehensive list of nations which contracted for Italian M1s, and many of the M1s shipped out like the ones I saw at Interarms in Alexandria ca. 1965 cannot accurately be tolled. Indonesian, Colombian, Chilean, Nigerian, and other crests supposedly exist in the US, but in tiny numbers.

As we've known for a long time, the Winchester machinery of legend—United States government property!—had been stored outdoors for years, and by the time it was shipped to Italy, was primarily usable only to reverse engineer the Italian production tooling.

Most early Italian receivers seem to have actually been made by Breda, regardless of logo on the left panel. This began to change about 1955.

Most of the Danish "FKF" contract specimens came in through Mel Bishop, who brought them in under trying and rather shifty circumstances. We have to thank him, though.

Ironically, more than two decades after the M1 receiver ban, it seems impossible to bring in more Italian M1 Garands. The civilian end of the ban is still, as of this writing, in effect.

Consequently, the Italian M1 is probably the rarest of the standard M1s, and they've always been one of the most interesting.

Also affirmed: many wartime US parts were supplied with the blueprints, which accounts for the odd, heavy milled trigger guard or narrow or obvious Winchester gas cylinder bearing Italian maker letter codes. They were buffed or microwelded, re-marked, and either set up on new rifles, or more often, secured in storage as spare parts, many serving throughout the entire career of the later BM.59.

To those who do not regard the Italian rifles as "real" M1s, such positions profoundly cheapen the rifle's greatness and cosmopolitan appeal. Moreover, it's also simply *wrong*.

Thanks to those who assisted with this update and upgrade.

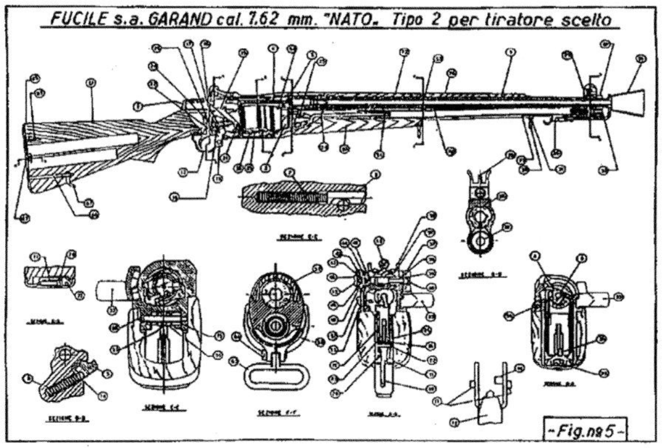

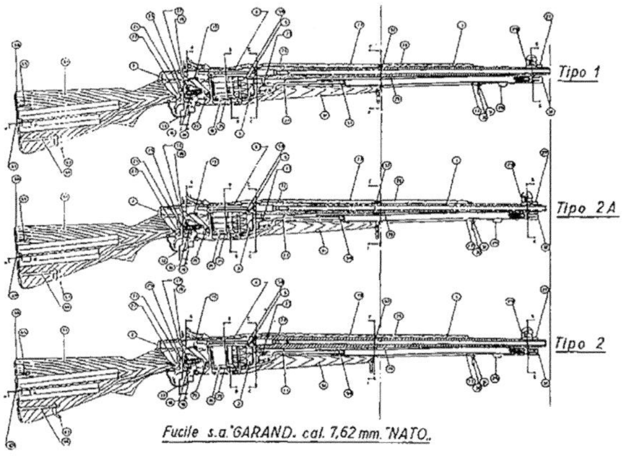

Beretta built and refurbished its own rifles as well as US-built Garands, many of which were reconfigured to its specifications, as in these drawings from official Italian manuals. Tipo 2 per tiratore scelto was basically a standard M1 D with a 23.5-inch reconfigured barrel in 7.62 NATO. Most of these retained 1 in 10-inch twist barrels. Tipo 2 and Tipo 2A were slightly different, shortened 7.62mm rifles of standard infantry configuration. Tipo 1 used new NATO specification 7.62mm barrels with 1 turn in 12 inches right-hand rifling. Most of these rifles remain in Italian service, though in diminishing quantities, mainly in noninfantry units.

Lower left view of a Beretta M1 Garand.

Arabic markings—most likely Yemeni—on an exported Beretta M1 Garand bespeak the vast and cosmopolitan history of the very last generation of true military M1 Garands.

While Fed Ord, Sante Fe Arms, and a few others also produced investment- cast versions of the Garand, it is Springfield Armory, Incorporated's version that is considered the best of the nonmilitary M1 receivers. Serial numbers commenced at 7 million. Early guns from the 1970s used many GI surplus parts; later rifles were virtually entirely produced by Springfield and its subcontractors.

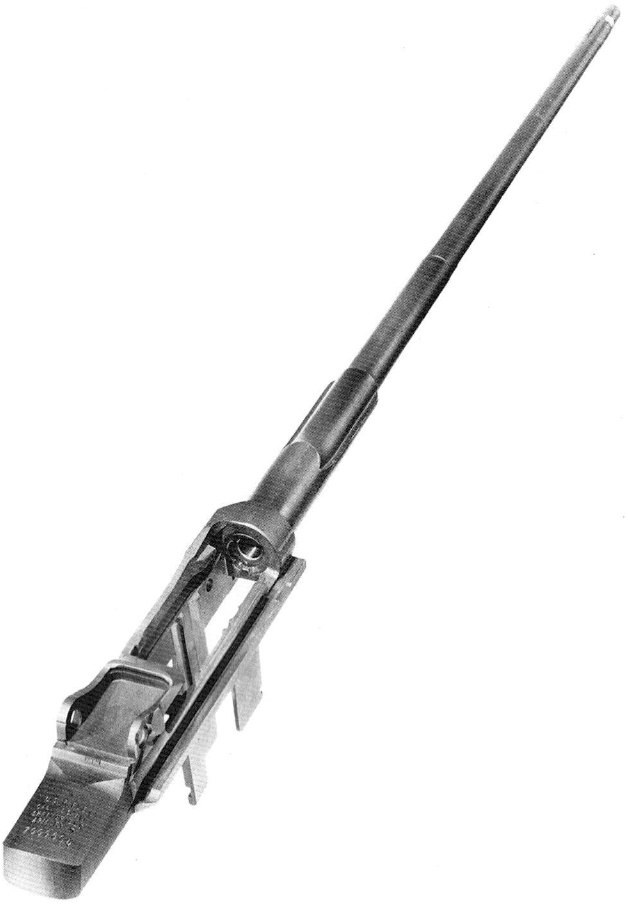

The very first commercial Springfield Armory, Incorporated receiver, serial #7,000,000, barreled with an early commercial unit.

SPECIAL-PURPOSE RIFLES AND RARITIES

As soon as the gas port rifles became the standard Garands and the system itself was fairly well worked out (about 1941), the armory began to plan for specialized variants and spin-offs. There were long lists of "T" series prototypes, almost all built up and modified from other factory rifles and inherently not available or of interest to collectors except as experiments. The sniper rifles and T26 were never truly "factory" items, but since scope-configured rifles were delivered from the armory, the sniper rifles developed there have substantial collector's status. The sniper rifles do not seem to have been selected for accuracy, and the addition of optics simply made aiming at greater distances slightly easier. Since the wartime and immediate postwar scopes were quite poor, most of the M1C and M1D rifles I have shot group better with careful use of the iron sights.

Even the M84—which actually began to see use about 1949–1951—showed poor flatness of field, serious color error, ultracritical eye relief, insufficient power, and bad parallax problems; it would not be acceptable today to even a casual shooter. There were better optics available, and one

Left view of an M1C Garand sniper rifle. This one may be a "brewed up" version, even though it came from the DCM in the 1980s.

of the mini scandals of the M1 program was the failure to utilize them.

Libby-Owens-Ford, Lyman, and Wollensak made most of the army- issue optics. The M81 and M82 were durable and compact but also suffered from optical problems.

The shooter who can locate a now-discontinued Leupold and Stevens Alaskan of 2½, 4, or 6 power and adapt the C or D mount to the larger optics will find the newer glass a far superior shooting and viewing unit—better sealed and more durable to boot. These employ ⅞-inch tubes like the originals.

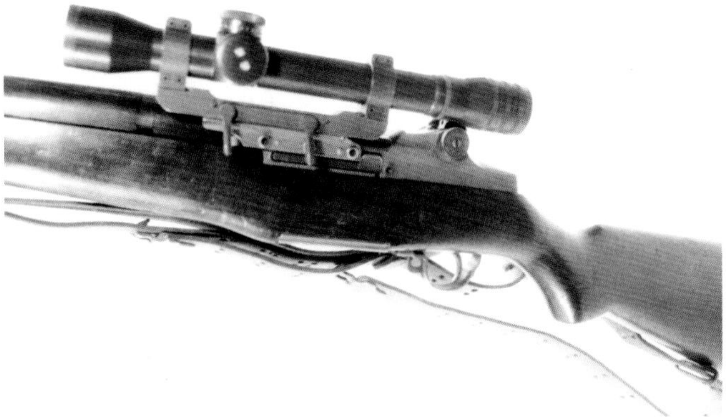

This is a very rare and fully documented Marine Corps MC1 (MC-1) Model of 1952 sniper rifle, with its superb Stith-Kollmorgen 4xD glass intact. The mount looks like the standard M1C mount, but it is longer and the dimensions are quite different. This is the only M1 sniper variant the author has ever been able to shoot better with optics than without, largely due to the fact that the earlier scopes have far more demanding eye relief positions and less brightness. I've only seen three, and was reminded in 2011 that I had fired one when I was a kid, about 1960. At the time, I thought all M1s had scopes and they were all just like that one. Wish I'd had some concept how rare these were, even then, I'd have appreciated it more. This specimen belonged to a collector friend, was photographed about 1998. This is a Griffin and Howe mount, to U.S.M.C. specifications.

The Marine Corps' MC-1 (formally, MC1) used the Griffin and Howe side mount of the M1C coupled to more modern optics. It is sometimes called the U.S.M.C. Model of 1952. It uses 1-inch rings and was sometimes found with Leatherwood and other very high-quality scopes affixed. However, these were mainly converted at Marine Corps depots, and little information exists on serial numbers. Therefore, they are difficult to document. They are also very rare, though some, complete with rings but without scopes, were part of Sherwood/Samco's M1 "reimport" shipments from Israel in the mid-1980s. The Marine Corps seems to have bedded many of these rifles. At least one I examined seemed to be fitted with a heavy custom barrel and most of the late National Match fits and adjustments. Stith-Kollmorgen, B&L, and even Unertl optics were apparently sometimes fitted.

Right-side view of a fully authenticated U.S.M.C. Model of 1952 MC1 rig, usually denoted "MC-1" in Marine literature. These rifles were apparently being generated and used long after the documented history trails off, or perhaps the recollections of the "old salts" I speak to are very hazy. Either way, no one seems to contest that they were the best of the M1 Garand sniper rifles, mainly due to the improved optics.

The T26 was never really a factory rifle, was never a "Tanker," and was never issued to anyone except for testing purposes (and no, your neighbor's is not the only authentic one that actually saw service). The T26 was an *airborne* project, and the intention was to replace the M1 carbine—which 'troopers like Gen. James Gavin strongly disliked—with a shorter version of the M1 Garand that paratroopers could deploy fully assembled on drops. The experiment was found to generate excessive recoil and muzzle blast in .30-06 and was brought to its conclusion way too late to see World War II service anyway. The "tanker" moniker is strictly postwar and strictly commercial, and it has absolutely nothing to do with reality.

In .308 or 7.62 NATO, though (especially with a compensator/flash hider attached), the 18-inch-barreled shorty can be a handy rifle and is small enough to carry in the field as a hunting rifle. With a plastic stock, the weight drops an additional two or three pounds. Springfield Armory, Incorporated and Arlington Ordnance sometimes marketed these variants, and they are quite good in .308. However, many of the Fed Ords are downright dangerous, and inspection by a first class armorer is imperative before firing.

A late WW2 "32" modification M1 Garand receiver bearing a very obvious "Fed Ord" import mark, acquired about 1994. Fed Ord was one of the peddlers of the "iffy" and often downright dangerous remilitarized Garand receivers, and as a result, much of their material is looked down upon by both shooters and collectors. Not too long before they folded, however, they acquired much of the Philippine store of M1 Garands, parts, and accessories, and some of them were actually quite good. I bought quite a few receivers for various projects, and as with this one, ultimately and not for a lot of money, produced some rather nice shooters. It's fine to look down one's nose at "import marked" M1 rifles, but even from a collector's point of view, they at the very least provide a source of shootable assembled rifles that relieve some demand pressure from rare originals and restorations.

The T26 was a shortened Garand experiment, almost useless in .30 06 but quite handy in .308. This is an Arlington Ordnance rebuild.

The T26 used a shortened operating rod and mechanism, and the front handguard was trimmed to about 2 inches. Many of the substandard Fed Ord rifles deleted the front handguard.

T26

The T26 is a commercial product only but was spun off a series of experiments originated at Springfield Armory and executed mostly at Ft. Bragg and Aberdeen Ordnance Proving Grounds. In the 1944–1946 period, the M1E5 folding stock gun—fairly standard, save for stock and 18-inch barrel—was found to work better when the gas port was enlarged an additional .007 inch. A small batch of the modified rifles in both fixed-stock and folding-stock variants saw fairly extensive testing, and reports were quite negative. Accuracy was also not good using standard ammunition, though loads with faster powders shot quite well.

The operating rod of the T26 is modified, trimmed, and recurved; the follower rod is trimmed to accommodate the thicker spring, which is seated farther back; and, of course, the front handguard is trimmed to just over 2 inches total length.

Lubrication with the 9+ pound rifle is especially important because the compression of all the physical forces on a shorter span increases the overall violence of the action.

M1C

The M1C was spun off the M1E7 project using a Griffin & Howe side scope mount plate, base, and rings, and the original scope was the Lyman M73 "Alaskan." Pins and screws secured this unit to the left side of the receiver, requiring five holes to be drilled into the receiver. By late 1944 the design was standardized, and some saw actual use late in the war. Virtually all standard scopes were nominally 2.5 magnifications, although actual optical measurement of various units proves that they, in reality, were anywhere from just under two power to almost three. Early units bore serial numbers, but it is not correct to say that scopes, mounts, and rifles must all match—especially not on authentic rifles that have seen service. To the collector, a word of caution: there are more fake M1Cs around than real; unless they are very thoroughly documented, buy these as rifles, not as collector's items.

Receiver: all documented units are Springfield Armory, from about 3,000,000 to 3,900,000.
Barrels: originals would be SA units from late 1944 to

approximately August 1945, but a replaced barrel of later date would not seriously diminish value.
Base/Mount: Griffin & Howe, stamped with serial number and often other ID numbers.
Optics: M73 Lyman Alaskan or military copy, M81 (crosshairs), M82 (tapered post), M84 a common replacement.
Accessories: flash hiders, cheekpieces, etc.

MC1 U.S.M.C. Model of 1 952 M1 Garand. This is the right-hand view of a correct M1952 rifle with its original scope, unmodified.

This is a Griffin and Howe-installed mount from the 1950s, installed on what was possibly a later issue Marine Corps MC1 with 1-inch rings but which might be a civilian version of that rifle from about the same time frame.

Original M84 scopes were far superior to their even weaker predecessors, but are still primitive, dim, and weak by today's standards and suffer from parallax as well. These specimens were reimported to the United States in 1988 and seem never to have been used or refinished.

MC-1 (U.S.M.C. Model of 1952)

The Leupold & Stevens "Alaskan" series of ⅞-inch tubed scopes, if you're lucky enough to find one, are far better scopes than any of the military units original to the M1C and M1 D, though spacers or custom rings are sometimes necessary to fit these larger optics in the correct position.

The muzzle end of a WW2 M1 with a camouflage covered U.S.M.C. steel helmet as background.

A post-1952 semi-clone subvariant MC-1 (MC1) Garand, photographed close-up with a covered steel helmet in the background. This one was apparently "brewed up" at a reserve unit in the 1950's, and was U.S.M.C. property, but most collectors find the commercial mount not original or not authentic.

MC-1s seem to have been prepared and/or modified to the approximate specification as late as the 1960s. Some others were modified from M1Cs received for U.S.M.C. service but were found unacceptable.

Most of the later guns incorporated match modifications, and some bore high-quality barrels apparently machined from commercial units at Marine Corps depots.

It is unwise, since there is really no such thing as a "standard" MC-1, to presume anything about a rifle presented as an authentic U.S.M.C. veteran, unless there is some sort of very secure, heavy documentation and verification. And verification does not consist of anecdotes from "buddies" or gun show troopers.

Characteristcs are difficult to specify, but some rifles use the original M1C mount and some use a larger version of same with double levers.

Most common scopes were the "4XD" Stith-Kollmoregen, usually marked MC and serially numbered, but not necessarily to the rifle. Later, Baush and Lomb, Leatherwood, and Unertl optics were often fitted, sometimes with additional support rings added to the middle band area for the long tubes. When this was done and at what level are almost impossible to determine.

I have only seen one MC-1 rifle that was not glass- or epoxy- bedded, and I have seen several in 7.62 NATO, with AMF or H&R barrels. These are usually very accurate rifles and are the only "sniper" versions of the M1 that are really very useful for actual sharpshooting. The M1C was considered inferior to the M1D by the services.

M1D

The M1D was too late for World War II, though the M1E8 developmental prototype was tested and the detail design worked up as early as 1944. Most authentic M1D receivers

Full view, M1D, as issued. This rifle was one of hundreds imported about 1985 by Sherwood, then in Northridge, California. All seemed to come from Israel, and they were in splendid condition. The M1D configuration sniper rifle does NOT require drilling the receiver, and if someone wants to use glass on a Garand, they are a more sensible alternative to the M1C. The optics are satisfactory, but most casual shooters will find they shoot better with iron sights due to viewing issues and parallax. However, there are lots of fakes and "re-do" rifles out there. If one pays a collector price on one of these, solid provenance should be required.

M1C in a firing position (posed) in Korea. The "E" series were developed and tested during World War II, but saw virtually no "in the line" use until the Korean War. (Photo credit: US Army)

are of World War II vintage, but there seems to have been some armory or depot conversion of later rifles as well. The scope mounting block on the M1D is on the barrel, which requires shortening the handguard. For shooters who merely wish to scope an M1, either this modified barrel (now available new from several suppliers) or the B-Square mount are best for the rifle's long-term value because nothing of interest to collectors needs to be modified to secure the optics. All armory conversions to M1D specifications seem to have been done in the 1951–1953 period, and all authentic M1D barrels apparently came from the Springfield Armory (US). There are no specific serial number ranges for M1Ds, though it is almost impossible that any M1 numbered over 4,500,000 or so could have been converted at the armory. These rifles were not selected for accuracy, and, again, because of the optical limitations of the most common glasses of the period, one is strongly advised not to expect much.

Scopes: M81 or M82, usually M84. A very few M1D rifles have been reimported with a 1-inch ring set, and I have seen one—which must've lived outside the United States for quite some time—with 30 mm rings.

Accessories: cheekpiece, flash hiders, as per M1C.

Note: Most M1Ds seem to have been refinished when converted.

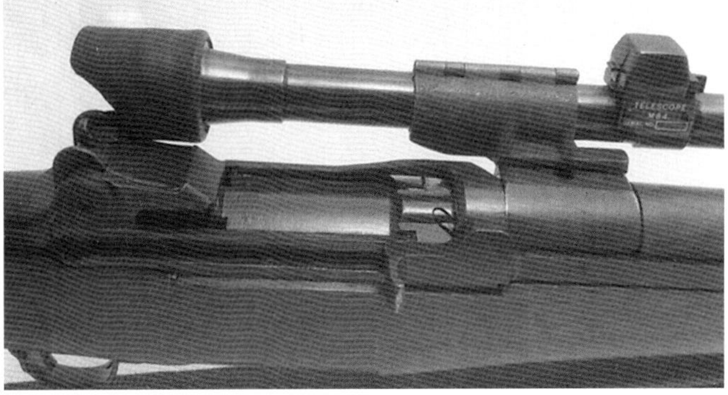

M1Ds are less valuable and more common than M1Cs, and there are many user-assembled M1Ds. These are not "fakes" unless someone tries to tell someone with an interest in buying such a unit that it is "original"—both issue and civilian M1D barrels are available. At least the value of the original receiver is not diminished, for, unlike the M1C, the "D" does not require drilling. The handguard, of course, does have to be shortened. This is the right detail view of the M1D mount.

M1D Left view of a proven, authentic M1D.

SPIN-OFFS AND DERIVATIVES OF THE M1 GARAND

The Garand was an extremely successful battle rifle, but once the soldiers and engineers and designers saw what they had, they sought to increase its magazine capacity and introduce a selective-fire version and even a squad support version.

The Beretta BM.59 used M1 technology and design directly. In fact, M1s were used to produce BM.59 rifles by remachining the receivers to accept a stripper clip and longer box magazine of twenty rounds, always intended to be loaded through the top. The American M14 used the receiver and sight design directly, but the receiver was about ½ inch shorter and not as strong. Yet the M14 lives on today, both as a very tiny number of GI rifles released to civilians and as a commercial product—such as the Chinese M14 featured on the following page, the Smith-forged M14 semiautomatic pictured in top and bottom views compared to a Garand receiver in side aspect, and various cast versions from Springfield Armory, Inc. (its M1A), Fed Ord, and others. M14 could never do for the military what was required—i.e., provide usable automatic fire in the field—but it's an excellent precision high-powered target rifle and is light enough to be carried in the field, with a legal five-round magazine, for hunting.

Everything that went wrong with the M14 happened because of the compromises made to lighten the weapon while endowing it with automatic capability at too high a rate.

The BM.59, though—which is essentially an M1, modified to accept new doo-dads—uses a shorter, heavier barrel and held up better and could shoot more accurately in full automatic mode. Many, however, were made and issued in semiautomatic only. Many persisting in service today use three-round burst control on "auto" mode.

Neither of these arms is part of the main M1 story, but they are the denouement of that long-running epic. Failing to explain their ancestry in this work would be a serious omission.

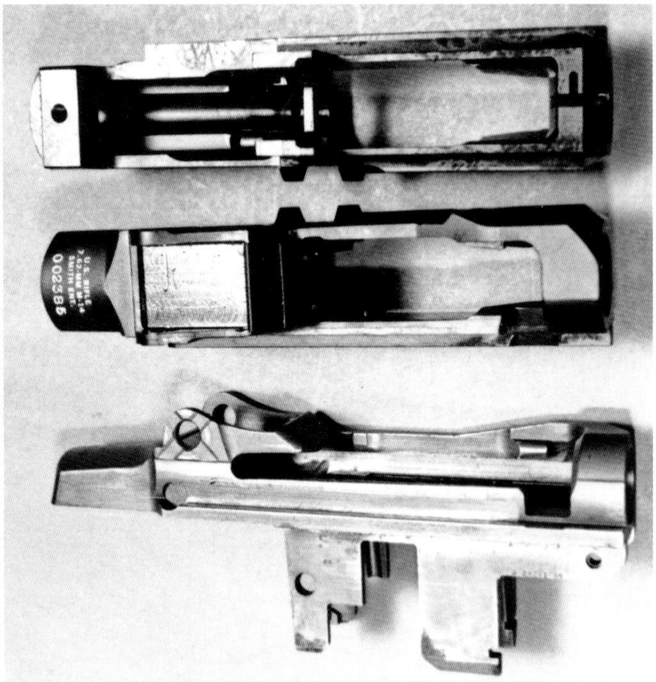

The M14, shown here in lugged semi-automatic versions from Smith Enterprises International, is the direct derivative of the M1 Garand, and indeed, in some views, it is difficult to tell the receivers apart. The lugged M14s are at the top. And no, they are *not* "M1As." That moniker is the copyrighted name of the Illinois-based civilian firm, not related to the armory, and is incorrect when applied to Smith, Armscorp, Fulton, or LRB pieces. Another factor: Unless something has changed since I consulted with SAI and SEI a few years ago, the operating rod raceway of neither rifle can be completely contoured using CNC machinery, and must invariably be hand modified and adjusted before final heat, treat, and finish. When I saw this being done ca. 1987, the work was done with stones, an operating rod, and feeler gauges. This fit is one of the reasons misbegotten cast receivers from some of the "lesser lights" of the parts business are such misery to get to a functional condition, but it seems *impossible* to convince novices and even a few would-be smiths of that simple fact.

The BM.59 used the M1 receiver directly, remachined, to produce both selective-fire and semiautomatic rifles for the Italian army and for export. This is the Nigerian service version, delivered from Italy in the late 1960s.

The author fires a Smith heat-treated and match-prepared Chinese M14 ca. 1 988. This is an all-forged rifle and, once the metallurgy has been brought to specification, is one of the very best M14 clones.

The M14E2—this one is a Springfield Armory- cast pre-1986 selective-fire clone—was a passable but too late attempt to make the M14 into a credible selective-fire support weapon.

A Smith-built M14 semiauto in match/sniper configuration with scope and cheekpiece, is also a credible hunting rifle.

There are civilian-owned and -operated M14s. This one is a TRW-built National Match, long since rendered incapable of fully automatic fire.

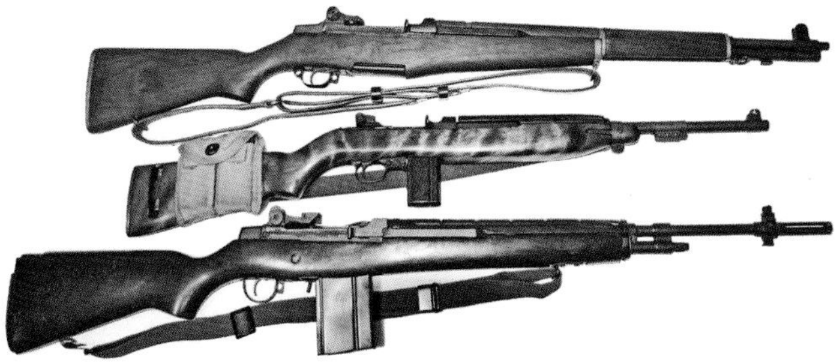

The rifles of the thirties and forties served alongside the seeming upgrades of the late fifties in the early days of the Vietnam War. These are, from the top, the CMP-supplied incarnation of a WW2 M1 rifle, a many-times-rebuilt M1 carbine with all the postwar furniture and a flashy birch butt stock, and, at the bottom, an SAI (commercial) M14 clone, the M1A cast-receiver version of the military rifle. In case someone wonders, NO, the M1A is not and never was an actual military issue firearm.

Shown on the author's old display horsehide about 1990, this is a full-house Smith Enterprises International forged receiver M14 (no, it is NOT an M1A—those are cast and made by the SAI commercial firm in Illinois) with all the bells and whistles and some Portuguese ammo in five-shot stripper clips.

CHAPTER 4

YOUR GARAND AND THE GARAND OF TOMORROW

PARTS COMPENDIUM—SPECIAL NOTES TO COLLECTORS

The world of firearms seems to be, even more so than the used car profession, the inheritor of the old horse trading tradition. Most of the pure scam artists frequent gun shows, dispensing profitable but erroneous hogwash; luckily, a lot of very good people also hang around gun shows.

Thing is, the flim-flam man will tell you anything to make a profit. The following are some good rules of thumb to keep from getting taken:

1. If a vendor won't allow you to take an M1 out of its stock, don't even consider buying it. It's okay if he wants to be secretive or protective about a Raven or a Jennings, but for what is being asked for Garands these days, if you can't examine the parts, just presume they aren't there. The one exception may be a tightly bedded match rifle, but even then, be suspicious.
2. Never believe anything that can't be documented or verified with printed information from genuine authorities.
3. With parts—especially high-dollar parts—remember that there are actual fakers out there making bogus goodies in huge quantities.

This section deals with some unusual or high-value parts. It is intended to give you a good idea what some things look like. I've included at least one fake in the hope that you can spot it when you see it, which you will. Ironically, most of the bogus parts I've seen are of very high quality, but they're being sold at collector's prices. On the other hand, the currently available, privately-produced clip latches and clips are usually below mediocre, and generally, if not useless, much adjustment is required.

Of the thousands of Garands I've seen at gun shows—every single one of which the guy behind the table assured me was "all original, all authentic"—the ones that were, literally, "all original" were those being sold by vendors I mention here. Some of those walking up and down the aisles were all original and authentic, but not all of those, either . . .

About 1997, at a gun show in Mesa, Arizona, a man was walking around the building with an M1 that actually had some rather nice parts on it—at least one from more or less every maker who made anything for the rifle. It was, however, badly worn and shot out. It did have old DCM paperwork. His tag read: "All original! Steal at six hundred dollars!" I might've offered him two hundred dollars for it, mainly for use as a parts source, and because it had a fairly nice World War II cartouched stock. Junk's junk, no matter what the source.

Very early "first model" sights, on the windage side, used bright-polished flush nuts. These assemblies were among the many features on the early M1 that had to be replaced quickly. Not only did they shoot loose, but a special tool was required to loosen and/or tighten the windage adjustment. Once it was loosened, the elevation eventually came loose as well.

This is standard configuration and nomenclature for early bolts, commencing with D28287 and, in this case, a -2 suffix. The dimple is a hardness test trace. Last line is steel supplier, in this case Republic.

On the first 100,000 or so Springfield Garands and the first few thousand Winchesters, the milled, grooved variety bands were utilized as standard.

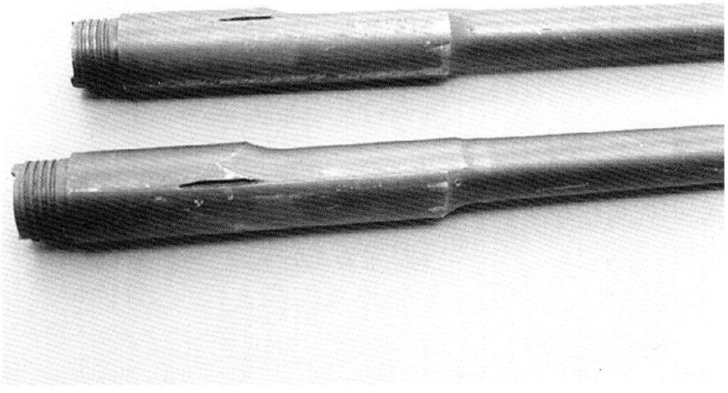

Early Springfield barrels such as the 9-40 unit on the bottom—one of the earliest production gas port specimens—placed the part number atop the barrel and the date and manufacturer upside down on the barrel's right. Top barrel is a 1943 specimen, for comparison.

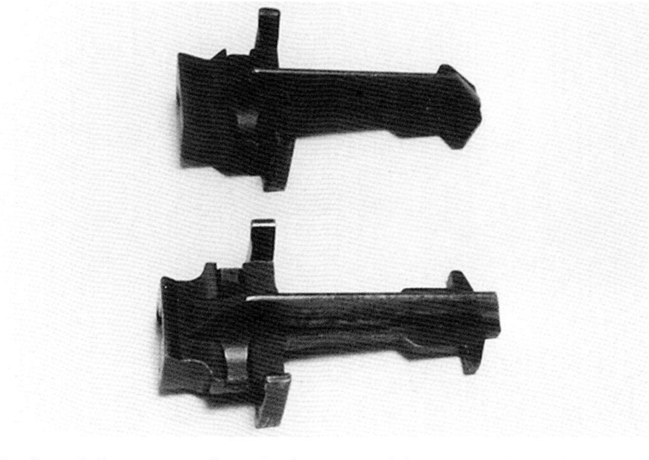

Earliest followers, such as the bottom unit here, ca. 1937–1939, were quite different from the standardized unit of about 1942 and afterward (top).

The rifle shown is one of many examined that combine all original Springfield parts ca. 1943–1944 but are fitted with Winchester barrels of about the same vintage. While one must conclude that these are some kind of field repair, there is a possibility—since this seems so common—that some of Winchester's barrels were fitted to Springfield rifles at the armory for at least a short period.

The indicating arrows on Winchester sight drums are referred to as "open," whereas Springfields like this one use "closed" arrows or, as I prefer, "triangles."

These are the "open" arrows of a Winchester windage knob.

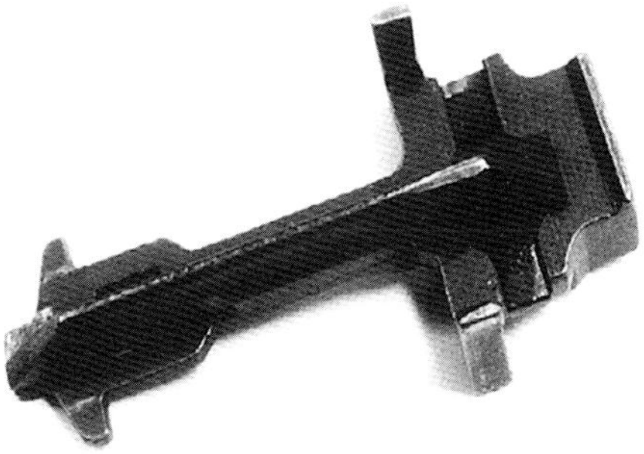

Rare first model Winchester follower, ca. 1941.

The original flush nut/short pinion M1 Garand rear sight is very rare, albeit not as rare as the short pinion/early locking bar types which immediately superseded this variant. Checkering matters, too. The nuts loosened with firing, tended to fall off, required a "two nipple" tool to tighten, and generally weren't satisfactory. This one is phosphate ("Parkerizing") finished. The rifle on which it is mounted is very early . . . and notice, that black line is a *crack*! I have seen them blued, in the white, and in a finish which may be case hardening color, and while I used to have a pet "maybe it's right" chronology on which was which, my current best guess is they were replaced so often in their service, 1936–42, that any order to which is which is largely guesswork. Also, it's implicit and obvious that they were being doctored and altered in the field and at the unit level, too. They resemble the T105E1 postwar sight from the right side, but only superficially. The left-side view (elevation knob) is basically the same as the latter "locking bar" types. There are several permutations of early sights, enough that many of us avoid using catch-all shorthand descriptions. Like the gas trap's replacement, the anecdotal evidence of the sight's failure is deep, and so is some of the overall hard documentation. Also note the squared off operating rod cutout in the receiver, about three-quarter inch ahead of the sight knob. Whether a coincidence or not, the earliest rifles seem to show up with the "flush nut" in the white, but we don't know if they began life that way or if someone later polished them . . . which seems unlikely.

All Winchester and very early Springfield hammers are bulkier, carry their part numbers on the side, and, until 1941 or so, carried an extra lube/access hole. This is a -1 Springfield. The excessive bulk had disappeared from Springfield's production by -5.

While this photo is a fairly good profile of the late M1 Garand/M14 hammer, with the upper unit being identical to a high-quality, late Garand hammer, its purpose here is not to illustrate the difference in profiles. The lower unit is an authentic Winchester, obvious by the heavy machine marks and "plump" overall configuration. Marked identically, the upper unit is a very nice, actually superior hammer, made very recently, but marked with a duplicate of the Winchester markings of the 1941–1945 period. To a shooter, at a fair price, the fake is fine, but it is definitely not an M1 original part and has no collector's value at all. Some collectors suspect these were made in China. One armorer of my acquaintance says they are Chinese M14 hammers.

Unmodified, unrefinished operating rod from an early Winchester. Note black finish, heavy wear pattern.

Topside markings of an original midwar Winchester M1 Garand barrel. Note index mark.

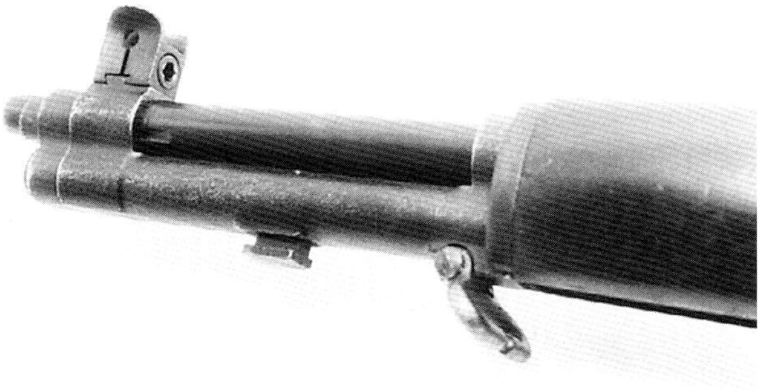

Like the later International Harvesters, Winchester front sights were out of specification, spread wider, or, if you prefer, more "bent" than all other manufacturers. I suspect this photo was reversed by an incompetent photofinisher, as many of the others in this ca.1982 photo shooter were also flip-flopped. Yes, folks, photography was not *always* digital!!

Very early Springfield and some early Winchester rear sight spring covers either had no depression groove or carried only a small dimple but were found not to hold securely and to wear excessively.

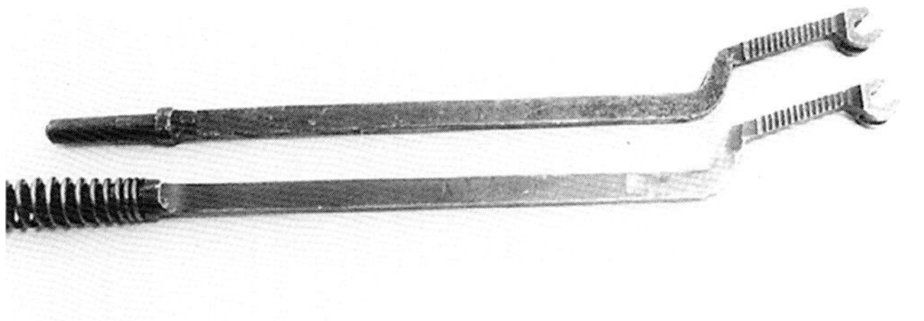

Early short fork follower rods. The bottom one—spring still in place—carries an "A" mark, typical of Winchesters. I have seen these marks on either side and both sides up. These early rods were milled, used no rivets, and were grooved. They were replaced because they tended to jump off the mechanism when used with grenade launchers. This type is authentic only to about mid-1942; later at Winchester.

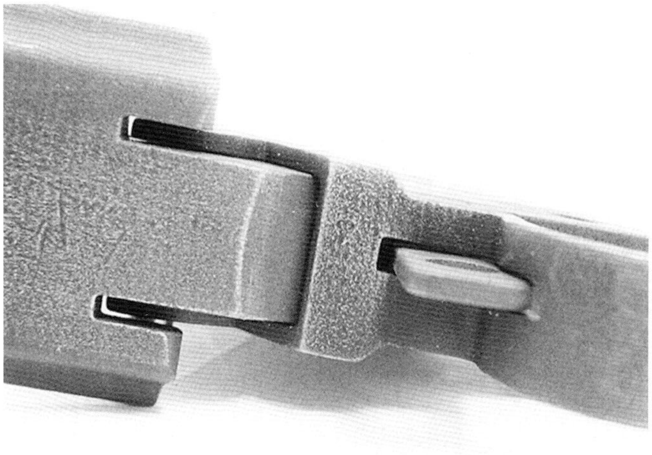

C 46025-3 was the last run of number-marked milled trigger guards from the armory, passing out of use by about late 1941 to early 1942. By late 1943, the superior, spring steel stamped units were standard—except at Winchester, which made the change only with its last lot of WIN-13 rifles.

Early "arched" lower band, on the lower rifle, ca. early 1943, compared to the late war/postwar "flat" version of the same part.

Many Winchester bullet guides are marked "A," sometimes "CM", and they are generally black. Some Springfields also carry the "A" subcontractor mark and are often quite dark. The lighter gray unit here, for comparison, is a later stamped unit.

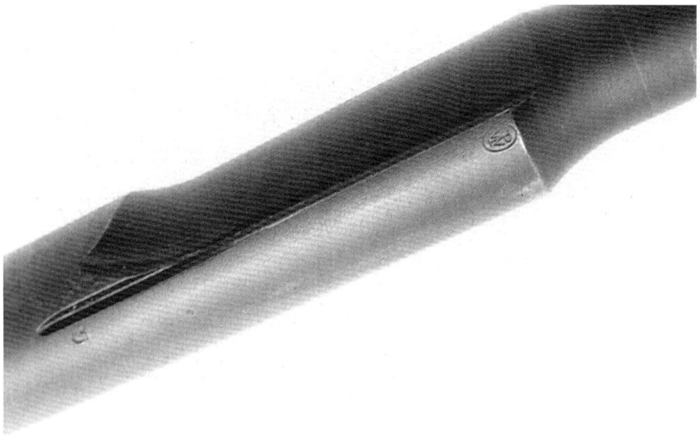

"WP" proof and detail index marks on a midwar Winchester M1 Garand barrel.

NOTE: The Garand buff is sincerely invited to copy and recopy the following data sheet (which will work best if you use a copier set up for two-sided copying and use one sheet for each rifle you inspect). Its purpose is to help you share data, aid in restorations, and evaluate specimens in detail.

This sheet is an adaptation of a similar one formulated by David Frenn and run (also with permission to copy) in the Garand Collector's Association Newsletter.

Don't be too amazed if, even after reading this book, you find some markings that are a mystery to you.

FRONT SIGHT SPAN CHART

Many front sights have been bent or ground upon and will not meet these specifications. But the chart below should provide some guidance.

Measurements will vary some due to fatigue, machining variations, abrasives used in finishing, and so on. M1 front sights made in Italy are to Springfield specifications. Those supplied initially (ca. 1949) and bearing Italian markings, like some gas cylinders and other small parts, will be of Winchester pattern, since some parts were included with the US M1 Garand package.

Some IHC rifles evince HRA front sights, and a large minority of HRA rifles deploy what are either Springfield or Springfield pattern front sights.

Measurements are high point to high point, across:

SA .625 - .6875 inch
HRA .70 inch
WRA .8125 inch
IHC .875 inch

(IHC spares and a few sometimes encountered on SA rifles seem to be an arsenal-supplied variant, perhaps from a subcontractor, and span .75 inch, exactly ¾ of an inch.)

M1 Garand Data Sheet & Property Record

date of acquisition________ Mfg.________S#_______________ Mkgs. notes_________
MISC ACQUISITION DATA____
Receiver: D#____________Heat Lot#__________Bolt Recess: rd___sq____two tone___
revision______rebuild marks_________finish color____________________
general type: M1C__M1D__MC1___"M1936"_____NM_____Civ Match______custom______
USN Mk.2Mod1___Comm. T26 fits_____Other______________
Bolt: D#__________Heat lot: Hole, bottom______hole, lug_______
firing pin, round____std_____mfg/codes/notes_____________________
BBL: side mkgs:_______________ chrome gas port______ NM_____M1D____7.62______
_______________other mkgs___________bore condition note_________
TEG READ________MZL READ or notes________________color/finish___________

SAFETY: D#______________Location #___________sub #_________extra hole________
flat edge___________ round edge____________mfg./mks notes:____________

Trigger: D#___________ other mkgs______Extra hole_____Sear mkg___finish/color:___

Trigger Housing: D#_______________Cloverleaf______Small hole_______ pad:lg___Sm__
finish/color notes_________________mkg_______mfg_________________

Trigger Guard: D#____________milled__stamped___ s w/hook____stamped w/o hook_____
mfg. code______ concentric rings______finish/color_____________

Hammer: D#_________________Location#: face___side____ exta hole____early notches__
finish/color_____________mfg_________
Hammer spring guide: ears____sans ears____finish/color_____________
Hammer spring housing: finish______number_____contours_____________

FRONT SIGHT: D#___________Blade guard span_____screw cap_____SA/HRA___WRA____PB__
finish/color___________ contactor____ IHC____NM____
Gas Cylinder: D#_________color/finish notes_____________________________
platform: narrow____wide____ sawcut____flat/round ring(circle one)
flat/tapered leading edge, bayonet lug (circle one) early______mzl
code letters___________mzl plg_______
GAS CYL LOCK: D#_________Misc codes_______Round(early)_____flat/humped_____
top bevel____no bevel____ color/finish__________notes_____________
Gas Cylinder Lock Screw: single slot___double slot(X form)____gas valve__mkg___
poppet________other notes, mkgs_________________________

Follower: D#__________Early______narrow front______wide front___________
slide: short nose_______long nose_____finish/color________mkg________#__________
Follower Arm: D#____________single bevel______double bevel_______prick punch____
contractor/i.d. code________no bevel______other mkg___finish/clr______
Bullet guide: D#/mfg____________________milled_____stamped______finish/clr_____
mkg/misc_____________ notched_________ notes:_______________

FOLLOWER ROD: D#_______________MKG___________Fin/color____________mfg__________
codes/#'s______short fork rd___flat____ short fork serr____milled____
long fork riveted__________notes______________ short fork riveted____

side 2, **Garand Data Sheet:**

Operating Rod: D#______________Mfg___________NM MKG.________Location mks__________
relief cut mod_____ handle side: flat___curved____ angle cut:slant__
finish/clr_____piston measurement_____condition_____ straight__
Op Rod catch: mkg/d#_______mkd on: inside____outside_____round front__sq front__
accelerator mark___finish/color_____letters, etc.________________
Clip Latch: D#__________Contractor mks.& letters:__________mk'd:outer__inner__
round front_____square front___ combination________open rear________
Op rod spring: round wire___ Keystone___ finish______
compensator spring____ sq. wire_______ finish______
rear handguard: D#__________op rod clearance cut___M1D____WRA___birch__wal__
other notes____
rear handguard band: d#__________grooved______milled_____stamped___WRA____clr__

---

lower band: d#______________milled/grooved__________arch_____flat pin_______
stock ferrule: D#__________milled_______stamped w/o hole____sm hole___lg hole__
no hole_____finish/color/codes/ltr_____________________________
rear swivel: notes and numbers, screws, etc_____________________________
front handguard: D#_____________early ferrule______N#____sharp/flat bottom
other notes:____

....

STOCK: walnut__birch__other___mkgs__________appx. mfg. date___________t.g.cut___
cartouche_________mfg._________(if known) ord. stamp: large__small___P_____
Def. ACC ST______Numbers, locations_____________________________
Butt Section: small hole over lg__holes same__mkgs, other____
buttplate: trapdoor___mkgs___________with border__w/o border___
no trapdoor ___notes/finish/color_____________________________
LOCATIONS AND SKETCHES:

REAR SIGHT NOTES

wndg knob #_______	elev. knob#_________________	base:mfg___code mkgs_________
fine chkr__________	fine chkr_________________	pt#_____color/finish_________
knurled___________	knurled____ mkgs___________	early:________________
lock nut__________	battle range ntd____________	late______________
cross bar, tran____	sht pinion_________________	cvr. mkgs____cvr grooves____
cross bar, std_____	long pinion:_______finish/clr__	cvr. prick punch_____clr/fin__
T105E1(Type 3)_____	pinion mkg____cond___________	location:outside__inside____
Coarse chkrd_______	coarse chkrd_________________	condition_______
AP NM___AP WRA_____	Arrows: open__closed__	with indents___w/o indents____
SA___HRA__PB__IHC__	With bottom grooves__w/o___	Notes: _______________
other_____________		
Notes_____________	Notes_______________	

LOADING FOR THE GARAND AND SIMILAR SEMIAUTOS

Reloading manuals are wonderful—they provide a safety net to the shooter/reloader and trim what could become a lifetime of work to a series of handy notations and intelligent suggestions. The latest Sierra materials, in particular, provide accuracy information based on exhaustive testing of Sierra's splendid line of bullets.

What reloading information seldom does, though, is relate the loads to the operation of automatic recocking systems—that is, high-powered semiautomatics. This means a pet load quite convenient for one's Mauser either won't operate the Garand's action, or it may beat up the gas system and operating rod, eventually leading to excess fatigue and/or breakage.

The loads listed here are designed and "peaked" to the Garand and its spin-offs and variants and are approximately ball equivalent—not necessarily in terms of pressure or velocity, but in terms of gas pressures generated in the gas system of this family of rifles.

You'll notice I haven't tabularized the velocity information; this you should test with your rifle. These loads were all tested at fairly high and fairly mild temperatures. We did no testing above 110°, none below 4°. With the exception of Hodgdon's VARGET, powders will generate different performances beyond these parameters. And by the way, ammo left in the sun on a hot day very quickly rises well above 110° Farenheit, so don't do that.

I specifically caution the reader against the indiscriminate use of either extant formula of 4350 or 4831 and any slower powders in the Garand or other gas-operated semiautos. These powders can work fine, but only at rather low velocity and power levels approximating .30/30.

This phenomenon is due to a coincidence of burn rate, expansion, and temperature in which these powders are hottest right where most rifles bleed off gas. Therefore, they can cause damage if used anywhere near full power.

Optimum bullet velocity windows were explained earlier in "The Practical M1 Garand" and, peripherally, in the historical overview. Another key factor in consistency—which, after all, is all accuracy really is—is a small one: the "pack" of the powder.

The arrangement of air space from shot to shot is always Data sheet.going to be more or less random—influenced by recoil, the violence of the action itself, position of rounds in the magazine or clip, and so on. But a powder that keeps the air space inside the round to a minimum will at least assure that the small influence of air space on burn and expansion rate is further diminished.

The following are some other tips that can contribute to accuracy with almost any rifle, but which are especially applicable to the Garand:

1. Find a way to either buy brass all of the same brand or, better yet, use brass finish, color codings, headstamps, and so on to code your loads. I try, for example, to keep all my .308 and .30-06 loads segregated in such a manner that I know any nickel-plated brass contains midrange match loads. I use Remington or Federal nickel- plated hulls.

I start *all* service loads on virgin Winchester primed brass. Heavy bullet loads—that is, long range ammo—is in Remington's conventional brass. Most of my experiments are done on GI hulls. There is no magic to my pattern. When doing "hot" loads or "gentle" stuff, I use nail polish of odd colors to code the cartridges either around the primer or in the extractor groove.

2. Within the above parameters, be sure each lot is fired the same number of times, trimmed identically, and handled the same. And you'll probably want to weigh the brass for ultra-precision loads. Remember, sensible handloaders use far more precise controls than any factory could afford to—not because it's cheaper (though it often is) but because the product works better. If it doesn't work better, you haven't read enough.

3. Extremely heavy and extremely light bullets require careful workup in the Garand and its derivatives. Light bullets (140 grains or less) require hefty powder supplies. Heavy bullets can beat up the guns, and my preference is to work very slowly with anything over 180 grains so as to develop just enough power to operate the rifle. There are very special procedures (talk to your armorer/smith) for potent, long-range loads, and there are some risks involved. But heavy match bullet loads are not available in factory fodder, so this is not an area where "off-the-shelf" is an option.

Lately, I have used ball powders almost exclusively for

any shooting that requires a lot of ammo quantity. BLC (2), 748, 760, H380 and some others measure very reliably and generate minimal fouling.

4064 and Hodgdon's new VARGET have lately become favorites for ultra-precison loads.

I use some Winchester primers, but I like CCI's "Benchrest" series for extruded powders and Federal's Match for ball powders in both .308 and .30-06.

Remington and CCI primers are relatively low pressure and must be used in their "Magnum" versions with ball powders. Federal and Winchester primers generate higher pressures and will work with ball or extruded powders.

The loads listed here should work fine in first quality commercial brass or military brass, though the thicker case walls of GI fodder produce slightly higher pressures.

NOTE: LOADS LISTED HERE ARE NOT IN ORDER OF BURN RATE OR RECOMMENDATION

147- to 150-gr. Military Ball or
Boattail Hollowpoint Bullets, Various Types
7.62x51/.308 Winchester

WW 748	45.5 gr.
IMR	39 gr.
IMR 4895	42 gr.
H 4895	41.6 gr.
BLC (2)	56.9 gr.
IMR 4064	44 gr. (VARGET very similar)
RE 12	44.9 gr.
RE 15	46.7 gr.
IMR 4064	46.1 gr. **

**Special accuracy load, from Sierra, for 150-grain BTHP for use with commercial brass only.

168-gr. Match BTHP, Various Brands

WW 748	43 gr.
IMR 3031	39 gr.
IMR 4895	40.5 gr
H 4895	40.1 gr.
IMR 4064	41.4 gr. **
RE 12	42.6 gr.
H380	47.8 gr.
BLC (2)	45 gr.

**Sierra accuracy load. VARGET very similar.

.30-06 Loads

NOTE: If you're using military brass, it's now quite old. You might want to check very carefully before using it. All these loads were worked up in Federal's nickel-plated "MUP" brass, which is of very uniform volume and weight.

.30 Cal. M1906 147- to 150-gr. Loads for Service or Match Style Fully-Jacketed Bullets

WW 760	55.1 gr.	IMR 4064	51.2 gr.**
IMR 4895	49 gr.	IMR 3031	48 gr
BLC (2)	50.7 gr.	H 450	63.3 gr.I
RE 19	60.8 gr.	MR 4064	50 gr. (VARGET very similar)

**Special accuracy load from Sierra, for 150-gr. BTHPs, in commercial brass only. VARGET very similar.

168-gr. BTBP Loads for Precision Shooting, Various Brands

IMR 3031	48 gr.	IMR 4895	47 gr.
H 4895	44.2 gr.	BLC (2)	46.5 gr.
RE 19	55.3 gr.	RE 15	46.6 gr.
WW 760	53.4 gr.	IMR 4064	45.9 gr.**

**Special accuracy load from Sierra. VARGET very similar.

NOTES: I have been using Winchester's inexpensive 147-grain boat-tail jacketed .30-caliber bullet, a bulk unit that sells for less than half what some of the others do. Loaders can use 150-grain loads, though some add .1 to .2 grains of powder. It is wise to quality control bulk bullets by weighing them and sorting into heavy, light, and medium batches.

These loads were worked up using Federal's 210GM primer.

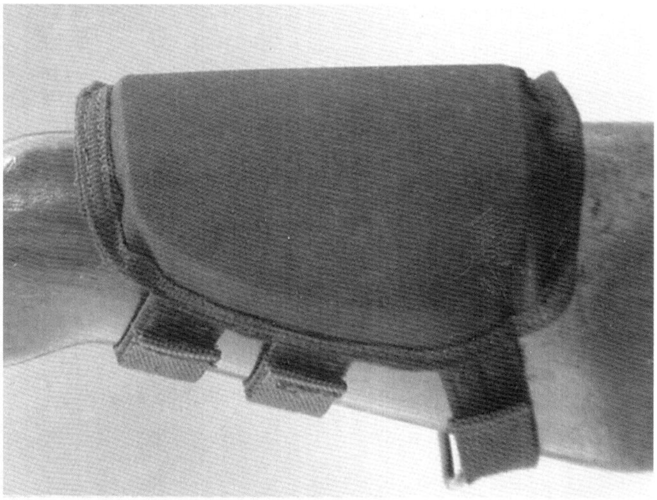

Smith's ambidextrous Kevlar/Cordura cheek-piece, designed to service almost any rifle, but especially tailored to the M1 and M14.

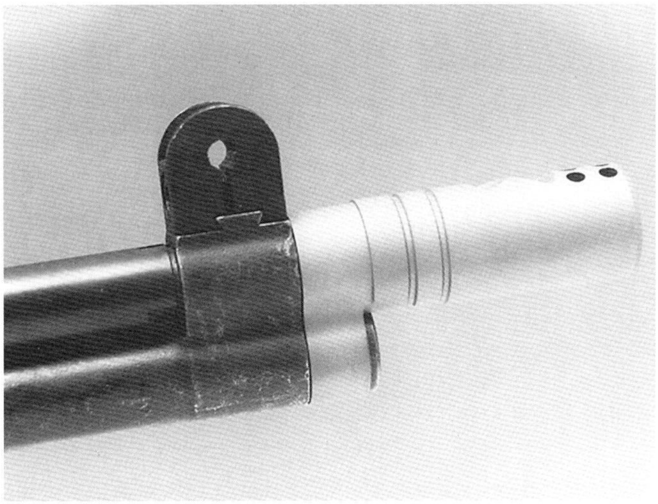

Smith's M1 Garand compensator, this one hard chromed.

Maker data panel, Winchestser WIN13—"D28291WIN-13" is the receiver right leg legend of the very last batch of WRA-produced M1 Garands, delivered at the very end in serial-number "patches" reserved for Springfield Armory, and usually arrayed in a hodge-podge of parts literally made up of whatever Winchester had lying around.

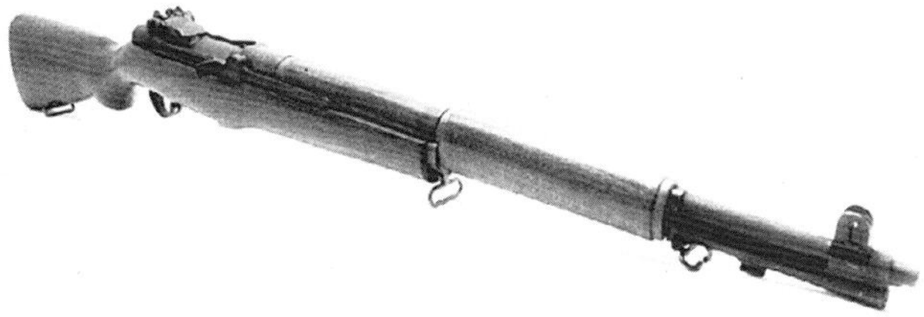

Bishop's standard format M1 stock of upgraded wood quality.

Reinhart Fajen made heavy match stocks for the M1 Garand.

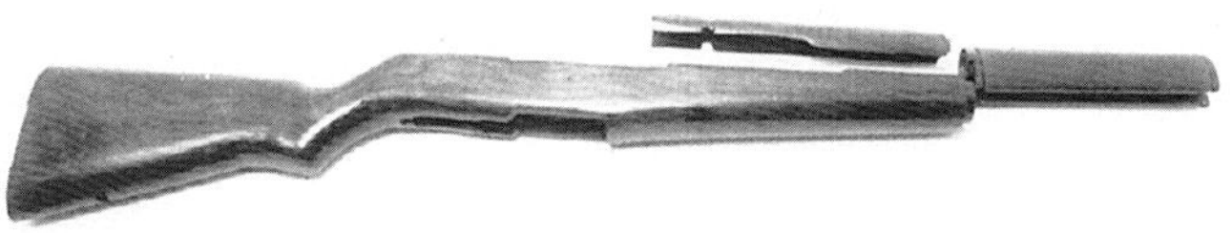

Complete set of M1 stock and handguards from Fajen, standard grade.

Typical late World War II barrel markings are represented by this 1944 specimen, found on a 2005 Civilian Marksmanship Program rifle, one of the Greek return rifles. Note that there are additional detail markings, including the part number, on top of the barrel.

The ball powders can work brilliantly in both M1 calibers. They measure consistently, and they burn cleanly and uniformly. W-W (Olin) 760 is very slow for the M1, but with very careful workup, decent accuracy can be had at reduced power levels. Documentation and chronograph work is imperative.

Federal's M1 Garand loads are more accurate than G.I. M2 ball, but also far less powerful. Point of impact is generally 1.5" or so lower even at 100 yards. However, the brass, contrary to rumors, holds up almost as well as heavier military fodder, *if* fired in tight chambered barrels.

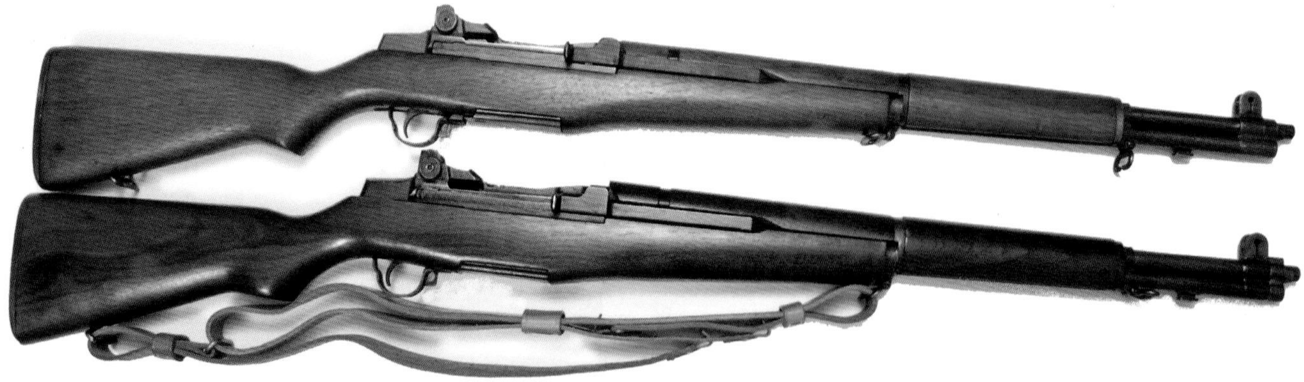

The top rifle is a near mint Springfield Armory official National Match rifle, caliber .30. It was tuned up slightly for test and carefully lubricated, then shot about two clips to assure stock seating. The lower rifle is a fairly casual, home-brewed .308. It was ready to go. Both using best handloads, the arsenal "NM" could barely stay under two minutes of angle accuracy, and that not for long. The .308 shot sub MOA consistently, some eight-shot strings being even more precise. So much for "pedigree."

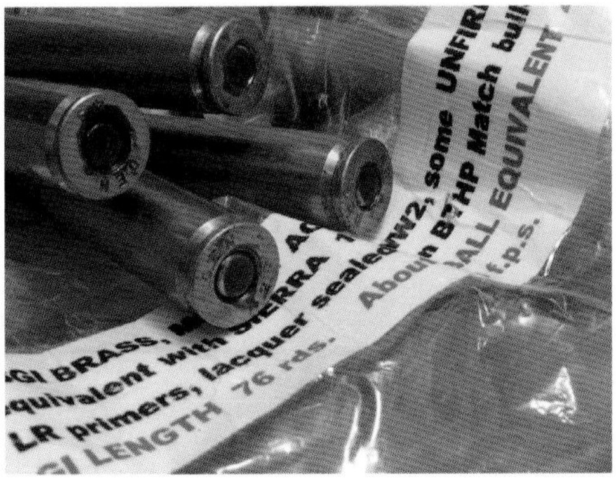

"New" can mean many things. These loads were done on brass that was old enough to retire—that is, sixty-five-plus years!—but unfired and used in "pull-down" configuration. This was loaded with tedious precision and attention to trim length, and topped with Sierra's 150-grain BTHP. The ancient corrosive primers were excised, modern non-corrosives added. Seated to full length. They shot groups HALF the size of most M2 ball and smaller. Of course the non-cannelured bullets (a cannelure is that striated set of pressed marks where real M2 bullets are seated into cases) and much more modern shape were some of that. Just to complete the authentic look of these, Lee Templin and the author even lacquered the primers and surrounding area with reddish-purple lacquer.

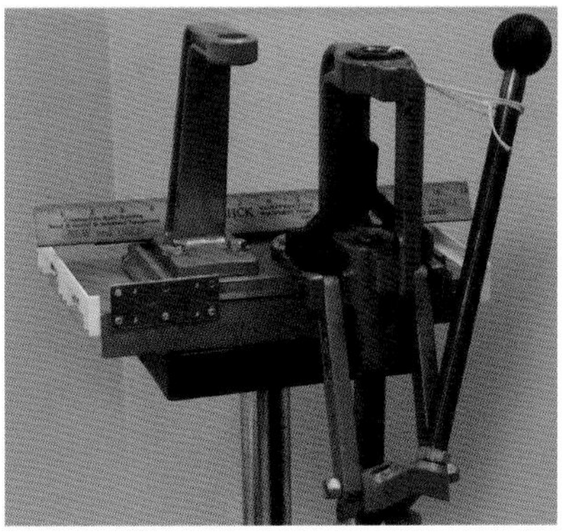

The author's old Rockchucker RCBS press and stand for his powder measure, tied off for storage, didn't take up much valuable floor space at all. The Rockchucker is a fine, powerful press, but it cannot be as fast as a multi-station (progressive) press. However, the unit takes up nineteen inches across the old Midway table base, is just over thirty-two inches, and can provide truly great ammunition. Yes, reloading generally saves some money, but eats time. *Precision* and *accuracy* are the main reasons to reload, not cost savings, at least with the M1. The author always uses his with some kind of tray or sheeting under the press, to catch cast-off spent primers.

Ancient pull-down G.I. brass (never fired, old G.I. bullets pulled, pocket reamed, new, non-corrosive primer utilized) from the forties is very uniform, even by today's standards, but Lee Templin and the author still weighed, measured, and "uniformed" every hull and powder charge, measuring and trimming and doing all the recommended steps, thus eventually yielding ammo even in the ancient Caliber .30 that was stunningly better than ancient ball or armor-piercing rounds.

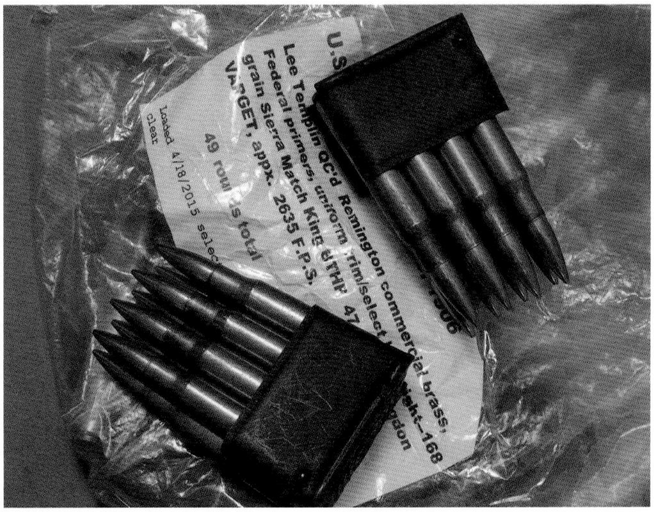

It seems so logical and almost automatic, but it's a safety and data imperative: Every round loaded and even factory rounds should be documented and labeled. Once tested and chronographed, data MUST be written, hard copy, with ammunition, and fully explained for use. Even the intention of the load should be clearly readable, such as "500-yard target load" or "low-recoil rounds." Everything should also be dated. In the author's case, even the designator can have meaning, as do primer colorant codes, especially when testing for publication.

BIBLIOGRAPHY

Perhaps the most useful publication for the Garand buff who wishes to immerse himself in this legendary firearm is the GCA Newsletter, from the Garand Collector's Association, the address of which is listed in the marketplace.

For the purist collector, nothing can equal Scott A. Duff's two- volume set on the old rifle: *The M1 Garand of World War Two and The M1 Garand: Post World War Two.*

The following two are inexpensive items, primarily useful for the shooter:

Rifle, National Matches. United States Army Weapons & Munitions Command, 1963. (Usually about $4.95.)

The M1 Rifle. National Rifle Association Publications, Washington, D.C. revised in 1985. ($3.95).

The books listed below demonstrate and explain the Garand and the principles behind the rifle. There are other publications with better technical illustrations, but these two contain a lot of information for a reasonable price. They are somewhat dated, and there are some research errors (easily corrected by referral to GCA publications).

Book of the Garand, Maj. Gen. Julian S. Hatcher. Infantry Journal Press, Washington, D.C. Updated in 1977.

Know Your M1 Garand, E.J. Hoffschmidt. Blacksmith Publishers, Chino Valley, AZ. 1975.

Many retired armorers retain copies of various War Department/Department of Defense Technical Operations Orders and manuals that pertain to specific parts and procedure. These are worth copying.

BOOK II

THE CLASSIC M1 GARAND

Preface

Three of John Garand's progeny under test in the mid-eighties. On the left, an excellent International Harvester, in the center a Smith Enterprises International M14, and on the right, a 1943 Springfield with a "reverse looped" 3-hook B.A.R. sling and new barrel.

This is *practical* history, not *industrial* history. Oh, as noted, there is some industrial material in this missive, but that is not the central matter or value.

Just as it's about a practical and historic rifle, it's involved with practical men and a historic rifle, and of course, the parts they played.

Lyman H. Pollock was one of the best, steadiest men I ever knew. When Alzheimer's claimed him in June of 2000, my overwhelming thought was how lucky I'd been to just meet the man. I was able to thank him and present him with a copy of my 1998 M1 Garand book from Paladin, but the latter Garand volume from that now-defunct publisher was just finishing up the editorial process when he died.

As the years wore on, he spoke less and less of World War II, and if he spoke much about it at all, it was the funny or heartwarming stories he'd repeat. We suspected he had forgotten a lot, too.

In 1986, with his sons along and participating, we took a rather robust collection of M1s and M14s and a few

A 1943 M1 rifle is shown with Lyman H. Pollock's World War II mementoes. Lyman was with 2nd Armored Division, 3rd Army, and drove a variety of different M-2 based half tracks. It was from him the author first learned the nature of Mister Garand's great rifle.

Often thought of as the manliest of firearms, this is at the very least an oversimplification. In the '80s these ladies were observed and photographed at the Rio Salado range in Mesa, Arizona, sighting in their very own M1s.

handguns to the Rio Salado Sportsman's Club range in Mesa, Arizona. It was April, not long after I began seventeen long years in that desolate, depressing part of the upper Sonora. Crisp in the morning, the day warmed up, and so did we all, shooting better as the day wore on.

He was about five-foot-five, weighed all of 130 pounds, but I could tell immediately that, despite his not handling an M1 in about forty years, he regarded the old rifle as an old friend, and his hands and muscle memory were working *just fine.* Both my "enhanced" service rifle and my "competition" M1 he ran at least as smoothly as I did, and I'd been shooting not more than two weeks earlier at Angeles Forest range in Los Angeles, with the very same firearms.

He was, offhand and kneeling, quite close to as reliable and accurate with the rifle as I was, and I was twenty-one years younger. I did some prone shooting, since my arthritis hadn't gotten to the point where it was difficult to assume and recover. Not so lucky, Lyman declined. Prone, I shot as well as off the bench, rested, oftentimes better. I also shot several times each week, and had for a very long time. Key fact: he'd learned the rifle well, long ago, and still retained the habits and knowledge.

We were partially packed up to leave, when he looked through the 20–60X spotting scope, noting at the 100 meter line an unperforated target.

He smoothly slapped an eight-round *en bloc* clip into the rifle, then as we spoke he slipped the safety back into "on" position.

My late good friend, Bob Katsch, about 1985, in a lucky shot where I was able to catch an ejected *en bloc* clip still in the air. Bob was a Korea-era veteran, who very much admired the Garand, and until this day, he hadn't fired one in thirty years. This was my 2.5 millionth "service enhanced" rifle that I rebarreled and mildly accurized.

A marking on a Winchester *en bloc* clip. I ran across several dozen of these about 2010, and sold them for $20–100 each. They're actually special *only* because they were made by Winchester in New Haven.

"Let me show you a little something I learned at Bastogne. See, we were shooting a lot, our shoulders got sore, and the *Volksies* weren't very good shots, so we stepped to gaps in any barricades, standing up, and we did this . . . "

I was still pondering, figuring "Volksies" referred to Hitler's *Volksturm Wehrmacht,* the NSDAP rightist equivalent of the home guard, and while still trying to picture their armbands and makeshift uniforms, eight rounds flew out of the rifle he held firm to his right hip, departing the M1 in perhaps five or six seconds, not quite machine gun fast, but still breathtakingly quick.

I went down, peeled off the last paper targets, and strolling back from downrange, held the group just generated over my chest. All eight were in the black of the big G.I. target, more of a scattergun pattern than a real group, I thought. Not impressive. Not at all.

Right.

Years later, having tentatively practiced off and on, I managed to isolate time, several more outings with a much superior set of rifles, taking two entire days to pound hell out of my hip bone, trying in vain to equal or exceed Lyman's standard. I never did. I never really came close. Thus came the epiphany.

He had learned the rifle and that particular skill not for a casual or recreational set of reasons. He'd practiced it, probably under fire, but most likely, beforehand not, complete with all the "aim the body, not the rifle" movements, such that doing it some four decades later, just for fun, was easy. And it was *just for fun* . . . he'd told me that about the Garand for decades, and now we'd enjoyed it together.

He'd told us about "treetoppers" in the Huertgen Forest, German Arado 234 jets at Remagen, German tanks knocking out over a dozen Sherman tanks and lots of half tracks before P-47s and Typhoons put them either on the junk pile or the run.

He'd told us, too, about relieving the German "satellite" labor camp/*konzentrationslager* and the horrors encountered there. It came out in little pieces in front of the television, usually on Sunday, as my older brother and myself asked him about what was being discussed on the historical programs.

He'd explained bailing out of "half a dozen" halftracks, usually because, "With a Tiger sitting, say, 25 yards ahead of you, boresighted right where you are, and two Panthers ripping alongside your column, there's nothing much else that makes sense."

He'd told us, too, about terrible injuries from broken operating rods. "Ice or mud in the last inch of the barrel. Tremendous pressure. Nasty stuff. Lots of blood." It was rare, he noted, but he showed us an old warning paper, folded sheet, mimeographed, I think, reminding troops to check their muzzles over the winter in case they were blocked. The paper fell apart about 1959, and he just threw it away.

Most of the stories we doubted.

There was no doubt of his tales for any reason other than his entire demeanor seemed way too "unmilitary" and easy-going, way too funny, entirely unlike the movie characters John Wayne played. His life was simple, straightforward, well ordered, but civilized, very, very civilian. When he left the service, he seemed to leave it completely. He'd been in Patton's 2nd Armored Division, briefly transferred out "for training and organization" to 8th Armored Division, then back to the Second. Never once did he go to a reunion, albeit he did once accompany a co-worker to a 32nd Division reunion.

After that gathering, about 1962, he wisecracked that, "Some of their artillery and a lot of their engineers wound up in Europe; everybody else was in the Pacific!" He found that "typical of the Army.'

Lyman was never one of those who digs through his medals and decorations periodically as if to verify he had been there.

While he faded, that line came to mind from Spielberg's superb *Saving Private Ryan*. It was uttered by the captain as he lay dying, his lifeblood trickling onto the cobblestones. "Earn it!" The film's title character, of course, had been saved by his peers, at great cost. The line, however, is also about earning a normal life.

In the tradition of Cincinattus, American wartime soldiers have primarily gone back to civilian life with relief. He did once enunciate, "Sometimes a fellow has to talk about the ugly stuff, or it haunts and chews." We recalled his conversations at length and involving the consumption of much local brew at family reunions, in particular with my uncle Perry Scott, a 101st Airborne veteran, several other uncles who'd been infantry in both theaters, and so on. Some of that was scary and ugly. They obviously spewed the messy stuff *only* with each other, apparently to relieve the nightmares.

He made brutal remarks about Patton, Holocaust deniers, fascism and ultra-right politics in general, and certain kinds of shifty business practices that reminded him of "the rot that almost destroyed the world." He had only an eighth grade education, but referred me to Fritz Thyssen's *I Paid Hitler* (1940) and other works on the origin of Nazism and fascism.

Looking back, six decades or more after those episodes in front of what we came to call the "boob tube," we came to realize why we so appreciated the M1, the Browning Automatic Rifle, even the foreign weapons of the period.

We cannot forever retain these men, their vigor, spirit, and stories. We can't really grasp the forces—terror, desperation, and that empty feeling that "this just might go on *forever*."

We *can retain* some of the hardware as symbols and souvenirs. The M1 was an American design, reliable, powerful, fast, accurate, and very seriously different from anyone else's infantry rifle.

It was designed by a brilliant, Canadian-born engineer, manufactured mostly in New England, and carried by advancing infantry all over the world. It changed tactics, spreading firepower to every soldier, with the full range of a real rifle and a rate of accurate fire close enough to a machine gun that it wasn't wise for enemies to place too much value on the automatic weapon belching rounds.

A rare Breda receiver.

The quality of our personnel wasn't created by the M1 Garand, but the slick rifle made it easier to instrument in the field. More than anything, it was the tough, resourceful enlisted man, the brilliant amateur, the one who hunkered down, fought like hell, protected his buddies, and kept finding new ways to make the enemy's life difficult.

In fact, though many editors have, without my permission, inserted George Patton's overblown, hyperbolic remarks about the M1 into articles of mine, even utilized the exaggeration as a sales device, I have never once quoted General Patton on *anything* in print, and seldom, if ever, even verbally.

It's a family thing, you see, for whenever his name came up, rather crude remarks about "blood 'n guts" (usually, "It was our blood and our guts, he only provided the hot air!") and things far more brutal would reverberate. Many who served in Second Armored Division during World War II felt that way, and after hearing some of the ugly stories, so did many relatives and friends.

The M1, vast numbers of improved radios, much more rolling stock—trucks, half tracks, towing vehicles, Jeeps—revised unit organizations, streamlined the incorporation of the B.A.R. into every squad, and often, into each fire team, the easy availability of the .50 Caliber support weapon for long range fire, and rafts of other upgrades encompassed the United States' infantry outfits. Every other military ground organization had tried to do similar things, but only the United States had spread massive firepower *downward* the way the US did, with the great M1 Garand rifle.

In the entire period of 1939–45, if an item was military and American, it worked, usually swiftly and efficiently, and this was especially so of the typical American fighting man.

We cannot conveniently or cheaply afford or preserve Sherman tanks or 105mm. artillery pieces. Most of us, even if we could afford those artifacts, lack storage space for them. But many of us own M1s; a lot of us own many.

Even if the rifle was made in Italy or long after the war, never once does one peer into the peep sight without thinking about the much earlier events.

It's one of those brilliant, vintage ideas one can constantly upgrade, play with, use to entertain oneself, and occasionally do what hard core collectors do constantly: pose the inevitable question, "What would this thing say if it could talk?"

Now, in the case of the rifles I own now, one in particular would enunciate: "I was made in Italy about 1955, spent a long time in Denmark, and then wound up here!" The last 1.4 million I built up for a close friend, however, showed evidence of two wartime refurbishments (these are often called "rebuilds", but more often, they're simpler than that!). It might have been training wear, but it sure had been fired a lot. The Winchester pictured in this work with my brother-in-law's World War II items shows heavy evidence of blood or salt water on its left side, and likely for quite some time. It probably didn't get that way in a rifle rack at Fort Dix.

This is a legacy at once simple and immediate and complicated and obscure. The "greatest generation" taught us that freedom is worth fighting for, and once in a while, *must* be fought for. Even now, I try every day to do some thing, however small, to make the community where I reside better and more liberated. This never involves firearms, and if it's done right, perhaps need never demand any kind of violence.

Don't kid yourself. Even in supposedly "firearms friendly" states, folks can move against individuals in a vehemently anti-gun way, often just to make a point. It's been tried, unsuccessfully, on me, and it's rather startling how the duplicity and hypocrisy are deployed to cheat people.

What collectors and shooters of the M1 Garand and similar equipment are trying to do is to both preserve and understand a legacy, and indeed, to develop it further, by breathing life into this venerable, sturdy, famous old tool.

In the past decade, family members of both genders and ages down to twelve have found this ancient old beast is surprisingly easy to use and feels modern, properly taught.

That's the legacy most of us ought to ponder and enlarge.

While shooting, imagine a Japanese or German or Italian infantryman, yanking and cranking a few rounds by hand out of his rifle, while, say, you and a buddy alternate 16 rounds for a while. It's not a real happy situation!

Long after I'm gone, hopefully, there will be others carrying on the legacy.

PRODUCTION OF THE M1

In total, six million M1 Garands might have been made. Well over 5.4 million US military, around 100 thousand

Mike Grimslid shoots a .308 H&R M1 Garand in 2012.

The author with Mike and Nick Grimslid, all holding their M1s, in 2004.

Italian units, and civil, cast specimens probably account for another 100 thousand or so. And those are minimal figures.

No truly reliable estimate of Italian production by Breda and Beretta is available, but there were Italian contracts known for well over 50,000 rifles, to include the Italian services, Denmark, Indonesia, Nigeria, Ethiopia, Yemen, Colombia, and supposedly Egypt and many others, albeit apparently many of those contracts and quantities are still regarded as confidential. Indeed, I'd been told the Italian-produced rifles numbered half a million or more. I've later learned, officially, that seems to have been about ten times higher than the actual totals. I like empirical evidence, and that seems very low even now—but I am *compelled* to use the figure, regardless.

M1's have been advertised for sale as early as 1948; Galef and Abel and others bringing rifles onto the US market at prices that seemed very high.

There has also been considerable production of cast-receivered versions produced by civilian firms, albeit no one at the moment this is written has M1 Garand receivers in production.

There in fact *were* production and service M1 Garands in 7.62x51mm. produced on both sides of the Atlantic, and in fact the rare 6,000,000+ range H&R the author purchased at a gun show in the 1980s was part of a "blip" set apparently intended to provide cartridge test platforms at the Harrington and Richardson factory. The prototypes were all in the .276 Pedersen Centerfire cartridge, a far more efficient and modern loading which was discarded because of endless millions of .30-06 rounds still on hand in US inventories.

There are few permutations in overall and barrel

Detail of a Tipo 2 barrel from March 1963.

length, and among these only the Italian "Tipo 2" is fairly common. There are weight variations, owing to the variable density of walnut. Standard barrel length is 24." Overall length of the rifle is 43.6." Normal weight is 9.6 pounds, but some rifles are slightly lighter, dense walnut rifles considerably more, and with bayonet, ammo, and sling, can be several pounds heavier. The eight-round *en bloc* spring ejected clip was controversial right from adoption, but the Ordnance Board had insisted upon an internal setup within these parameters.

The .30/06 M1 Garand was a re-design of the .276 Pedersen centerfire original, designed for the current M1 ball ammunition with its 172-grain bullet. Later, a typical M2 ball propelled a 147- to 152-grain jacketed bullet at just over 2800 feet per second, albeit it was noted from the rifle's very inception that the one turn in ten-inch, right-hand twist rifling and precisely cut bores tended to shoot more accurately with heavier bullets. My rifles, with one turn in twelve-inch custom barrels evince less errant "flyer" rounds.

THE MARKET, RIFLES, AND SOME POLITICS

It helps no one, really, that since the Columbine massacre, it is larger magazine firearms that many have decided are the technological "bad guys" of the industry. There are folks looking for simple solutions to complicated issues, and neither mental illness nor a particular type of weapon is a suitable diagnostic conclusion that covers mass violence. What matters is we need to be aware the M1 might one day be targeted, regardless of whether it's ever involved in any actual violence or not.

We're running out of M1 Garands worldwide, regardless, so by definition, traffic will slow down very soon. Then, too, as the last personnel who trained with them in the late '60s and early '70s die off and retire, interest may wax and wane like the moon, and perhaps relative prices might decline.

Denmark, Greece, Turkey, most of Latin America, the Philippine Islands, several smaller Asian entities, South Korea, and most of the remainder of the world have returned their M.A.P. program rifles. Italy reconfigured most of theirs into Tipo I and Tipo II rebuilds in 7.62x51mm., detail welding the markings but retaining US serial numbers, and eventually scrapping many. The reality is, there are very few M1 Garands that will be introduced to new civilian owners in years to come, and eventually, perhaps in my lifetime, the Civilian Marksmanship Program will also run dry.

Fajen and Bishop are now part of the Midway Arms Empire, and will never again independently produce wood rifle stocks. Only Boyd's reliably produces butt stocks and handguards in the US, and solid G.I. wood is almost gone, having long since ceased to be inexpensive.

A few others produce Garand stocks, Wenig among them, but their production is small. I was unable, despite extensive attempts at contact, to obtain a Wenig specimen for photography, despite willingness to pre-pay. The few I

Right side overall view of a low-numbered .308 CMP "Special" with Criterion barrel and reproduction M.1907 leather sling, purchased in 2013.

Closeup right view of a reproduction "locking bar" rear sight installed on a CMP .308 M1 "Special" ordered in 2013. The decision was made, mainly as a pastime, to make this rifle into a visual representation of an early war M1, albeit of course, it was in an obviously CMP stock with that cartouche, and in another loading entirely. This is for "eyeball" appeal. Were it to be shot constantly, it would bear a fine adjustment NM2A sight set, and the locking bar set would be back in the parts box for the next hair-brained project.

Nick Grimslid's gift M1, a .308 rifle that the author contrived (it is very close to being a true competition rifle) to make appear "authentic World War II" externally. The cartouche is re-struck by a local smith on a fatigued old stock, the rod is the correct vintage but safety modified, the handguards just fatigued enough to look real, but the barrel is a wonderful stainless steel Wilson, its last several inches painted with high temperature enamel to look "normal." It was a gift to the young man upon the occasion of concluding his tour in the United States Marine Corps.

The stainless-steel Wilson barrel of a .308 M1 Garand.

have owned were excellent, but the company can be difficult to contact. There are intermittent Italian and even Latin American mahogany wood products for the rifle, but these are not easy to find or acquire.

Wilson no longer produces the wonderful barrels they used to make for Fulton and others. The current Fulton products, of course, are excellent. Springfield Armory, Incorporated, no longer sells barrels independently. Citadel has moved to far northern California, but their latest production ca. 2017 or so has been very good. We have been unable to determine if the heavy units or their former, very nice M1D barrel/collar kits are still produced, or even if they will be again. The myth of "cheap Chinese M1 barrel and M1D kits" was never real, nor are most of the malarkey confabulations along those lines. There are, after twenty-some years of poking the odd toe into the marketplace, some excellent Chinese sight parts, butt plates, and so on, even being sold by the CMP itself. But barrels from Criterion and Krieger, including the relatively new "service" weight/match quality Krieger, continue in production. There are *no* Chinese barrels for the M1 Garand, and it is unlikely there ever will be.

There *are* open civilian market, unmarked M1 Garand barrels made in Germany, from Lothar Walther. As one might expect, they are very pricey, but reports from users (I was unable to acquire one for test) are glowingly positive. Other high-priced independents, including Douglas and Barnett, produce barrels for the Garand.

For those who wonder, with a carefully prepped rifle

in .308, a heavy barrel, excellent ammunition, and solid bedding, yes, the M1 Garand can be an M.O.A. or better rifle. But one cannot get there casually, and staying there demands preparation and maintenance.

Hugh Sutherland and a couple of others who have acquired such rifles from me, even unbedded, have explained that such accuracy is attainable, just as I explained to them it was. Sutherland's barrel is a tested Citadel "heavy" in .308, tightly chambered, and the free floating was done by hand over weeks of time. It was to be "my special rifle" forever, until my car needed major repairs. There are several others in new hands, still performing at that level, and yet there are those who persist and loudly explain this is "not even possible." One wonders: why do the targets, witnesses, co-participants, and tapes exist?

BMF is gone. So is their straight pull kit.

It's important to spread the "gospel of the rifle," and along those lines, I've worked to introduce Mister Garand's machine and a wide variety of permutations to family members, even though my own shooting skills are eroded by arthritis, C.O.P.D., ulnar and carpal tunnel and other old age issues. Still, the more reverence and good feeling

An old Danish Breda receiver the author built with heavy Citadel barrel, relieved original handguards, and "tightened up" but not bedded butt stock now belongs to Hugh Sutherland, who notes that it shoots sub-minute-of-angle groups with rather ordinary ammunition. It is, of course, a commercially tight-chambered .308, one of the test rifles from my molycoat and barrel wear testing which had to be sold off when it became obvious that decade of testing was never going to see publication. Several of my old test crew had noted it was that accurate and better with decent handloads. (Hugh Sutherland photo, with his permission)

toward this old rifle, the better off we'll be. It's never been a common rifle for criminal activity, being too large and heavy and powerful for that sort of operator . . . and yes, very soon, firearms suppression by type and by name and characteristic will again take hold.

Count on it.

WASTED EXPERIMENTS

From 1992 until about 2009, I spent a great deal of time and money shooting Garands off the bench, heavily sandbagged and rested, testing various incarnations of molycoated bullets. This was done very carefully, every round documented, every target saved. Bullets were weighed and measured.

That entire study has now graced a landfill or been burned to ash since about 2012. It was a fad that came and went, and what we discovered was that the precisely applied coatings did not have any deleterious impact on accuracy, but those "tumbled on" coatings done by indifferent amateurs could be frightening erratic at high velocities. This mattered less, as one might expect, with heavier bullets. This mattered hardly at all with pistol bullets.

Finally, toward the very end, and because of the tight controls, it was determined that molycoated bullets, used consistently, do diminish throat wear on the M1 Garand and other rifles. And that effect is substantial. It pointed to almost doubling the usable life of a standard barrel. However, many users pointed out, the meticulous bore preparation before commencing fire to avoid "skid effect" was enough of a nuisance that, with the added cost of preparation, the material was unworthy of further experimentation.

It mattered hardly at all. Most of the products have become obscure, discontinued, and largely forgotten.

The last of my factory-coated Sierra bullets are now in .308 brass, and will go through my Breda rifle this summer of 2019.

This section will develop more information on contracted delivery dates (the somewhat apocryphal "born on" dates collectors seem to crave!) and on the nuts and bolts of details like tuning the M1 Garand trigger.

There was, some may recall, a time when I had remarked that, "I would not be surprised if there were no Breda M1s!" That was "tongue in cheek" or if you prefer, "grain of salt" stuff. At that time, I'd never seen one. I have since owned several, all former Danish specimens. They're quite rare, and always will be. Indeed, any Italian-made military M1 Garand other than a Danish Beretta will remain very uncommon. The high numbered (best information is that very few Italian M1s were EVER numbered above 10,000, none over 15,000) receivers, Tipo 1 and Tipo 2 receivers seem to be reconfigured, marking microwelded US Military Aid receivers, and in fact the first one I handled, marked "Breda," was very obviously a Winchester by serial number and shape conformation.

The Beretta "uncrested" units brought in by the SAI/ Reese group were real Beretta, but were *never* military.

There is, in fact, a massive body of evidence suggesting that few, if any, Italian-made M1 receivers ever saw duty in that form in the Italian military. My Italian ordnance and collector sources stipulate that as fact, albeit it is interesting that many of the NATO rifles that showed up at Interarms in the 1960s bore US receivers, all the rest of the array being Italian produced.

A Danish issue Beretta M1 in 7.62x51.

A Danish issue Breda receiver, developed by the author as "The Mutt," with laminated custom stock, South Korean gas cylinder, German Sauer and Son bolt, Winchester follower, US IHC safety, "RA" marked "National Match" operating rod, several Springfield and H&R parts, some Beretta bits and pieces, and generally something from almost every M1 Garand contractor (not all the small parts—that's simply impossible!) somewhere. It's a precision .308 with one of Wilson's last stainless steel 1 turn in 12" barrels, painted black over the last ten inches or so of the barrel.

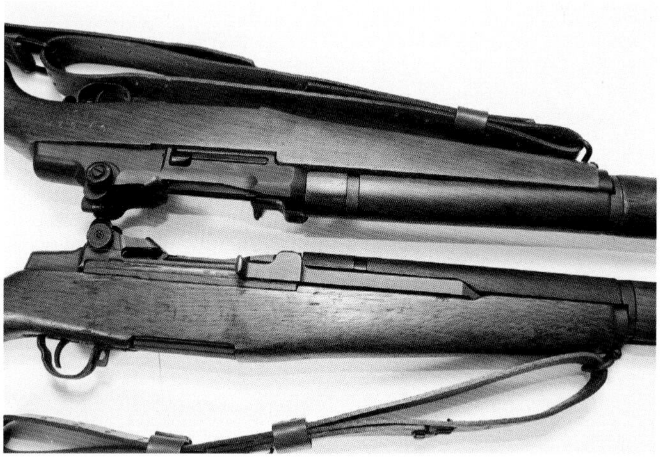

Comparison shot TIPO II on top (these are BOTH in .308/.62x51, with commercial configuration chambers), high quality civilian full-length match conversion below. Note the position of the lower band and the amount of wood behind the lower handguard ("rear") band ("clip"). It's subtle, but it's there. By the way, this very dark phosphate is not "Greek black"; it is either original finish or a very good approximation thereof. Most original phosphate is similar to this. That light to medium gray stuff is virtually always a refinish, and usually very recent, most of the time purely civilian. Nor do all parts on M1s match, save in a very, very few cases—the metals are different, they take finish differently, and different kinds of finish were frequently applied to the same rifle. The "matched finish" military rifle is almost entirely the product of the hyperactive imaginations of fledgling collectors.

PART I

THE ONGOING HISTORY OF THE M1 GARAND

The Complete M1 Garand" was designed from the outset to be the first single book to address the M1 as a shooting machine, collector's item, and artifact, in a volume directed to the reloader, technician, competition shooter, and perhaps even a kid contemplating purchasing the old war horse. In the past, there were books for collectors, books for shooters, manuals, and technical/mechanical books, none of which had enough overlap to automatically be applicable for everyone who enjoys the M1.

But the history of the rifle didn't end in 1957 or even in 1992. The gun confiscation lobby wants to end that long parade, much as it wants to end the history of firearms in general, at least among people who are not wealthy, and an elitist calumny that the M1 is "ideal for gangbangers" has resulted in a ban upon the further civilian importation of the M1. Other than the patently obvious fact that people who say such ridiculous things have never lived in the ghetto—which I did, for most of twenty-three years, where mechanisms with the bulk and weight of the Garand are regarded with looks of absolute bafflement—such fantasies demonstrate how targeting and scapegoating work for the forces of elitism. As well, the currencies of exchange in the cutthroat world of the crack dealer, the speed freak, the burglar, the casual criminal, and the lower elements of disorganized crime are chemical, legal tender, and cheap or stolen handguns and large- magazine short guns of much smaller dimensions. If there's ever been a low-level armed robbery or drive-by shooting with an M1 Garand, it's buried very deep in somebody's records. Not, mind you, that facts, logic, and truth mean anything to the elitists who, when the rest of us have been disarmed, will still be able to afford cadres of gun-wielding goons.

The M1 is the most popular high-powered target semiautomatic in the world, and probably the strongest. It is also

The M1 is a rifle that can tear up a digit, and it requires some background in mechanical principles to operate properly. Even loading clips is beyond the capability of many crooks, and getting them into the rifle would remain a puzzlement.

the last actual issue US military rifle that can be owned by a civilian without the financial and paperwork nightmares of an National Firearms Act (NFA)- registerable receiver.

Much against my better judgment—because such items are frequently thought of as chapter and verse—I am including in this volume date charts and guidelines for US-produced M1 rifles, emphasizing World War II production. These are guides only and must be treated as such. The notes in the charts, drawn from Garand Collectors Association (GCA) documentation, Duff, dozens of other sources, and my own research on the rifles themselves, are probably more important than the dates themselves. Firearms, especially during World War II, were not built to please collectors or fill logbooks; barrels available were put on receivers as available, and sometimes even major changes in production did not arrive kerblam on one particular serial number. More important is the general production pattern, very simply expressed by the real rule of the M1's production life: from inception to the end of military forged-receiver production, everything got better. The difference between a -2 receiver of 1940–41 and a -35 of 1945 is profound.

The difference in quality of detail fit and finish between, say, 1942 and 1955 is at least as great.

Thanks to the importation of considerable numbers of parts kits and a few more receivers, we now know a great deal more about Italian production in general, and the Danish lots in particular. It is unlikely that we'll ever know everything about Italian M1 production and markings, since these guns were ordered in many small variants and permutations of marking and numbering, but it is now possible to detail Breda production and accurately show Danish receiver markings, both of which I at one time thought might be fictional.

CHAPTER 1

THE TACTICAL HISTORY OF THE M1 GARAND: SOME THOUGHTS, RECOLLECTIONS, AND ANALYSIS

The "fire-and-maneuver" tactics that made the World War II American infantry unit so formidable evolved in direct response to the nightmare of World War I. Many traditionalists in the military had opposed all the changes necessary to institute these new concepts and, ironically, some of those people wound up benefiting from the new concepts of movement, fire base, communications, and logistics.

All the competing designs in the development of the M1—and the M1 itself—were designed around a new family of 7mm cartridges similar to the concepts, originally British, intended for the Pattern 13 and, in turn, similar to the .280 Ross. These cartridges featured faster burning powders, excellent accuracy, high orders of sectional density, and somewhat reduced muzzle blast and recoil. (Copper fouling, however, would have been a problem.) Early on, the radicals behind all this activity envisioned, as well, all-tracked infantry and support; radios and communications gear everywhere; and everything fast, flexible, and efficient.

The American military, from 1919 to 1941, was comparatively tiny. But despite the calls for isolationism emanating from the American right wing, by 1932 any rational analyst of world affairs knew there would be another "big one," most likely covering two oceans and, therefore, much bigger than the last one. The services and designers toiled quietly and on a shoestring until the Great Depression sucked the life and the money out of virtually all but the smallest development programs.

Revisionist historians often like to mull over how much better off the United States might have been had more money been directed to the military during the Depression, rather than toward civilian programs, but the facts and the hardware involved would have meant that by the time we entered the war in late 1941 we'd have had vast quantities of inappropriately trained personnel and obsolete, expensive equipment quite incapable of fighting the real war. Masses of P-26, P-36, and P-40 fighter planes to fight the war of the 1940s might have inspired confidence somewhere, but the simple truth is that new designs just coming off drawing boards were what was needed, and had a huge inventory of the earlier hardware been purchased already, the long-term effect would have been to set back the progressive programs that actually mattered. For example, despite the fact that leading-edge tank designs that originated here were developed elsewhere, the armored vehicles our government could have acquired early would have been obsolete by 1940 and the United States simply could not spend the money for capital-intense durable goods, and dared not spend on the sinkhole of dead-end military goods. America's wounds from the Great Depression required healing, and priorities were in directions other than military monuments, and for pressing reasons which, short-term, relegated military equipment needs to prudent planning.

But the smaller programs could be advanced and financed. Tactics could be developed, and foreign tactics could be studied, adapted, and refined. US industrial power was part dormant in the 1930s, with our labor force in a desperate struggle for survival. The economy improved in fits and starts from 1933, and civilian demand—far more productive and constructive than military spending—gradually rose. But increases in military spending were few until 1940. The fire-and-maneuver concept was straightforward, and it called upon skills still fairly common in the United States: the rifle and the rifleman were the basic unit of

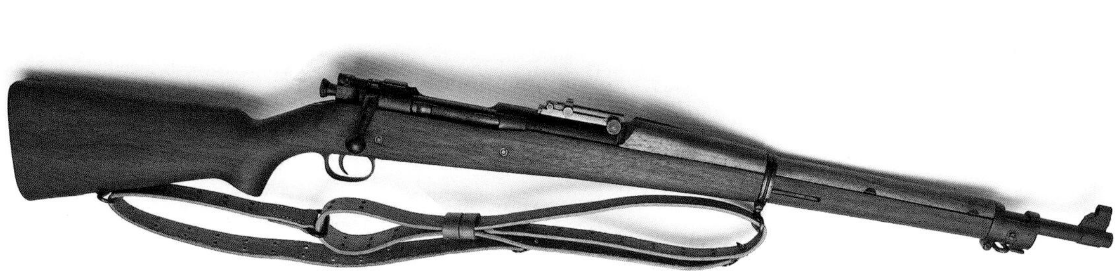

The M1903 Springfield (basically a modified M98 Mauser) was the M1's service predecessor. Although an excellent rifle, it couldn't even compare in World War II firepower terms, and after World War II it was found to not be as inherently accurate, either, in anything like service or standard match form.

advance, with all other personnel and devices serving as support. We had the other weapons: the B.A.R., the Browning .30s in the weapons units, the Browning .50s at a higher level. But the bolt-action rifle—and it didn't matter which bolt-action rifle—simply couldn't be operated quickly and efficiently enough to spread firepower delivery down the chain reliably.

There are those who dispute this. A British marine once explained to me in depth that he had participated in a firepower demonstration during which his unit, using No. 4 Mk 1 Enfield rifles in .303, had "out-shot" American personnel with M1s. Although he was telling the truth and had the photos and targets to prove it, that was a very special case. Bear in mind that the Enfields carry 10 rounds. This was the early 1950s, and most of his team comprised NCOs—tough, experienced World War II veterans—who'd been firing those rifles for seven to ten years. The Americans were mainly recent draftees.

Every British rifle was brand new or freshly rebuilt, whereas the American rifles were of varying qualities and vintages and had been in Germany since the end of World War II. And yet, the scores were quite close, with the US GIs generating slightly more bull's-eyes, which was more than offset by a number of rounds in the white or off the paper entirely. And of course, there was a factor I've noticed in shooting both rifles myself: in rapid fire, the British rifle, more so than the M1, generally trails off in accuracy due to heat buildup after about 15 rounds. And as an observer of this same demonstration remarked, the various hand and shoulder movements involved in operating the bolt-action rifles made their shooters much more visible at range. Most people seem to agree that the amount of training required to deliver rapid fire accurately with most any semiautomatic rifle is far less than with bolt actions of any type or design. In short, the exercise was a wonderful demonstration of what the very best training and experience can deliver with one weapon, but the other competitor proved quite capable of delivering similar results with far less specialized preparation.

British Enfield No.4Mk.II rifles such as the Brits often claimed could "outshoot" the M1—and under sufficiently contrived conditions, they could and did.

Bear in mind that military bolt-action rifles had been around for sixty-odd years, and the Enfield system itself for more than fifty, when this comparison took place and was apparently repeated at NATO bases all over Europe. The gas port version of the M1 was less than fifteen years old, and, though well developed, many of the rifles involved bore original barrels at least ten years old.

Much of American military thinking had been bound to mechanisms similar to the bolt action. It was said that semiautomatics would greatly increase ammunition demand. This was correct, but logistics improvements provided plenty of ammo. It was said that troops would relax fire discipline on the theory that anything missed on the first round could be hit with the next. "Experts" recalled the Mondragon and various Mauser and other full-powered semiautomatics, dismissing them as "fragile," "erratic," "inaccurate," and "purely specialist's weapons." Those actually in the firearms industry, which also experienced the Depression at its worst, stepped forward to advise that they already had various designs.

In the period 1964–67, I was already an M1 owner and shooter. I sought out veterans and armorers and, when possible, pumped them for information. Using the microfilm resources of my university library and twice even venturing to the Library of Congress, I meticulously dug through mass-media and specialized sporting/shooting publications for references to what was already my favorite rifle. With the rifles I actually owned and fired, I found it difficult to rationalize much of the exposure that the M1 received up to about 1941. Generally scathingly negative, and never very specific, there were references to inaccuracy and unreliability and even inferences of catastrophic failure. I copied and transcribed and compared, and noted with some confusion that very little official literature seemed to confirm or even address these matters. And I was baffled that none of the mass-media coverage included any mention of the new tactical developments. Obviously, this was not my entire life, but being relentless in general and inquisitive by nature, I asked the smiths of my acquaintance for information. And I got it.

Jake wasn't real jolly, and he could be very uncommunicative, but when he communicated, it was in short sentences and very clear: "Combination of hogwash and little bits of truth!" He snatched an odd-looking, dusty M1 off the rack from among his eight or 10 Garands, and I immediately noticed its squared-off gas cylinder and muzzle apparatus and its four digit serial number. We wiped it off and talked as he secured it in his vise fixtures and began to remove the gas cylinder, which was nothing I'd seen before on an M1, though I dimly recognized the blocky part. "See the funny rubbed spot here?" he asked, pointing to a shiny spot about one-third of the way back along the receiver's operating rod raceway.

"Well, rubbing there, especially if you didn't load clips with the first—and therefore, the last—round to the right, along with some other little glitches, would freeze the @®Ù#@ action on the seventh round." He finally screwed the gas cylinder off, and I noticed that the barrel was shorter than mine was. He exposed the gas trap blast cone. "This damned thing probably woulda worked okay with new .276 ammo with faster powders, but it was a #®Ù@&*& nightmare with .30 caliber, especially match ammo and old stuff!" (He would explain more afterward, which I'll cover later.) He meticulously cleaned the interior of the gas cylinder before putting the rifle back on the rack. "I can't replace that gas cylinder, and I never shoot that gun—not since '40, anyway. It's really a prototype, and it's the first M1 I ever shot much. So it might be valuable someday." It would be almost twenty years before I saw another gas trap M1, though oddly, I'd seen some of the old gas cylinders in store at a nearby army base, and I didn't, until that moment, have the vaguest idea what they were for.

Vertical profile shot of a ca. 1939 M1 Garand gas trap rifle.

"See, the military don't like to change nothin'! And anytime anything does change, there's always some $#@&Ù®Ç who wants to make lots of money off it, and he's always got some better way to do this, that, or the other thing! Sure, it always works better, he's had it layin' around for years, that other idea is stupid, and, by the way, did he mention, it also costs a helluva lot less?"

I still didn't quite comprehend his meaning.

"Didja ever wonder why all this nasty crap about the M1 stopped more or less the very day Winchester got the private contract? Whole bunch o' businesses wanted government work, so they'd plant stories—any damned thing, long as it was partways true—and that's why every little glitch or wrinkle with anything new got made into a catastrophe, whereas if some o' their crap *#&%$#' exploded, well, hell, that's somebody else's fault!"

COMBAT

Fire and maneuver was the very opposite of the Continental European concept of the automatic base of fire, wherein the machine gun is primary and everything else support, but it, very simply, spreads firepower and encourages aggressive movement at much lower levels. In fact, the Japanese concept was similar to ours but so heavily steeped in errant philosophy that tactical instrumentation was much different. Yet the Japanese were studying and attempting to copy the Garand—apparently based on procured rifles and/ or stolen blueprints—very early on.

The M1 ejects its flimsy sheet-metal clip at the end of eight rounds, and the distinct "ping" was sometimes viewed as a disadvantage. Some World War II veterans claimed they'd toss an empty clip to the ground after a couple of rounds just in case the enemy might take this as a reloading signal, but I've been told by at least two veterans that no one reacted at all. Perhaps enemy soldiers never heard the sound, or perhaps they were unwilling to take what would have been a terminal chance to show themselves or break cover. But clips of eight rounds, quickly replenished, in the hands of a well-trained squad supported by at least one B.A.R. is a great deal of full-house firepower, quite capable of suppressing movement out to 1,000 meters with no further support. The rhythm and rapidity of fire, all by itself, will keep an enemy formation ducking and dodging, and therefore movement forward becomes a possibility. This is not to say that a German formation could not do the same, but it created much more of its entire density of fire from its one or two machine guns, which were also much more easily located. The percentage of fire delivered by the machine guns was far higher. Taking out the machine gun or its crew, obscuring the automatics' fields of fire, avoiding the main source of bulk firepower . . . these were more easily refined for use against such formations than against American units.

But, of course, this massing of fire suggests something similar to area or volley fire, and the traditional military shooting technique has always called for firing only when a specific target is in the sights. This controversy predates the M1 by centuries, but in the twentieth century numerous rifles had become available that could kill easily at 1,000 meters and beyond. In particular, the US Marine Corps opposed the change in fire concept originally and expressed no interest in the M1; not too long thereafter, it became their

Early on, the M1 carbine wasn't directly incorporated into standard infantry units but wound up being the standard weapon for anyone who had other support duties—radiomen, assistant B.A.R. men, officers, and sometimes NCOs. This, though, is a later M2 carbine, which by the time of the Korean War had been neatly folded into a fire-and-maneuver tactical package.

"baby," and though the training did not change very much, in the field, covering and suppressive fire—in tremendous volume—became as effective as the British, decades earlier, had hoped their "grid volley fire" might be. The M1 could never spray down the landscape like a submachine gun or the German MG42, but especially working in groups, from good cover, there was minimal body movement required to fire and reload, and in terms of rounds or power, well-trained men, especially men who trained together and knew each other, could move against far superior numbers with some alacrity.

There are no panaceas. Nothing is perfect. While the difference between one man with a Pattern 17 Enfield or M1903 Springfield and one with an M1 is fairly substantial, the difference between an experienced squad with bolt-action rifles and an experienced squad with M1s (presuming similar support) is rather astounding. The Germans, the Soviets, and the British all admired the increased American firepower delivery system and eventually used different solutions to achieve similar results in some selected units, or merely added submachine guns to increase the number of rounds fired by most units. But only the United States could boast full-power, high-outflow, long-range weaponry in every combat unit after the middle of 1942.

I have interviewed enough German and Japanese veterans of that conflict to know that the fascist enemies were fully aware of this.

This old US Army official 4x5" Ektachrome from 1942 relays some interesting details that probably meant nothing at the time. His M1 is less than two years old, the flush nut on his rear sight is "in the white," and his gas cylinder is reaching the same stage. The early finish on cylinders was paint, supposedly high heat enamel, but not very durable. A collector or shooter who wants to refinish one for cosmetic purposes shouldn't feel too terribly bad about using modern high temperature paints, which are much better, or other "dip and dunk" pickling or plating processes, to refinish that part. After all, regardless of whether a potential enemy sees the reflections, the shooter can pick them up and lose sight picture in strong backlight. Another detail: we tend to think of earlier stocks as being very slender. This one isn't really so trim. Reason: it hasn't been sanded to near disappearance, which most old originals were.

CHAPTER 2

THE INDUSTRIAL AND DEVELOPMENTAL HISTORY OF THE M1 GARAND

The '03 Springfield was essentially a Model 98 Mauser slightly modified from the original German design to suit American tooling and manufacturing techniques, and with sights specified by US Ordnance officials. The Pattern 17 Enfield was very similar, but a British design simply adapted to the American .30-06 round. Their predecessor, the Krag, was a very traditional Danish/Norwegian design, again adapted to American sight preferences, with the caliber changed. The old Model 1873 Springfield and its various successor and spin-off single-shot rifles were straightforward developments of very traditional caplock designs. In short, until the Garand came along, American military long arms were not very innovative and demanded minimal tooling and manufacture research.

Springfield Armory, however, had developed much of the industrial discipline associated with mass production and interchangeable parts, and, indeed, the large-scale machine production of finished products was frequently referred to as "armory procedure." Much later, Henry Ford became erroneously associated with the "assembly line," and the nineteenth-century accomplishments of the mother armory in Massachusetts were largely forgotten.

Much of the Garand's contouring, fitting, and, most important, true parts interchange depended on the strict application of what was called "armory procedure," which meant leaving encoded tracks of heat treatment, drawing number, steel manufacturers, and the like on major parts, such as the cryptic notations on this 1944 -32 receiver.

The Garand demanded some fairly subtle contouring and milling, and the specification was upgraded virtually continuously from about 1932 until 1945 and, much more gradually, even in the 1952–57 period. Many of these small permutations were covered photographically in *The Complete M1 Garand*, and it seems that some of the various contour changes had to do, perhaps, with fixtures or jigs intended to secure the receiver during test or manufacture.

Duff's comprehensive volumes include far more in the way of detail than we have room for here. His research was primarily done at Springfield Armory and is found in official military records. But there are some general observations that are productive in analyzing this great rifle's long, successful history.

Perhaps the most significant single change was quite early, ca. 1941–42, when the base specification was rewritten to call out 8620 steel, rather than the traditional "41" series ordnance steel. This steel had been used in some firearms applications before, but it was mainly thought of as a tool and spring material. When the hardness and heat-treatment specifications—which were rigorously followed at Springfield Armory and not so rigorously at Winchester—were changed in approximately 1943, the receiver had reached a point of optimum strength that remained basically unchanged in receivers of similar design through the Beretta BM series and the American M14.

All military M1s were produced from pressure forgings. With some exceptions, all civilian receivers have been produced from investment castings. Simply put, the difference between the two is bubbles—and therefore strength. Forgings are essentially crushed while hot and thus compressed to an approximation of the necessary shape. Castings are simply poured. Forgings are somewhat denser, albeit careful heat treatment can make up for some of the differences in strength. And the M1, like most products of its time, was considerably overbuilt. Still, no cast M1 or M14 or "M1A" receiver can truly be called "Mil Spec," because the first specification page begins, "Forging shall be of 8620 steel, heat treated. . . ."

Incidentally, I have seen the original drawing file on the M14 at Smith Enterprises (then in Mesa, Arizona, now in Tempe), and much of the M1 file as well. These documents, though in the public domain, constitute a vast file—weighing well over 130 pounds for the M1 alone—and describe precisely the manufacture in detail of each part. The attendant documents and orders at least equal the drawings in volume.

Smith has produced forged M14 receivers, and after long consultation and actual observation of the manufacturing process, I inquired, "Isn't the M14 kind of a 1930s-style creature?" The answer was real simple: "Yes!" But some parenthetical data were immediately added. On both the M1 and the M14, the manufacturing baseline can be achieved with CNC (Computer Numerically Controlled) machinery, though many smaller items can be wholly manufactured using CNC and other more modern techniques. Still, the final fitting, contouring, and prefinishing detail is done by hand, measuring, filing, buffing, inspecting, measuring again, and so on,

The stainless-steel gas cylinder of the M1 led to various letter-coded experiments to get better finish adhesion, few of which have ever been deciphered, but which eventually led to far more durable finish methods.

Original November 1943 barrel, marked in the definitive (but not ubiquitous) World War II manner. Markings evolved for the convenience of armorers, not collectors.

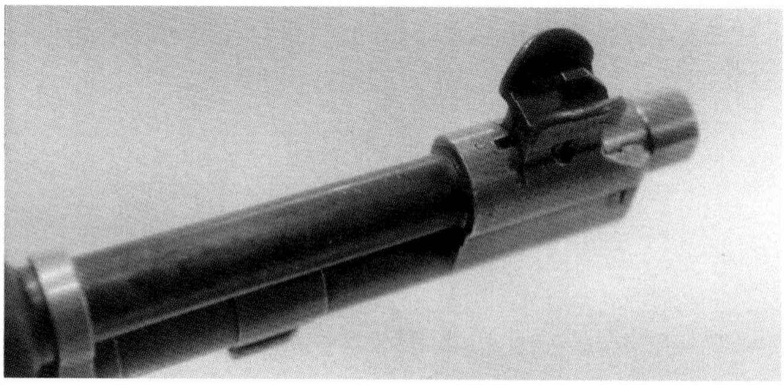

The gas trap gas cylinder and its attendant parts, including the barrel, cannot truly be interchanged with later rifles in the normally understood sense of the word.

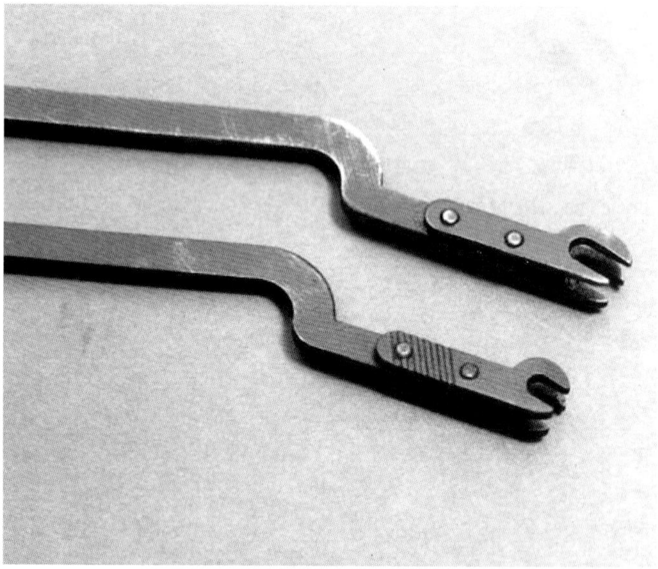

The follower arm rod of the M1 improved in strength but became more difficult to mount and dismount, with the "long fork" version on the top, compared to a riveted "short fork," ca. 1942–43, below. To shooters, there's no functional difference.

because the manner in which the receiver interacts with other attendant parts is quite subtle. No matter what, the manufacture of an M1 receiver is virtually the same process, even though the operating rod and various other parts are significantly different. As of 2019, no one has ever successfully finished the operating rod raceway via CNC machinery. The M1 was also the first American military rifle to employ stainless steel, primarily the gas cylinder itself and the gas piston on the operating rod. Getting the finish on this material to last proved to be elusive, which is why so many gas port cylinders bear small, cryptic letters. Finish experiments were conducted at the armory almost constantly until at least 1948, and no perfect solution was ever found, which is why so many gas cylinders today are shiny bright. Oxides, which were far better than the early "pickling" processes, went on the last.

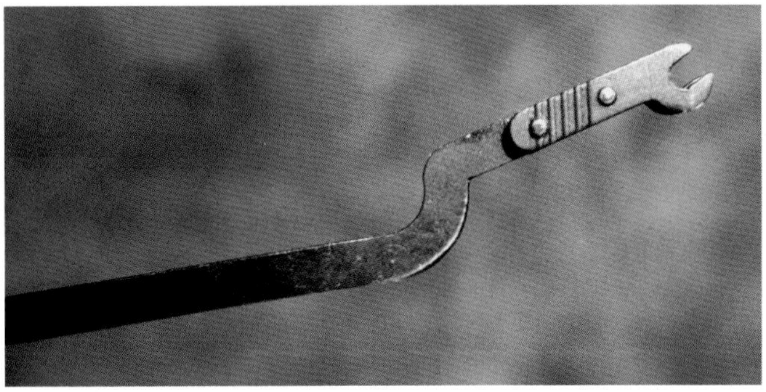

The riveted short fork follower rod is correct for most midwar Springfield Armory M1 garand rifles, and is actually handier for most uses than the later (but stronger!) long fork riveted version, which was found to function better with grenade launchers, in particular. "Handier" means it is easier to dismount when stripping the rifle. These tended to dismount more often when used with the launchers. These have become very hard to find, and the price is high enough that I have seen a couple of fakes. These were replaced in production as the war ground on, having entered production to replace the original 1-piece milled unit. They show up intermittently on Winchesters to the very end of production. The long fork riveted, sans serrations, appeared as early as '43, but it wasn't until well into '44 that it became standard. Collectors sometimes wonder why "original" M1s don't color match. They mostly *cannot*, and important but physically smaller parts like this were produced, polished, and finished entirely separately from receivers and barrels, and heat treated differently. No one cared if they matched or even came close. These have been witnessed, new, all the way from a rather light silvery gray, to nearly black, and about all parameters in between.

Generally, every part on the M1 rifle got continuously better. Extraneous machining operations were eliminated, oddments of excessive contouring disappeared, and the receiver got stronger, along with virtually every other part of the rifle. While it's generally correct to say that virtually every M1 Garand part can be interchanged with every other M1, there are two exceptions—one very obvious, the other slightly more subtle. First, neither the barrel proper nor the gas cylinder and attendant front sight assembly of the gas trap rifles can be interchanged with later units, though it would be theoretically possible to put the entire gas trap apparatus intact on more or less any M1—barrel, cylinder, sights, all subordinate front end parts. The other one—which I had forgotten about until I ran into the CMP rifle whose trigger assembly appears here—is one we don't think about much until we actually encounter the parts combination: the original trigger housings, up until 1941 (and much

This is the fairly typical layout of a World War II complete M1 Garand trigger housing group, fully assembled, showing the safety parts marking.

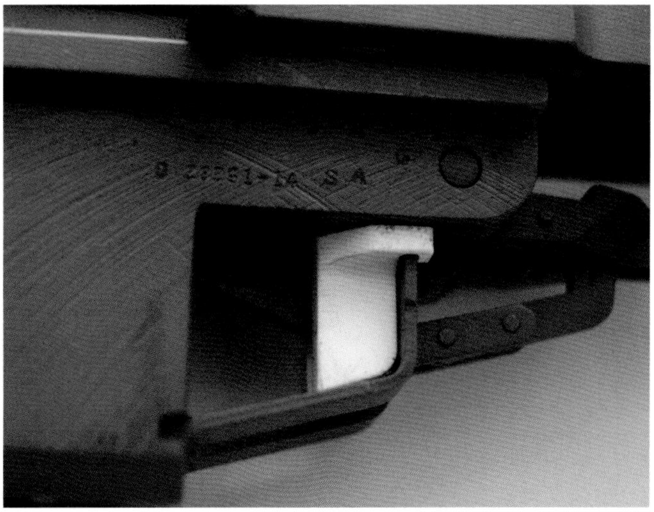

Closeup of a "dash 14" SA receiver from the CMP in .308, with its military style plastic magazine block installed. Strictly speaking, these are not necessary, but save the shooter who has both calibers of M1 the embarrassment and awkwardness of trying to remove a .30 caliber cartridge improperly inserted into a rifle set up for the shorter, more efficient, more modern cartridge.

later at Winchester), utilized a larger "stop" machined in for the older, weaker "flat-top" safety. A "flat-top" safety can be used in any trigger housing, though collectors and shooters would both want not to do so, but the newer safeties will sometimes not fit, or fit entirely too tightly to the original trigger housings with unmodified stops. Because of their value, of course, such trigger housings should not be modified; they should be sold or traded or used with original flat safeties, but never remachined. Almost always, the larger safeties can be fitted, but with a lot of effort. Better to simply trade off the very old housings to someone who needs 'em!

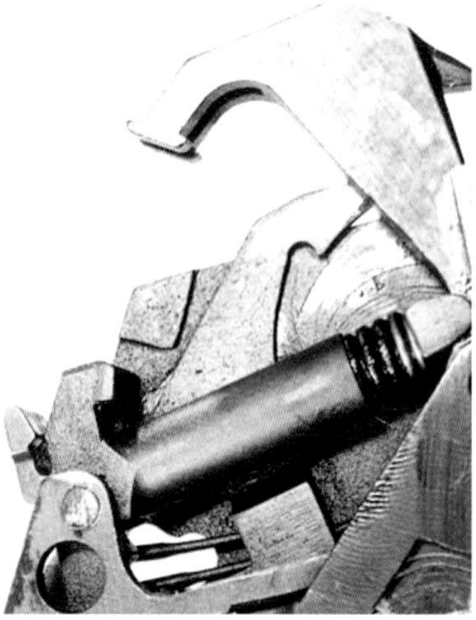

Old, original, unmodified trigger housings designed for "flat-top" safeties whose stop pads have never been reconfigured, such as this one, will sometimes not fully function, due to clearance issues, with the much more common "round-top" improved safeties.

The photographs here examine some parts development—the "extra rail" configuration receivers, a few contour permutations, and so on.

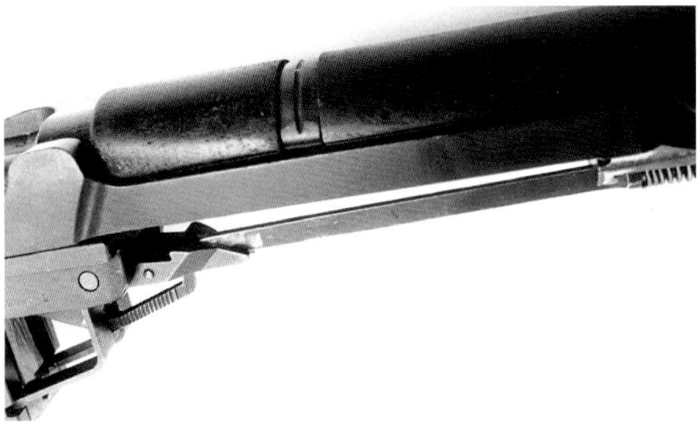

Though Winchester's output of M1s was smaller than Springfield's (this is Winchester's very first rifle, 100001), Winchester never incorporated many of the changes that were almost constant at the Springfield Armory, and this 1940 WRA isn't much different from a rifle of five years later.

Again, I want to stress this: as in the rest of the shooting sports, it is more imperative than ever that shooters and collectors come together, not just to present a "united front" to the gun confiscation lobby, but to help each other in day-to-day events, restorations, and shooting events.

Closeup of the Winchester buttplate. Note the distinct border around flat-ended "checkering."

The Winchester bayonet lugs do not have the frontal "toe" of all other M1s *unless* one has been beaten, milled, or filed over the years by someone.

CHAPTER 3

NEW M1S FOR THE 21ST CENTURY: THE DANISH KITS AND BEYOND

For about two years, starting about 1999, Century Arms, the Canadian-owned firm with offices in Vermont and Florida, imported parts kits of M1s, complete except for receivers. Apparently there were originally just over 20,000 rifles that formed the base of this group, of which Century was the main importer.

A selection of CMP rifles, set up and ready for the range.

Denmark returned the lion's share of those it had received free of charge under MAP to the US government, in accordance with the original agreement. These, in turn, were made available through the CMP to qualified purchasers as complete rifles. However, the receivers Century purchased mostly stayed in Canada. This glut of parts spurred more domestic receiver production. A few complete rifles trickled into the United States by various means before the ban on importation of the Garand receiver took effect.

Denmark's long association with the North Atlantic Treaty Organization (NATO) and participation in exercises with US troops meant its armament took on a quite cosmopolitan inventory. Since NATO members generally were required to issue arms in NATO caliber from the early 1950s, many collectors had presumed that M1s in stock would have been converted predominantly to the 7.62x51 chambering made standard in 1953–55. But this proved not to be the case.

THE PARTS

Long before my books came out from now-defunct Paladin Publishing I contacted Steve Kehaya at Century Arms to begin obtaining parts kits and information. Until recent "musical chairs" began in the editorial offices of the many firearms magazines for which I used to write, it was my custom to generate two to five M1 articles annually as updates. And I found it possible to squirrel away some decent M1 receivers for future projects, which, as of late 1998 or so, were sitting around gathering dust.

There is a vast economic difference between buying individual parts and getting everything in a kit. About this time, complete M1 kits could be acquired from $125 to just short of two hundred dollars. A decent barrel, all by itself, will get into these price ranges wholesale, and an operating rod will run not very far below that. Bolts? Twenty dollars to sixty dollars! Add the small parts, pins, wood . . . purchased individually, the parts then could cost five hundred dollars or more.

The fifteen or so kits I purchased made obvious the Danish acquisition pattern, which was later corroborated by other collectors. Most of their US-made M1s were acquired in the early 1950s. By the middle to late 1950s, rifles from Italy, with their unique Danish markings, were being purchased new. And, apparently, quite a few were purchased well into the 1960s from third-party countries or US inventories, separately from the MAP acquisitions. I made a point of going through parts purchased by other M1 buffs, and what I found basically confirmed this information.

A 1960 production Danish VAR replacement barrel markings.

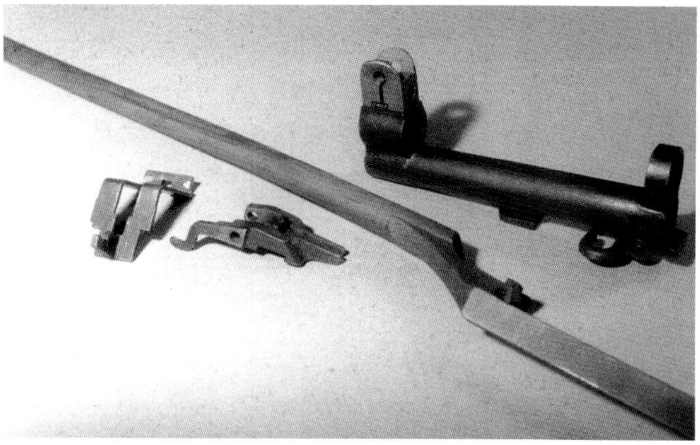

The Danish M1 kits from Century provided a great many high-quality parts. All gas cylinders, operating rods, and other moving parts, such as the operating rod catch and bullets guides, bolts, and so on proved to be of very high quality.

The Danes seem to have manufactured two major parts only: barrels and buttstocks. The barrels bore the same proofs that rifle and machine gun buffs had noted on fine Madsen arms for years and were mainly from the late 1950s and early 1960s. The wood made in Denmark was European beech, strangely reminiscent of the K98k of a generation earlier, but closely cut and well made and surely prettier than the American birch stocks.

Danish stocks were generally stamped with the serial number of the receiver just ahead of the butt sling swivel, sometimes adjacent to the receiver heel, and many stocks had been drilled and countersunk for what must have been British-style unit ID discs, most commonly in the "heel" of the pistol grip. This was done on American- and Italian-produced wood as well, though most commonly on the beech units. These serial numbers allowed some conclusions to be drawn about the times and nature of service lots.

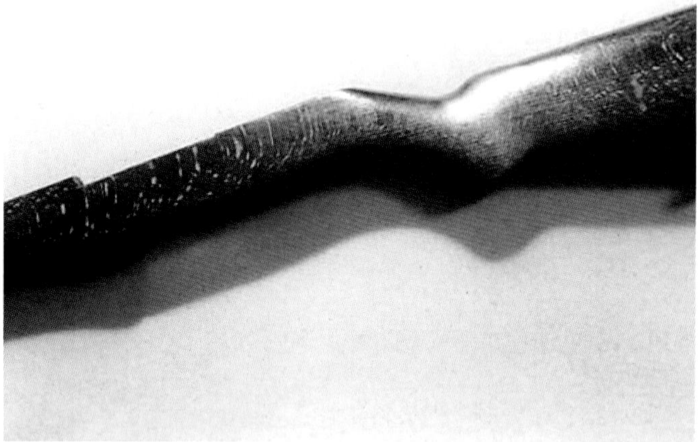

The Danish-made beech stocks were nicely fitted and very sturdy. Virtually all the M1 buttstocks from Denmark carried the receiver's serial numbers ahead of the rear sling swivel.

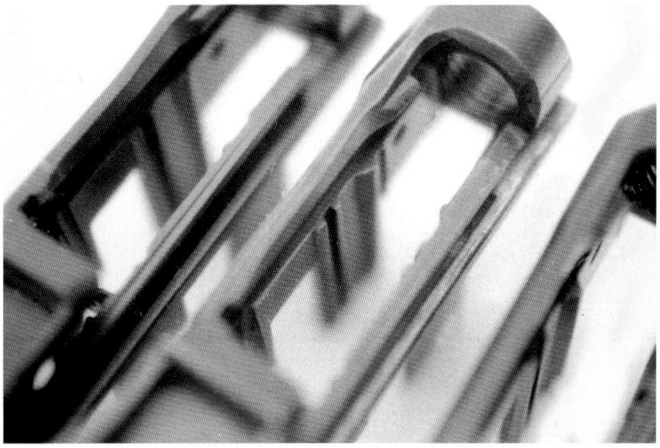

Some of the early parts in the Danish kits made it possible to restore receivers that had been sitting for some time, such as these three, to complete working condition. Note the extra "guide rail" ahead of the follower grooves on the center receiver, which some collectors think might be for an accessory never actually introduced or for some kind of production fixture that did not stay in use for long.

Closeup of the part number on an International Harvester M1 Garand hammer. All IHC parts are in high demand as restorations proceed.

Most numbers manufactured were well below the 3.8–3.9 million figure generally thought of as very late World War II production. A lot of four-digit numbers suggested Italian rifles, and usually these were with kits including Beretta and Breda parts. I have not yet seen—and I've gone through at least 25 kits—a number over 4.2 million and have seen perhaps half a dozen American parts associated with US-built rifles after 1952. To enumerate: one International Harvester (IHC) hammer, one 65 series Springfield operating rod, one H&R hammer, one postwar Springfield Armory (SA) bolt, and a safety.

A considerable number of "type 3" (actually T105) sights and D35382 relieved operating rods from the immediate postwar period, mixed with a fairly high percentage of "locking bar" rear sights, suggested shipment of a lot of unmodified and/or once-rebuilt World War II US rifles.

Slightly overlit so texture and markings can be seen, these are "Type 3" or the "final" form of the locking bar rear sights, in their Springfield Armory form. Winchester's "open v" direction indicator arrows used throughout their production (and very briefly on a few early SA rifles!) are only slightly different. The "Type 1" used a much smoother locking bar and the old short elevation pinion. The "Type 2" generally used a smaller, smoother, more gently contoured bar. Yes, there are small permutations of each, and most were *very* dark in color as required by the specification. No, M1 Garand rifles do *not* "finish match." And *all* the early rear sight configurations were vastly inferior to the postwar T105E1 self-tightening, internally sprung units.

I retrieved a wealth of World War II parts, however—some of them very hard to find and quite valuable. I was, in fact, able to build up a 3.3 million rifle, with an approximately correct barrel and stock, by careful sifting. Also found and worthy of mention: a near-mint, uncut WRA operating rod, a complete set of very early Springfield bands and operating rod catch, several very early bolts, and lots of early gas cylinders. I observed only two World War II Springfield barrels but many replacements, ca. 1947–52.

Not many Winchester barrels were among the Danish kits, though this one, which belonged to a collector, was in virtually perfect condition, all by itself worth more than he paid for the entire kit.

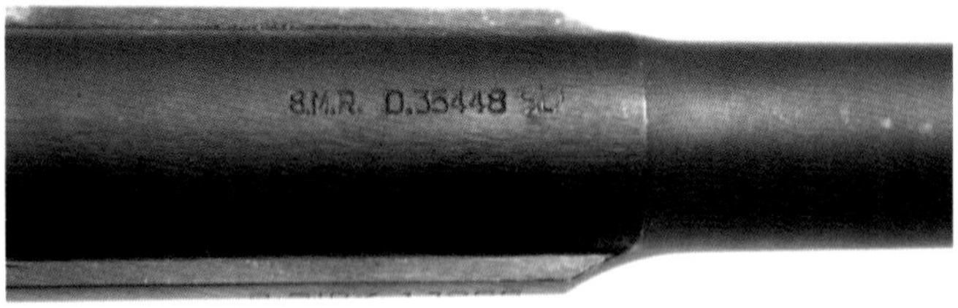

Breda barrels were quite common in the shipments from Denmark via Century. This one was apparently built by Beretta to service a Breda rifle, as it also carries the B.SID notation generic to Breda M1s.

The Danish barrels showed signs of very high quality, and I found several Breda barrels, which I had never seen before. I would later find myself shooting a Danish barrel on one of Century's receivers, now finally (effective July 2000) available separately, and that experience would confirm my measurements and observations.

Typical Danish-made barrel, of very high quality.

All of the Danish parts were in at least solid condition, most were excellent, and I did not encounter a barrel whose throat erosion gauge reading was worse than 3.5. And there were some interesting experiences.

Apparently upon rebuild, the Danes renumbered parts not customarily numbered. Virtually all the Italian bolts bore rather large serial numbers, and few of the American ones did. One Italian bolt sported two numbers. The band and stock hardware of one rifle that I thought to be very early appeared to be covered with heavy rust; I sprayed the lot with Break-Free, let the assortment soak in the hot Arizona sun for days, and then boiled and boiled and boiled, sometimes with detergent. The effluent from this proved not to be rust at all, but some kind of seemingly evergreen-based preservative, which permanently stained everything it touched. Underneath was an almost perfect set of hardware, which appeared to be in a near-black finish, matching yet!

I also began to find beautiful, heavily flame-grained French walnut handguards, so stunningly colored that they looked odd with any stock I owned. These mainly bore "PB" bands and ferrules, and I am quite sure they were original to Italian rifles. I traded these off too early, then got a buttstock in the same stunning wood. I found only one cracked stock. There was only one birch buttstock.

My cache of Italian parts grew steadily, and I stumbled onto a Danish Beretta receiver and purchased it immediately, calling upon Derrick Martin to barrel it with almost indecent haste. This I tested with an Italian barrel initially, then set that .30-caliber unit aside and rebarreled with one of Springfield's units in .308/7.62 NATO and an original Beretta steel magazine block. (More about this later.)

Breda and More

The Danish-issue Breda I examined and have attempted to picture here is one of the very few that entered the United States before the ban took effect. It is it is basically the same as the Beretta Armi Roma Italia currently in my rifle rack. I've now had the opportunity to examine Italian rifle receivers of the general M1 configuration from a rather large time frame, and I can draw some educated guesses. On all Italian M1 and BM59 receivers, examination with loupes and microscopes for tool marks, machining style and techniques, and the general manufacturing "fingerprints" strongly indicates that all were produced almost identically, inferring a common manufacturer, identical tooling, perhaps even common hands and eyes. I will not burn it in stone or write it in blood (remember, "*never say never*"), but it appears that the early receivers were all produced in the same place or, at the very least, under the same management. However, peripheral parts bearing different makers' markings seem to be made with slightly to moderately different machinery and tools. Eventually, enough was figured out and verified: Breda was producing receivers well before the Gardone Val Trompia firm, and made most of the early Berettas.

It is virtually certain that rifles were shipped to the end user from separate locations/sources. There seemed at first to have been parts mingling on original rifles, but that seemed later to have been in error. What did vary was letter codes Breda used, including BMB and BMR, mixed on rifles that seem to be original and undisturbed. Early assessments were primarily "logic error," but it told analysts that parts were swapped out during cleaning quite early in the rifles' lives.

One of a family of US M1s re-marked minimally Italian BM59 rebuild. Many other US receivers were microwelded and over-marked with Breda or Beretta "Tipo 2" nomenclature as well. (Photo courtesy: CMP.)

Many used the wartime base part number; others the "65" prefixed version. There seems to be no logic or pattern to which goes where.

By the twenty-eighth modification of the M1 Garand receiver, in the late midwar interval, the Garand rifle was a very strong machine indeed. Parenthetically, all sorts of "oddball" markings appear in the leg area, other than the heat treat/alloy codes, and if one tries to track them all down, it is guaranteed it *cannot* be done. The author has found random numbers, letters, and what appeared to be initials, plus what might've been jokes . . . and no puzzles were solved.

The lettering with which parts are marked seems to have gone through many almost random permutations as well. "PB," in particular, appears on bands, ferrules, buttplates, gas cylinders, and gas cylinder lock screws in several sizes and type styles, and the other markings also show some variation in type style and size.

Also interesting: I've seen a number of Italian parts, marked with simply the part number, sometimes the World War II part number, and no other identifier of any kind. I've seen at least two gas cylinders that had to be late American wartime production, because of the other letters and hardness test marks, but bearing "PB" aft of the stacking swivel.

Very few World War II barrels were found among the Danish kits, but all proved to be in excellent condition.

A beautiful, flame-grained Beretta handguard, with an original "PB" handguard band (clip), proves that not all M1s bore straight-grained, mundane walnut. Yes, that is Italian or Circassian walnut. It took about nine years before the author was able to put together a similar flashy stock set and grace it with a Danish-issue Beretta receiver.

Indeed, the Winchester narrow wartime cylinder on the WIN-13 I photographed some years ago, a DCM gun, had been aftermarked "PB" at some time in its life. No one will ever explain all these anomalies, but the die-hard collector should remember that Beretta rebuilt M1s as early as the 1940s and apparently received some brand-new US- produced parts along with their tooling. Again, it bears repeating that rifles are built to shoot, not to conform to collector's specifications.

Markings

The receivers found on the Danish rifles do not differ in configuration from other Garands, but the markings go a long way toward confirming what previously had been educated guesses. The Italian receivers built for Denmark all bear a crown and "FKF" shown in the photos on page 143. FKF may somehow relate to Danish King Frederik IX, and the crown definitely denotes "by royal authority." But

The author's "Beretta Armi Roma Italia," shown here after being converted to 7.62 NATO and used to test Springfield's new barrel in that caliber.

Breda's rendition of a Danish-issue M1. Examination with microscopes and instruments suggests common manufacture of all Italian receivers, though not of other parts.

the most likely meaning of FKF is Forsvarets Krigsmaterial Forvaltning, meaning, (approximately) "Defense War Material Authority."

The Breda barrels are usually marked with "BMB" and a variation of the part number, and "B.SID" and what appears to be a lot number or heat-treat batch, then a date. The one I shot said (topside, ahead of the chamber), "B.M.R. D35448," with the Italian cross proof, and on the right, where the operating rod slot would allow it to be viewed when in wood: "B.SID.71 1955" (1955 very obviously being the barrel date). Despite the World War II part number, flats and gas cylinder port are chrome-plated, meaning the tube meets the postwar new production and rebuild specifications. This particular barrel carried the Beretta code but was apparently originally produced for the Breda rifle. There was obviously some kind of interplay between the two manufacturers, even at this early date.

More precisely, my correspondence with Beretta and articles in the Garand Collectors Association newsletter have confirmed that the B.SID denotes "Breda Siderurgica," code for the Breda Iron and Steel conglomerate based in

Brescia. "BMB," of course, is "Breda Meccanica Bresciana," at that time a state-owned manufacturing facility directly related to "BMR," or "Beretta Maschina (or Meccanica) Roma," the Rome-based firm that seems to have produced mainly smaller parts. Among my unusual treasures (and now on my Rome- marked Beretta) is a "BMR"-marked extractor, the only maker-identified extractor for the M1 I have yet seen, though I've seen some other strangely marked ones.

One .30 barrel among all the kits I looked at was merely marked "PB" with the postwar part number, no date, and a few small stamped inspector's marks and a cross proof. This, I suspect, might have been a Beretta replacement barrel.

All the barrels met the American specification in terms of grooves (four), contours, dimensions, and so on.

A COMBINATION OF NEW MERCHANDISE AND OLD ARTIFACTS FOR SHOOTING PLEASURE

The military M1 receivers of the past are now available as slightly overpriced parts from the CMP and whatever left-overs dealers have salted away from the "gravy days" of the M1 imports, or perhaps salvaged and torn down from rifles with tired barrels. In 1998 and early 1999, I was able to procure a couple myself and, as I prepared this book for publication, I was happy that I had because it turned out there was much to be done.

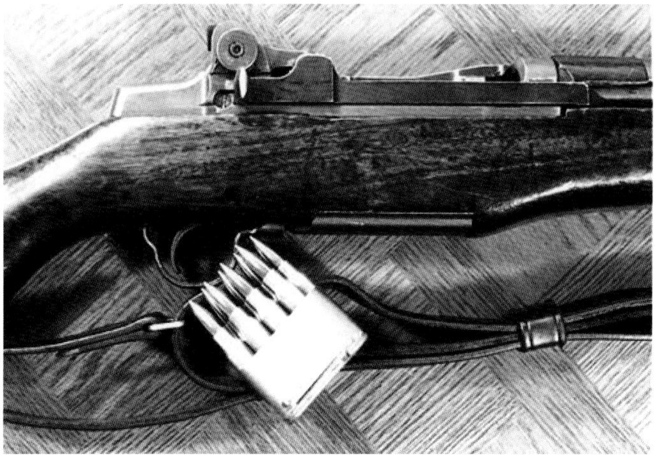

Regardless of caliber, all M1 clips are the very same unit. This one is loaded with .308 cartridges.

Receivers

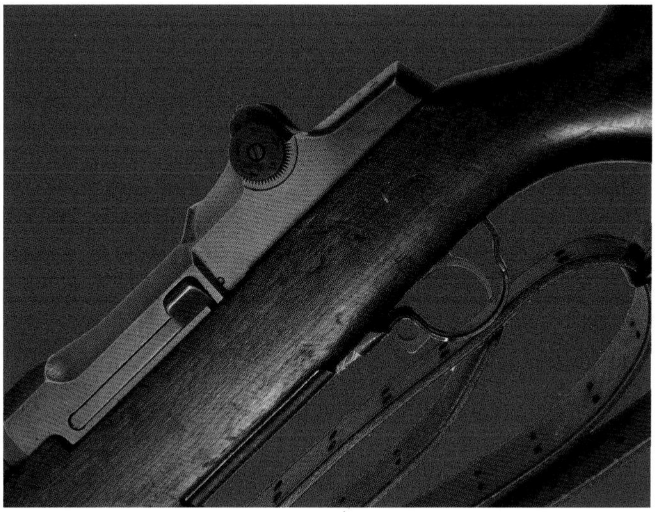

A re-heat treated 1.5 million WW2 SA M1 Garand receiver.

The receivers I'd put away for future use and reference were a Springfield "reheat" 1.4 million, a 3.8 million late-war Springfield, a 3.3 million SA, and, of course, the aforementioned Beretta Roma. (More about those later.) But I also had lots of parts. And my intention for this tome was to put much of the other material I'd squirreled away on brand-new receivers, test it, and save the best for myself. The 3.8 million eventually wound up being tested here, along with my Beretta, with Springfield's new four-groove commercial barrel. The idea was to test some other new tubes on brand new receivers. So much for good intentions.

Only Century actually delivered any. The Entréprisé, pronounced the French way as "on-tray," not "Enterprise," advertised for quite some time, existed only in prototype form. The Entréprisé firm folded almost two decades ago. They never learned what I am still told by everyone in the industry: The ultra-subtle operating rode raceway *absolutely cannot* be final-formed by CNC (computer numerically controlled machinery). Its final forming MUST be via hand fitting. Everyone who didn't realize this is out of business or no longer produces M1 or M14 receivers. The IAI, which has not been advertised but has been shown around the country, might have reached the US market before the Entréprisé which inherently cannot, as the company has entirely disappeared. The Springfield Armory, Inc. receivers, are now off the market again, and probably will be forever. These new receivers never reached fruition.

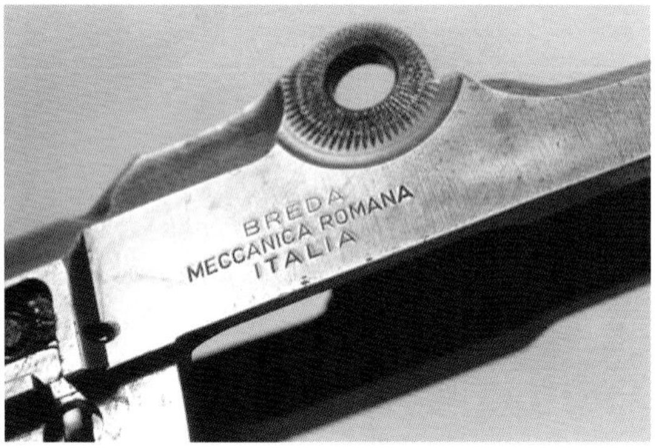

Left receiver panel data on a Danish-issue Breda- built M1 Garand.

Breda produced many early Beretta receivers. This is the early "leg code."

My Century Arms gun featured a Danish barrel. I checked over the cast receiver very carefully. Markings are small, on the left side of the receiver, as seen on page 145, and the finish is a nice phosphate. Adjacent parts have been refinished in a dark phosphate. I checked lockup and verified timing before shooting. The rifle was in .30-06, and so I dipped into my supply of Federal 3006GM and Century's PMP for a brief test shoot at "The Bowl" north of Mesa. This was necessary because the range was closed that day. It proved to be a very short test of function due to the presence of a number of shooters who had no grasp of safety procedures and our general discomfort with people drinking large quantities of beer while they actually shot firearms. The rifle cycled properly, seemed fairly accurate, and placed the valuable brass where we could find it before we left. I was somewhat miffed that the new receiver showed only the center alignment windage witness/reference marking, rather than the fine cuts on the old originals, but once we got the rifle rough sighted, this was less irritating than I had imagined.

About a week later, having cleaned the rifle, I took the same ammunition supply plus some Sierra molycoated 168-grain handloads using my optimized "Varget" load (the same one published in this book, 45.1 grains, with Federal's Match Large rifle primers. I am very stingy with .30-06 ammunition, since it costs so much more than .308. My friend Dave Lanza primarily executed the handloads, with input from Lee Templin. The bore had been meticulously cleaned of all copper fouling before shooting and then de-oiled and moly-prepped just before firing. The plan was to shoot about 350 rounds, then hand the rifle over to Lee Templin for further testing, upon which it was my intention to report further if any significant deviations developed. They haven't.

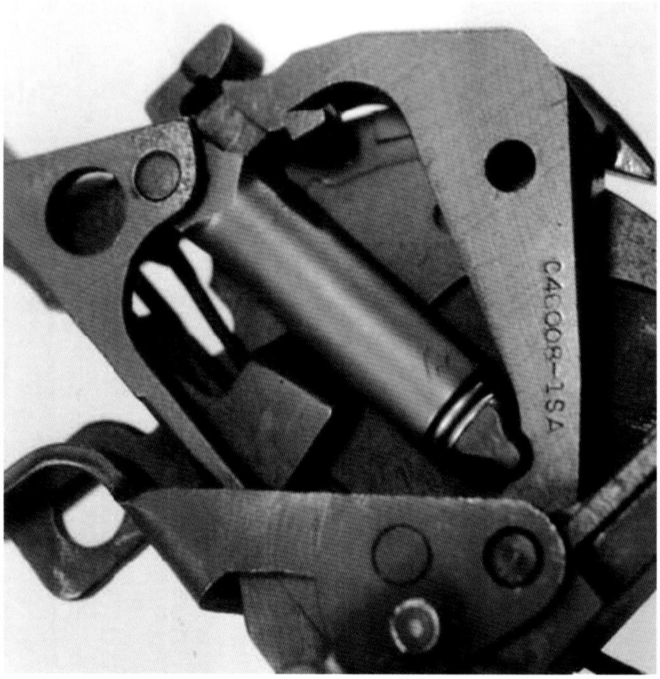

A very early hammer marked "C46008-1SA" with the extra hole, accompanied by many much later parts, found in one of the Century Danish kits.

Entréprisé Arms prototype receiver.

Even before the first test, in what has become almost a ritual, I went over the stock and used DUCO wood hardener and little bits of Crazy Glue (that's right, regular, ordinary Crazy Glue) in areas where stock fit seemed sloppy. This is not a real substitute for glassbedding a rifle, but it is enough to stabilize a receiver temporarily for a short-term test without having to spend a lot of time or money. I particularly look for light passing under the receiver horseshoe, and, if necessary, build up that area, which in this case was necessary. In porous areas, I use the hardener and sometimes bits of filled epoxy before I even consider the rifle ready to be fired. I might not do this with a pure-as-the-driven-snow collector's rifle, but when I am testing barrels and/or receivers—and in this case, it was both—I do not want wood to be a factor at all.

Likewise—and this hasn't been necessary on anything built up from Danish parts kits—I will, at the first sign of wobble on a gas cylinder assembly, punch-peen the channels that receive the gas cylinder. Remember, any sideways wobble in the gas cylinder will destroy accuracy, even if everything else is perfect, and there's no point in shooting expensive ammunition without looking to these two small, easily-dealt- with potential problems.

Another check: are the rear sights secure? It has been a while, but a worn-out sight cover can cause even the very stable Type 3 rear sight assembly to move with recoil. I've also had cracked shafts and worn-out threads, though, again, none of this showed up with the Danish equipment. But it still must be checked. Wishing to test the rifle rather than myself (I am nowhere near as steady as I used to be and far more farsighted), I was determined to fire every round with the rifle carefully rested and bagged. This is asking for a sore shoulder, for confining recoil to a horizontal plane increases the rifle's thrust into the deltoid area.

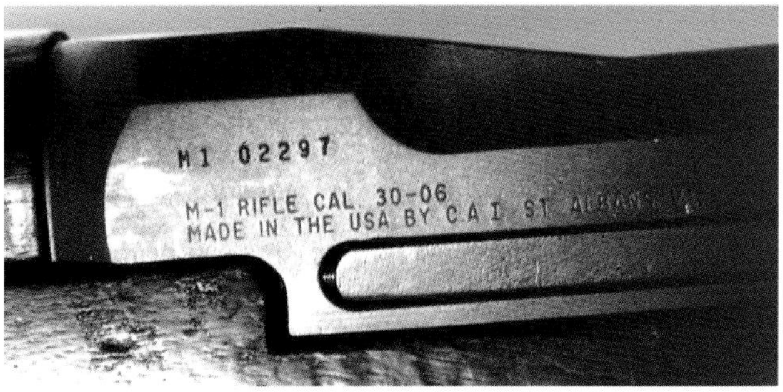

Logo of the author's early Century receiver. Nothing topside on the horseshoe at all. . . . This was an assembled rifle, and worked very nicely. I got one from Century, another locally. The ones bought later as receivers generally were difficult to set up and required excessive fitting. Century no longer has these available.

Naturally, before shooting, I removed any and all thin oils from the M1 and properly greased the rifle with my favorite wheel bearing grease. I have not used what most people call gun oil on a firearm for almost twenty years. I do not consider it a lubricant. For the M1 Garand, and for any other fast-firing weapon, it will not stay where it is put and serves no meaningful purpose. I do sometimes use oil-based solvents for various purposes (mainly cleaning), and before storing guns I often use a high-grade motor-oil patina in bores and chambers, preferably Mobil 1 Synthetic.

To avoid case separations due to hydraulic adhesion, chambers must be cleaned of such lubricants before firing. I am convinced that wet and dirty chambers are also a factor in the "slamfires" mentioned later in this book. And bores should be "de-oiled" properly before molycoated bullets are fired. It was while I was preparing the Century receiver for its second test that an associate—who owned my first M1 book but apparently had never read it—confessed that he was having function problems with his M1. (Reason: *improper lubricants.* Oil leaves; grease doesn't.) So I greased it properly, took it to the range with me, and fired about 75 rounds of his handloads, never experiencing any of the problems he had described. I ran off a copy of the trouble-shooting data in the book and wrote on top of it: "Rifle fine. Lubrication sucks." I have moderated my views somewhat and now use white lithium grease on guns that will not see heavy use. But for purposes of fast-operating firearms, the rule is real simple: *oil is not a lubricant!*

Even during World War II, the GIs who got the best service from their Garands were using concoctions of soft pencil lead and high- temperature cooking grease on the operating rod raceway. Nobody had to tell them that; they found out very quickly that oil doesn't work!

Then along came the lubriplate greases. Those were okay, and little was required. But modern wheel bearing grease is even better, and cheaper, too.

I wanted to shoot all the molycoated bullets first on the prepped bore, and, for the sake of those who don't handload, follow with the factory stuff. I shot my initial groups at 50 yards, since the earlier episode had not really confirmed that the sights were close to right, and the heat was sufficient that mirage might not reliably allow me to see bullet strikes at 100 yards with the spotting scope.

Having blasted mainly at the 300-yard gong with the rifle that "wasn't working"—and having had no malfunctions of any kind—I put out the little small-bore target I like to use at 50 yards and slowly tracked into the target bull. Eleven shots in, I was striking just above dead center of the little red stick-on center and cutting half-inch three-shot clusters.

Satisfied that I was sighted properly, I rotated my spotting scope over to some other targets at 100 yards and played with the power settings. I could discern the .50-caliber holes from someone's huge muzzle-loader, but another gentleman was shooting to my left with a .270-caliber heavy target rifle, and the mirage was such that I could not tell his bullet holes from tiny crinkles in the paper. In fact, unless that huge rifle was missing completely, my first impression was that I couldn't even discern his groups. Later, I realized that I could in fact find his five-shot clusters, which were excellent, but everything much smaller was "iffy" . . . so my decision was to try this rifle, that day, at 75 yards, which I proceeded to do, placing my targets during the next cease-fire.

At 75 yards, I got no group larger than 1.25 inches with the Sierra molycoated bullets, and we are discussing eight-shot groups here. Five would sometimes be under the traditional 1- inch standard, center to center. The 3006GM 168-grain loads shot almost identically.

Again, when testing ammunition and hardware, I clean between types of ammunition, including at least a moderate copper solvent cleanup, even if I have not been using metal-jacketed bullets. Call it superstition, but I refuse to test a product of any kind under anything save clean conditions, and I believe in fouling shots only within the short span of a magazine or so.

Pretoria Metal Pressings (PMP) ammo, then imported from South Africa by Century, went for around nine to ten dollars a box in many stores, half or less the price of 3006M, so I didn't expect a great deal from it. Also, almost everyone I know who shoots the M1 has the distinct and documented impression that bullets of 155 grains up to about 180 grains usually shoot best, and the PMP fodder was loaded with a 143-grain Spitzer.

However, it shot very nicely—nothing over 1½ inches, and several five-shot subgroups under an inch (and this with an untuned rifle and some wind). There were no flyers (unusual for me, since I generally generate a few on my own), and there were no failures to function. I resolved to touch up the trigger a bit before passing the rifle on to Lee Templin, and to look at the barrel and receiver to see if anything had happened (e.g., cracks, odd bits of metal). I did find some brass "dust" down in the magazine well, typical of a crisp, new, extractor, freshly finished, and made a note that if I shot it much more, I would smooth those mating surfaces very gently.

Upon later detailed cleaning of the gas system, I found powder residue to be no more and no less than one would expect from this level of firing. Examination of the brass showed nothing unusual. The main thing I learned was that the Danish surplus barrels, if in sound condition, can deliver accuracy within match specifications without being in a match-prepared rifle. Detailed disassembly revealed an unusually tight front handguard and actual contact between the stacking swivel lug of the gas cylinder and the handguard. Modifying these tiny fits, all by themselves, would probably have resulted in at least slightly better performance.

The rifles sold at that time for $389 to $479 in stores. Of course, I cannot guarantee that your barrel will be as good as mine. What I can assure you is that the rifles are, in fact, assembled by someone with a solid knowledge of the Garand, and that some of the details not checked by others seem to be subjected to Century's inspection. This is important.

I am sure someone, somewhere will have some kind of negative experience with somebody's new receiver. This happened, we all forget, even with original GI rifles. And with Fed Ord material it was chronic.

These rifles—because of their civilian receivers—will never have the collector's value of GI M1s, but they are credible shooters. I have since eyeballed, handled, and even taken down to small parts a variety of M1s in inventory at area stores and in the hands of shooters, and I have yet to find any of the errors of casting and assembly that one expects to see sooner or later with a relatively embryonic product. So for the person who wants to shoot but flinches at the price of an all -GI M1 or a prepared match rifle, the Century-receivered rifles appear to serve as useful, handy alternatives. This does NOT mean that independently sold receivers, which are sold unfitted, will work well or easily.

Barrels of Barrels

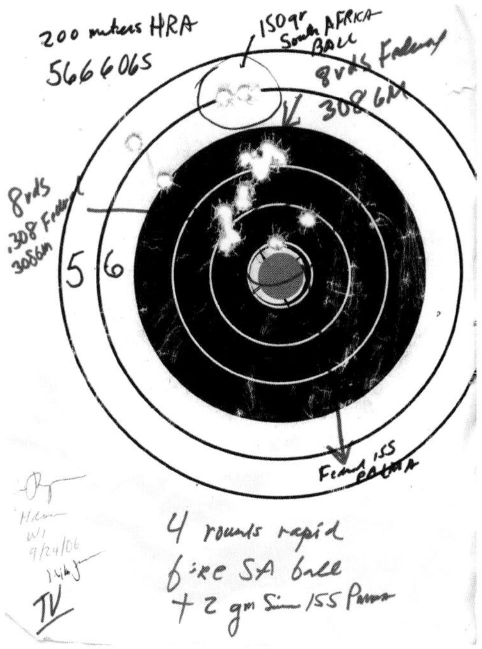

Since Ackley's early findings, and confirmed by bench rest and long distance competitors over more than six decades, there's no question that the inherent accuracy of the 7.62x51mm. NATO/.308 Cartridge is, given equal loading care and rifles of near equal quality, far higher than that of the US Cartridge, .30, Model of 1906. This is, as all accuracy distills, a question of consistent velocity at the muzzle. The newer, shorter cartridge features a very consistent "total burn." That's not about air space or the lack of it, it's overall propulsion burn. No wonder. The original cartridge for Mister Garand's rifle was the .276 Pedersen Center fire, almost exactly the same length as .308, and featuring a similarly efficient burn. It was a brilliantly accurate round, and worked much better with the "gas trap" apparatus than the .30 ever did. It was MacArthur's 1932 order to change the design to the old cartridge that ended that opportunity to update and upgrade. This sighting-in target involves a 200 meter try-out, the very first, of an H&R rifle brought up to date with a new barrel. The .30 06s do NOT generate this kind of accuracy before break-in, and usually not afterward, either. This was an inexpensive Citadel barrel. Note witness information and date, etc.

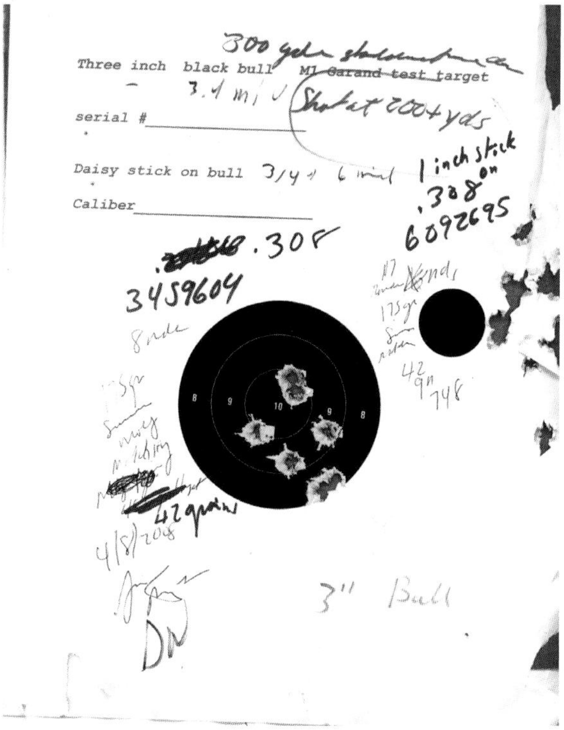

This is the 3" bull "locator" target that my test team used to use, normally, at 300 yards to 300 meters; this one, however, shot at just over 200 yards using one late rifle with a military NM barrel, the other with a civilian unit, with a few minimal relief and bedding adjustments, including "hard finishing" the key bedding portions with polyurethane. Note load information. No .30 06 there that day could equal this, and this was the sighting in workup.

I had only just finished an exhaustive test of Citadel's best grade match M1 barrel and Springfield's last generation match barrel when I found out Citadel seemed to have disappeared, and the Springfield upper level stuff had changed considerably. Too bad. Both were pretty good products. And besides, I had spent a small fortune on ammo for testing products that no longer existed, at least not on the open market, though there is no telling how many of each may repose at the back of some smith's shop. I therefore acquired SA's new standard barrel, this one somewhat more like the GI unit than the old six-groove, and the Fulton Armory standard grade in both .308/7.62 and .30-06. As this is written, my master plan calls for the .30-06 FA barrel to be bolted to my last spare receiver as soon as I build up an ammo supply for the older cartridge. It turned out that Citadel had moved and cut off all retail contact with customers. As of 2016, they have moved to far northern California. Their best is superb, but it matters from whom one buys. The SA I ordered only in .308, planted on my

Beretta Roma rifle, and duly tested it, and the .308/7.62 Fulton barrel went right on my 1.4 million "reheat," whereupon testing began immediately.

"Immediately" is not entirely true. I use a very conservative polish technique on new barrels before even beginning to break them in. Some people call this "lapping," but I don't use lapping compound or other traditional supplies. I use automotive liquid polishing compound on patches, making literally thousands of passes; meticulously wiping out the dried residue with oversized patches until the bore is virtually mirror-like, always according to directions; then cleaning with solvent and synthetic motor oil and rubbing again; and finally degreasing thoroughly and preparing the bore with whatever molycoat preparant is at hand. This treatment, which is really just very fine polishing and should not change anything one can measure with normal instruments, eliminates some of the eccentricities of an M1 barrel's early life.

New barrels tend to copper foul badly and shoot erratically for the first several hundred rounds of their shooting lives, and if there are eccentricities near the gas port on the M1 and similar rifles, this will tend to be exaggerated. Again, this happens with all rifles due to microscopic burrs, inclusions, and tool marks, which tend to be mitigated and disappear as the rifle is shot and can merely be highlighted by gas-operation systems with such anomalies near their ports. But there is a subordinate theory that such surface irregularities cause other irregularities, in turn harming both barrel life and accuracy. I refuse to fully endorse this theory, but on the other hand I will state it as a suggestion and tell you, affirmatively and for sure, that this little operation will provide the best part of an M1's accuracy much earlier and make a rifle under test much easier to clean. Therefore, even if all of the other asides and theories are wrong, I have a small hand-labor process that allows the saving of the stinkiest part of the work on the dirty end of shooting.

I should probably add, since I was unable to fully work up the FA .30-06 for test. Much of the reason was my fitting a Marlin postwar barrel from among the Danish kits to the other late war receiver, the 3.3 million, to do a little work that sprang from curiosity. I had fired some oddities, including a button-grooved tube that bore a Marlin commercial logo and oddments of military markings that may have gotten into military inventory via some enterprising, curious armorer decades before my purchase; an "SAC" of apparently approximately World War II vintage, which I was told was made by Savage; and an "MAC," with full World War II-style markings, lacking even the chrome flats and gas port. These I had purchased for very little money at Surplus Disposal at Fort McCoy in Wisconsin many years ago, and, according to some people, these cannot exist, let alone in military ownership. Same with the "SBC," which I saw and noted there, and bought, but sold before ever fitting it to a rifle. The "MAC" and the "SAC"—I have since located another "SAC" and photographed it—bore vintage military markings, and seemed to be of World War II or possibly much later vintage. Along with the button-rifled Marlin, they shot very nicely with ball ammunition, but the button-rifled Marlin opened up with heavier bullets.

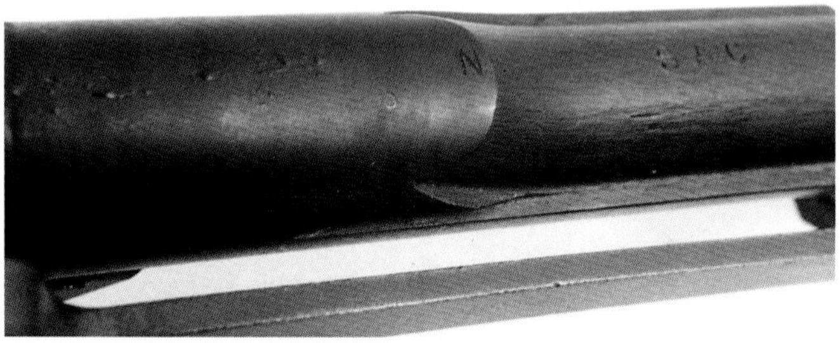

"SAC"-marked barrel of World War II style and configuration. The author has seen a couple of these. Also seen, bearing part number 35448 and mostly in government ownership at the time are "SBC," "RA," and "MAC." There is some doubt that Remington made M1 receivers under the "T" programs, but some collectors think Remington made barrels. Many collectors think these were made by Savage Arms Company, under "gray" DoD contract.

Italian steel magazine blocks may be fitted to any M1, to avoid the troublesome jams that eventuate trying to feed .30 06 ammo to a .308/7.62 rifle.

I also purchased and then resold what appeared to be a postwar barrel marked "RA," not dated, but with the World War II part number. At the time, I thought this sort of disposal would go on forever and never envisioned myself doing books like this. Thing is, the Marlin postwar tube found in one of the kits measured virtually new on the throat erosion gauge, and I wanted to try it with high-quality handloads. The tube was slightly disappointing, to quickly summarize this test, which was not done with this book in mind. It more than met service specifications, but with ammo at $1.50 per round, like 3006GM and the very best handloads, one expects to see at least one five-shot array with all rounds touching. Yet, despite my best efforts and allowing the best rifle shot I know to blast out eight rounds, 1½ inches seemed to be the best result, and that with a great deal of preparation. Now, it is possible that this barrel, had I polished it like a truly new unit or broken it in gradually, might have approached the level of postwar commercials. But my experience is that military barrels—save LMRs, some National Match units, very late H&Rs and, of course, the Danish unit just mentioned—seldom equal even low-priced current units. And why should they? There are almost fifty years of machining technology advances and measurement behind the newer units, not to mention anything that might have happened, even to a technically new unit, over all that time.

Shooters should gravitate toward newer barrels in either caliber for two very sound reasons: (1) vintage military barrels have high collector values if they are in solid condition and are irreplaceable, and (2) new commercial units will virtually always (a rule to which the exceptions are very notable) shoot much better.

Which brings me to a brief summary of the new barrels under review.

The Springfield Armory unit makes no attempt at mimicking military markings, though external dimensions forward of the handguard slots are absolutely correct.

The Springfield unit carries the maker's name and ".308" in the right operating rod cutout. Its gas port measured approximately 5⁄64 inch, correct for .30-06 but about 1⁄64 inch small for .308/7.62, which calls out .100 inch. A standard 3⁄32-inch drill bit is close enough, and I enlarged the port. Note, however, that if you are a long-range shooter who wishes to push large bullets supersonically at great range, you should talk to your smith before modifying the gas port. There seemed to be more metal, about .0016 inch, over the chamber area, and I could not fit a standard GI rear/upper handguard to the unit. This did not matter, since I already had a hollowed-out unit on hand. These hollowed- out handguards—you can use a router; I use 60-grit sandpaper—will increase accuracy all on their own by reducing pressure on the barrel and improving airflow around it. With anything that I know will be shot much, the handguards are hogged out, though I seldom remove the front handguard tin liners anymore except on a true, pure match rifle. I have experimented with drilling many small holes in that unit and buffing until it is just short of transparent, but removing the liner means that the stock ferrule and bands and even the handguard itself can eventually shoot loose and begin to bounce around. This is irritating, ugly, and not good for accuracy. I am seeking, frankly, a better way to do all the front handguard work-ups, without a lot of endless misery, and when I find it, I will execute it on all my rifles.

The Fulton Armory barrels bore military markings (the .308, with the late number for 7.62 barrels, F11010457, was dated 9–98, and coded "FA"). Its gas port was properly sized, and external dimensions were right off the GI drawing.

The "match" Springfield .308, which then graced my friend Pat Fisher's 3.8 million rifle that used to be mine, was of almost identical configuration to the standard barrel, though the internal polish was of a higher order, and the gas cylinder fit was miserably tight.

The .30-caliber Fulton unit also employed military-style markings, only the correct postwar part number, D6535448, was in the operating rod slot and the date was 12–98.

The flat forward of the threads, usually called the shank or shoulder, needed to be turned down slightly before the barrels could be fitted to receivers in good condition, this from about .008 inch on the Springfield to roughly twice that on the Fulton units (both of the Fultons will require the exact same amount of reduction). The seeming excess material is added to some M1 barrels to accommodate fatigued and sand blasted receivers. Many 'smiths simply ignore the "fat." This is a sound approach and was done on many late GI replacement barrels for precisely the same reasons.

Both received my hand-polish treatment. It's worthy of note that the Fulton, depending on from whom purchased, usually sells from thirty to fifty dollars higher than the standard Springfield, though for somewhat less than Springfield's match tube. Finish on both was very nice, the Fulton approaching the black of the wartime Winchesters, the Springfield a nice, uniform dark phosphate.

I fitted both rifles with Italian steel magazine blocks, so as not to accidentally try to jam a .30-caliber clip in either, since at this stage I thought I would be actively testing both calibers simultaneously. I used "NM" modified gas cylinders on both, along with the aforementioned relieved handguards, and tightened up the stocks via my customary "quick" method. Both guns received the smoothing operations described to ejector and extractor and my "foolproof" trigger job, as did Pat's 3.8 million rifle bearing the "match" Springfield barrel. Precleaning and prefiring lubrication procedures were followed as described earlier with the Century gun.

My ammo supply was vastly more liberal in .308/7.62. In addition to 168- and 155-grain Sierra molycoated match bullets loaded in selected brass ahead of Varget charges, I had a good stock of 168-grain 308GM from Federal Italian steel magazine blocks may be fitted to any M1, to avoid the troublesome jams that eventuate trying to feed .30-06 ammo to a .308/7.62 rifle.

Also on hand were several cases of British "Radway Green" ammo originally loaded, I am told, for British Army Special Air Service (SAS) snipers. This stuff had been shooting beautifully in some more casual experiments, and I was eager to try it in a part accurized and considerably smoothed Garand.

Each rifle was fired, rather casually, at the 300-yard gong before being even seriously sighted in, then borecleaned and prepped for molycoated bullets. The 155 Sierras very rapidly proved to be extremely accurate at 100 yards, both rifles putting eight rounds at least once under the 1-inch magic parameter. Later, the other ammunition would prove not to be far behind.

From the beginning, the Fulton proved to be slightly more accurate and, in fact, precisely equaled the performance achieved later with the match version of the Springfield barrel, although in rapid fire (which I got around to later), the very slightly heavier Springfield barrel shot identically—perhaps a matter of luck, or perhaps something to do with the harmonics of a heavier barrel, albeit very slightly so, in rapid fire.

Before I became exhausted (which isn't very long at 110° Fahrenheit), I began to do some fairly interesting plinking at the 300-yard gong. The Fulton delivered at least one five-shot cluster small enough that I could not discern, with the mirage at 100 yards, whether I had missed. Center to center, it was ⅝ inch. Oddly, it was with the British ammunition, not the far more expensive commercial stuff or the expensive handloads. The "Radway Green" did not seem to hold this accuracy out at 300 yards quite as well as the other loads. But then, one doesn't expect lighter bullets to retain their accuracy quite as far out, though the difference here was very small. It was still very good ammo for the price.

I made a point of shooting both rifles several more times before coming to any firm conclusions. The Fulton "standard"-grade barrel, at least mine, performed fully to match specifications and beyond consistently—again, on a rifle not fully match prepared. This is impressive performance. The Springfield was not far behind and, indeed, in my hands and those of other shooters would periodically shoot as well and even, very occasionally, a tiny bit better. Both represent a high order of quality and dollar value.

Both firms offer an extensive list of services for the M1 as well. All my installation work on these rifles was done by Derrick Martin, one of the few smiths who has yet to mount one of my barrels askew.

I will continue my research with barrels and ammunition for as long as I can get the work done. Again, I have to emphasize this point: neither of these barrels is the equal

Stainless Krieger in 7.62/.308.

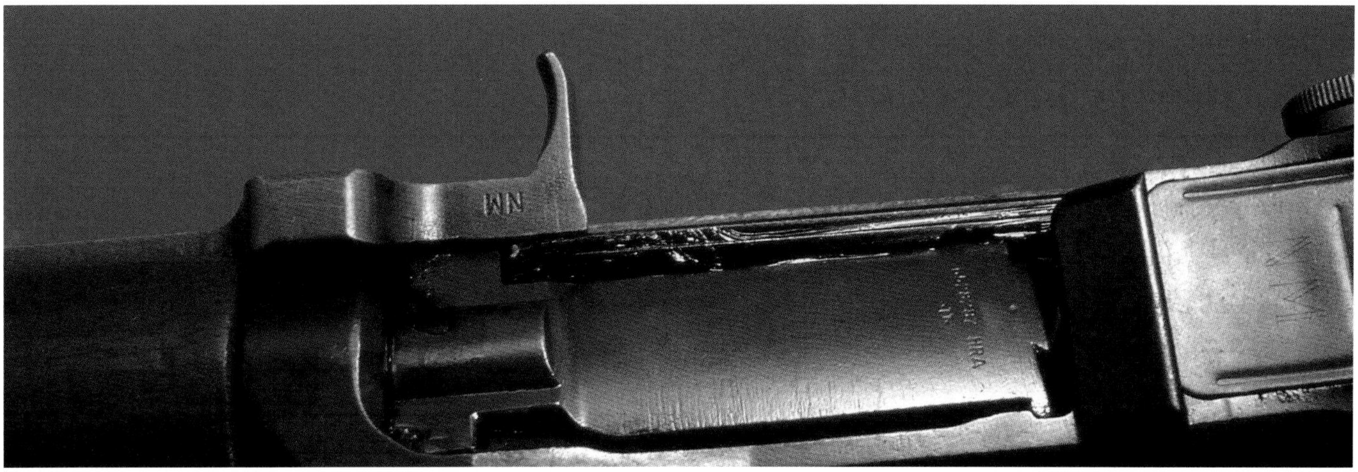

Another H&R rifle, this one built to competition status in the modern sense by Derrick Martin of Accuracy Speaks, in Mesa, Arizona. The "NM" marked operating rods followed the rifle's production by several years, and other than the marking, only the updated welding and better concentricity and roundness testing make them better in any way, and even that is debatable. What isn't debatable is, they are newer, and saw less use, so for rifles to be heavily used, one can be reasonably sure they have more wear life remaining.

of the big Krieger, but most shooters will seldom notice the difference. And, of course, most of that difference will come when the barrel is hottest. And these barrels cost less than half the price of a Krieger.

We'll discuss some other concepts and toys later in this book; but, again, for the shooter of the M1 the world certainly has not ended.

CHAPTER 4

M1 GARAND'S MULTIPLE "FLAWS": A REALISTIC VIEW OF PERCEIVED PROBLEMS

Not all of the negative press the M1 received in its early days was false. The rifle did cost three or more times the price of the '03 Springfield, and its introduction was accompanied by some unreliability and a great deal of exaggeration thereof. But all of this has to be put in some kind of historical and factual perspective.

Garand's early designs were for a brands new 7mm cartridge. But by about 1932, because of huge inventories on hand and the prevailing Depression economy, it was decided that the new rifle would have to use .30-06 ammunition, much of it dating from 1918 or earlier.

Very early gas trap trigger housing group, assembled, this one from about 1938 or 1939. Note the polished hammer spring plunger, still "in the white." Most of these got finished in their long, colorful careers.

GAS TRAP IS A POWDER TRAP

None of the gas trap rifles ever built—in the United States, Germany, Russia, Belgium, or Britain—stayed in issue very long; most, in fact, were never issued at all. And they had problems in common.

In the Garand, the gas trap is more straightforward than most. The barrel ends some 2 inches behind a false muzzle, leaving a profound tube-shaped 2-inch reaction area for hot gasses. This very volume of gas, with slower burning powders—as my smith Jake explained in his shorthand—was what caused Jake, and the other half-dozen or so veteran armorers and team captains with whom I discussed the early M1 rifle, such profound problems in the field and in competition in the period 1936–40 that it constituted a crisis. Burning powder, ash, residues, and even bullet fragments accumulated in that relatively vast chamber, and what Jake called "secondary ignition"—just like dieseling in your gas-engined car—caused erratic performance, erosion at the muzzle, and build-up of complex fouling, such that the entire assembly really should have been removed for detailed cleaning after every few clips. The slower the powders, the more profound this symptom.

There seems to be no confirmation of this information among official documents at Aberdeen or Springfield Armory, but every smith of 1930s to early 1940s vintage who was involved with the rifle in its early days used almost the same words. The speed with which the gas trap's more traditional replacement, the old gas port system (used on machine guns since the 1890s), was instrumented and standardized suggests that the negative results of the reversion to the old .30-06 chambering were well known in the field. By 1938, experimental gas port rifles were already under test, and not long after the middle of 1940, no more gas trap rifles were scheduled for production.

Similarly, the German G41, in both its Walther and Mauser incarnations, used a somewhat more subtle gas trap, employing barrel sleeves and even larger blast chambers early on, but the system worked on the same foolproof principle, and the machinery did all the same things. (With almost identical results, I hasten to add!) Their rifle—also intended to replace their bolt-action piece universally—saw some production and some issue, but once it was in the field, the same problems developed and it was preempted by another gas port semiautomatic, the G43/K43 series.

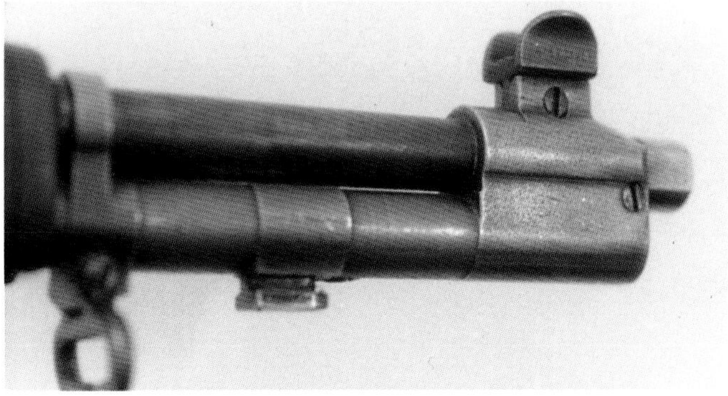

The gas trap never did work out in .30 06, though it might have worked fine with the experimental, interim .276 cartridge, using faster powders. The very latest of the gas trap cylinders cranked the outside "ears" aside slightly, but the more laborious takedown required remained.

From the onset, the gas port system worked better and required less attention than the gas trap system, which, once in production, was dumped for the more traditional type in use on machine guns since the 1890s. The upper one here is an early war unit, the lower one an International Harvester.

Jake was quick to point out that any kind of secondary ignition, especially when it is close to the muzzle, let alone right at the muzzle, in the immediate area of the bullet, causes terrible accuracy problems, beginning with bullet distortion and ending, downrange, with terrible vertical stringing. This can also be a safety problem. One veteran told me that early M1s often smoked heavily from their false muzzles, especially when fired with match ammo, long after they were returned to their range racks.

But like most of what is or was wrong with the M1, the gas trap system was a flaw because of outside factors. For instance, had the 7mm round for which the 1929–32 rifle was designed persisted and become standard, the gas trap probably never would have become an issue, let alone a problem. One of my many correspondents has fired his gas trap rifle with my handloads using BL(C)-2 powder and 168-grain bullets and reports no difficulties whatsoever in several hundred rounds of firing. But he notes that with issue ammunition (and this is a direct quotation), "The gas cylinder stinks and smokes and is a misery to clean, and it must be cleaned!"

This has nothing to do with corrosive ammunition, although when one views a crosssection of the gas trap, there is a strong possibility that the muzzle and adjacent areas would require detailed solvent and water cleaning to obviate wholesale rusting and pitting. Rifle powders before about 1936 were virtually all of current 4350 speed or slower, and the closer one gets to World War I stocks, the more common that speed range becomes. With a 22-inch barrel, burning and unburned particles of extruded powder—some as large as a retractable pencil lead in diameter—can actually cause physical interference, not to mention ballistic problems. Even a quick read through Speer's latest Reloading Manual (especially the powder illustrations) will give some idea of the potential effluents.

It is not at all amazing that virtually no footprints of causation remain at the official level. I keep hearing that there were only ever a handful—perhaps from two to five—T26 18-inch-barreled M1s in issue or under test, and that the related M1E5 "folding stock" project was similarly tiny. And yet for thirty-six years now, I've talked to men who claim they were variously exposed to such rifles. More interesting, I saw both new-condition 18-inch barrels and a collection of rather beat-up folding stocks for the Garand at Fort McCoy (then Camp McCoy) as early as 1964. I inquired about surplus disposition, speaking to a gentleman whose name, coincidentally, was Jim Thompson, and he looked at the specimens and tags. There were lots of them, in a huge pile, being sold at scrap prices. "All I can tell you," he replied, "is that they come from a couple of navy bases and from Fort Bragg." At a dollar or so apiece, I probably should have picked up some specimens, but I was looking for other, more practical toys at the time.

The bland statement that "the replacement of the gas trap cylinder seems to have been for other than functional reasons" has long been an easy write-off of what seems to have been something of an emergency. I have tested the theory, as have others, and the "slow powder/secondary ignition" physics are ironclad. However, it is the artifacts that prove the point: there are way too many guns numbered below 52000—that is, built until about September 1940—whose barrels and gas cylinders seem to have been replaced within one calendar year to validate a theory that replacement of gas trap mechanisms was anything but a very serious emergency. Winchester—and its very first "school" rifle appears in detail in The Complete M1 Garand—was never even given the gas trap drawings.

The entire front sight of the earliest series of rifles comprises straight verticals, including the shading "ears," meaning there was a strong possibility of mistaking one of the outside flats for the sight proper. The "furniture" on the gas trap cylinder was modified at different times and the sight slightly altered, but by 1939 all indications from the hardware suggest that engineers were aware that there was no point in attempting to improve the system.

Still, when the rifle was on John Garand's drawing board, the .30-caliber cartridge was not a factor, and it is likely that the earlier cylinder would have worked with a higher pressure curve (that is, more efficiently, with faster burning powders) cartridge. The Japanese—who are known to have had specimens of both types of rifle under test by early 1942 and who were trying to generate a semiautomatic rifle, though apparently not as a very high priority—seemingly had problems with their gas traps, too. Their surviving prototype rifles spun off the Garand use the gas port exclusively. Apparently, they had reached the same conclusion independently of the armorers and competitors in the field in the United States.

Most of us will never have to worry about keeping a gas trap operating, anyway. They are extremely rare and probably too valuable to shoot.

THE M1 IS TOO HEAVY

I am probably the last person in the world to accept that the M1 is "too heavy," since I put a lot of effort into trying to increase the weight and to modify the weight distribution of match/competition M1s. Almost any M1 weighs at least 10 pounds without the heavy leather sling, and a good many hover around 12 pounds (and more loaded with sling and bayonet). The "book" weight, from Small Arms of the World, is 9.5 pounds.

It was the Garand's weight and the excellent gas system that made the M1 the easy-shooting machine it was by soaking up recoil and generally stabilizing the rifle.

Here's a weight comparison of the Garand and some of its contemporaries (these are all empty weights).

RIFLE	WEIGHT (LBS.)
German G41(W)	11.08
German G4l(M)	11.25
German G43	9.50
German MP44/STG44-45	11.50*
German K98k	8.60
US Thompson M1928A1	10.75
US Johnson M1941	9.50
US Browning Automatic Rifle M1918A2	18.50
US M1917 Enfield	8.18
US Model 1903 "Springfield"	8.69
Soviet Tokarev M1940	9.48
Soviet Mosin-Nagant M91/30	8.70
Soviet SKS	8.80
Soviet PPSh 1941	8.90
Italian M41 rifle	8.21
Japanese Type 38	9.25
Japanese Type 99 (short)	8.60
British SMLE No. 1 Mk 3	8.62
British No. 4 Mk 1 rifle	8.80
US M1 carbine	5.50
US M1A1 carbine	6.19
Belgian SAFN Model 49	9.48
Typical FN FAL	9.06**

*These vary in weight even more than the M1.

**Due to variations in furniture, barrel weight, and so on, this represents the low end of FAL weights.

These weights are all from various editions of Small Arms of the World and my stock of military manuals. But what this comparison shows is that everything of power similar to the M1 that can be shot comfortably (and that omits the British No. 5 Jungle Carbine and the German G33/40 from that group, I think) is within about a pound of the Garand. Nearly everything semiautomatic or selective fire, regardless

M1 "too heavy"? That's a matter of taste. This match rifle, in extra-fancy flame-grained walnut, weighs almost 13 pounds, and the author would like to add a little "nose weight."

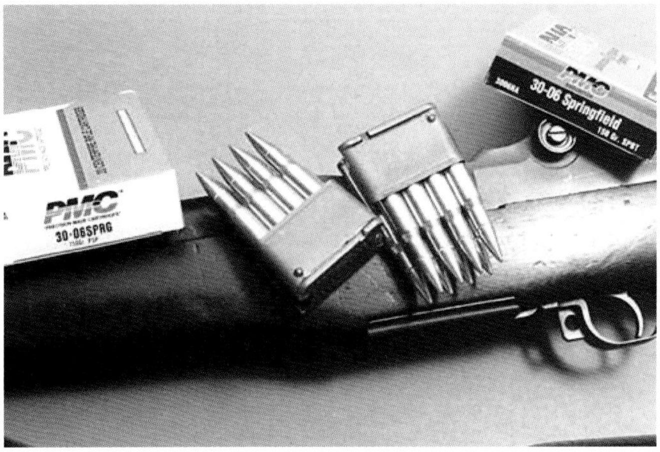

John Garand was stuck with an internal magazine, but it became the subject of much research by mid-World War II. The closed bottom of the M1 contributes to its integrity against dirt.

of power range, is about the same weight or heavier. Not only could a carbine- weight .30-06 or .308 be built, but it's been done; however, shooting such a lightweight repeatedly is a brutal thing, and such bits of fluff should be reserved for hunting.

I cannot and will not give somebody a pat answer that M1 is or is not too heavy—or, for that matter, too light. That's all about taste and physical endurance. Bear in mind that everything that went wrong with the spin-off of the Garand, the M14, happened because of overzealous efforts to lighten it without refiguring some very simple physics. M14s, in their original service form, weigh 8.7 pounds, but eventually, those intended for support automatic fire, such as the M14A1 and some sniper versions, gained well over four pounds—and often a bipod. The M16 is surely lighter than the M1 but, at 500 to 1,000 meters, is nowhere near as deadly. Much of this doesn't matter in modern warfare, and it surely doesn't matter to a casual plinker. But the M1 was not intended for plinking, though it's very, very good at it.

MAGAZINE CAPACITY

Having saddled John Garand with an internal magazine requirement, ordnance authorities very rapidly began to experiment with insertable box magazines of increased capacity. Fine. This culminated in the M1E, the BM.59, and, for that matter, the M14. But Garand was stuck with the requirement.

Japanese prototypes almost immediately jumped to a ten-round box that could be topped off from strippers. However, this brings up the interesting question of the introduction of dirt into the mechanism from the bottom, which on the original M1 was virtually impossible unless the firing/trigger mechanism was removed. Most bolt rifles of the time, the British rifles excepted, carried six or fewer rounds but could be refilled before the magazine was empty.

For the times, however, eight rounds was plenty, and the general integrity of the action—that is, its "dirt exclusion"—was superb. But it sure would have been nice to be able to replenish the magazine from the top.

THE HANDGUARD SYSTEM

Because of the way they are used, military rifles require handguards. Even with them, hand and forearm burns are common after heavy firing, and semiautomatics with big, long operating rods like the Garand's would catch on a lot of things and throw a lot of dirt without handguards. The M1, however, almost always shoots better with no handguards on at all. This was suspected for a long time but was finally proven by a series of detailed experiments that led to the National Match specifications and adjustments detailed in The Complete M1 Garand. The wood and metal fittings not only contribute to heat buildup along the barrel but expand and twist and generally put stress on the barrel and adjacent parts. Still, to delete the handguards in a service situation would cause far more problems than it would solve.

The lower—really, the rear upper—handguard (the one immediately forward of the M1 receiver) is a particularly nasty beast, along with its "band," actually a spring-steel retaining clip. It retains just fine if you can get it on a new handguard at all, and if you can then get it onto the barrel. I have used various fishing line openers and modified circlip pliers on them over the years and even briefly owned the military wrench, but none of these is foolproof.

Hogging out both handguards will immediately contribute to accuracy, because the less contact there is between these and the barrel and receiver, the less obvious the torque/heat effects on the barrel and attendant assemblies.

Experiments were done from the early 1940s on to produce an "all-in-one" handguard set—sometimes of painted aluminum and sometimes of dyed-in-the-mass plastics—wherein the handguards and middle band were a single formed unit. Some of these even deleted the band/clip entirely. And they worked, but the plastics of the time tended to distort and cook, and the aluminum had to be refinished frequently and had the additional disadvantage of transmitting heat to the surfaces very quickly.

For the technology of the times, however, wood worked best, was available, and protected both the user's hands and body and the rifle's metal, so that we still have a great many rifles. So the "handguard flaw" involves a certain amount of misery for those of us who work on the rifles and clean them diligently, and a modern, high-heat version of the experimental one-piece set might be superior—if someone would produce such a beast in a manner that did not significantly alter the look of the rifle.

AH, SWEET MYSTERY OF TRAINING

Morons can operate the M1 only at considerable risk. And they can never seem to get it apart. This is just one of the many reasons the M1 has no real history of use by criminal gangs. The hand-eye coordination and sense of feel required to insert an eight-round clip without leaving some skin and blood inside the rifle's guts are, I'm sure, quite beyond the capabilities of any of the gangbangers in my neighborhood. Not too long ago, these lowlifes had a sort of gunfight with at least five long guns and a dozen pistols, in which the only shots fired came from a little .25 automatic and an old revolver. Nobody was being easy on anybody, and nobody hit anybody, either. They just couldn't properly load most of the hardware, and one dimwit in particular seemed unaware that he had to cycle the bolt on his SKS to get the first round where it had to be.

For someone who has no discipline or cannot read or follow instructions, the M1 is perhaps the worst rifle in the world. And for that, I am very glad. I've had only one incident in which an M1 caught a digit with its bolt, that about ten years ago, when I was cleaning a particularly sweet match rifle. I got a phone call that required me to pass on quite a lot of information, and, of course, I should have set the rifle aside as soon as the phone rang. But I didn't. Having completed the bore cleaning and while chatting merrily away, I used a finger as a reflector off my high-intensity light to check my work. It must have struck the follower precisely correctly to release the bolt and operating rod, because my next sensation was a great deal of pain, and the weird sensation that my right index finger was growing even as it bled.

I not only had to open the rifle and clean it up but also dress the wound and, while not really in the mood, make sure the blood didn't do more damage than sloppy cleaning could ever do. The man on the other end heard the noise and my expression of pain. It wasn't a phone call I could postpone, and I couldn't let the rifle or my finger just sit. And I kept rolling over repeatedly in my head that old admonition, "Never forget your training!"

My finger acquired the shape of a .30-06 round, albeit puffed up, and to this day has a small "bottleneck" from being effectively "chambered.". . . I can thus claim that I have never had "M1 thumb," but I have a permanent "M1 finger."

Stripping the M1, especially the bolt, operating rod, and trigger group/firing mechanism, requires training and repetition and considerable care. Also necessary are some mechanical intuition and a sense of feel that's adequate to know when something is not right. I once upon a time stupidly presumed this could be taught to anyone; it can't.

Perhaps the greatest "weakness" of the M1 Garand is that it requires some training, knowledge, discipline, and instinct to use, let alone maintain. I consider that, by the way, one of the rifle's greatest strengths, for it is an apparatus virtually useless to those who are unsuitable to own anything more dangerous than a spoon.

CHAPTER 5

THE M1'S DELIVERY CHRONOLOGY: WORLD WAR II AND POSTWAR

Readers may recall my carefully avoiding a date chart for M1 Garands in my earlier book. The reason is that such charts are, in a way, a trap: someone restoring a rifle may presume that they are somehow ironclad, perfectly accurate, and therefore a sort of religious law, never even to be challenged. So the first thing you need to know about this date chart (adapted from Duff's material—which is as close as you get to complete and accurate—and various other sources, plus a lot of my own notes since 1964) is this: when a receiver was built or contracted for is merely a small part of the rifle's history!

By no means do receiver dates correlate precisely to barrel dates, nor should they.

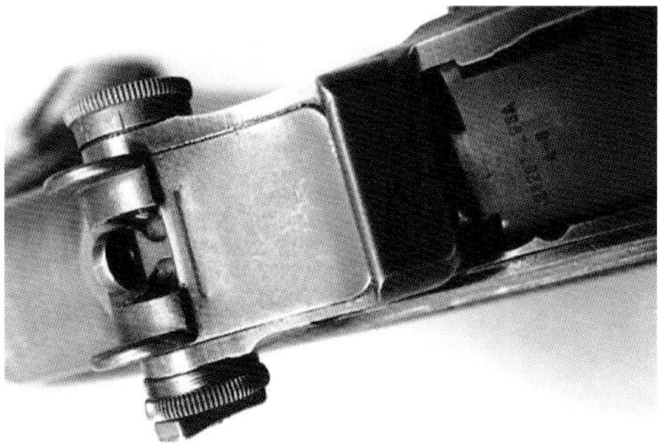

Collectors should do some analysis before presuming anything is wrong. This World War II rifle, numbered over 3 million, carried a sight cover much earlier. But the rifle seems never to have been rebuilt, and the finish matches perfectly. This doesn't mean it's original, just that this slightly reconfigured part has been on the rifle a long time and may be correct, even though much earlier than the rifle.

Barrel production was frequently 30 to 60 days ahead of or behind the production of other parts, especially receivers. And if a rifle was rejected or required adjustment for some reason, it could wind up leaving the factory with a barrel considerably later than its theoretical receiver date. Receiver dates and production groupings are, therefore, just one small part of the story.

Even though other collectors have told me similar stories, I am not any happier to have spent a long time looking for the "right" barrel for a particular rifle, only to find, either in the literature or by experience, that, in fact, the tube with which it arrived was the correct unit. You feel particularly stupid if you've gone to the trouble and expense to find the "correct" barrel and mount it and you no longer own the one that was truly right.

There are other factors: I recently received a letter from a man who was deeply concerned that his rifle with an approximately 100000 receiver serial number had none of the correct parts on it, and in fact stock, barrel, and so on were all ca. late 1944 to early 1945. Not only did I tell him not to worry, I also told him to appreciate the likelihood that he had a World War II combat veteran. Again, there's no way of absolutely proving that, but the general practice during World War II rebuilds was to waste as little as possible, and virtually everything on this rifle had apparently required replacement. Some accidents could cause such a condition, but combat damage is a very strong possibility. Since, I have seen a lot of other "jump cut" rifles, which is why I now have a nickname for them. Those are rifles of the correct subtype or "dash marking" on the right lug or "leg" for one approximate date, but ALL fittings and "furniture" from another, sometimes about a year later. This is often because of a receiver being set aside due to some kind of malfunction on or before test firing. That serial number would be then folded into another production batch, much later, meaning that it's actual "born on" or "first issue" date is far later than the way-too-neat charts everyone regards as gospel.

Just as a slightly later barrel should not be of much concern, so small parts a month to a year earlier than the supposed receiver date shouldn't cause a collector to panic. Usable parts were never thrown out, and unless some flaw existed in a design, extant materials were used up as located. Even though this date chart is here under some protest (from me!), a good friend pointed out that a rifle's delivery date contributes to its legacy. And there's a purity to this that anyone can appreciate. I have therefore attempted to include enough notes and exceptions to make this material helpful.

World War II M1 production was nicely documented, and it is the very precision of these contract/delivery dates that sets the "trap" that sometimes confuses collectors. So as good as the data are, their key limitation is inherent: *it's only a delivery date*! Really, it's a contracted delivery date. A part here and a part there do not make a rifle "incorrect." In some thirty-six years of fooling around with Mr. Garand's rifle, I've noticed with some regularity very late World War II rifles in nice, apparently original condition, bearing 1946 barrels, some with postwar "D35382" operating rods and "Type 3" sights. There is absolutely no way to prove it, but, at the very least, there is a strong possibility that these rifles were not fully assembled until many months after the war.

In the period 1932–36, 80 toolroom prototype rifles were produced, numbered to 80, and it may therefore be considered that production—slow at the onset—actually began in August 1937. This chart uses the numerical month abbreviation and the last production number for that month, thus using the "shorthand" similar to that actually used on the barrels. However, barrel dating was not present on many rifles before 1940, sometimes into 1941.

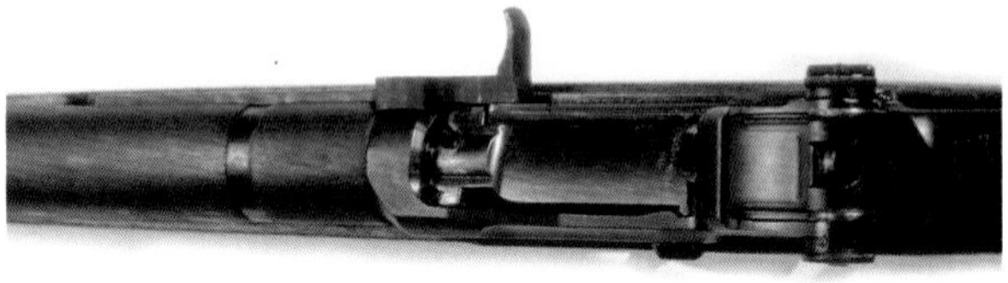

Topside horizontal shot of an undisturbed 1944 Springfield Armory (US) M1 Garand rifle. This one was a pre-GCA '68 unmarked (no stamped-in import marking) import rifle, whose owner had the 1965 paperwork. Most of these came from European countries, selling off reserve, "cash and carry" rifles, long since paid for in hard currency and not Military Aid Program material.

SPRINGFIELD 1937–1945

DATE	SERIAL #	DATE	SERIAL #
8–37	120	12–37	1034
10–37	539	2–38	1338
4–38	2213	11–37	699
6–38/7–38	2911	1–38	1186
9–38	4386	3–38	1809
11–38	6072	5–38	2406
1–39	7715	8–38	3537
3–39	9893	10–38	5242
5–39	11511	12–38	6972
9–37	307	2–39	8762
		4–39	10703

NOTE: At this time, reports from the field began to show up suggesting great difficulty in getting reliable performance from gas trap mechanisms, and various prototype gas port guns began to reach the field. Often, guns from mid-1939 to about September 1940 seem to have been "rebuilt," before ever leaving Springfield Armory, to the more reliable gas port configuration.

6–39 . 8–39 10–39 12–39 2–40 . 4–40 . 6–40 .

6–39	12848	6–40	46221
8–39	14823	7–39	12911
10–39	19410	9–39	17010
12–39	23567	11–39	21293
2–40	30008	1–40	26729
4–40	38034	3–40	33790

SPRINGFIELD 1937–1945

DATE	SERIAL #	DATE	SERIAL #
8–40	59868	9–40	68054
10–40	78306	11–40	90177

NOTE: Winchester contract kicked in December 1940. Winchester assigned "missing" serial numbers (Springfield had produced rifles numbered to 100000, then jumped to 165501), including instructional rifles beginning with "first" Winchester shown in The Complete M1 Garand. Springfield production for the month ended at serial number 169073.

1–41	183519	2–41	197911
3–41	211228	4–41	228527
5–41	248757	6–41	269686
7–41	296252	8–41	324301
9–41	349442	10–41	377258
11–41	401529	12–41	429811
1–42	462737	2–42	498216
3–42	542494	4–42	588879
5–42	638679	6–42	691401
7–42	749779	8–42	809016

9–42	872343	10–42	940250
11–42	1008899	12–42	1090310
1–43	1169091		

NOTE: The second Winchester contract kicked in February 1943, so one "end" number is 1200000; lot numbers resume at 1357474 and continue to the last February issue, 1396225.

3–43	1469177	4–43	1547452
5–43	1629565	6–43	1710012
7–43	1786469	8–43	1877654
9–43	1978407		
11–43	2204430	10–43	2092825

NOTE: In December 1943 there was another Winchester contract crossover, wherein numbers ended (first lot) at 2305849, resumed at 2410000, and finished at 2420191 at the end of the month.

1–44	2543412	4–44	2810628
3–44	2723004	6–44	2981126
5–44	2900312	8–44	3114434
7–44	3051952	10–44	3242497
9–44	3180532	12–44	3359159
11–44	3302641	2–45	3531489
1–45	3450503	4–45	3717867
3–45	3672442	6–45	3875601
5–45	3797768		
2–44	2634316		

NOTE: Various records draw various conclusions in this late period after June of 1945.

Very early Springfield receivers and most of the rest of the rifle closely resemble Winchester's output.

Small differences evolved in gas port Springfields from late 1940 (top) to 1942 (middle) and early 1943 (bottom).

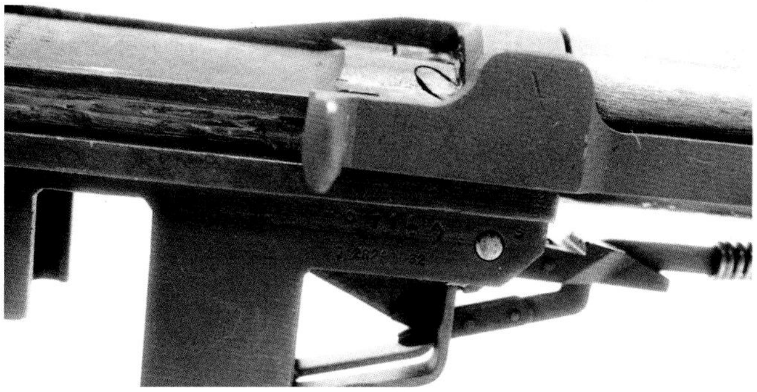

All Springfield-produced M1 receivers noted heat treatment data, though not always in legible form.

Receiver 97308, with early "flush nut" sights.

eceiver #208518.

SA receiver #481614.

Two midwar Springfield M1 receivers in the 2.5 million range.

The mill marks on this -17 M1 receiver, from about 1942, bespeak a worn out blade and are unusual for that late in M1 production at Springfield.

Receiver #462975, in a rebuilt condition, mounted in a laminated Boyd's stock.

In mid-1945, production slowed down in terms of complete rifles, and the last World War II number is considered to have been in the 3888000 range. Many of these are found with barrels dated just a few months later than that date, suggesting that they were not completed until well after the war. Also, at the very end, many experiments and new M1 developments at Remington and elsewhere caused a kind of confusion similar to "last casualty" malaise in the field, wherein the formerly meticulous record-keeping disappears, though guns were being delivered new to European-based units as late as 1947.

WINCHESTER 1940–LATE 1945

Winchester was a business first and foremost, and, as such, its prime goal was profit. Since Winchester barrels were not customarily dated, instead carrying the part number and a version of standard commercial proofs, the receiver dates are not quite as vital to putting together a restoration.

In addition, Winchester and Springfield sometimes slightly overlapped each other's production allocations. Approximately 30,000 Winchesters were produced in the range 357474 to well over 1387XXX (precise number unknown) in August/September 1943, and quite a bunch in the 2540000 range. These "duplicates" were frequently stamped with an "A" or etched below the number. The WIN-13 series receivers are primarily in the 1.6 million

The part number on top of Winchester M1 Garand barrel.

serial number range and comprise some very strange sets of parts, including some operating rods that are unmarked.

Winchester production began with 100,101 (shown in detail in *The Complete M1 Garand*), part of the "school" or "instructional" lot. Early and many late Winchesters were finished inky black; many late versions and the WIN-13 series bore hodgepodges of phosphate and dulite finishes.

A comparison of a Springfield receiver from 1945 to a Winchester of similar vintage. Note, however, that many original Springfield receivers of the period 1942 and before were virtually as dark as the Winchesters. The Springfield receiver has surely been refinished.

DATE	**SERIAL #**	**DATE**	**SERIAL #**
12–40 to 1–41 "school lot" numbers 100101 to 100501			
2–41	100831	7–41	115501
4–41	104901	9–41	122081
6–41	111501	10–41	126130
8–41	20111	12–41	137960

3–41	102701	11–41	131130
5–41	107801	1–42	144110
2–42	149130	3–42	155310
4–42	162190		

NOTE: May 1942 was a contract "jump" point where the initial finished unit should have been 165500, then resuming at 1200001, finishing with 1203692.

6–42	1210472	4–43	1323872
8–42	1228982	6–43	1349982
10–42	1254002	7–42	1218972
12–42	1276102	9–42	1241002
2–43	1294762	11–42	1266502
1–43	1282762	5–43	1336882
3–43	1309772	7–43	1364982

NOTE: August 1943 was another contract "jump" point, where the initial lot finish was at 1380000, resuming at 2305850, finishing the calendar month at 2305932.

9–43	2318032	10–43	2334032
11–43	2523942	12–43	2533642
1–44	2379642	2–44	2394642
3–44	2409642	4–44	2424642
5–44	2439642	6–44	2454642
71–44	2469642	8–44	2484642
9–45	2499642	10–45	2513822
11–45	2523124	12–45	2533142

NOTE: January 1945 to the end of February 1945 was another contract "jump" point, this time constituting 2540XXX numbers, and groupings ending with 1601150 to 1605600 and, apparently, also 1607100, getting the WIN-13s out the door over the next few months. largely after the war. The WIN-13s were never really contracted for but were part of Winchester's insistence upon using up remaining parts, forgings, etc.

3–45	1613000
5–45	1627000
4–45	1620000

The very first Winchester off the "school contract," 100001, with its data legend on the horseshoe burnished to show markings.

Gas cylinder detail on the very first Winchester M1.

Winchester receiver #1332557.

Close-up of the muzzle end of a ca. 1944 Winchester. Note the single-slot gas cylinder lock screw and the wide "bent" sight "ears."

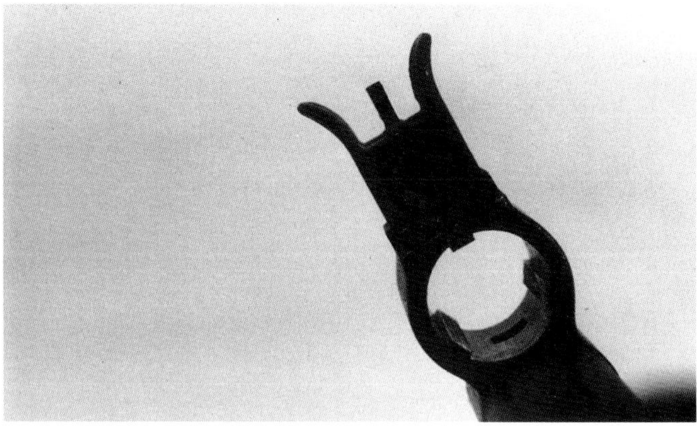

Rear detail of a Winchester M1 sight, off a WIN-13, mounted a very late Winchester wide base gas cylinder.

Winchester's WIN-13 receivers overlapped SA numbers and incorporated some of the changes from SA production of three to five years earlier.

A great many Springfield rifles like this one sport barrels and operating rods of Winchester production, and may have been part of some kind of parts interchange testing, actually released in issue. The author has also seen several of the reverse—Winchesters bearing Springfield barrels and operating rods of exactly the same date as when the Winchester receiver was supposedly delivered.

Winchester never built a gas trap rifle. That system had been discarded by December 1940. But most of the detail parts were of early pattern, and many stayed that way to the very end.

The very last Winchester bore an unknown serial number somewhere over 1640000 and was completed in June 1945.

A further Winchester anomaly of some interest to collectors: In *The Complete Garand,* I noted having seen several Springfield M1s bearing Winchester barrels and operating rods of precisely the same vintage and detail, suggesting that the long-held suspicion that parts-interchange programs were conducted at both manufacturing facilities was much more than a rumor. Since 1992, I have seen several more. Somewhat unnerving—and easier to speculate about because of the attendant upgrades—is the fact that I have seen several Winchester rifles, apparently undisturbed, bearing dated Springfield barrels and operating rods correct for precisely that vintage. This *prima facie* evidence suggests—but does not absolutely prove—that these interchange test rifles were released into general issue.

POST-WORLD WAR II DATE INFORMATION: EXCEPTIONS AND NOTES

From 1945 to 1952, most production activity on the M1 dealt with prototypes, some by Remington, apparently newly built; others converted as convenient from earlier receivers; and a very tiny amount of production evidently almost hand manufactured, some of it apparently intended to edify machinists and personnel at new contractors. Considerable effort was directed toward getting Beretta's Garand program moving. International Harvester was prepared to get into the program with perhaps more enthusiasm than its ultimate production record ever justified.

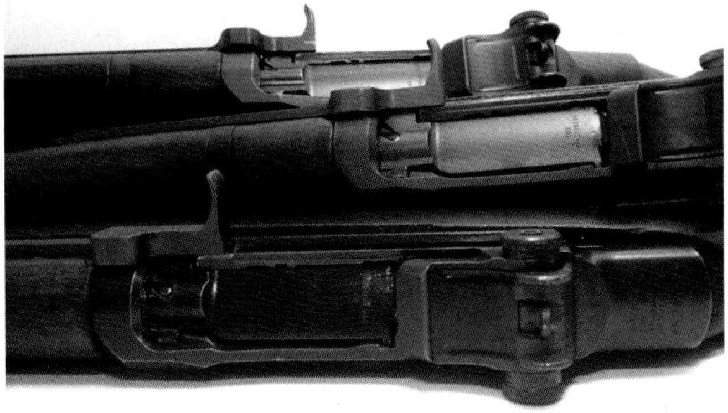

From front to rear, representatives of all three US postwar Garand manufacturers (International Harvester, Springfield Armory, and H&R), all from about 1955–56.

However, the accuracy of postwar records is nowhere near as tight as the World War II material, especially at IHC, where production "discipline" seemingly bordered on chaos. Thus, what most date charts of postwar vintage do is take contract length, divide by months, and come up with approximate dates. Even so, barrel dates and even makers often line up only very loosely. So here I've included "durations" and allow you to do the math, in concert with the gross production chart elsewhere in this missive. And where I have been able to pin down some data that would be of use to collectors and researchers, I've included appropriate notes.

Again, none of the following data should be seen as ironclad rules. Guidelines, perhaps.

- 1952–54: SA batch 4200001 to 4399999
- 1953–54: IHC batch 4400000 to 4660000
- 1953–54: H&R (HRA code) batch 4660001 to 4800000 (unassigned: 4800001–4999999)
- August 1952: SA "NATO" standard batch 5000000 to 5000500, out of sequence, apparently intended for European subcontractors/armed forces
- Mid-1954–56: IHC batch 5000501–5278245

- 1954–55: SA batch 5278246–5488246
- 1954–56: H&R (HRA) batch 5488247–5793847
- 1955–57: SA batch 5793848–6099905

4.65 million IHC gap letter receiver.

A 4.68 million H&R rifle.

From August 1956 to early 1957, an H&R "blip" batch was reassigned from the Springfield batch to H&R for a 400- to 500- rifle contract overrun. (I have seen four of these, one with an HRA 7.62x51 barrel, the others with rather odd, but apparently original, earlier H&R tubes in conventional .30 caliber.

Interesting Subgroups

The receivers ranging from 4440000 to well over 4445000 were International Harvesters actually produced in 1953 by Springfield Armory.

The receivers ranging from 4638XXX to about 4660000 were the "gap letter" "IHC" receivers, actually produced at Springfield in 1953–54. Likewise for those ranging from 5198034 to 5213034, in about 1955–56.

No precise numbers exist for the receivers bearing IHC logos actually built at H&R, but the range in which these are sometimes found includes 5213035 to somewhat over 5217000. This was also 1955–56, and apparently some of these originally bore "HRA" barrels.

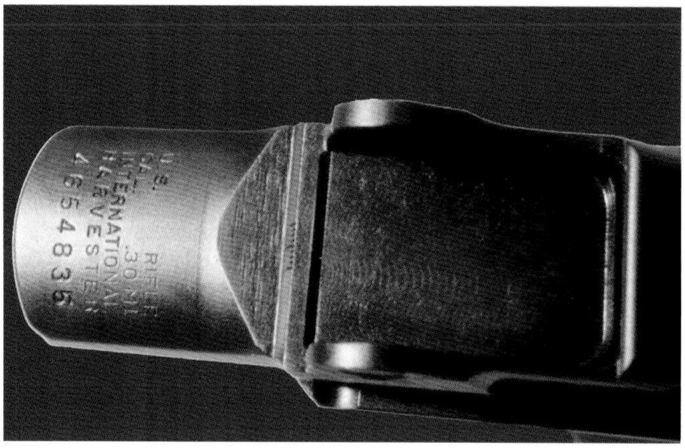

International Harvester M1 Garand rifles are intriguing because of their small output and somewhat turbulent production history. Bailouts and emergency production assistance resulted in markings permutations like this "gap letter," actually produced under the tutelage of the Springfield Armory. Notice the odd spacing of the lettering. The excellent Line Materials subcontracted barrels generally made them good shooters despite quality issues. A great deal of what is known about the parts array is a little more abstract than collectors sometimes realize, and some of us suspect (but do not *know*!) that some of the HRA and SA parts found on the rifles were, in fact, original.

A fairly early International Harvester receiver. Those pits on the rear sight aperture are finished over, but it seemed to be an original, correct unit. While it's likely those fissures were caused much later, it isn't uncommon on IHC's to show finish over pits. Still, those particular ones seem to have been caused by someone beating on the sight with a punch, rather than by corrosion, and they probably would upset a potential buyer.

A 1954 "competition" SA receiver in the 5.2 million range, on the left, and an IHC ca. 1953–54 in the 4.52 million range.

A 5.63 million H&R, received from the CMP with all H&R parts save the bolt, a condition very quickly rectified.

As a group, M1Cs are postwar modifications of wartime receivers in the range 3200000 to 3800000. A few doubtful Winchesters exist, with nominal chance of authenticity. But those with the highest possibility of authentic provenance would be those that coordinate precisely in the same production time frame.

Such lists are necessarily incomplete. However, they help explain things like the recently observed IHC parts cache I inspected, all of which bore heavy, characteristic greenish phosphate over fairly heavy pitting. International Harvester had bad quality control problems, which apparently horrified military inspectors and the armory, and I have seen misground receiver contours, among other faults, on IHCs. Still, they are fascinating to collectors because of the many permutations and variations. And it is a testament to Garand's engineering skills that the rifle would still work, and rather well, grossly out of specification and beyond the mundane parameters of even a mediocre craftsman.

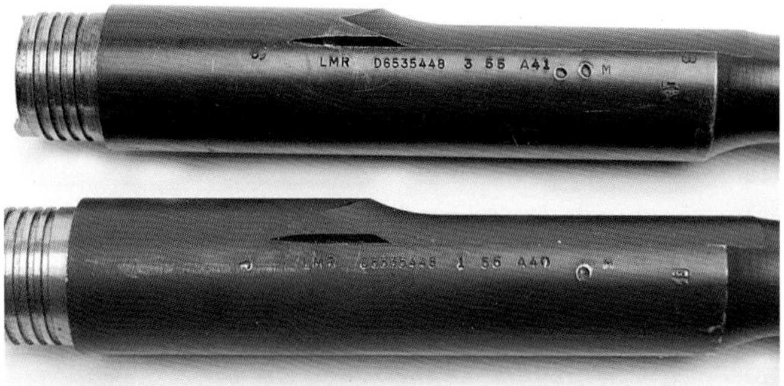

A couple of LMR barrels.

All contractors produced spare parts as well as receivers and complete rifles. And we continue to run into anomalies: SA barrels on H&R receivers, of precisely the right date and apparently undisturbed; LMR barrels and HRA barrels in similar places; and so on. I recall reading Dave McClain on some subject or other in the GCA newsletter saying, "Never say never," and while I won't go out on a limb and suggest that all such rifles were delivered that way, I'm not foolish enough to say the opposite, either! Not too long ago I handled a very nice, very late International Harvester rifle in virtually mint condition, whose owner was a veteran. He had owned the rifle since 1960 and had a bill of sale. The barrel bore the earliest date I have ever seen on an "LMR," and he asked me at the end of our conversation, "Is it right?" I said, "It's great!" Which it was. Anything else I'd told him would have been guesswork.

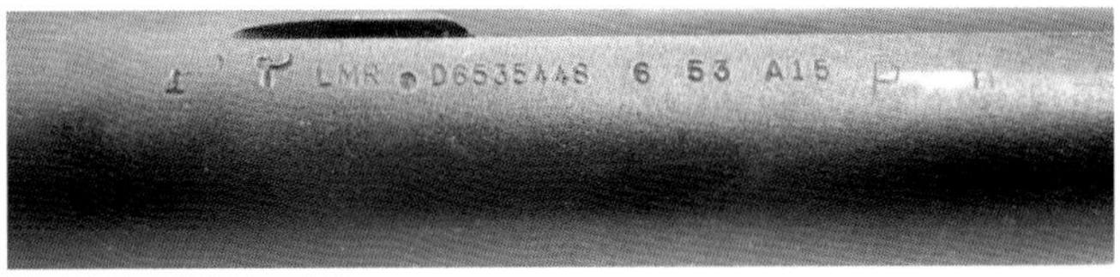

The very best of the Garand government issue service barrels were the latest, including most from the 1960s, even to include the Italian tubes and the V.A.R.'s from Denmark, and of course, the Line Materials units normally associated with International Harvester. The AMF, HRA, and SA 7.62x51 conversion barrels, of course, performed better still, but involved a cartridge change. This is a rather early "LMR." The "R" is for "rifle." Had the firm produced a pistol barrel, the code would've supposedly been "LMP".

Note: The lubrication guide contained in the CMP's "Read This First" guide to the M1 Garand is adequate, but many shooters, mindful of the increased historic and monetary value of their rifles, go considerably beyond those fundamentals. For example, the operating rod raceway on the receiver's right is usually lubed in the groove for its entire length with panthermic wheel-bearing or other such greases. The detent in the operating rod behind the "knuckle" where the right-hand bolt lug engages is worthy of a substantial dollop of grease. The hammer spring plunger (the shaft inside the spring), its tube or "barrel" (inside, of course!), and the spring are generally also coated. Many match shooters likewise apply grease to the frontmost five inches of the operating rod tube, as well as to the "hook" of the operating rod catch. Where the follower ("recoil") spring reposes inside the operating rod benefits from heavy grease, and since that area can also be a moisture trap, most shooters preclude the possibility of damage and lubricate there quite heavily. Modern wheel-bearing greases, machine assembly greases, and a variety of others can and will serve well. And as a preservative, modern museum conservators and advanced shooters most often find waxes, which do not migrate with gravity, are vastly superior to oil in any and all preventative applications, including car waxes and products as fundamental as ordinary grocery store paste wax. I use Johnson's paste wax and whatever auto material first falls under the hand, and it has been decades since anything of mine acquired rust while I owned it. There are countless cases where oil was relied upon and repeatedly failed. The cause is, again, gravity, which means thin liquids move down and dry out. There have been articles in the GCA Journal on this topic that put this even more in context and provide much more data than is appropriate in this volume.

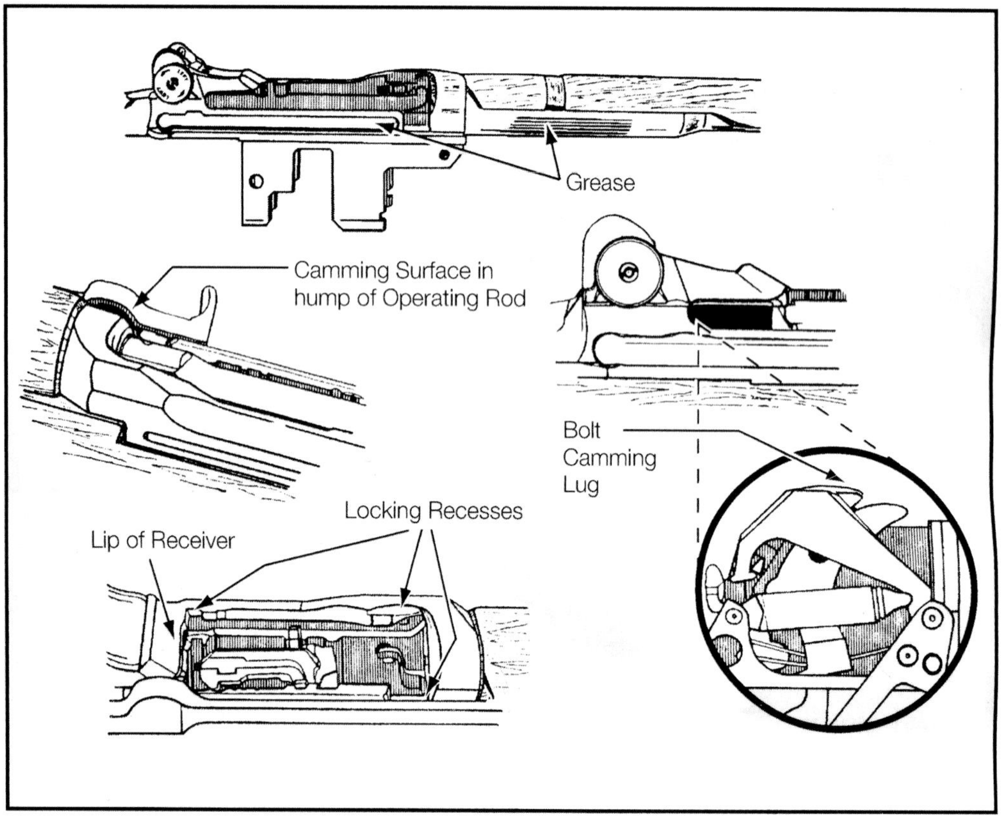

Fig. 39 – Points to apply rifle grease.

The CMP's greasing guide is very conservative and traditional. Most precision shooters also grease the last 7 to 8 inches of the piston end of the operating rod, inside the gas cylinder. The so-called "snaggletooth hook" of the operating rod catch and a fairly major smidge under the operating rod's slide-by area of the barrel's right surface (this is shown on the chart, but not emphasized), where usually the markings are found, is usually also greased. No reason to spend absurd amounts of money on "gun-labeled" products exists. Any panthermic wheel bearing grease greatly exceeds the specification. Many good smiths also use a patina of grease on the rear sight's friction surfaces.

PART II

COLLECTING AND SHOOTING THE M1 GARAND IN THE NEW MILLENNIUM: MYSTERIES SOLVED, TROUBLE AVOIDED, TARGETS HIT

It's hardly amazing that a mere tool becomes almost a cult object. Look what happened with cutlery, plates, vintage cars, the Jeep, and even bottles. The M1, of course, is still used for its main purposes: precision shooting and training in the general discipline of firearms responsibility. A couple of my friends think M1s are just plain ugly, and I don't dispute that, either. To me, they look precisely the way a rifle ought to look, and I wax mine and clean them just about every time I think of it. Indeed, when *The Complete M1 Garand* finally hit the market in 1998, I had spent so much money preparing that tome that I'd sold every rifle I owned just to make ends meet.

This part of The Classic M1 Garand is about enjoying and maintaining the rifle and, incidentally, making sure your thumbs (based on my mail, some of you have far more than two) and your face remain fairly intact—that is, *safety*!

There isn't much here about ammunition and reloading (most of that was covered in the previous volume), though I have included some updates.

And we'll address the touchiest parts of maintaining and smoothing the rifle in detail, with some fairly controversial but nearly foolproof procedures.

M1 Garand Collector's Piece

The mystique of the M1 Garand is no puzzle. It's the very last US general issue military long gun that can be owned by a civilian with a minimum of paperwork, and it's long and illustrious service included the most dangerous, widest conflict in human history, the Second World War.

Technologically, it was the very first infantry rifle of the United States that was truly innovative. It was preceded, of course, by the Springfield M1903, a M98 Mauser derivative, an earlier Norwegian-designed rifle, the Krag, and a series of domestic designs which were, for their times, very, very average. Functionally, the M1 demonstrated in 1946 just how superior it was, shooting National Match scores will ball ammunition which, in aggregate, surpassed any of those executed with the Model of 1903 in the decades preceding with actual match ammunition.

John Cantius Garand's original .276 Pedersen prototypes aren't much related to the refined rifles that rolled off the lines at Springfield Armory (US, Massachusetts) or Beretta over the ensuing years, but the idea of a fast functioning gas operated semi-automatic rifle with most of its functioning innards carefully sealed inside the traditional stock and handguards which seemed so radical in the early 1930s lives on over eighty years later, still shooting, and still impressively demonstrating a standard of excellence that's difficult to duplicate.

ALL M1 Garands accept the very same eight-round *en bloc* ejecting clips. This view shows nickel-plated Federal brass "Gold Match" .30 06 on the left, precision handloads on GI brass, with Sierra bullets, on the right. Any Mauser based full-power cartridge can, for enough trouble and money, produce a functional M1 Garand variant, and one of the author's best was in 7x57 Mauser, as close as one can get to the ORIGINAL M1 cartridge, .276 Pedersen center fire in factory fodder.

Just how difficult that duplication is was made pretty clear to me by the production staff at several facilities producing the M14 receiver (no, NOT M1A's—that's a copyrighted SAI product—Smith, Fulton, Armscorp, and LRB produce M14s!) and well-schooled in the M1 advised me that the operating rod raceway, for example, is so subtle it CANNOT be properly set up by CNC (Computer Numerically Controlled) machinery. This may have changed in the last few months, but Ron Smith of Smith Enterprises International put it bluntly: "Those who tried failed."

Still, from the very first production gas trap rifles of 1936, by that time in the old 1906 caliber .30 cartridge, to the last Berettas to leave Gardone Val Trompia (Lombardy) about forty years later, the rifle was improved, enhanced, and developed, and ironically, the last units delivered and used in service (some Tipo 2s may still be in service in Italy) wound up chamber for 7.62x51mm. NATO, a cartridge far closer to the original than the ubiquitous .30-06.

Two M1 Garands in .308, a "Tipo 2" on the right, and a standard length rifle on the left. The "Tipo 2" rifles are supposedly still in reserve in Italy with non-infantry units, albeit whether they're ever issued at this late date has to be open to question. They were mostly built on "cash and carry" US receivers. Shortened from the rear ½ inch, they are fine rifles, and as of late 2019, complete kits with modified barrels, operating rods, handguard, and brand new stocks were still available.

Every single part on the rifle changed and evolved. The receiver alone underwent about 35 noted upgrades/revisions before the end of World War II.

A single magazine article cannot possibly encompass all the changes to the rifle or impart the entire chronology.

To the collector, though, here are some key designators:

Pre-War: At the US Armory in Massachusetts, until about serial number 48,000, the gas trap gas cylinder and extant early systems prevailed. The last gas traps to leave the

Armory seem to have been CDD (contract delivery dated) about August of 1940. There was NEVER a "gas trap" Winchester. On earliest rifles, most parts, even small ones, were numbered if sufficient surface space was available, and yes, there are such things as numbered buttplate screws. The general surmise (that's a "pretty solid educated guess") is that some of the impetus behind this detailed numbering was to teach assembly staff to identify parts. Almost all original finish on M1 Garands is very dark, virtually all of it phosphate. The medium gray stuff so common now is almost *never* original, and usually is fairly recent, often civilian. Pre-war receivers attached to mixed up, many times rebuilt rifles, wherein all updates and corrections have been executed, command only small premiums unless exceptionally low serialed or fairly close to correct. All pre-war rifles bore the flush nut/short pinion rear sights so rare and valuable now, and so very impractical in actual use. These are part numbers, not serial numbers.

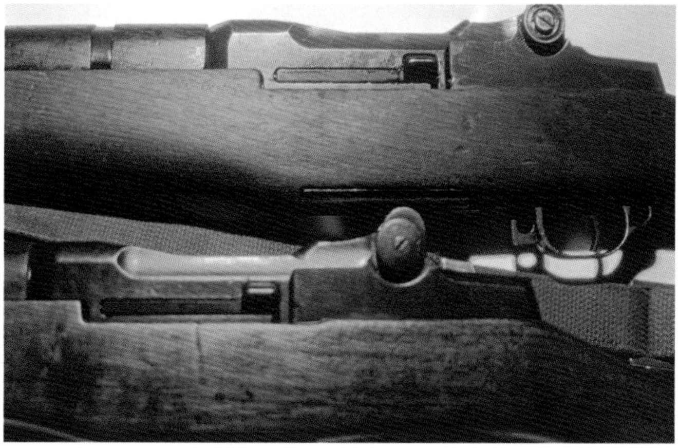

Two "import" wartime M1 Garands, right after degreasing, ca. 1993. The front one still retains its locking bar rear sight. Either, with a good barrel and tight stock fit, is a decent choice as a casual shooter. The upper one was the purest of all mixmasters, containing at least one part from every contractor, but sporting a near new, very crisp, late LMR barrel.

Wartime: Winchester production entered the program in 1941 and that New Haven firm had generated roughly 30,000 rifles by Pearl Harbor time. Their primary production was centered around the "dash two" receiver and upgrades, when made, were invariably late. Machine quality never equaled the Armory, The Armory, by 1945, was up to "dash 35" revisions, whereas Winchester's "WIN-13" specimens at the very end were approximately the same as the SA "dash three" receivers of more than three years earlier. Rough machining on W.R.A. parts is the rule. Save for early '42, all wartime rear sights were of the lock bar type, at first short pinion, developing into the final "Type 3 locking bar (large with squared edges) that was employed, albeit there are several marking and configuration setups. All wartime unmodified operating rods are fairly rare, and more subject ot bending and/or breakage than "cut" or postwar specimens, most cautious collectors choose not to shoot them heavily, if at all. Because of the smaller quantities and many variations in small parts vintage, and of course the Winchester name, the New Haven firm's rifles command price premiums. They are not, however, better rifles, and they especially are not better shooters. Correct wartime rifles with solid, original barrels are difficult to find, and many collectors—when and if they own such rifles—either do not shoot them at all, or do so with key, high priced, high wear parts off the rifle. Wartime production ended at around 3.9 million, and there is compelling evidence that many of the highest numbered World War II rifles were neither completed nor issued until as late as 1947, although receiver "CDD's" (contract delivery dates) end about August of 1945.

All inspected and issue WW2 vintage butt stocks originally bore letter-cartouched stocks, save of course 100001, Winchester's very first "school" M1, which stayed at New Haven, never actually being inspected for acceptance by Colonel Waldemar Broberg.

This is the small "DAS" (Defense Acceptance Stamp) as found on almost all but the very last H&R (HRA code) M1 Garand rifles and, according to one collector, a very few IHC specimens.

Postwar US: No new M1 receivers were produced with CDD's between August of 1945 and late 1952. The lettered cartouche acceptance mark was phased out early on, being replaced by the "eagle and stars" defense acceptance stamp. Armory production began at 4.2 million. Harrington and Richardson, who had been producing replacement barrels, was introduced into the program, with superb overall results. International Harvester also entered the program, albeit it took several "bailouts" to keep up production, and as a result, the numbers are small, there are many variations, and the rifles carry rather high values, especially if correct and original. The safety relieved operating rod became standard, as did the vastly improve T105E1 internally locked and sprung rear sight. Virtually every small part on the rifle had by this time been improved and enhanced. By '56–'57, US production was complete, and the M14 entered production, in stages.

Italian Production—The first Italian M1 Garands were produced in about 1954. Figures on total production are sketchy, and collectors are not truly sure how many were produced, this being complicated by the fact that virtually all Beretta serial numbers were four digits and letters, to the instructions of the ordering country, meaning that there are many with duplicate serial numbers. The second Italian manufacturer, Breda, seems to have disappeared from the program there by 1956. Italy, Denmark, Indonesia, Colombia, Ethiopia, Somalia, probably Egypt and Morocco were Beretta customers of which collectors seem certain, but there seem to be many more. Last deliveries seem to have been as "cut rate" pieces addended to BM.59 contracts, all the last in 7.62x51mm., some twenty years or more after the armory ceased US domestic production. Many US supplied parts were supplied to Beretta, largely Winchester-produced, which accounts for a fairly large supply of W.R.A. bits and pieces carrying the ubiquitous "PB," including milled wartime trigger guards, which were never actually produced in Italy. Rumors to the contrary, it has been affirmed to a certainty that the "machine tools from Winchester" sent to Italy ca. 1951 were *never actually utilized*, being in very poor condition after outdoor storage, albeit they were studied and reverse engineered to facilitate production, initially announced as taking place in Rome. Many collectors, however, having studied the receivers with microscopes for machine tool "tracks," suggest that *all* Italian receivers seem to have been made by common machinery, probably hands, and likely in Gardone val Trompia. This is definitely NOT the case with other parts, which carry several different "fingerprint" patterns. Seemingly all non-Italian true military Italian-produced Garands will be bear national crests and identifiers. Some imported in the late 1970s to the '80s bear no national crests at all, constituting Beretta's last few "leftovers" purchased by the Reeses for resale in the US

Bolt and surrounding area of a Danish-issue Beretta M1 Garand. Very uncommon, the Beretta Garands are very collectible, commanding high prices under pressure from both shooters and collectors. Being delivered new well into the 1970s, some say even later, they're the very last of all the M1 Garand rifles to be actually militarily issued. The Danish crested rifles are the most common. All other national crests (and all non-Italian-issue rifles would have some kind of crest!) run even higher. Some were imported in the '80s with no national crests at all, those being the "leftovers" from Beretta's earlier serial production. Those are still authentic Beretta products, but at the very bottom of the value of the dollar value scale. Those were brand new when imported to the US, and many were not even assembled until they arrived.

To determine what is correct and not it is necessary, especially with early rifles, to have industrial histories and perhaps the GCA JOURNAL handy. And new things keep coming up. For example, I have in the last twenty years or so run across a lot of rifles bearing receivers from a few months to just shy of a year "younger" than every other part on the rifle . . . that is, say, a mid-1942 rifle bearing everything "correct" from, according to the books, early 1943, yet bearing paperwork indicating it couldn't have been fooled with much, and never having been touched by a collector. I *think* (but I do not *know!*) that these are receivers torn down from rifles rejected for some reason, set aside, and assembled later, sometimes quite a lot later. Quite a few purist collectors have come to similar "guesstimate" conclusions . . . but all that is, truly, constitutes a probability. Such a hypothesis is the best available explanation, but will *never* be conclusive.

This rather tight fitting butt stock might very well be a Winchester, albeit almost all of its original markings seem to have been obscured. It bore no less than FOUR "P" and "circle P" firing proofs, a DAS that looked wrong but probably wasn't, an ordnance wheel of the size normally found on mortars, and several odd rebuild marks, all suggesting that this critter had been mated to many rifles and been in Anniston, the armory, and Ogden, plus a few places I couldn't identify. It came on this late CMP service grade rifle. What is known about it for sure? It began life in World War II, and it's walnut. Beyond that, it's all guesswork. For the author, this was the perfect "shooting stock."

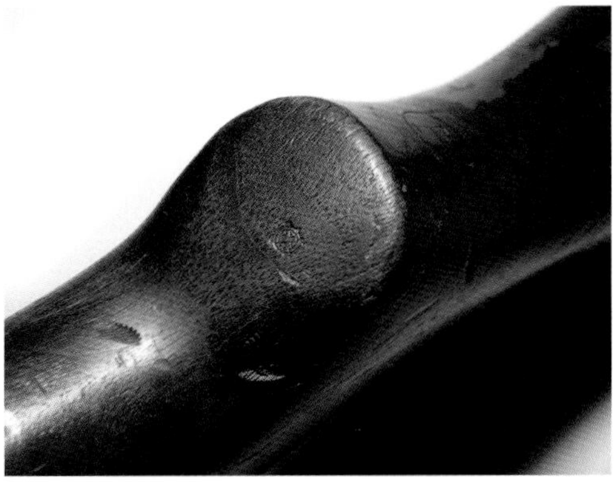

The red paint is NOT the British stuff used on lend-lease rifles, but is obviously there to denote some "special" i.d.

A well worn circle P firing proof on a Winchester GHD butt stock.

So some little rivulets will always contain some "mystery."

That's part of the pleasure of it all.

THE OVERALL VIEW

A collector could, with about ten rifles, tell a fairly compressive story of Mister Garand's rifle. But those correct rifles could easily reach a very high dollar evaluation.

For example, any gas trap that is usable, identifiable and carries an original cylinder and a handful of other pre-1941 parts is worth as much as a new compact car. If correct and very good or better, figure around the price of two rather well-equipped compact cars. This is why, for representative purposes, there until recently were businesses surviving by making decent quality reproductions, largely so that collectors can at least show visitors what an early rifle looks like.

Actual Springfield Armory "National Match" rifles carry a dollar premium as well, albeit shooters who genuinely mean to compete need to go another way. The NM2A rear sights and improved 7790722 operating rod and many of the other late changes such as grim tight fiber glass/epoxy bedding and full free floating of the barrel, as well as the vastly superior .308/7.62x51mm. loading used in the last Navy and Air Force competition rifles were not available in the Armory-produced match rifles from "production days", and anyone competing with such a rifle would not be competitive. A few collectors specialize in the later type rifles, but again, value is such that heavy shooting would not be prudent.

It isn't easy and it isn't cheap, and there is a lot to learn.

But the M1 was in service so long that many National Guard units, including the main ones in the area of Wisconsin where I live now, went right from the M1 to the middle period of M16 . . . that's about three decades of duty.

And then there are *all those movies!*

Mystique? Nah.

CHAPTER 6

ANSWERS TO M1 PUZZLES FOUND IN THE MAIL AND ELSEWHERE

Lance Baumgartner fires the author's G.I. H&R M1.

When I was teaching adult education back in Wisconsin, way back in the 1970s, I appreciated the many and varied questions the students asked because they kept me on my toes and active in the fields in which I taught. But, boy—when you write a book, some days it's like a barrage! On top of that, the articles I've published in Gun World, various Guns and Ammo annuals, GUNS, and some of Cowle's history magazines have generated tons of correspondence. What this chapter will do is pluck out some of those queries that are of general interest (usually ones I got repeatedly) and relay the answers here for your perusal.

Frankly, I dislike the "Q&A" format used in magazines (even the ones I've written myself), because what they mostly do is let a writer pick and choose based on the information at his fingertips. So what you'll find here is combinations of questions I've been asked, and in some cases I can only cast a little light on them. As for those aspects that I fail to address, I suggest that someone else may want to do a little research, for which I lack both the time and means.

JOHN GARAND

People are perpetually asking me questions about John Garand the man, and I have precious little to contribute. The N.R.A.'s *The M1 Rifle* includes a thumbnail biography, and most of the other works in the bibliography of The Complete M1 Garand offer tidbits. Someone should do a combination technical/engineering and personal biography, because the brilliance I see in this rifle suggests a fascinating personality. But I never met the man.

What few papers of his I have seen indicate a very versatile mind, sharp wit, and a high order of broad-spectrum knowledge far beyond what we today think of as being stereotypical of engineers, often unfairly depicted as "nerds." He was apparently a tad eccentric as well and, at one point, had his living room reconfigured as a skating rink. Born in St. Remi, Quebec, Canada, in 1888, Garand had left Canada with his parents by the turn of the century. By age 20, he was a tool and gauge maker at Browne and Sharpe, and by 1914 he was acting foreman and machine designer for Federal Screw Corporation in Providence, Rhode Island.

Garand was in New York City during World War I, at which time he turned his talents to the design and development of firearms. He was intrigued with automatics being subject to so many malfunctions. Soon after approaching the Naval Invention Bureau, he went to work for the National Bureau of Standards and developed a primer-actuated machine gun. Impressed by Garand's designs and detailed concepts, Army Ordnance moved him to the Springfield Armory in 1919.

Because of Army Ordnance interest in such systems—which always worked well under perfect conditions but never seemed to be reliable in the field—Garand's early designs employed primer activation systems, in which the primer actually initiates rearward action movement.

Most of these would not function without waxed or lacquered cartridge casings. Then, in 1925, the Army Ordnance Board discerned that conventionally prepared ammunition must be used in all new designs. By 1932, the Ordnance Board and Army Chief of Staff Douglas MacArthur ordered that any new designs must be chambered for the vast socks of caliber .30 Model of 1906 ammunition, much of which was of World War I or older Vintage. Garand's Rifle, Caliber .30 US, M1, was formally adopted by the US Army on 9 January 1936.

It's when one gets into the details of the M1's firing mechanism that Garand's brilliance for detail is truly appreciated. Nothing very much like it—modular and complete—had been used before, and it has been flattered many times since by being endlessly copied in other designs. Unfortunately, as is the case with most American firearms designers—with the possible exceptions of William Ruger and John Browning—both John Garand and the greatness of his work seem to be, if not truly forgotten, then grossly underappreciated. Though he worked on some of the "T" series prototypes, he was never even consulted in the final phases of the design and production of the M14, and many ordnance officials were entirely too eager to suggest that the M1 and the later M14 were entirely unrelated, and even to imply that Garand was only peripherally involved in either project. This ridiculous bit of fraud must have left a bitter taste in Garand's mouth, but apparently he said nothing. I, for one, doubt whether the M14 would have had anywhere near the terrible teething troubles it did had Garand been directly involved. And the rifle might have been a little sturdier.

Garand died on February 16, 1974, at age 86.

I am not a biographer, and I lack the means to research Garand anyway. Such work would have to be done far from my Wisconsin home, which I do not mean to leave for my remaining years. It would've been fascinating. And, really, we're all some twenty-six years late . . . perhaps at least fifty years too late.

BAYONETS AND BLADES

M1 accessories, all by themselves, have become an independent collecting field, and although I try to avoid getting deeply into accessories, there are some that are both functional and decorative.

German-made, NATO-issue ten-inch M1 bayonets, ca. 1954, marked with the US Army Ordnance "flaming bomb" symbol. These are not fakes; they are real issue for the rifle, postwar, foreign, but interesting and fully usable.

These are Native American "code talkers" on Bougainville, 1943, proudly displaying their M1 rifles and bayonets. Front row, second from the right, in the camouflage, is a young Marine with a Reising. Notice the M.1907 slings on all the rifles, the 16" bayonets, and for the militaria buffs, what appear to be hand painted camouflage helmets. (Official U.S.M.C. photo)

The ten-pocket "Mills"-type ammunition belt with snap pockets—of any vintage from the turn of the century (i.e., nineteenth to twentieth) to recent Korean and Chinese copies—is extremely handy. The latest "copies" do not include grommet holes for hanger accessories and work just as well. In fact, as you read this, I have Scotchgarded one for regular range use. The one pictured with the accessories in *The Complete M1 Garand* dates from 1916, belonged to a "China Station" marine in the late 1930s through the late 1940s, and apparently saw service in both world wars, as did the bayonet (the blade, anyway—more about that, later).

M1s eventually saw service with web slings, but mostly after World War II. In over five decades of looking, I haven't seen more than a dozen or so shots of combat outfits using cloth rifle straps, almost all from Hodges' First Army, very late in the war. Indeed, as late as the Korean War, Marines in particular rarely deployed anything but the leather M1907 sling.

Few US infantry units in Europe received web slings before the war ended in early May of 1945. Even fewer had the two types intermingled. This outfit, photographed supposedly on 3/20/1945, was from Hodges' First Army, then near Cologne, and they sport a mixture of straps. The old caption on the sleeve says, "near Frankfurt," but it seems unlikely that the date and location are both correct.

Web slings were produced but rarely got to fighting outfits, save perhaps a few very new ones. One Gyrene said: "Them rag slings, they'd fray and tear and rot and stink. Let the boots have 'em!" And so, for the most part, that's what they did.

In the Garand Collector's Association Journal, Summer 2014 (Volume 28, issue 3), that noted the passing of Congressional Medal of Honor recipient Walt Ehlers, Jebb Harris wrote:

"As for camouflaging shiny gas cylinders: 'I don't think we ever had time for it. I don't ever remember guys trying to cover them up. I imagine, maybe if you were a sniper you would.' The slings were all leather, not web."

His reflections are solid, and not P.R. based.

I heard the same thing from all my local veterans, including the hard-nosed former Marine Raider who made the slightly cleaned up remarks in the early versions of my work. Don Nichols, US Army, who died in 2017, said, "We had web in training, once we left the states, I never saw another one on a US rifle! Everything was leather M1907s."

These weapons were harvested from those lost and abandoned in the field and others no longer of use to the dead and wounded. Tanks for cleaning and phosphate and tooling to rebarrel and fit parts was lined up, right on the beach, and everything that could be salvaged was recycled. Note there is not a bolt action Springfield in the pile (or in any of the other shots in the collection, either!), nor was there a single web sling. (United States Marine Corp photo, marked 3/22/1945)

Very late in World War II, US Army personnel watch aircraft pummel the enemy on German soil. Note the shiny sling hooks and fittings. Almost all combat infantry used the M1907 leather sling, and the slings were generally older than the rifles. Rifles were equpped with straps at the unit level, and many World War I brass-fixtured slings saw service over twenty years after they were produced. That appears to be what these personnel are using. (US Army, Germany, 1945)

December 15, 1944, and engineers of the 463rd take a pre-Christmas break just before the von Rundstedt Offensive (the infamous "Battle of the Bulge") commences the very last serious German offensive of World War II. Their rifles carry M1907 leather slings, again with shiny bright, possibly brass hooks. Most engineering outfits used the Carbine, but of course, there were always infantry attached and ready to stop infiltrators. (US Army, 1944)

Parris Island US Marine Corps Recruit Training Center, July of 1945, in a carefully set up shot by public information personnel. Note that even the canine mascot had full access to leather slings, M1907, and again, these have shiny fittings. Also notable is the very dark finish on these M1 Garand rifles. It is very unlikely any of these Marines ever heard or saw shots fired in World War II, as the war was over in about a month. (United States Marine Corps, July 1945)

It was in colder/temperate climates like Camp McCoy, Wisconsin (now "Fort McCoy") where ice and frozen mud precipitated the operating rod separations so heavily cautioned against in their local literature. Blocked muzzles precipitated far higher than normal pressures and speeds of the reciprocating materials, which of course made everything far worse. It was 100th infantry Battalion paperwork and medical reports from that facility which led to these discoveries back in the 1960s. These fellows, however, are training in Summer of 1944. The mud, however, is obvious enough, as are the M1907 leather slings on each and every M1. (US Army, 32nd Division photograph, July 11, 1944)

Some did enter service in the last few months of the war, having been at one time for engineers, rangers, training, and some specialists, and saw service, in the Atlantic, mainly with boat crews and with Hodges' First Army, mainly at the very end, such as the fighting in Cologne. But the leather M1907 dominated during the war in combat outfits, and every photo I've seen affirms that hefty majority.

The interesting facet of the Internet "chat room commandos" who populate a lot of online venues and forums is, they mis-state what I say, never mention heroes like Ehlers (whose position is much harder than mine!), and just generally pontificate based upon sleazy rumors and absurd, ridiculous assertions.

M1907 slings in military service used brass or steel hooks and hardware, with heavy rivets securing the hooks and flax stitching securing the keepers. The list of known contractors is vast, and I have purchased from government stocks slings made by at least 20 manufacturers—some of them obviously "off- the-shelf" commercial items.

My favorite slings for my most pampered rifles were made by Leslie Tam in Honolulu, incorporating some

The original hooks of most USG.I. Model of 1907 leather slings were continuously curved, which made them quite stable but difficult to adjust. The modern heavyweight commercials use a slightly curved variant, much faster to adjust but not as stable. There are originals with the newer style, but no one knows why both were in issue. This type was dominant on older originals.

Saipan Marines, June, 1944, carrying their M1s, every rifle strapped up with a Model of 1907 leather sling. This is an old, restored U.S.M.C. official photo, interesting because it depicts a lot of weapons with a veteran outfit, obviously back from laying phone wire, and evincing about every infantry weapon of the period. The B.A.R. man seems to be scowling at the photographer. Notice there's not a submachine gun in evidence, and the specialists can be spotted by their carbines and the additional gear stowed at waist level. It's by no means certain, but one of the captions suggests the leftmost Marine is an officer, and he's carrying a Garand, with bayonet fixed. The Marine Corps originally rejected the M1, but decided after "acquiring and experimenting" late in the Guadalcanal campaign, that decision was, if not foolhardy, then certainly retractable. Almost immediately thereafter, it became "their rifle," and the M.1903 disappeared virtually completely.

vintage hardware along with some new fixtures on very heavy leather, and my Beretta now sports a match style, with numbered hole settings and is emblazoned with the Marine Corps anchor and globe. Why, you might ask, put something like that on an Italian rifle, of all things? One area where sophisticated collectors and I agree is this: a good part of the fun in accumulating these wonderful toys is appreciating the cosmopolitan nature of their use and adoption.

Other Gear

As for camouflaging shiny gas cylinders: "I don't think we ever had time for it. I don't ever remember guys trying to cover them up. I imagine, maybe if you were a sniper you would." The slings were all leather, not web.

Bayonets

"We trained with the long ones when we first went in, but we had the shorter ones overseas. We trained with a lot of antique stuff. We sharpened our own bayonets, they didn't come that way." On June 10, with a whoop, he charged machine gun and mortar positions.

"I had my bayonet fixed. When the Germans saw me...my God, their eyes got big and they started to take off. Of course, I was as scared as they were. I didn't know there were eight or 10 of them back there at the time." He had shot several by the time some of his squad arrived to finish them off.

Walt Ehler with bayonet. As for camouflaging shiny cylinders, "I don't think we ever had time for it. I don't ever remember guys trying to cover them up. I imagine, maybe if you were a sniper you would. The slings were all leather, not web."

Close-up of logos on one of Leslie Tam's match slings.

Okinawa, 1945, official U.S.M.C. photograph. Marine infantry, taking what must've been a longed-for and well-earned break. Notice there's no submachine gun in the photo of what seems to be a squad. The "fire and maneuver" tactics dictated the use of the B.A.R. or Browning to "fire" and suppress the enemy, while "maneuver" and the enemy's death or destruction was done by the rifle. Specialists carried the Carbine. Again, notice the leather M.1907 slings, ubiquitous with infantry of the time.

Many manufacturers can provide commercial or high-quality clones of the M1907- style sling, and at very reasonable prices. There are some very white, dry "military" M1907s marked "MRT" with which I have had problems in the field. Two of them have broken on me. Since I use slings both as carrying straps and shooting aids, I hate when that happens. These are around for sale at sensible prices, but I have decided not to purchase any more because sooner or later I will drop a rifle and break something, and then I will be furious.

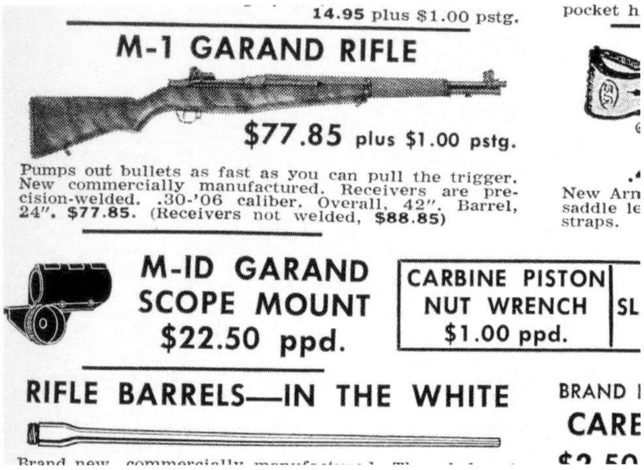

The author ordered his first M1 Garand, a remilitarized, welded specimen, in 1963, for $77.85 from P&S sales. It was a wonderful, accurate rifle. By 1964, he'd ordered an original for $88.85. It wouldn't shoot. A quick examination by neighbor, machinist, and industrial arts instructor Bill Flanagan settled the "why." The bright, shiny barrel was uniformly fatigued and near death. Bill had one on hand and installed it. This is the advertisement from which both were ordered.

My first M1, purchased in 1963, had a wonderful barrel, but was a welded, "remilitarized" receiver. The next year, I got an "original" unwelded version, but its barrel was incredibly tired. I rebarreled it, at what I thought was tremendous expense, before we started filming on *The Valiant Americans.*

No, this isn't World War II, and isn't the South Pacific. It's the Minnesota side of the northern Mississippi River, and the four fellows in this shot are amateur actors in a 1964 film production attempt. That's the author, just emerging from cover, second from the left, with his very own M1 Garand.

Other than his minor acting role, his job was to maintain 3 Thompson Submachine Guns, 11 M1 Garand rifles, 4 M1 Carbines, a .50 caliber M2 HB, a B.A.R., a Browning M.1917A1, and a whole collection of Japanese weapons. Combine that with lots of sand, water, plant life, sixteen kids, all of whom *know* they won't have to clean the firearms or even the uniforms, and a volunteer can learn a lot of things, most of which he never set out to discover. The most important one would be: *never volunteer.*

The first time I had tried the traditional forearm sling wrap on my old Springfield, I had cut my forearms badly. I found an oiled leather strap did not do this.

I also found if I did plenty of curls and presses and bench presses and worked my "squeeze springs" in my exercise regime, I could wrap that sling very tight and shoot much, much better. Still in my teens, offhand shooting was remarkably good and easy.

However, like everyone learning on his own, I gained some habits and superstitions. I mostly used the 3-hook or extra-long variants of the M1907 leather strap. When I could, I rigged them such as to have the sharp ends of the hooks facing out, therefore rigging them backwards. I used as many as five keepers. And I tied off any loops with leather thongs. I wanted that thing tight on my arm, wound back around my triceps. It worked, but old veterans found this very strange.

Not too much later, across the state in Milwaukee, an older gentleman who had worked at "The Saddle Company" sold me several hundred leather slings, all marked "MILSCO" with various dates.

Disliking cotton straps I sort of inherited, and then I developed it.

It's never gone away, either.

Bayonets are nice display accessories, though prices are going steadily upward, especially for GI items. Southern Ohio Guns apparently still has, at this writing, the entire Danish supply of US 10-inch bayonets, both the M1 and the M1905E1 shortened 10-incher. With the exception of the late M5 and M5A1 bayonets, based on the carbine design and whose blade configuration was until very recently standard with all US military bayonets, any bayonet designed for the '03 Springfield fits the M1 and is at least nominally appropriate.

The author's ca. 1986 "enhanced service" rifle, built up on a 1943 receiver, still with locking bar rear sight and narrow gas cylinder, on a bed of virtually entirely World War II U.S.M.C. artifacts and ordnance. The only things in the photograph which are definitely NOT WW2 are the rifle's gas cylinder lock—a postwar "high hump"—and the brand new commercial custom barrel. Yes, most of the web gear is marked "U.S.M.C.", too.

However, virtually any bayonet used on the M1 after 1936, even if built in 1905, would have been phosphated ("Parkerized") and fitted with black plastic grips. Original M1905s were used with the M1 so configured, and wartime production of the 16-inch M1905 (usually called, unofficially, the "model of 1942") was the same basic hunk of steel. Shortened versions of either are usually referred to as "M1905E1," and very few of the wartime production lot were ever shortened.

A very late World War II rifle in correct condition, but oddly, bearing an early ungrooved rear sight spring cover. The cover probably isn't original to the rifle, but was in a very similar finish to the rest of the sight gear (virtually black!) and the wear pattern told the author it had been there a very long time. When he gave the rifle to his late brother, he explained this, and the decision was to leave it on. Generally, it's imprudent to start swapping out parts based upon what one is "pretty sure" is correct, because very often new information emerges.

A gas trap rifle or any rifle below roughly 150,000 would be most appropriately fitted with a retrofinished M1905 of the full 16-inch configuration, though, of course, this doesn't mean such arms were always issued that way during World War II. And a study of World War II photographs reveals that 10- and 16-inch blades were issued throughout the war, any given unit usually having all of the same length, with only airborne units actually getting any preference, their needs calling for the 10-inchers almost exclusively due to space considerations on aircraft.

The 10-inch bayonets are referred to as "M1" bayonets, even though many were also issued with the earlier Springfield '03 and the contemporary '03A3.

In one of very few World War II combat shots that isn't arranged or posed, a Marine rifleman gulps down precious water on the Betio Atoll (popular name: "Tarawa"), in which water, contaminated and not, played a rather formidable part. Notable is the 16" 1942 style or older M1905 refurbished bayonet. The shiny hooks on the sllng are also notable. At this point in the war, Marines still used hand grenades painted yellow. (U.S.M.C. photo, 1943)

A little analysis is called for here. People are forever telling me they have difficulty keeping their bayonets sharp, even used with self-sharpening sheaths. There's logic to this. Until recently, bayonets were never intended to be cutting instruments, and they were not knives, despite their physical resemblance. They are spearpoints, to be handled and manipulated and used as spearpoints. That is the theory, anyway, behind

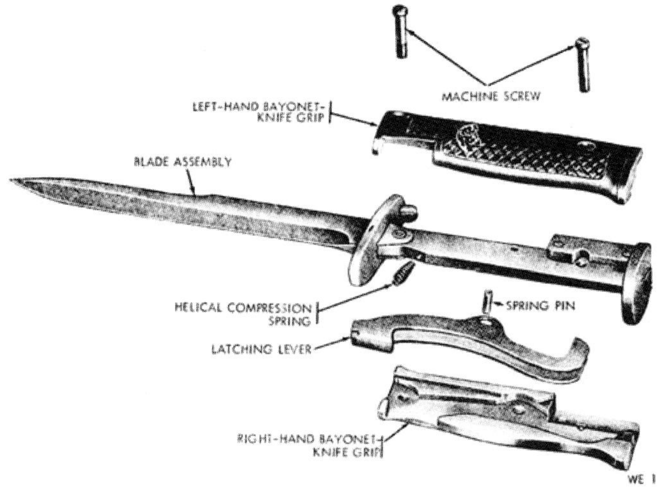

Figure 5-45. Disassembly/assembly of bayonet-knife M5A1.

Exploded view of the original M5 from US Army Training Manual 9-1005-222-35. The M5 series bayonet was the only blade ever designed specifically and exclusively for the M1. The M5A1 is much more common.

Closeup of a standard postwar gas cylinder/sight assembly, with "high hump" gas cylinder lock and standard front sight.

Unusual rear view of an IHC front sight from the rear "hoop" on its original cylinder.

their rather relaxed heat treatment. If bayonets held an edge and were used as they were supposed to be, a lot more soldiers would have a lot more scars and missing digits. Traditional bayonets can be used for some hacking functions and moderate prying, but if hardened to a true knife specification—as were some early "M1942s"—there is a tendency for the blade to break, especially at the 16-inch length.

Of the last generation of bayonets for the M1 rifle were the M5 and M5A1, which do not have a loop in the hilt that fits on the muzzle of the barrel but rather a stub that goes into the gas cylinder lock screw. These can still be had for sensible prices, and they are, in fact, the first generation of standard-issue bayonet blades from their inception designed to actually be used as knives.

The M5A1 was produced by many makers and in several different countries. The same "scabbard, bayonet-knife,

M8A1" and its successors fit this blade and virtually every other US bayonet produced since about 1948, and a lot of others as well. If, for some goofy reason, you feel compelled to shoot your M1 with a bayonet fixed, you are in for some surprises. Most service rifles shoot better, and with considerably less felt recoil, with the blade mounted. This is not true of match-prepared rifles, except for the recoil reduction, which is a simple matter of the physics of the center of gravity. The M5 series is far more modern, sporting a large release/latch lever and tab, but has nowhere near the romance and panache of the much larger World War II blades. However, it is a much more utilitarian knife and is actually convenient around the house. I have just located a Beretta M5A1 and was amazed to find that the same owner had a 10-inch Beretta-made and marked "M1" bayonet, which I did not previously know had ever been produced outside the United States. Within days of that 1998 occurrence, I realized I already owned a Norwegian-made blade, in an old US scabbard, and that in fact several other countries produced 1ten-inch M1 bayonets.

In Korea, the Philippines, and Chinese Taiwan, the longer bayonet blades were reconfigured to the M5/M5A1 profile, apparently for convenience, and many of these are on the market at relatively bargain prices as of this writing.

GAS CYLINDERS AND SIGHTS

Several of the photos of M1 "business ends" in The Complete M1 Garand were intended to give a general idea what correct hardware of various vintages looks like. However, I didn't want those captions to become books in and of themselves, so I explained most of the detail in the text. Here I'll be a little more specific. The rather more obviously "bent ear" front sights are IHCs and Winchesters and look a great deal alike. International Harvesters are nominally 15⁄16 inch from extreme outward measurement to extreme outward measurement; Winchesters—which, if not refinished are usually virtually black—measure 13⁄16 inch in the same plane (although, I hasten to add, enough sand blasting and refinishing will change these approximate measurements considerably). Virtually all other M1 front sights from all other sources will be very close to 11⁄16 inch unless they have been damaged or crushed.

Just below the sight, the "straddle" measurement across the dovetail, on the gas cylinder, over which the sight slides

"Business end" of a late M1 Garand, this one of the IHC rifles QC'd by the armory. This one may or may not be "disturbed" but the "x-form" poppet gas cylinder lock screw and "high hump" lock are typical of all postwar M1 Garand rifles. The front sight is assuredly a Springfield, of about the same vintage, and is not "collector correct" for the rifle...but may still have been there since this oldie left for issuance.

when it's being fitted, is ½ inch for the early gas port- style gas cylinders and approximately 19⁄32 inch for all late-war and postwar units in the same area. One can see this difference. If the dovetail hangs out to the left and right of the sight, it's a late style; if flush with the sight base, it's the early style. The late style is probably stronger, but the reason for the change was to provide greater front-end windage adjustment without having to radically modify anything else in the rifle.

Winchester gas cylinders are mostly of the "early" configuration and can be spotted because the flat on the rear "hoop"—the upper one that contacts or comes very close to the handguard ferrule—is either off center or not there at all. Not surprisingly, the early profile gas cylinders appear to the very end of Winchester production. Wide ones are far more common than I once thought. The "rear hoop" permutations vary a lot, and are not quite unique to the New Haven manufacturer. This is true of some early Springfields and some gas cylinders that were sanded too severely in rebuilding. The Winchester cylinder also has no beveled "toe" on the bayonet lug underneath the operating rod tube, in contrast to all others. Virtually all World War II Springfield gas cylinders and most Winchesters will bear small hardness punch marks, usually on the bayonet lug's bottom surface, and these appear in random numbers and depths. The small letters that appear on all sorts of Springfield cylinders, even many postwar units, are the leftovers from various finish experiments intended to develop a better, more durable finish for the big stainless-steel part, which, in service, tended to become bright metal fairly quickly and caused complaints almost immediately from the field. The final solution, as nearly as I can tell from microscopic analysis, seems to have been some kind of black-chrome-related plating (very dark), which appeared on many very late rifles. But I do not know for sure if this, too, was merely a refined experiment applied in rebuilding or if it was being done at the armory. In any case, this process seems to have produced an extremely durable finish.

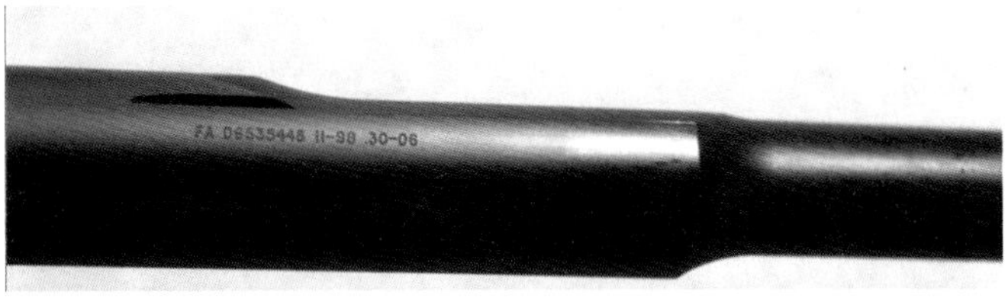

Fulton Armory barrel in .30 06, basically an enhanced GI specification unit.

A Springfield Armory (US) barrel from November 1943, found still attached to its original receiver on a CMP rifle the author received recently.

All Italian gas cylinders carry the maker's letter code mark, although, interestingly, I have seen at least two gas cylinders that were definitely American-made and wartime carrying the "PB" identifier. One of these was on a DCM-supplied WIN-13 and seems to have been the original gas cylinder for the rifle, which I suspect—but cannot prove—was rebuilt or refinished and inspected at Beretta at some time or other.

AUTHENTICITY AND PERIPHERALS

I am forever being asked about the use of terms like "correct," "original," and "authentic," with regard to restorations, and although I will not go into a lot of the specifics here, I will explain some economics and try to give some practical data.

Anyone who thinks that a great deal of money can be made by restoring rifles should think again. It can be done—usually by luck and diligent, patient scrounging—but it is not easy. My projects along those lines have almost always lost money, and generally a lot of it. There are some scoundrels out there who will modify existing parts, remark civilian barrels, and resort to welding and reconfiguration in an effort to produce something that, if not downright dishonest and fraudulent, is certainly questionable.

Yet there are situations in which a serious collector needs a specific example to complete his array and has no choice. Much against my better judgment, I recently agreed to help a correspondent in bringing a four-digit M1 back to its fully "original" gas trap configuration. This would have been incredibly stupid to even start, except that he had discovered a gas cylinder, intact, complete with its original sights, screws, and all fittings, and his rifle had already been rebuilt to gas port configuration in September 1940 and apparently hadn't been touched since.

In other words, with perhaps seven hundred dollars out of pocket, he was very close and needed only a barrel and the original handguard ferrule, which turned out to be rather easy to find.

Probably the best advice I gave him was not to fool with his original vintage 1940 tube from the gas port conversion rebuild, since it is and was one of the earliest gas port barrels extant, but to have a brand-new barrel made from a Douglas blank. By the way, most 1940 barrels were not dated by the usual stamping, although they're easy enough to spot. But this one—which was verifiably authentic—had the usual markings of that time and was marked "9–40" (very large, perpendicular to everything else, and above the chamber, of all places). I have seen a couple of other barrels, all early, with similarly emblazoned dates in large letters—including one on a Winchester (though 180 degrees flip-flopped from what he described) under the handguard. One collector suggested that these barrels were dated by inspectors on some selection basis, probably just one per heat-treatment lot, before the rationalized manufacture dating system was put in place. Point is, if you see it, don't panic—it seems to be what I have learned to call "extraneous/peripheral" markings (or, if you like my original term, "mystery marks"), the purpose of which was forgotten, most likely, before the first soldier held the rifle but which have been observed too many times to be illegitimate. Explanation required:

Most modern collectors find those marks off-putting, but many have realized they were done by units and inspectors contemporary but outside the armory itself. They are period and authentic markings, but never "original" in the strictest interpretation. They're not fakes.

You see, fakery is the attempt to profit by ascribing artificial value to an object. "Mystery marking" is just stuff applied for some short-term purpose and should have no meaning at all, except as an interesting footnote. For our restoration barrel, we came up with a honestly marked but "undisturbing" compromise marking. Had it been left blank, it might very easily have shown up, fifty years from then, with an "authentic" 1940 inscription.

I stressed to my correspondent that if I were to be associated with his rifle in any way, although I had no objections to his putting parts together, I wanted no one to think that barrel was original and authentic, save perhaps from a few yards away. This was very neatly solved. The smith who installed the barrel used no right-side barrel markings at all except the crossed cannons, but of nonregulation size, and put the actual date of installation parallel with the bore, along with the owner's initials, at 6 and 12 o'clock locations. This rifle won't change hands, barring some terrible tragedy, for the next quarter-century or so, and the 1940 tube is still on hand. But this is a case of luck and providence.

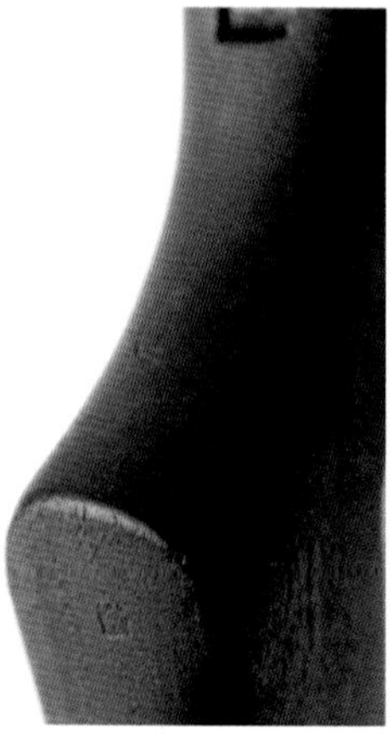

The small heel ordnance "crossed cannon" mark in back of the pistol grip on a 1944 "GAW" cartouched M1 Garand butt stock. These are usually worn off or reduced to a mere scar. They often never got stamped at all, and often the "circle P" firing proof was lightly stamped, or on replacement stocks, never stamped at all. Seeing one this crisp is quite rare.

Elaborate restorations, especially of early M1s and Winchesters, almost never work out financially, unless one is just a few parts away. A friend's CMP H&R came along in the middle of 1999, and it was complete and correct, save for a Winchester bolt. Guess what! That Winchester bolt didn't live there very long!

But trying to pull together a full-house restoration, especially of an early World War II rifle with nothing actually in hand save the receiver is an expensive nightmare, and correct, original, cartouched buttstocks, in particular, have become brutally expensive. Barrels are often a monstrous stumbling block. It was my original intention, by the way (since so many fake and "modified" barrels are floating around these days), to measure and hardness-test a rather huge batch of barrels and present the results here. This proved to a be a fool's errand because, even among authentic specimens of similar vintage, there are tiny changes in machining style—placement of certain curves and so on—such that it would have amounted to a great deal of work to accomplish nothing. But there is an alternative for the collector with access to a smith's takeoff barrels and some that are basically elaborate tent stakes: examine all the specimens possible with a micrometer, look for tool mark patterns, and compare all to specimens on the market. Be always on the lookout for places on barrels that seem to be too thin, turned, flattened, overstamped, or filed . . . a good trick is to roll a barrel on a hard, flat surface and look for wobbles and bumps. Use an 8- to 10-power magnifying loupe, and look very, very closely at markings and surface eccentricities.

To shooters, it's all much easier: Check throat, muzzle, and shoot. . . .

USING AND SMOOTHING THE CIVILIAN M1

Your rifle is no longer in military service. It's yours, in the traditional capitalist sense of the term. Hopefully, it's fought its last firefight.

Yet, without converting your rifle to something else or substantially altering its unique looks or basic functions, you, like most shooters, want it to perform well.

The firing mechanism and bolt of the M1 are two of Garand's areas of triumph, but your applications for them are not quite the same as those contemplated more than

The M1's ejector and spring assembly, almost ready for final polish.

The M1's extractor, slightly beveled to M14 specification, ready for touch-up.

Bolt face of the M1 Garand, with the author's center punch testing extractor tension. The already polished ejector lies just below.

seventy years ago. The M1 characteristically flips brass much farther from the rifle than is convenient for a civilian shooter who wants to recycle his brass—and spews it all over the place, too. In combat, it's a good idea to get brass out from underfoot and out of the immediate position.

The M1's extractor is very positive and quite massive and has a tendency, especially when not clean, to "ding" the occasional case rim. Again, this was a military rifle, and brass condition after firing was well down the list of priorities. Clearing the chamber, though, was imperative. These problems are easily solved.

We'll start with the bolt. Once it has been removed, study the extractor surfaces that contact the cartridge rim and test the tension on the ejector with your finger. Take a look at the photos of the ejector (top left) and extractor (top right), and briefly study the photo at left, which shows the bolt face with both the ejector and extractor in place. Don't take anything apart yet.

You're going to need at least the following, and save everything for the trigger work, too:

- A punch or M1 tool or both, or an old screwdriver you don't plan to use for screws anymore
- The finest steel wool you can get
- At least one spare ejector and spring
- Probably some thin cutting oil or other surface lubricant for use with the abrasives below
- A collection of flat, mild abrasives (stones, very mild files, even emery boards will do, nothing coarser than 220 grit, preferably no coarser than 400)
- A bottle of cold blue, the directions to which you should follow whenever you're removing surface finish—not to fool anybody, but to provide some corrosion resistance where bare metal has been exposed (you'll use this during the trigger work, too)
- A few sheets of emery paper, the wet and dry kind, of 220 and about 400 grit
- Whatever collection of paper towels, brushes, soap, hand cleanser, and/or scouring powder you find handy for cleaning yourself and your tools, parts, and rifle

- Toothpicks, pipe cleaners, mild wet abrasives (automotive polishing compound is handy), some small brushes, and perhaps also a high-quality dental pick
- About +3 or +4 diopter viewing glasses or an 8- or 10-power magnifying loupe for viewing parts close up (simple magnifying glasses are generally not adequate)
- A spare firing pin (also a good idea, regardless of this procedure)

In particular, note the "dip" or detent just over one-third of the way back on the ejector body. That little depression has to line up with the shaft on the extractor for the bolt to go together, meaning the spring ejector has to be depressed during disassembly. Before tearing down the bolt, again study the extractor in situ, and note the contact surfaces. Those are the ones you're going to polish.

Center punch aligned with extractor at bottom of bolt, ejector depressed, almost ready for removal. It's wise to aim the ejector someplace safe, preferably where it can be found.

We're illustrating here from the military manual the disassembly technique using the fixture. If you have this device, great! Chances are you don't, so remember that this happens fast and that the ejector leaves in a hurry, so always aim the bolt face into a bucket or restrain the ejector like grim death. The M1 tool carries on its arm a semieliptical projection designed to compress the ejector precisely to the right depth and restrain its path out, and that's a good shortcut. An empty cartridge with the same base as .45 ACP or a little smaller is very handy. Finally, after some thirty-seven years, I am actually able to disassemble and even assemble the M1 bolt once in a while with nothing more than my bare hands and a center punch. But I don't rely on doing that, and you may not have thirty-seven years to learn. Everything depends on the alignment of that little slot, and it will stay stable only under pressure, albeit pressing in on the extractor will tend to slightly realign it if you're close enough.

Before beginning, assess your mechanical skills. Many people find it easier to strip the bolt in a vise, and I have also seen homemade fixtures. Watch what you're doing, read and reread the instructions, and proceed with the tear-down when you have plenty of time. It's the reassembly that's awkward. Don't even think about using power tools, and if you have problems with mechanical functions in general, pack up the whole thing and take it to your gunsmith.

Using your driver, punch, or M1 tool, compress the ejector the appropriate depth; aim the bolt face someplace safe, keeping pressure on the ejector throughout; push or drive the extractor out toward the top of the bolt (as illustrated in the photo at left); and, as gently as you can, ease out the other parts, including the firing pin and the extractor spring/ spring plunger.

Much of the rest is instinct and analysis. So again, before applying any tools or abrasives, go back and study the photos and illustrations. Generally, nothing is done with the extractor spring/extractor spring plunger assembly except to clean it up and put a little grease in its detent before reassembly. If your eyesight is not perfect for close-up work, get yourself an 8- to 10-power loupe and study the parts, looking for burrs, pits, stuck-on bits of filth, abrasions, and tool marks. It is common to snip one or two coils off the ejector spring, then restretch it, especially in .308, before reassembly. (I only do this if I know from experience that a rifle chambered for the shorter cartridge is tossing brass way too far.) Then meticulously clean everything (preferably working with the tiny parts in a strainer if you do this in a sink with water) and again look for flaws and abrasions of any sort.

The easiest part is flat and simple, and that's the firing

pin. Check the tip for anything unusual, and if it's sharp enough to cut your skin or in any way convoluted, do not hesitate—replace it immediately! Firing-pin eccentricities contribute to the slamfire phenomenon (discussed later), and the nose is what actually strikes the primer. Check the long span for signs of cracks or fractures, and if you see a line but can't determine whether it's a crack or not, the next step should help clarify things. (If the firing pin does prove to be cracked, replace it immediately!)

Now, we go to work on the pin, and this is easy. You're going to polish it until the sides show no tool marks; you don't have to be able to comb your hair with it, but every tool mark is a potential snag at some time in the rifle's life; get rid of them, and that life will be longer and safer. Cold blue the shiny parts.

You'll want to spray some kind of Teflon spray into the bolt's detent after you have flushed, cleaned, and done what you can to inspect that raceway. Or you can use a tiny touch of grease on either side of the pin when you do the reassembly.

Now take another long, slow look at your ejector and spring assembly (refer back to the top left-hand photo on page 183); grab some pipe cleaners (and/or toothpicks if you're particularly industrious) and make that spring shine like chrome plate (or as close as you can get), preferably inside and out; and moderately deburr the ejector itself using automotive polishing compound, steel wool, and rags. *Don't even think about changing contours on the ejector, especially the ridge!* (I do this while watching TV—almost like absent-mindedly whittling, often for several hours.) Then clean the parts carefully with brushes and dry. All metal filings must be removed before reassembly (avoid using emery paper or files on this part). And again, reblue and lubricate the channel before reassembly.

The extractor won't be changed much either, but because the finish process often results in tiny phosphate inclusions on the extractor that cause it to abrade brass, you're basically just going to remove some finish and any obvious tool marks, very gently, in the areas where the cartridge touches or is likely to touch the part. You don't want any lube on the exterior of the extractor, but you can clean that up, if necessary, after reassembly.

A 5.6 million Harrington and Richardson rifle, import marked, acquired in almost unused condition, all collector correct except for the operating rod, photographed here while the stock was being degreased.

It's a good idea to use this opportunity to clean up the bolt face. Don't try to remove pits; if they are there and they offend you, replace the bolt and check your headspace. But do remove any blobs of material stuck there—they do get stuck there, more than anywhere else in the rifle, at 50,000 pounds of pressure per shot—and degrease, then use cold blue to at least slightly control corrosion.

You can also check firing-pin protrusion, if you have the military gauges or other adequate precision measuring tools, and the repair standards table on page 186 provides safety-related measurements.

Also, while your rifle is disassembled, without the springs and operating rod, put your bolt back in the receiver and, preferably using feeler gauges, check the lug clearances, wiggle the bolt around, and study its movement. Worn, peened, and improperly machined bolts, especially in the lug areas, are both a safety and a wear problem. Look for excessive play.

If you haven't already lost your ejector, you still may in the reassembly process. Be sure you get the extractor spring/plunger assembly in properly, mash down on the ejector with whatever contrivance you have at hand, and, following the steps in the illustration on page 187 and the manual, reassemble your bolt.

If you are conservative, relaxed, use no power tools, and keep everything clean and spiffy, this process cannot harm your rifle and should treat your brass much better. Sometimes, though, another condition—say, excessive gas in the system due to a corroded port—may cause brass to be slam-danced into oblivion and badly beaten, but at least now you should eventually be able to find it.

CHAPTER 7
REPAIR STANDARDS

7-1. General

The repair standards included herein give the minimum and maximum measurements of repaired parts; those beyond the limits will be replaced by new parts.

7-2. Specific

a. Bolt Assembly.

Fig. No.	*Point of Measurement*	*Repair Standards Minimum*	*Maximum*
5-17.	Firing pin protrusion	0.044 in. (overseas)	0.060 in.

b. Gas Cylinder Group.

Fig. No.	*Point of Measurement*	*Repair Standards Minimum*	*Maximum*
5-23.	Gas cylinder bore	0.5320 in.	—

c. Follower Group.

Fig. No.	*Point of Measurement*	*Repair Standards Minimum*	*Maximum*
5-14.	Operating rod gas piston diameter	0.525 in.	—

d. Trigger Housing Assembly.

Fig. No.	*Point of Measurement*	*Repair Standards Minimum*	*Maximum*
5-5.	Trigger-trigger pull	*M1*	
		5.5 lb	7.5 lb
		M1C and M1D (Sniper's)	
		4.5 lb	6.5 lb

e. Barrel and Receiver Group.

Fig. No.	*Point of Measurement*	*Repair Standards Minimum*	*Maximum*
5-31.	Throat of chamber	0.306 in. (overseas)	0.310 in. (hands of troops)
5-32.	Barrel gas port	0.5991 in. outer (overseas)	

By the way, it's a good idea to prepare a spare ejector and firing pin to keep on hand, particularly if you have more than one rifle.

Since we discussed firing pin protrusion and so forth, by the way, some of the more commonly used specifications from the repair standards table are presented on this page. You need to know, though, that some civilian gas cylinders and, therefore, pistons, have larger bores and that civilian barrel throats usually use much gentler leades and throats; the figures here apply to GI units only.

SMOOTH, RELIABLE, DURABLE: THE BRILLIANT M1 FIRING MECHANISM AND HOW TO DO A TRIGGER JOB WHERE YOU ALMOST CAN'T BREAK ANYTHING

The M1's firing mechanism has several fascinating characteristics, of which perhaps the best is that it is *very* easy to employ both a "service" trigger and a "match" trigger on the same rifle, interchanging them in less time than it takes to explain how to yank down the trigger guard, which is covered in this volume in great detail.

Removing the trigger housing assembly is where

field-strip begins. It contains not just the trigger, but the hammer/striker, sear/ disconnector, and safety mechanisms, as well as (snapped into the housing itself) the clip ejector. And the whole apparatus, while not impervious to water or dirt, is a much better seal to the bottom of the mechanism than is found on most rifles of similar or later vintage.

I'm going to explain here a trigger-smoothing and slight lightening technique spun off of that described in the N.R.A.'s *The M1 Rifle*, and we'll employ virtually all the tools and supplies I detailed in the top-end, bolt-related job we just described and discussed.

Study the three photos in this section and the chart detailing the firing mechanism. The chart is an illustration from the US Army's rifle, national match, in its final version, and shows, from the top, a cocked trigger housing assembly on safe; a cocked unit, ready to fire, in match incarnation; and, at the bottom, a schematic and parts lexicon, in fired or ready- to-strip condition. OK, don't take yours apart yet, but take it out and play with it, studying the look and feel of the parts from all aspects. In particular, brace the hammer on its release, then press it back with the trigger still depressed and note how the sear/disconnector functions in various regimes, release the trigger once it's locked rearward, and so on.

Now, there are some things you need to know before going on. Many of these parts are very, very hard on their surface but much softer and more malleable below a few thousandths of an inch. We're removing no substantial amounts of material, simply cleaning up and polishing, then doing the same kind of lubrication and detail refinish we did in the last section. You'll need a few more doodads, too:

- Some pieces of ¼-inch or slightly smaller dowel material or something similar, 4 to 7 inches long
- A set of feeler gauges that will allow you to measure any eccentricities that might cause you to reject a given firing mechanism that's out of true, or to try to adjust it

You might want to fix your housing in a vise to clean it up if it has visible burrs and machine marks, or use the securing holes to screw or peg it to a large wooden flat.

Let me briefly summarize, while you're looking at your housing and the drawings, what is ideally done.

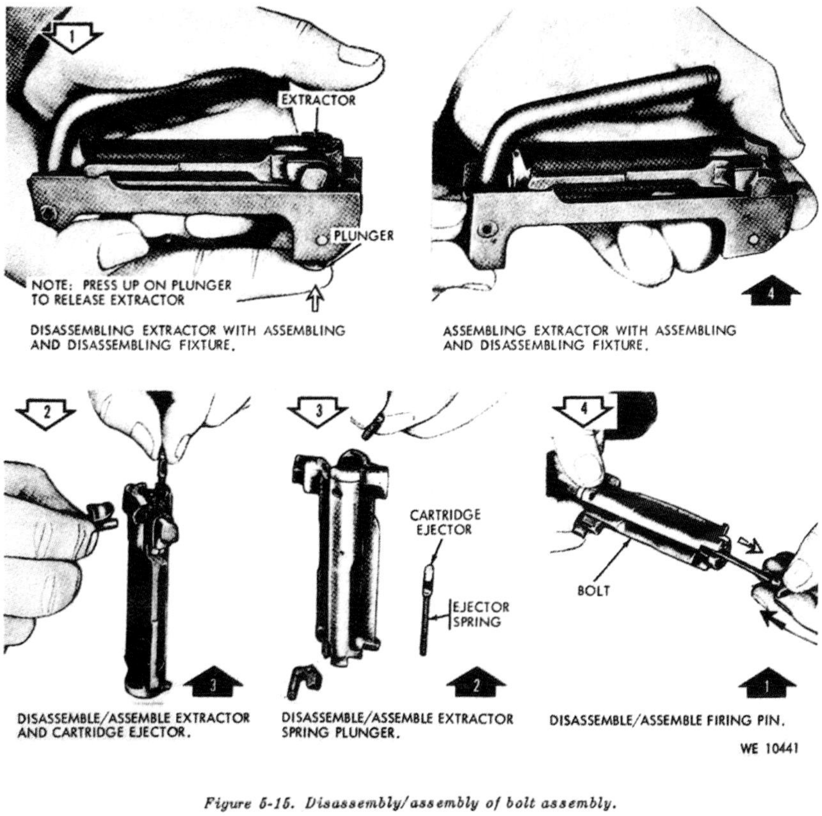

Procedure for disassembly and assembly of bolt, from US Army TM 9-1005-222-35.

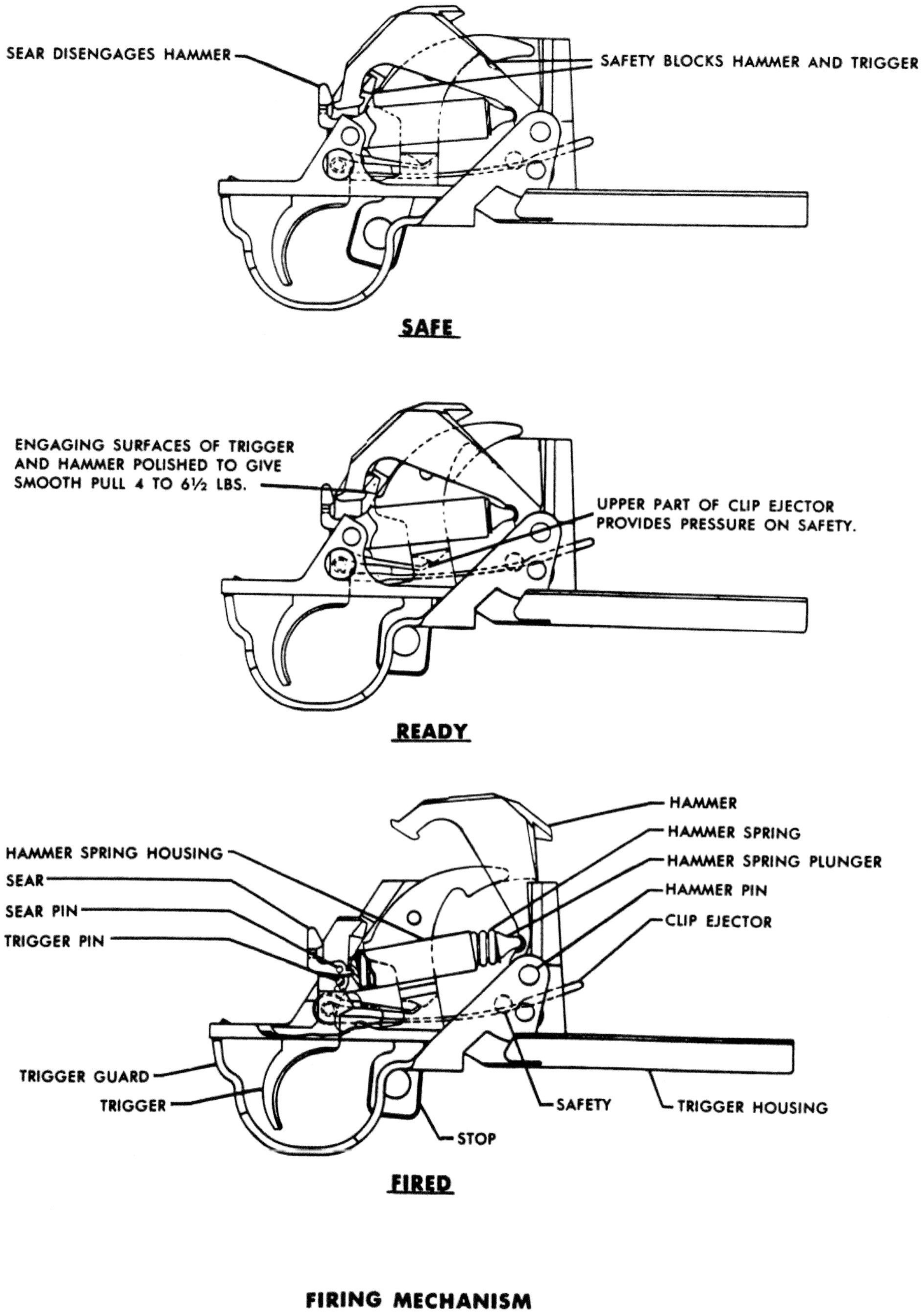

Firing mechanism chart, from US Army TM 9-1005-222-35.

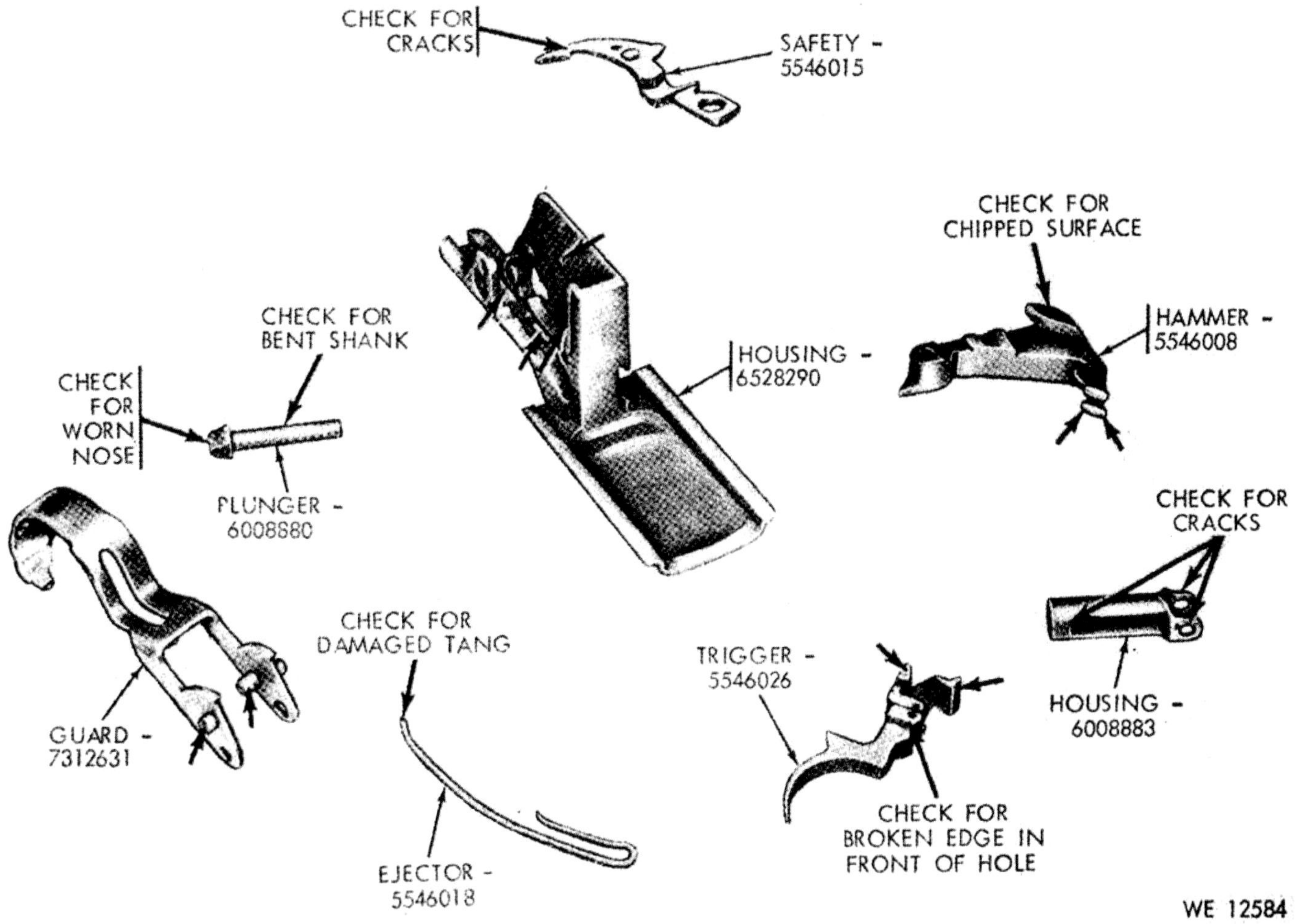

Trigger housing assembly inspection points, from US Army TM 9-1005-222-35.

The trigger/sear/disconnector assembly will not be disassembled, but some work (very little) will be done with *very mild* abrasives, some of it with the whole device in its fully assembled condition, if necessary; work will be done on all four surfaces, if required. The housing itself rarely needs any work, and the clip ejector need not be removed unless such work is required; study, watch, and listen for signs of grating and friction. All four hammer hook surfaces will be polished, but very tenderly. The safety may require finish or burr removal, especially on the inside surface, but often does not. The hammer spring should be very nicely polished but not subjected to anything coarse at all. The hammer spring housing can be polished very bright inside, but be careful; this is very thin, brittle material, so work with oil and polishing compound and steel wool very slowly. Some people polish the nose of the hammer spring plunger to a bright finish, which does not affect trigger pull but supposedly has some impact on locking time; I usually don't bother unless I see some actual disruption.

No need to mess with the rest of the parts, unless something has happened. (See the illustration below for safety notes.)

Check for approximate parallelism at all locations of the hammer hooks. That is, you should not be able to measure any substantial difference between the lock/friction points of front or rear, right or left engagement points in the "null," or cocked and ready. I have seen distorted and bent housings, which were truly unserviceable, but in particular, the trigger/sear/disconnector mechanism can be damaged very subtly such that it is out of parallel and must therefore be replaced. Indeed, it's not a bad idea at all to keep a spare hammer and trigger assembly or even a whole, fully assembled firing mechanism and/or a hammer and hammer spring housing on hand.

Overzealous filing, machine grinding, and attempts

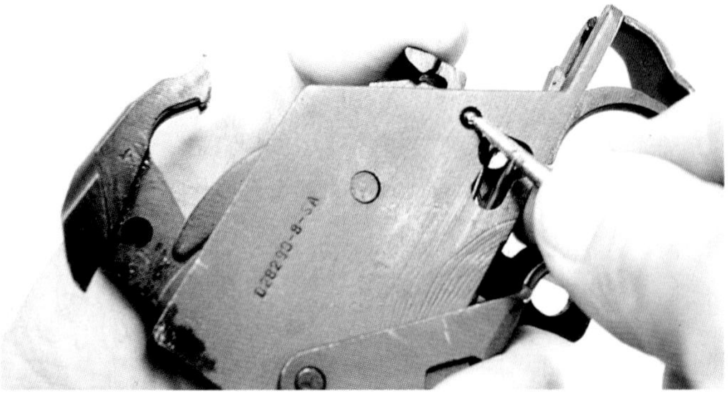

Driving the trigger pin out with a punch, trigger mechanism held forward, with the unit uncocked. Note burrs on the upper portion of the hammer, which proved not to cause friction or interference.

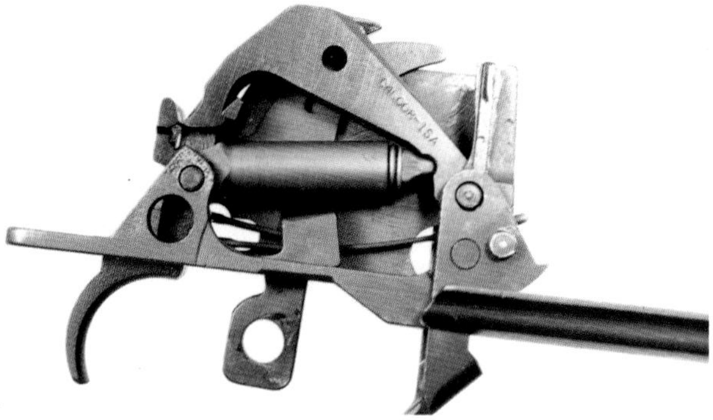

Complete trigger housing, viewed from right side, in cocked condition. Note the very tight front hammer hook fit and early -1 "extra hole" Springfield hammer and postwar "no ear" plunger head.

to remove too much material, especially on a part that's already defective, are the primary cause of parts failure in such a job. If you're one of those guys who can't wait to get out his big, old mill file, *don't even start on this process!*

Long before beginning, study the disassembly procedures (see the illustration on on this and the preceding and following pages) and the photo above. This photo shows the center punch actually beginning to dislodge the trigger pin, but, more important, it shows an early, extra-hole hammer that, on its upper center quadrant, contains some burrs and machine marks that might require the use of some polishing techniques. Whether it does or not (and it didn't, by the way) depends on the adjacent surfaces and clearances, which are highly individual. Do not remove burrs that do not interfere with or touch anything. Such removal might make things look nice, but it's wasted time. The photo above shows the same assembly, cocked, from the other side. Notice how tight the engagement is on this unit, which, ultimately, was only very tenderly polished.

Make *sure* the closed side of the hammer spring housing faces *outward* upon reassembly, and press forward and down or you may never get this nice "light through the hole" position required to start the trigger pin in its seated position.

Again, remember, you should find very few metal shavings, but they need to be removed and any bare metal touched up with cold blue and lubricated before reassembly. Regular inspection with your magnifying devices is absolutely imperative every few strokes or rubs of whatever polishing medium you have opted to use.

Please don't try to make all the mating surfaces absolutely identical on the hammer hooks—and if you reconfigure anything, you are in trouble already. Again, this is detailed reburring, polishing, and touch-up.

Use stones to start, with oil or grease, if encountering heavy burrs, moving quickly down to 400- grit emery, then to steel wool. A good portion of what causes scraping and grating in M1 triggers is the heavy phosphate, and once that's gone, it is amazing how nice a trigger can be. Indeed, as military rifles go, the M1 is almost always quite good.

I would not do these procedures on a true collector's rifle but would instead acquire an entirely separate firing mechanism, perhaps even of the same vintage "parts package," and set up a separate "shooting" trigger housing assembly/ firing mechanism. But that's up to you.

Clumsy, overaggressive work here can cause all sorts of malfunctions in the M1, including random "machine gunning," slamfires, and failure to fire. Being a little too conservative simply means that one gets minimal improvement. I suggest—though it takes a very long time to work this way—assembling, disassembling, and testing the entire mechanism many times, doing a very moderate amount of work between each test period. This will help you learn the technique, too.

The main thing is to inspect constantly with the magnifier. When tiny traces of the finish are left and everything else gleams, you are definitely done and maybe a little over the edge. And be particularly tender on the hammer hooks.

There is one procedure that J. B. Roberts suggests, which I have only used a couple of times and do not necessarily recommend. I include it here just in case you find it necessary to get where you have to. It's in the N.R.A.'s The M1 Rifle, quoted directly as follows. (Note that I use 400-grit where he uses 220-grit, and I check my work every couple of runs.)

I first stumbled across the leather M1907 sling and similar units back in 1963, at what was then Camp McCoy. We purchased a rather huge lot of "strapping and tack," stuffed with wadded up paper, for practically nothing. The box was not much smaller than a typical refrigerator, and was very heavy. Inside were leather slings, over half with three hooks, bearing dates from 1917 to about 1942. They were over half the "Model of 1907, Modified" sling designed for the B.A.R., which was actually quite popular with half track crews because it was more stable and it was easier to secure the rifle over pack gear.

For a long time, I presumed all those with only two hooks were cut down, and that all the standard specimens had three hooks, originally. That was wrong, but it was 1963, and there was precious little literature.

Viewing *literally* hundreds of thousands of WW2 images, very few show web straps, again, almost all at the very end of the war, and in Europe *all* were from First Army, especially the action in Cologne, near the Cathedral.

The late Walt Ehlers said it plainly: "All our slings were leather, not cloth!" My late friend, Don Nichols, was a little more obscene, but did mention some of their training rifles used web slings in the US Every Marine veteran I knew said their slings were "Leather and leather only", including the former Carlson's (2nd Raider Battalion) Makin Island Vet, who finished the war with weapons company, 4th Regiment, and whose remarks I quoted earlier. He *hated* web slings, having cut a forearm on one during an infiltration exercise on the west coast not long before his last landing.

But Internet storm troopers will argue, including those who spew up old film of March 1945's ugly street battle to prove they were "all over the place" and "early in the war" and "with Patton at Cologne" (Patton was many miles away!). All that's required to make stupid remarks in such venues is the *chutzpah,* fingers, some hormones, and a willingness to spew ignorant twaddle.

A Marine rifleman on Bougainville lines up a shot. This shot may be prepped, but then again, that clip in the air suggests superb timing by the photographer. Note he isn't using the "sling forearm wrap" so heavily stressed by the Corps, but the high elbow comes right from their training syllabus. (U.S.M.C., 1/10/1944 marked)

The fact remains: The standard rifle sling for the M1 Garand in combat infantry outfits was the M1907, with a few exceptions, until and often way beyond the end of World War II. The photographic evidence is overwhelming, and the witness testimony is unanimous. Styles and colors varied.

Slings were not shipped with rifles, they were distributed at unit levels, and there were WWI brass-hooked M1907s being issued even long *after* World War II. Straps were cheap, made in huge numbers, and outfits issued what they had. It was almost always leather. If one looks at some of the shots I have from Parris Island, it's obvious most of them used the earlier style brass hooks, even on Okinawa.

This tack sharp 3 1/4" x 4 1/4" sheet film shot was found labeled, "32nd Division Infantry about to attack a Japanese hard point pillbox from behind." Trouble is, these are Marines, and it seems this might not even be Okinawa. What *is* interesting is, every single rifle here, well into some battle, has a nice, dark gas cylinder, tending to lend credence to what several old Marine veterans told me: between oil lanterns and liberally issued flat black paint, there was effort expended in combat to keep gas cylinders dark and flat. Also, everything in the shot that isn't a carbine, including the Thompson Submachine Gun, carries a leather M1907 sling or variant thereof. (US Army archives, shot about June of 1945)

Not everything Mister Garand's rifle did was dedicated to actual combat. Here, on Okinawa, a transfusion is administered, set up by a Navy Corpsman, using the rifle as a support stand. (U.S.M.C. photo, June 18, 1945)

Though circulated with several different captions, this seems to be a posed shot with 82nd Airborne Division personnel, from 506th P.I.R.

December, 1942, and US Army 32nd Division Infantry on Buna stand by for Japanese counterattack. Everything has leather M1907 slings, and this is about the last "line" shot of the 32nd locatable where any variant of the '03 Springfield appeared anywhere near a fight. (32nd Division, US Army, December 28, 1942)

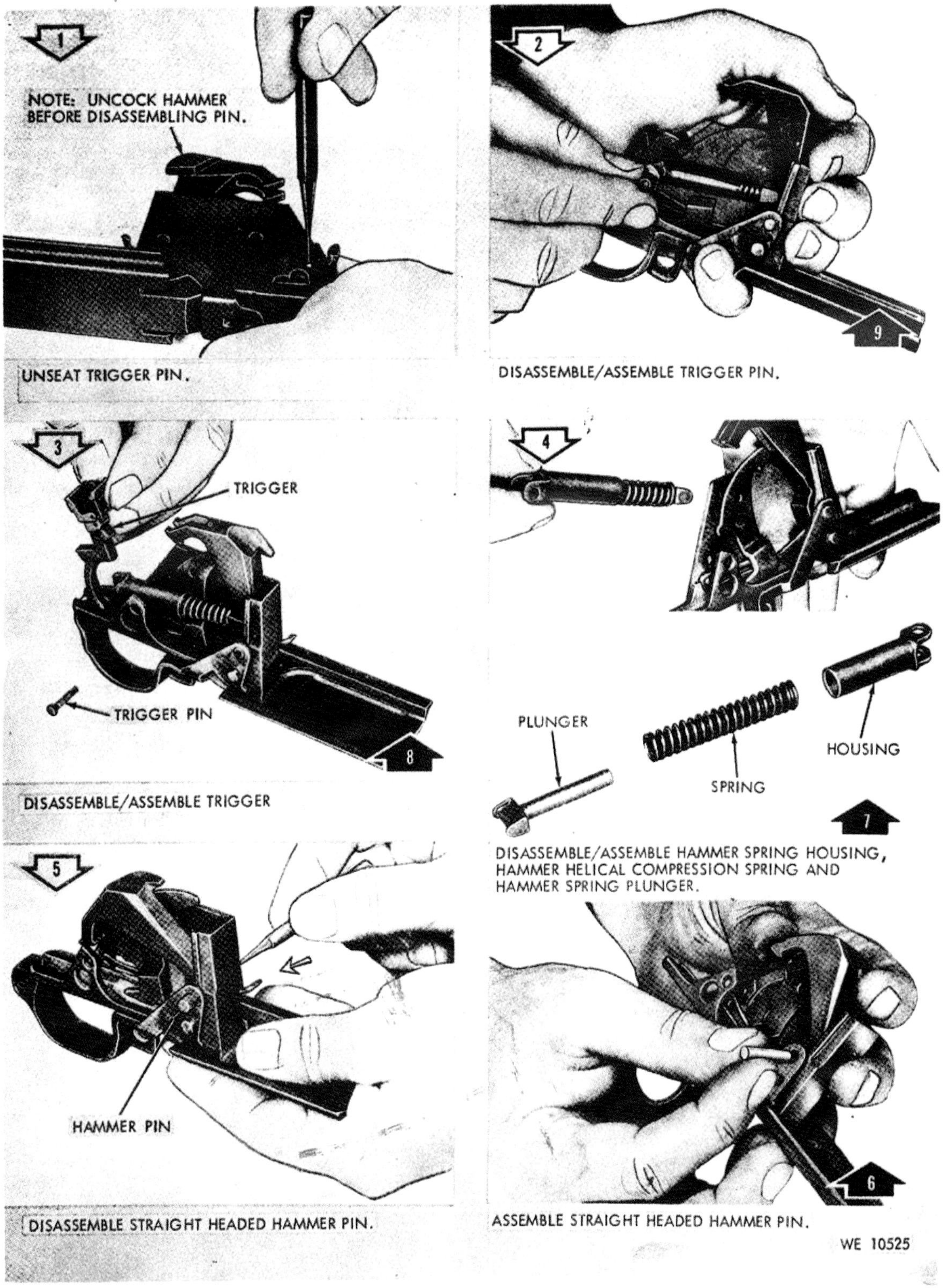

Figure 5-1. Disassembly/assembly of trigger housing assembly. (1 of 2)

Trigger housing disassembly/assembly procedures, from US Army TM 9-1005-222-35.

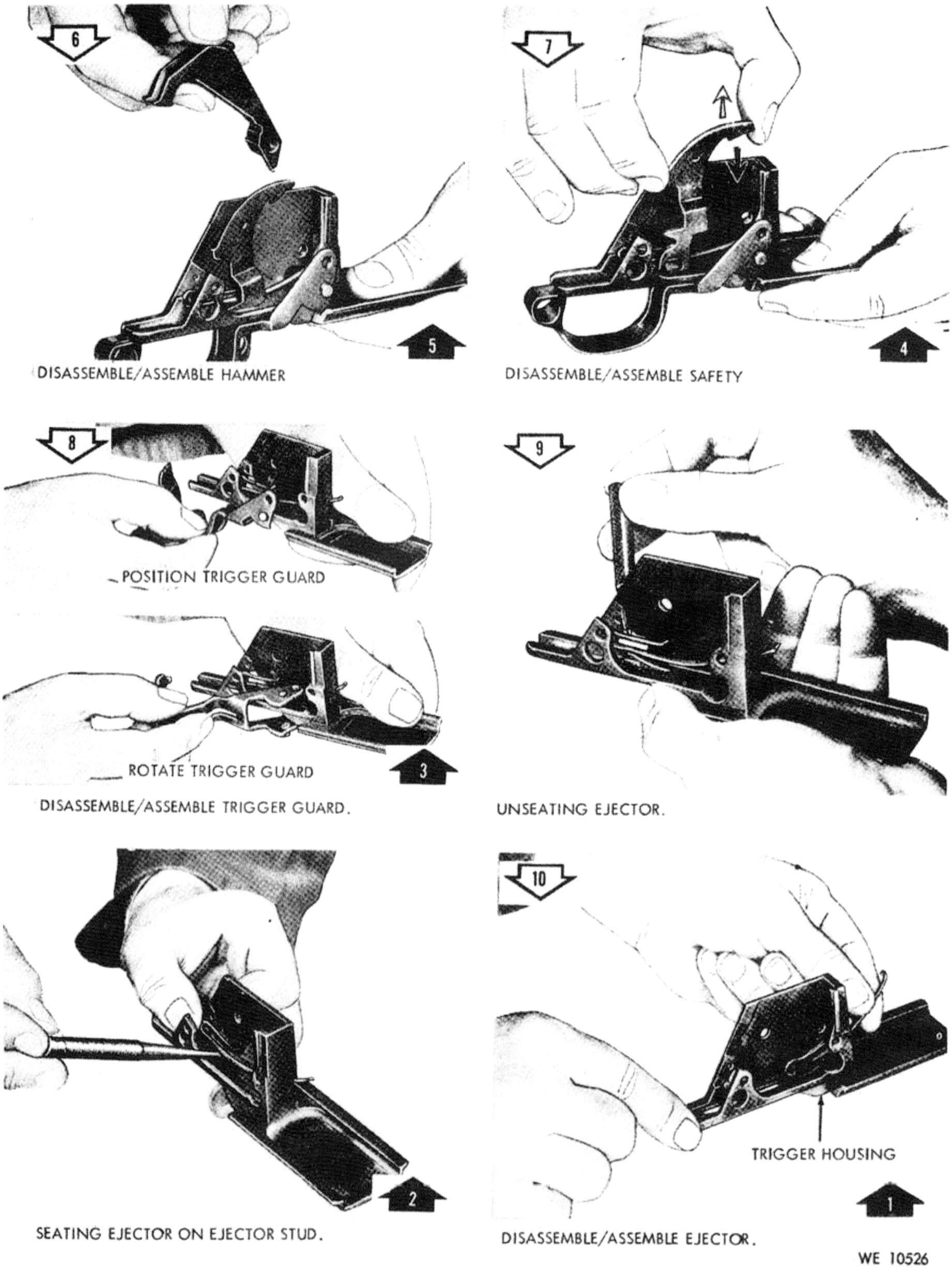

Figure 5-2. Disassembly/assembly of trigger housing assembly. (2 of 2)

Trigger housing disassembly/assembly procedures, from US Army TM 9-1005-222-35.

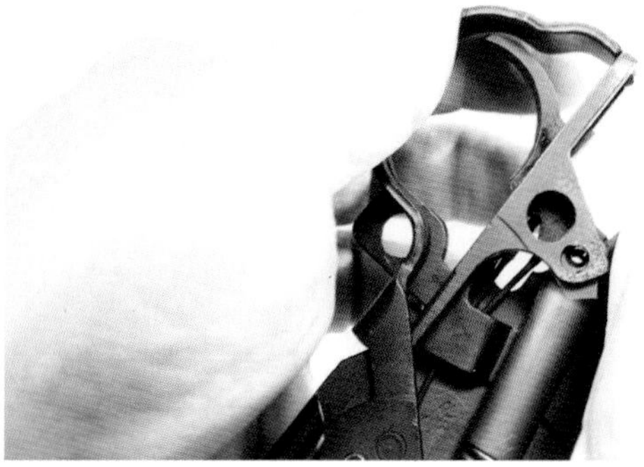

Trigger mechanism ready to have the pin reinserted. Note that the clean hole is emerging, which can be seen through, and that the "closed" side of hammer spring housing is in the correct orientation.

Take a 1 "x 8" strip of 220-grit, Wet or Dry or emery cloth, and insert it between the rear of the trigger and attached disconnector, abrasive side against the trigger. This is done with the trigger housing assembled, the hammer uncocked. Hammer spring tension in the assembly will hold the cloth in place. Making sure the abrasive surface touches only the trigger, slide the cloth back and forth, using about half the length of the strip. Check the weight of the pull about every fourth stroke until the trigger will hold . . . weight.

Roberts stressed the 4.5-pound weight, but I have been told that the current match standard is 4 pounds. Double-check if you're actually in competition, which, as of this writing, I'm not.

Many will find chalk, Prussian blue, and other marking mediums convenient for finding points of binding and abrasion. I find—and it may be experience or dumb luck—that I can usually find the sources of roughness by eyeball and hearing. Again, constant checking of polish levels with the magnifier is a fail-safe device and must be used.

At the first sign of deep bewilderment, overeagerness, or a deep desire to warm up the bench grinder or belt sander, take a walk. Then find your nearest armorer or smith who works on M1s, and have him do it. You are mainly removing finish, very little metal, and only the actual high points that cause binding and abrasion in the mechanism.

Some shooters have had their entire trigger mechanism's internals (once set up) hard- chromed, and though I thought this was crazy at first, I have learned that it actually precludes wear, especially when coupled with heavy grease lubrication of the correct sort.

This mechanism is almost foolproof, which you should figure out from observation. If you go very slowly, inspect regularly, and have some mechanical skills, things are very unlikely to get messed up.

FUN AND SAFETY: AMMO AND AVOIDANCE OF DANGER

In the past couple of years, I've heard a lot of reference to "slamfire," a dangerous condition in which the Garand or any similar rifle discharges a round by movement of the bolt forward. Sometimes this results in a second round's discharging—and it can be catastrophic—when the bolt is not locked down and the operating rod fully forward.

Springfield Armory provided me with a copy of a Wayne Faatz article in American Rifleman (reprints of which can be ordered from the magazine). I will not reanalyze his or the N.R.A.'s data, save to point to improper detailed reloading procedure, softer than military-issue primers, case-sizing details, occasional case separation, and various glitches with firing pins and ejector modification. In fact, his article is part of the reason I briefly ceased shortening ejector springs unless I have a definite problem. (He also notes that shooting glasses should be worn at all times, which I sometimes foolishly presume everyone does automatically.)

I do not disagree with any of his work or conclusions, but I do have something to add. I have seen two slamfires, or, rather, the remains from them, one in each of the popular calibers. The factor that I suspect is at the root of some of the problem—though by no means all of it—is dirty or oily chambers, which, in a high- pressure rifle, especially a gas-operated one, can cause cases to stick on their way in or out and adhere in strange ways or places, even contributing to gross separations. This is called "hydraulic adhesion."

Both of the slamfire-caused specimens I saw had fallen victim to factory ammunition. I did some further calling and digging, and not a single one of the victims I contacted regularly used the standard chamber cleaning recommended by the military. This involves a chamber-cleaning brush with a patch over it, followed by the brush itself, cleaned completely of oil, with additional applications of absorbent patches. Oil especially, but also brass debris, powder fragments, and any foreign material must be removed and chamber polish maintained.

Commercial match barrels are usually very tightly chambered. This contributes to both accuracy and brass life. And, therefore, any foreign matter in the chamber means a cartridge's smoothness of entry and, therefore, speed is affected at the worst possible time. Oil here is a no-no.

Ammo

Federal has in its catalog a new version of 308GM using the 155-grain Palma Match bullet, though it is very unlikely this bullet will ever be loaded in .30-06 as a factory item. Sellier & Bellot has introduced a lot of very good ammunition in both calibers, and perhaps just as important, some of its "export" military format stuff in .308 is being sold at very sensible prices.

PMC/Eldorado has upgraded its whole ammunition line, including the 168-grain match bullets, as standard items in both chamberings.

Perhaps most important some years back was that Sierra offered virtually all its .30-caliber bullets in molycoated incarnations. They were tested and the results were superb and fruitful. Most important of all, I can now say that molycoating and judicious cleaning of the M1 can at least double the useful life of an M1 Garand barrel, and probably do considerably more. I'm basing that on a barrel fired with only copper jackets, an identical one fired only with molycoated bullets, and the erosion generated after about 5,500 rounds. However, the products shut off, and the results, no longer of interest, will never be published.

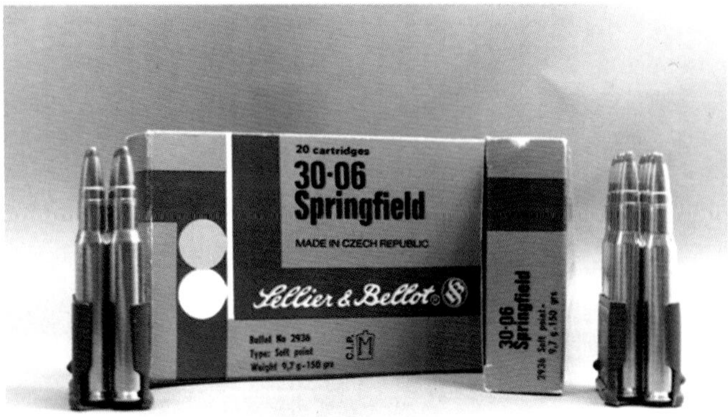

All the various Sellier and Bellot ammunition I've tried, even the hunting-style soft points, functioned cleanly and well in the M1 Garand, in both salient calibers.

Significantly, Lapua has introduced their Scenar bullets in various sizes, and loaded ammunition. All of it is quite expensive, but of the products commonly available in the United States, they were the most uniformly accurate I've ever tested. I generated several thousand rounds, and finished the testing just before my first re-consolidation of my ancient load books and these volumes.

The Cold, Cold, Cold

I am also able to report that some of the unrelieved Citadel barrels (those that showed such machine stress that, when hot, they would shoot as many as 11 clicks left or right, and some of which were actually magnetic) have shown much improved performance via cryogenic treatment . . . that is, they actually shot where they were aimed! These units sold for as little as fifty dollars in the period 1990–97 or so, and the very best of them were excellent. But they were graded. A couple of unscrupulous dealers unloaded what were effectively rejects through advertising and at gun shows, and so a great many of these flawed tubes are still sitting around waiting to surprise somebody.

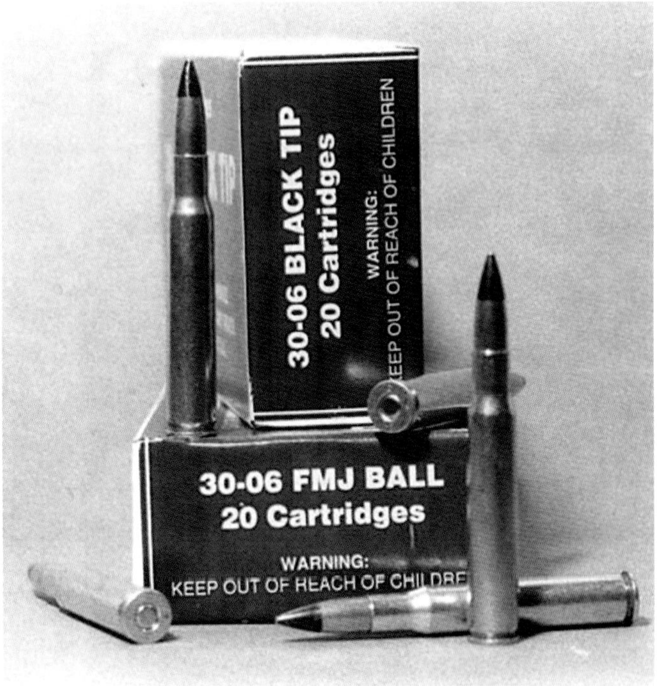

Civilian "remanufactured" .30 06 on Lake City cases.

Radway Green, British fodder, once available from Century Arms. This was L2A2 ammo for the Envoy series of sharpshooter and precision target rifles, and was very accurate. I burned all mine in my M1's. It is more accurate than any of the Lake City ball in 7.62x51 I fired.

Belted Israeli ball ammo, purchased from the now-defunct Navy Arms surplus about 1997.

APPENDIX I

SOURCES: A POOLED BIBLIOGRAPHY

Perhaps the most useful publication for the Garand buff who wishes to immerse himself in this legendary firearm is the GCA Newsletter, from the Garand Collector's Association, P.O. Box 7498, North Kansas City, MO 64116.

For the purist collector, nothing can equal Scott Duff's two-volume set on the old rifle*: The M1 Garand of World War Two and The M1 Garand: Post World War Two.*

The following two are inexpensive items, primarily useful for the shooter:

Rifle, National Matches. United States Army Weapons & Munitions Command, 1963. (Usually about $4.95.)

The M1 Rifle. National Rifle Association Publications, Washington, D.C., revised in 1985. ($3.95)

The books listed below demonstrate and explain the Garand and the principles behind the rifle. There are other publications with better technical illustrations, but these two contain a lot of information for a reasonable price. They are somewhat dated, and there are some research errors (easily corrected by referral to GCA publications).

Book of the Garand, Maj. Gen. Julian S. Hatcher.
Infantry Journal Press, Washington, D.C.
Updated in 1977.

Know Your M1 Garand, E.J. Hoffschmidt.
Blacksmith Publishers, Chino Valley, AZ, 1975.

Many retired armorers retain copies of various War Department/Department of Defense Technical Operations Orders and manuals that pertain to specific parts and procedures. These are worth copying.

It's not possible to pen a major compendium of technical and interpretative data without some errors popping up. As well, *too literal* applications of dates and sequences on parts invariably leads to a considerable numbers of collectors, particularly, generating what amount to "errors" to conform to texts, rather than first applying reasoning and deduction.

I've even seen all original rifles "doctored" by the "faithful" to conform to standards of "correctness" that never really existed. One unscrupulous type in particular welded up and surface "tooled" some "WIN-13" stamped trigger guards based upon an error in J. C. Harrison's missive that, for a while, fooled quite a few folks.

Frankly, I should *still* never have given away my copy. Harrison's *Collecting the M1 Garand* contains a lot of errors. Its spiral-bound format and superb line drawings and overall organization is excellent. Mine had all sorts of marginal notes, stuck in yellow "Post It" additions and corrections, and date modifications, but there really is a place where line drawings clarify better than even the best photographs because they delete the variables of lighting and finish wear, and that is particularly so with markings, where a worn stamp can cause a litany of messy misinterpretation. When the family member to whom I gave my copy (actually, I *lent* it to him!) died in 2011, it was, along with my copies of Duff and several other tomes, given away by other family members to Goodwill.

Bruce N. Canfield's rather massive *The M1 Garand Rifle* (from Mowbray, 2015) is infinitely better than his earlier effort, which included the unrelated Carbine. With 872 pages and over a thousand illustrations, it seems mostly very solid, albeit much of the data on foreign service and Italian-produced rifles is severely limited and perhaps erroneous. Surely I can empathize. It's literally impossible to cover all the nooks and crannies of the M1's service, well into the 1980s and later, and even more obvious, very few folks are interested in what would be many thousands of pages. So too much detail based upon "iffy" recollections and partial information is inherently nonproductive, as well as unachievable. Much of even the best information on these machines is "iffy" due to translation issues and math garbles . . . so even my stuff is "grain of salt."

I have always enjoyed the N.R.A. work, *The M1 Rifle*, but it's anathema to collectors since it totally ignores markings and parts matching or anything to do with originality. Albeit dated overall, the process of bedding the stock for this particular rifle is better explained there than anywhere else. The other "nuts and bolts" approaches and techniques are solid, too.

The notes and mimeographed or "dittoed" orders and so on from armorers taught me a good deal more than the industrial histories, in practical terms. The "gas trap question," operating rod separation incidents (rare, apparently always involving frozen mud/ice plugging the last 1" or so of the muzzle end of the bore), the introduction of birch stocks about 1960–61, safety notes on condemned and/or "withdrawn" parts—these were matters affirmed *long* before I understood what they meant, back in the days when I was simply a shooter.

The Garand Collector's Association, of which I have been a member for many years, is primarily for hard core collectors, and contains more retrospective data than some care to even consider, and periodically, a fascinating industrial/technical piece that's truly compelling. Some I detail and discuss in the interior of this missive.

But there are others worthy of comment and note:

Summer 2014 carries the last interview with Congressional Medal of Honor recipient, the late Walt Ehlers, wherein he noted that his personnel never touched up their gas cylinders (some U.S.M.C. outfits apparently did!) and that, "The slings were all leather, not web." There are other insights about the rifle and about tactics, too.

Spring 2014 and the preceding issue contain pieces detailing "Butt Plate Evolution" (two parts), and is superbly illustrated. Of course, one of my associates, a hard core collector with a reputation for being abrupt, said, "Lots of stupid mistakes in that one!" I think he, at least, *vastly* overstated. I can't find any, but then I'm not one for exotic butt plates.

In the fall 2004 issue, Scott Duff himself discusses in detail, in a piece entitled, "Low Serial Number H&R", what had been a rumor among collectors for decades, the part time and maker anomalies on early Harrington and Richardson M1 rifles. Some wartime parts presence was acknowledged, to include some from the armory and oddments of W.R.A. bits. Only a few years before, to say that aloud among collectors was to be accused of what amounts to heresy. Applied therein mainly to rifles in the first batch after 4.66 million, I have in fact seen bits and pieces of the same array considerably later. No idea whether that was caused by inept restorations, or in the case of one which came from Arlington Ordnance in the 1990s, just a matter of coincidence.

A pair of fairly typical ca. 1942 M1 Garands as found in the 1990s. These came from Arlington Ordnance, and had not undergone quite as many extensive rebuilds as many others.

As this project in the late middle of 2019 readies itself for ink and web relay, we await important word from Italy on some details which might very well change many educated guesses and opinions over the last six decades or so.

No, all is not "set in stone."

That's why this is a practical history.

APPENDIX II
THE MARKETPLACE

"The Marketplace" comprises mainly names and addresses, along with notes, so that you can find most of what's been discussed in the text.

The only place to get much selection in custom M1 Garand stocks in laminate and various grades of walnut is

Boyd's Gunstock Industries, Inc.
25376 403rd Avenue
Mitchell, SD 57301
https://www.boydsgunstocks.com/

Century at one time produced M1 receivers. Most of their assembled RIFLES were fine, but the receivers offered separately did not perform as many of would've liked. If the current (ca. 2019) edict changes, the firm may even begin importing them again. They also import a wide variety of surplus ammo, and thus may service the venerable rifle in many ways.

Century Arms, Inc.
430 South Congress Avenue, Suite 1A
Delray Beach, FL, 33445
Phone numbers: (561) 265-4500 and (800) 527-1252.
https://www.centuryarms.com/

There is no more Department of Civilian Marksmanship, but there is a private firm, sort of, with considerable volunteer help, that ships M1s and various other items, including parts, and now offers grades of M1s. Gone are the 18-month waits, but also gone are the very low prices of the early 1980s. Partly gone, too, is the direct N.R.A. affiliation, though one of the ways to qualify is still via an accredited high-power competition program. For literature, contact:

The Civilian Marksmanship Program
P.O. Box 576
Camp Perry Training Site, Bldg #3 (shipping)
Port Clinton, OH 43452
Phone: 419-635-2141
Fax: 419-635-2802
E-mail: info@thecmp.org

The Anniston Distribution Center is different:
Civilian Marksmanship Program
1401 Commerce Blvd
Anniston, Alabama 36207
Phone: (256) 835-8455
Fax: (256) 835-3527
E-mail: custserve@thecmp.org

Barrels such as those tested here on my 1.4 million rifle are available, along with other M1 goodies and barrels in higher grade, from

Fulton Armory, Incorporated
8725 Bollman Place # 1
Savage, MD 20763
http://www.fulton-armory.com/index.aspx

The Garand Collectors Association is almost essential for the serious Garand collector, and handy even for shooters.

The Garand Collectors Association
P.O. Box 7498
North Kansas City, MO 64116
http://thegca.org/

Even if Krieger doesn't produce the best M1 Garand barrel in the world, I haven't seen the one that's better.

Krieger Barrels, Inc.
2024 Mayfield Road
Richfield, WI 53076
https://kriegerbarrels.com/

Derrick Martin was one of my primary consultants and my favorite smith. And unlike a lot of gunsmiths, he's also still an active competitor. This is the comprehensive, versatile shop, begun by Derrick Martin. Derrick retired in late 2018, but assures me his successors are fully his equal.

Accuracy Speaks Gunsmithing
3960 North Usery Pass Road
Mesa, AZ 85207
http://www.accuracyspeaks.com/index.html

Very high quality M1 Garand barrels, service profile, "in the white", available in .308 and .30 Model of 1906—expensive, but among the finest of the standard weight units. Lothar Walther also manufactures superb Mauser and other military and civilian format precision barrels.

LOTHAR WALTHER PRECISION TOOLS
3425 Hutchinson Road
Cumming, Georgia 30040
http://www.lothar-walther.com/

A very heavy Krieger barrel, mountedon a Smith-refinished H&R receiver, in one of Boyd's laminated M1Garand stocks.

Midway has offered reloading supplies to dealers for a long time and has branched out. It owns the Bishop and Fajen names, though there is not much likelihood that there will be new product in the future. It also sells wood and accessories for the M1, including Boyd's, and features, in stock, such items as Kager's M1 hooded duplex reticle front sight.

MIDWAY
5875 W. Van Horn Tavern Road
Columbia, MO 65203
https://www.midwayusa.com/

MPI produces the only commonly available M1 polymer stock I know of.

MPI
5655 NW St Helens Rd
P.O. Box 83266
Portland, OR 97383–0266
http://www.mpistocks.com/

There is probably nobody who handles more Garand parts than Sarco.

Sarco, Inc.
50 Hilton Street
Easton, PA 18042
http://www.e-sarcoinc.com

Smith produces some M1 products, does high-quality dark-phosphate finishing, produces M14 receivers, and provides full-service M1 smithing. Smith also stocks many M1 parts.

Smith Arms International
1701 W. 10th Street #14
Tempe, AZ 85281
http://www.smithenterprise.com/index.html

Standard Parts' Greg Sytkowski handles high-quality used, new restrike, reproduction, and surplus parts for the M1 Garand and a few other rifles. His is not a large enterprise, but his products tend to be among the best.

Standard Parts LLC
1405 16th Street

One of Smith's dark- phosphate refinishing operations delivered this H&R in a nearly black color, quite close to its very late original finish.

Suite 0601
Racine, WI 53402
Phone: (262) 902-6823
standardpartsLLC.com

Larry Stewart operates a well-ordered store full of fascinating military antiques and curios, to include a vast selection of items pertinent to the M1 Garand and other US and foreign firearms.

Stewart's Military Antiques
108 West Main Street
Mesa, AZ 85201
https://stewartsmilitaryantiques.com/

The finest, custom-made, specially marked M1907 variant slings such as the items pictured herein can be had from

Leslie Tam
1411 St. Louis Drive
Honolulu, HI 96816
http://www.lestamslings.com/

The Garand is itself a tribute to the citizens who made it, the genius who designed it, and the creative, mostly civilian troopers who lugged it to victory in so many horrible places so very long ago. But this rifle is far from being a mere monument, and the accomplishments of that generation and the rifle must be recognized and reinvigorated.

Enjoy!

One of Leslie Tam's logoed custom M1907 slings.

ABOUT THE AUTHOR

—By an old-hand M1 collector.

Jim Thompson is an internationally published firearms writer, photographer, and consultant whose immersion in the world of firearms and deep experience as a serious shooter and experimenter began about 1957. He purchased his first M1 from P&S Sales in 1963. His dedication to precise historical research combined with his practical, empirical insight has yielded significant contributions to the fields of military history and weapons development.

In May 2013 the author marked fifty years of M1 Garand ownership by test-firing a heavy-competition M1Garand, which he built for his grandson, Adam. The rifle used a heavy custom barrel and a postwar Springfield Armory US receiver, and was executed in the vastly superior 7.62mmx51mm/.308 chambering.

Thompson is not a hidebound traditionalist, nor is he sufficiently corrupted to believe the easy conventional wisdom of the past. He was more inclined to believe real ballisticians than voodoo/macho theorists without credentials, and more inclined to test finishes chemically than to accept whatever was written in factory notes. One editor remarked that he was the first one to "quote the best ballistics labs in history, Ackley and White," in an article, and then present actual "chemical analysis of finish materials from M1's, to prove the 'oxide theory' and explain what had been unsubstantiated rumors, which the same editor remarked, "generated strange hate mail from some very odd people".

His first national firearms publication was ca.1983. He has outlived over fifty editors, two publishing companies, and saw his work "hit ink" in many countries and roughly 200 publications as writer/photographer. He remarked recently, "I don't know anyone at any of the magazines any more, and the children I contacted when I tried had no idea of what I was speaking."

Thompson's philosophy has been to pursue chronology and authenticity to assist the collecting fraternity, but also to be fairly brutal in describing that which is practical and essential. For example, he notes that *most* M1's which flow from the CMP have been in foreign hands and issue at least once in their long lives. Thus, he notes, since they have been abroad, their return to the US is, literally, an "importation." In the most legalistic sense, of course, there was no ownership change, so in that sense they aren't imports. However, many hucksters in the firearms community and a few very confused folks imagine that anything without an importer's markings is a "bringback" or has only ever had a single owner/national user until arriving upon the civilian market. The distinctions matter. Some folks have even suggested their European-made firearms are "non-imports" if they are not marked in the manner prescribed in the 1985 changes to GCA 1968. That, too, is incorrect.

Terms like "correct," "as issued," "as first issued," "restored," "rationalized," and "all G.I." have specific meanings, which unfortunately are frequently, Thompson notes, used in dishonest or deceitful ways, sometimes simply misunderstood. With a lot of M1s, he continues, establishing which is which and what is what simply cannot be done.

And yes, there are mysteries which will never be solved. A very well-traveled stock that, Thompson recalls, showed in an old veteran's estate sale was, according to the industrial histories, made by Winchester. Sanded repeatedly, it carried the traces of a very old Springfield Armory stamped cartouche and several much later markings, including a "boxed eagle" defense acceptance stamp. Even odder: it proved to be not birch, surely not a "fake" (fakers make eyeball replicas of items to make a profit, not to annoy people, Thompson notes!), not the odd "fruitwood" (cherry) sometimes seen on a few wartime prototypes, but maple. It is doubtful that will ever be explained.

Thompson also avoided including date charts with his volumes, early on, claiming any such "CDD's" (contract delivery date) were far from ironclad, and later, that so many of what he calls "jump cut" rifles augured mightily that things were nowhere near as neat as the industrial histories liked everyone to surmise. He also bemoaned the fact that the literature on the Italian rifles, even including that flowing from the "mother country," does not seem accurate or inclusive at all. The Breda figures, in particular, seem awkwardly arrayed, and the author has seen firearms and crests that aren't in ANY of the published literature from both makers. He suspects they produced far more than the hard literature seems to say.

Similarly, he notes that serial numbers alone on M1's, especially Italian ones, aren't really much of a key to "born on" dates. Many Winchester and even much later H&R M1's overlap/duplicate Armory serial numbers. The re-marked and rebuilt Italian rifles, with identifiers changed, use the old, original US serial numbers, and sometimes, bits of the markings. Every known Italian production contract—there seem to have been at least a dozen—theoretically began at zero, so as late the late 1970s, new, very low numbered rifles were being made, with duplicate serial numbers. At least one Indonesian contract group seems to be the only exception. One collector of Thompson's acquaintance claims to have three rifles with the same four-digit serial number—one E series Beretta of Yemeni origin, a old Springfield Armory rebuild gas trap, and a Breda for a South American nation. There is surely a Danish Beretta bearing the same number, and an Indonesian, and a Nigerian, and so on. There is almost zero chance those will ever get to this nation, and not much more chance they still exist, but Thompson notes: This isn't history or the reading of tea leaves, it's math and industrial reality.